Education Library, ...
Iter...
KU-682-665

Archaeology has often been put to political use, particularly by nationalists. The case studies in this timely collection range from the propaganda purposes served by archaeology in the Nazi state, through the complex interplay of official dogma and academic prehistory in the former Soviet Union, to lesser known instances of ideological archaeology in other European countries, in China, Japan, Korea, and the Near East. The introductory and concluding chapters draw out some of the common threads in these experiences, and argue that archaeologists need to be more sophisticated about the use and abuse of their studies.

The editors have brought together a distinguished international group of scholars. Whilst archaeologists will find that this book raises cogent questions about their own work, these problems also go beyond archaeology to implicate history and anthropology more generally.

Nationalism, politics, and the practice of archaeology

Nationalism, politics, and the practice of archaeology

edited by

Philip L. Kohl and Clare Fawcett

CAMBRIDGE
UNIVERSITY PRESS

Published by the Press Syndicate of the University of Cambridge
The Pitt Building, Trumpington Street, Cambridge CB2 1RP
40 West 20th Street, New York, NY 10011–4211, USA
10 Stamford Road, Oakleigh, Melbourne 3166, Australia

© Cambridge University Press 1995

First published 1995

Printed in Great Britain at the University Press, Cambridge

A catalogue record for this book is available from the British Library

Library of Congress cataloguing in publication data
Nationalism, politics, and the practice of archaeology / edited by
Philip L. Kohl and Clare Fawcett.
p. cm.
Includes bibliographical references (p.) and index.
ISBN 0 521 48065 5
1. Archaeology and state. 2. Archaeology – Political aspects.
3. Nationalism – History – 20th century. I. Kohl, Philip L., 1946–.
II. Fawcett, Clare P.
CC136.N38 1966 930.1–dc20 95–1635 CIP
ISBN 0 521 48065 5 hardback
ISBN 0 521 55839 5 paperback

VN

UNIVERSITY COLLEGE LIBRARY SWANSEA

Contents

Part III Eastern Europe and Eurasia

Part IV East Asia

Part V Commentary

Maps

Contributors

DAVID W. ANTHONY, Department of Anthropology, Hartwick College, Oneonta, New York

BETTINA ARNOLD, Department of Anthropology, University of Minnesota

E.N. CHERNYKH, Laboratory of Natural Science Methods in Archaeology, Institute of Archaeology, Moscow

MARGARITA DIAZ-ANDREU, Departamento de Prehistoria, Universidad Complutense de Madrid

LOTHAR A. VON FALKENHAUSEN, Art History Department, University of California at Los Angeles

CLARE FAWCETT, Department of Sociology and Anthropology, St. Francis Xavier University, Antigonish, Nova Scotia

HENNING HASSMANN, Department of Antiquities, Prehistoric Museum, Dresden

TIMOTHY KAISER, Department of Anthropology, University of Toronto, Ontario

PHILIP L. KOHL, Department of Anthropology, Wellesley College, Massachusetts

KATINA LILLIOS, Department of Anthropology and Sociology, Ripon College, Wisconsin

SARAH M. NELSON, Department of Anthropology, University of Denver, Colorado

VICTOR SHNIRELMAN, Center for the Study of Nationalism, Department of Sociology, Central European University, Taboritska, Prague

NEIL ASHER SILBERMAN, Branford, Connecticut

ENZHENG TONG, Department of Fine Arts, University of Pittsburgh

BRUCE G. TRIGGER, Department of Anthropology, McGill University, Quebec

BERNARD WAILES, Department of Anthropology; University Museum, University of Pennsylvania

AMY L. ZOLL, Department of Anthropology, University Museum, University of Pennsylvania

Acknowledgments

Many people – too many to mention – helped us complete this volume; only a few can be explicitly acknowledged here. Antonio Gilman, the then Program Chair of the Archaeology Division of the American Anthropological Association, promoted the symposium in 1991 that resulted in this book. Jessica Kuper, our Editor at Cambridge University Press, correctly urged us to restrict the number of contributions and keep the entire enterprise within a manageable scale. We have tried to adhere to the high standards upon which she insisted and have incorporated the numerous positive suggestions of the two anonymous reviewers for Cambridge University Press. Elena Krasnoperova helped standardize the Russian transliterations, Lothar von Falkenhausen performed the invaluable service of ensuring that all the references in Chinese were accurate and uniform, and Junko Habu assisted with translations from Japanese. We would like to thank Wellesley College and St. Francis Xavier University for technical and financial support throughout this project. Edna Gillis and Sarah Doyle helped greatly in the preparation of the final manuscript; the latter's assistance in compiling the integrated bibliography was particularly invaluable. Barbara Gard deserves special mention for her close reading of the introductory chapter. Finally, we must acknowledge the support and forbearance of all the members of our growing families: Barbara Gard, Owen and Mira Kohl, Eric Atkinson and Marc Fawcett-Atkinson; without them, this book never would have been realized.

Part I

Introduction

1 Archaeology in the service of the state: theoretical considerations

Philip L. Kohl and Clare Fawcett

This book developed out of a symposium examining the relationship between nationalism and archaeological practice which was organized for the American Anthropological Association meetings, Chicago, November 1991. Several of the articles published here (Wailes and Zoll, Arnold and Hassmann, Anthony, Kaiser, Kohl and Tsetskhladze, von Falkenhausen, and Fawcett) represent expanded versions of the papers presented in that symposium; the others (Diaz-Andreu, Lillios, Shnirelman, Tong, Chernykh, and Nelson) were later solicited by the editors for this publication, as were the general commentaries by B.G. Trigger and N.A. Silberman. Initially, we planned to obtain an essentially "global" coverage of issues relating to nationalism, politics, and the practice of archaeology, and more than two dozen archaeologists were contacted in hopes of obtaining such coverage. The articles that appear here deal exclusively with European and East Asian archaeology, an unintended focus representing the contributions of those scholars who responded affirmatively to our invitation.

It is unfortunate, of course, that certain areas are not covered. We particularly regret lack of coverage on the nationalist practices of archaeology in Israel, Turkey, and other Middle Eastern countries; in North and sub-Saharan Africa; in South Asia; in Mexico; and in Peru and neighboring countries (e.g., conflicting interpretations of Tiahuanaco), but it is also obvious that the issues associated with the relationship between archaeology and nationalist politics, whether considered historically or in terms of contemporary developments, are ubiquitous. The areas covered only illustrate the more general phenomenon of nationalist archaeology which one can find embedded within almost every regional tradition of archaeological research (see Trigger and Glover 1981).

It can be argued that there is an almost unavoidable or natural relationship between archaeology and nationalism (section II below) and that this relationship is not necessarily corrupt or intrinsically suspect. It is not surprising, however, that the blatantly political manipulation of archaeological data is particular acute today in those areas, such as the Caucasus and Balkans, which are experiencing ethnic wars associated with the dissolution of old regimes and the emergence of new nation-states. The rise of ethnically based nationalist sentiments throughout eastern Europe and the former Soviet Union and the construction of various mythologies that accompany them make this collection of case studies timely. We hope that they will also serve to demystify dangerous nationalist myths and, in this way, help to defuse some of today's all too prevalent ethnic tensions.

Silberman (pp. 249–50) correctly observes that the nation-building use of archaeological data even occurs in countries, like the United States, that lack an ancient history or a direct link with the prehistoric past; the concept of "'ancient-ness'" is relative and "may lie in the eye of the beholder," making eighteenth-century Monticello or Mount Vernon for US Americans of European descent or the nineteenth-century Little Bighorn Battlefield for both European and Native Americans as emotionally satisfying and time-honored as much older remains from Europe or Asia. More subtly, the borders of contemporary nation-states necessarily influence the tradition of archaeological research, and archaeologists who naturalize them may consciously or unconsciously appropriate another culture area's prehistoric past (as, perhaps, can be argued for the remains of the American Southwest in respect to Northwest Mexico or greater Mesoamerica; see Weigand n.d.).

This fact of the near universality of a relationship between nationalist politics and the practice of archaeology, of course, precludes the realization of our overly ambitious goal for considering it everywhere it occurs. We will be more than sufficiently pleased if this current study stimulates archaeologists working in different areas not treated here to consider how nationalism and other political concerns may affect the practice of archaeology in the areas in which they work. We welcome other collected volumes on this largely overlooked, if implicitly recognized, topic.

I Archaeologists in the service of the state

Trigger (this volume) reviews the long historical relationship between nationalism and archaeology, particularly in Europe during the latter half of the nineteenth century, and stresses many positive features, insisting that nationalism and its relation to archaeology is complex. Under the impetus of nationalism, archaeology abandoned a primary focus on evolution and concentrated on documenting and interpreting the archaeological record of specific peoples. This new focus often led to a much thicker description of material remains and "had a positive effect on archaeology inasmuch as it encouraged archaeologists to trace spatial variations . . . more systematically than they had done previously" (p. 269). More significantly, particularly in colonized countries, the rise of nationalist archaeology –

"when combined with an awareness of the dignity of all human beings" (p. 277) – helped provide resistance to colonialism and racism, both of which often wore an evolutionary disguise.

One can admire the positive role of an ethnically inspired archaeology that helps build justifiable pride in a specific cultural tradition and stimulates research into the past development of that tradition. The articles collected here, however, are principally concerned with the *abuses* of the relationship between nationalist politics and archaeology, with the *problems* that may emerge within distinctive regional traditions that are associated with concepts of cultural or racial superiority and, particularly, with the questionable agendas of certain political movements and nation-states. The case studies presented in this volume clearly show that archaeologists in the service of the state frequently have manipulated archaeological remains to justify the ownership of land claimed to have been held "from time immemorial" or to support policies of domination and control over neighboring peoples.

Problems, of course, emerge in determining the border between responsible and unacceptable research into a group's remote past. As Silberman insists, archaeology may always be an unavoidably political enterprise. When, then, does one deem the use of the remote past as *overly* politicized or *excessively* nationalistic and on what grounds? Do we criticize Saddam Hussein's deliberate manipulation of Mesopotamia's glorious past to justify his attempted annexation of Kuwait, or condemn the late Shah of Iran's triumphal celebration of 2500 years of Persian monarchical rule, held a few years before his own dynasty collapsed, simply because we dislike these figures and disagree with their unsuccessful policies? Are the constructions of our own pasts or national identities more acceptable because they are ours?

The cases reviewed here provide guidance and clarify, at least, two issues. First, although archaeological interpretation may constitute a form of narrative and may always be both a scientific and political/literary enterprise, most contributors would insist that there are evidentiary standards by which archaeological reconstructions can be evaluated and emphasize more Silberman's qualification of the discipline's "obligation to adhere to scholarly standards of logic and evidence" (p. 250). For example, Anthony's deconstruction of the noble Aryan and the Great Mother ecofeminist myths in Indo-European archaeology is predicated on the ability to distinguish plausible from unbelievable reconstructions of archaeological data. He forcefully decries the fashionable relativism of post-processual archaeology and insists: "If we abandon our standards for choosing between alternate explanations, we abdicate any right to exclude explanations that promote bigotry, nationalism, and chicanery" (p. 88) and "Nationalist or racist agendas are only encouraged in an intellectual environment where the 'real' world is visualized as a web of competing ideologies, all of which are equally true and all of which are equally false" (p. 185). In other words, the historical and contemporary distortions of archaeological practice discussed here graphically illustrate the limits of the archaeology as storytelling metaphor: one story is not as convincing as another. Some archaeological tales are not innocuous, but dangerous in that they fan the passions of ethnic pride and fuel the conflicts that today pit peoples against each other.

Celebration of the inevitable political content of our discourse also is fraught with perils. Tong's discussion of the politicization of archaeology in Communist China, particularly during the Cultural Revolution, is chilling, as is Shnirelman's treatment of earlier, but eerily similar developments in Soviet archaeology during the thirties. Shnirelman emphasizes S.N. Bykovski's political awareness of the changes he helped institute in Soviet archaeology during its short transition to an internationalist, anti-imperialist, and anti-racist archaeology. Bykovski's position seems fashionably post-processual: "Consciously or unconsciously, a historian performs a political task expressing his political interests and inclinations in his choice of a particular topic, in his methodological tools, and in his representation of historical data" (cited in Shnirelman, p. 125). Why were the consequent developments in Soviet archaeology so problematic and the seemingly admirable goals Bykovski and others set for themselves so easily and quickly subverted? We suggest that one answer lies in these archaeologists' willingness to act "in the service of the state"; their abandonment of evidentiary standards and adoption of the obviously incorrect – as seen retrospectively – linguistic theory of N.Ya. Marr made it all too easy to purge them when state policies changed and Soviet internationalist archaeology was replaced by Russian chauvinist archaeology (and a new cohort of archaeologists also acting, of course, in the service of the state). Behind "useful fools" like Bykovski lurk more astute and useful official "academic authorities," such as Xia Nai in China (Tong, this volume).

A similar lesson can be drawn from nearly all the case studies presented here. Whether one looks at Stalin's Soviet Union, Salazar's Portugal, Franco's Spain, Hitler's Germany, Mao's China, Gamsakhurdia's Georgia, or Milosevic's Yugoslavia, an archaeology closely identified with state policy all too readily becomes a distorted archaeology that bends and ignores rules of evidence to promote the glories of the ethnic group in command.

Sometimes the relationship between archaeology and state policy may be more covert than overt, more subtle than direct. Fawcett, for example, traces the changes in Japanese archaeology from a subsidiary discipline in the service of the divine imperial cult prior to 1945 to the massively state-financed salvage programs of today. In the course of this transformation the relationship between state demands and archaeological practice became less direct, less overtly manipulated by political authorities. Nevertheless, as archaeologists compromised their independence through their acceptance of state support, the discipline inexorably was invested with a new task: documenting the antiquity and homogeneity of the Japanese people. Archaeological information now has been incorporated into a broader public discourse which resolves around the definition of this new Japanese national identity.

As the chapter by Arnold and Hassmann particularly makes clear, the effects of political interference may continue, creating their own peculiar legacy (the "Faustian legacy" here) that characterizes and pervades the discipline for years. Post-war German archaeologists are reluctant to discuss either the past or present political implications of their discipline. As a consequence, they tend to concentrate on the description and typological classification of materials and to avoid theoretical discussions on broader topics of evolutionary and historical development which have occupied archaeologists in North America, Britain, and other parts of the world over the past several decades. This conservative tendency can be attributed to a caution born of the memories of the racial and nationalist deformation of theory by the National Socialists. Today, however, the overall effect of such conservatism is debilitating.

Ironically, as archaeology becomes less politicized, support for basic research may lessen. Díaz-Andreu's chapter on Spanish archaeology shows how archaeology was subverted by the ethno-nationalist ideology of Franco's regime to create an aura of homogeneity throughout the country during a period of strong central control. More recently, other ethno-nationalist ideologies have played an important role in creating senses of identities for people in the autonomies of Catalonia, the Basque country, and Galicia. In both cases, archaeological research, its publication, and the preservation of historical and archaeological sites were affected by the ethno-nationalist agendas of the government. Her chapter describes the generally salutary effects of the adoption of more objective standards of research and interpretation, termed here "modified positivism" and "pragmatic reformism" (not exactly a Spanish processualism, see also Ruiz Rodriguez (1993)), for combating different ethno-nationalisms in post-Franco Spanish archaeology. Unfortunately, as research on ethno-nationalist themes has waned, so too has interest in archaeology declined among both politicians and the general public.

Von Falkenhausen's chapter illustrates how changes in the institutional and financial support of archaeology in post-Maoist China affected both the nature and scale of research and transformed the dominant interpretation of archaeological remains. Specifically, the growing regionalization of Chinese archaeology has resulted in the breakdown of the mononuclear model of the origins of Chinese civilization. By giving greater emphasis to the importance of regional developments, Chinese archaeologists are able to legitimize a much larger part of the country as ancestral to the cultural mainstream, thus encouraging the integration of people throughout China. This growing regionalism is supported by administrative reorganizations and new infrastructural bases of support, such as provincial museums. By emphasizing the importance of the prehistory of their particular region in the development of Chinese society, archaeologists can draw funding from the central government to themselves and away from neighboring regions, while they can also convince the regional government to devote more funds to their archaeological projects.

Archaeology thus appears as a discipline almost in wait of state interference. Dependent upon considerable support for their primary research, archaeologists seem peculiarly vulnerable to state pressures. Can one resist such demands? What roles are archaeologists able to assume, if they refuse to become implicated in state policies? Again, often a fine line separates legitimate from questionable research. Responsible archaeologists are able to determine the *limits* of the evidence they control, what they can and cannot reconstruct with reasonable confidence from the archaeological record. As empirical scientists, archaeologists can distance themselves from objectively non-verifiable myths which resort to divine intervention or similar explanations of the past.

Post-processual relativism provides no guide for determining when one should encourage the conscious construction of national pride and when one should condemn it as excessively chauvinistic. In fact, generalizations are extremely difficult to formulate. In any archaeological or historical analysis, each case must be examined in terms of its specific historical circumstances and be judged by a minimal *universal* standard which requires: first, that the construction of one group's national past not be made at the expense of another's; and, secondly, that concern and respect be accorded all cultural traditions.

As Kohl and Tsetskhladze argue for the highly politicized archaeology of the Caucasus, archaeologists need to be aware of the political implications of their work and be sensitive to the contemporary social setting of their studies of the remote past. They need to recognize and articulate the limits to which the archaeological record can be pushed when identifying prehistoric ethnic groups and the territories they once occupied. Finally, they can distinguish between archaeological and historical reconstructions affecting a people (in terms of group consciousness or historical claims to a territory) and governmental state policies affecting those people. In good conscience, one can admit a potentially damaging archaeological reconstruction as the most plausible and objective interpretation of the evidence and then condemn the state policy that bends and distorts that reconstruction for its own questionable political purposes. A similar point is made by Anthony when he distinguishes the ability to protest a racist explanation on ethical grounds from one based on accuracy and conformity with "the facts." Presumably in most cases, these grounds coincide.

II Archaeology and the construction of national identities

That there exists a relationship between nationalism and archaeology is not a novel idea. As Trigger points out, nationalism has influenced the kinds of questions archaeologists have been willing to ask and the sorts of data they have collected since it became a political force in Europe and other parts of the world, particularly during the last three decades of the nineteenth century. The relationship between archaeology and nationalism has been, nevertheless, a somewhat under-conceptualized, if not prohibited, topic, particularly among archaeologists working in the North American or certain European archaeological traditions, although this is not true for all parts of the world. In Israel (Elon 1994), for instance, the political value of archaeology for nation building purposes has long been appreciated, while in Japan the relationship between archaeology and nationalism has been thoroughly discussed since the end of the Pacific War in 1945 (Fawcett 1990; Tsude 1986).

Trigger's historical overview presents the issues of archaeology and nationalism within the context of a dichotomy between, first, the "rationalism, universalism and positivism" of French liberalism and, secondly, the "romanticism, particularism . . . and idealism" of German reaction which have dominated Western thought for the past 200 years. Trigger recognizes the impact of social, economic, and political factors on the interpretations archaeologists make of the past, while rejecting the extreme relativist position taken by some post-processual archaeologists. Ultimately, he believes that the growing empirical data base excavated by archaeologists year after year should constrain archaeological interpretations. Archaeologists should steer a course between the rigidity of an extreme positivism, which over-emphasizes the regularity of human behavior, and a radical relativism, which denies our ability to break through our individual and communal prejudices.

Since its inception, archaeology has been deeply involved in nationalist enterprises, above all in the construction of national identities. Silberman places the beginning of this relationship back to the time of the earliest stirrings of the Renaissance and a kind of proto-Italian reaction against the High Gothic movement, but the relationship becomes much clearer when nationalist political movements emerge as a political force throughout Europe in the nineteenth century and archaeology matures and becomes institutionalized as an academic discipline. C. Thomsen and J.J.A. Worsaae set up and tested their Three Ages of Stone, Bronze and Iron while collecting and organizing artefacts for the Danish National Museum. Even late nineteenth-century diffusionists, like O. Montelius who believed that the archaeological record documented the passage of civilization from the ancient East to northern Europe, were primarily involved in the reconstruction of the prehistory of their own nation-state (such as Sweden for Montelius). The relationship between nationalism and archaeology seemed so natural and close at so many levels – from the ideological to the material – that it remained largely unexamined, much less questioned, throughout the nineteenth century.

The cases presented here demonstrate, not surprisingly, that the close connection between archaeology, nationalism, and the construction of national identities has continued unabated in the twentieth century. Lillios, for example, provides a detailed case-study of the mechanism by which Copper Age archaeology in Portugal was influenced by nationalist ideology during the years of Salazar's regime (1932–74). Although Salazar stressed the Age of Discoveries (fifteenth and sixteenth centuries AD) as Portugal's greatest time of glory, he was committed to national history and, consequently, formed the Portuguese Academy of History which sponsored archaeological as well as historical research. Lillios shows how research on the Portuguese Copper Age by dedicated followers of Salazar's authoritarian regime, such as Manuel Afonso de Paço and Eugénio dos Anjos Jalhay, glorified this period as a prehistoric "golden age" which resembled, in greatness, Portugal's Age of Discoveries and, of course, the Salazar present.

Similarly, Nelson argues that, for historically ascertainable reasons, ethnic questions have always been paramount in Korean archaeological studies. The result of this focus on a Korean homogeneous ethnic identity has been that explanations have inevitably relied on the unlikely premise that from the earliest times intact groups of "Koreans" migrated into the Korean peninsula from either Siberia or China. Korean archaeology has been and continues to be detrimentally affected by the contemporary political desire to see Korean culture in the past and the present as highly distinctive and homogeneous, a view scarcely sustainable from a more impartial evaluation of the evidence, one not fixated on questions concerning Korean ethnicity.

Archaeological sites are such potent symbols of national identity (e.g.,

Masada in Israel, or Zimbabwe in, significantly, Zimbabwe) that peoples today are frequently willing to fight over them. Archaeology and ancient history help define a people as distinct and occupying (or claiming) territories that were historically theirs. Thus recently we almost witnessed the outbreak of hostilities over the appropriate name for the breakaway area of the "Former Yugoslav Republic of Macedonia"; to the Greeks, use of the classical name of Macedonia by the peoples occupying this former republic represented an unacceptable historical appropriation of Greek history (the glories of Alexander and his successors) and also immediately suggested to them territorial designs on their northern territories. The ancient, archaeologically documented past is alive for many peoples throughout the world to a far greater extent than is often appreciated.

Wailes and Zoll espouse the more encompassing term *ethnic archaeology* in their review of the ethnically biased interpretations of early medieval Insular art. Their chapter presents a central theme around which European history and archaeology have been explicitly or implicitly constructed, viz., the transformation of human societies from barbarism to civilization, and they argue that this transformation has generally been understood within an ethnic frame of reference in which some groups are seen as "retarded" or "primitive" and others "progressive" or "advanced." Although the debate about the time and place where Insular art emerged has long been couched in terms of ethnicity, barbarism, and civilization, Wailes and Zoll feel that Insular art, in fact, symbolizes the appearance of a new cosmopolitan civilization emerging in Europe during the early medieval period and question whether the early monasteries and Christian communities were ever as ethnically pure as later apologists would like us to believe. In a similar vein, Trigger (this volume, p. 276) observes: "It [nationalism] is also a phenomenon of recent origin. It is therefore a concept of importance to modern people, including archaeologists, rather than to the people who created the archaeological record."

As Kaiser's discussion of the hopelessly complex history of the Balkans makes clear, the terms nationalism and ethnicity may almost be synonymous, virtually obviating any need to distinguish between nationalist and ethnic ideologies. This correspondence, however, is a peculiar product of the Balkans' specific, ethnically troubled history. More generally, we prefer to refer to *nationalist*, not *ethnic*, archaeology, for it is more specific and rooted in the shared history of the emergence of nation-states and the development of archaeology as a discipline. It is useful to distinguish nationalism from other forms of social and cultural group consciousness, such as ethnicity *per se*, and situate its rise within larger historical processes that began roughly during the past two hundred years. Since archaeology as a professional academic discipline emerged during this same period, it is not surprising to find a relationship between the "study of old things" and the development of nationalist consciousness.

The question of how national consciousness reaches the extreme levels of intensity we witness today must be explored historically. To paraphrase Hobsbawm, nationalists create nations (that is, groups thinking of themselves now as nationalities), not the reverse, a fact illustrated by the famous statement of Massimo d'Azeglio delivered at the first meeting of the parliament of the newly united Italian kingdom: "We have made Italy, now we have to make Italians" (cited in Hobsbawm 1992a:44).

Likewise, it is doubtful that most "Greek" subjects of the Ottoman Empire, who were mainly peasants living at the southern end of the Balkan peninsula, would have become agitated over the naming as Macedonia vaguely demarcated territories to their north prior to the nineteenth-century political liberation movements which freed them from the Turkish yoke; such movements, in turn, were initiated and led by *intellectuals* – foreign and local – whose yearning for political freedom was stimulated and abetted by their Romantic vision of classical Greek culture, a vision continuously reinforced throughout the nineteenth century by archaeological discoveries of the ancient Greeks (for a comparative analysis of nineteenth-century nationalist movements that stresses the role of intellectuals in their development, see Hroch 1985).

Prior to their nineteenth- and twentieth-century awakening, most "Greeks" would have exhibited an ethnic consciousness similar to that recorded for "Ukrainian" peasants by a British observer in May 1918:

> Were one to ask the average peasant in the Ukraine his nationality he would answer that he is Greek Orthodox; if pressed to say whether he is a Great Russian, a Pole, or an Ukrainian, he would probably reply that he is a peasant; and if one insisted on knowing what language he spoke, he would say that he talked "the local tongue." One might perhaps get him to call himself by a proper national name and say that he is "russki," but this declaration would hardly yet prejudge the question of an Ukrainian relationship; he simply does not think of nationality in the terms familiar to the *intelligentsia*. (Colonel Jones, "The Position in the Ukraine," cited in Suny 1993b:50–1)

National awakening thus is associated with political movements which were directed towards the construction of independent nation-states or for more autonomy within such states. Throughout most of the world archaeology has played and continues to play a critical role in the creation of national identities essential to these projects. For the reason of its integral association with the construction of national identities, we follow Díaz-Andreu's discussion on the relationship between nationalism and archaeology. According to her, "the development of archaeology as a scientific discipline in the 19th century can only be understood in the creation of a national history; that is, a history directed at legitimizing the existence of a nation and, therefore, its right to constitute an independent state" (p. 54). Most of the recognized "regional traditions" of archaeological research are, in fact, *national* traditions which have developed within the framework of specific nation-states. The pervasiveness of the relationship between archaeology and nationalism is, from this perspective, most understandable. Since ancient historical sources are always grossly incomplete and, more importantly, since many contemporary or aspirant nation-states altogether lack early historical records, it is obvious that archaeology will continue to play a critical and inevitable role in the forging of national consciousnesses. Put simply, nationalist archaeology will continue to flourish as long as we live in a world of nation-states.

The inherent ambiguity of archaeological, especially prehistoric, data for the identification of a people paradoxically strengthens this role or, more accurately, enhances the potential for abusing it. Dangers of subverting the natural relationship between archaeology and nationalism are always present. Since archaeologists typically uncover murkier and more remote pasts than historians, we are even more subject to critical scrutiny. Hobsbawm (1992b:3) tellingly has evaluated his own profession by means of a striking metaphor: "For historians are to nationalism what poppy-growers in Pakistan are to heroin addicts; we supply the essential raw material for the market." Archaeologists (and perhaps linguists, folklorists, and ethnographers) must be compared with the concocters of even more powerful hallucinogens, which distort the past to the likening of nationalists intent on demonstrating the uniqueness of their people. Chernykh's postscript on recent developments in Russian archaeology demonstrates that many of the fierce nationalist movements unfolding today throughout the Soviet Union are *actually led* by archaeologists, philologists, and ancient historians, a fact illustrating the intimate link between past perceptions and present realities. In light of this, Hobsbawm's metaphor may be in need of further revision: rather than just the producers of raw materials, historians and archaeologists may occasionally resemble more the pushers of these mind-bending substances on urban streets, if not the mob capos running all stages of the sordid operation.

We cannot review the enormous corpus of literature that presents various theoretical perspectives on nationalism (see, for example, the reviews and analyses of Smith 1971, 1986 and Gellner 1983). Our discussion follows those studies which distinguish nationalism from other related concepts, such as ethnicity, and which treat it as an historically rooted phenomenon associated with the rise of nation-states during the nineteenth century and the emergence of an articulate nationalist intelligentsia utilizing the then newly available means of mass communication, such as newspapers (e.g., Anderson 1983; Hobsbawm 1992a, 1992b). The rise of nationalist sentiments typically is associated with the appearance of broadly based popular movements, demanding their national rights and liberation, and they sometimes form along distinctive lines in protest against colonial rule (e.g., Chatterjee 1993). The perspective adopted here assumes that all forms of nationalism are social constructions of reality; they are "imagined communities," subconsciously fashioned and/or consciously invented and manipulated by social groups, who themselves are emerging for reasons associated with economic and technological developments of the modern era.

III The underacknowledged topic of nationalist archaeology

Nearly every practicing archaeologist is aware of this inherent relationship between nationalism and archaeology; nationalist archaeology is almost always recognizable. Why then has it remained such a largely unstudied and unacknowledged phenomenon in the archaeological literature? More precisely, why are studies only now beginning to appear that are devoted to this fascinating and important topic? To answer these questions, we briefly review the history of the avoidance of this topic, adopting for convenience the Anglo-American classification of the development of archaeological thought through its culture-historical, "new" or processual, and now – at least partially in some restricted areas of northwestern Europe and North America – post-processual phases. Our discussion is necessarily schematic and treats almost exclusively archaeological works written in English.

General lack of interest in exploring the relationship between archaeology and nationalism during archaeology's pre-processual era may have been related to the nature of traditional culture-historical research, particularly in North America and in Europe. The relationship was so pervasive and taken for granted that its study seemed superfluous. Culture historians, in many cases, however, attempted to trace the development and origins of extant ethnic groups, and their work, thus, could be used to support nationalist causes. The highly nationalistic use of archaeological data intensified during the years preceding the outbreak of the major national conflicts of this century, the two World Wars. Understanding this, Childe moved away from culture history partly because he saw that Kossina's work was being used in Nazi Germany to support racist and fascist policies. He also argued that historians and prehistorians should view history and, by extension, archaeology as a science basing their "judgments on the facts unbiased by personal feeling" (Childe 1941:2).

Like Childe, the new processual archaeologists of the 1960s and 1970s, including Binford (1972), Clarke (1968), and Watson *et al.* (1971), saw "science" – which they defined in terms of the logical positivist theories of explanation and hypothesis testing – as the way to rid archaeological interpretation of the personal influences haunting the culture-historical approach. Unlike Childe, however, these processual archaeologists rarely acknowledged the link between the subjective opinions of individual scholars and broader political, economic, or social trends. Because of their largely unexamined scientific pretensions, processual archaeologists rarely bothered to discuss the political implications of their work. In their view, science – and hence real archaeology – should not be influenced by ideology.

The link between archaeology and its social, political, and economic context surfaced in the 1980s when authors such as Trigger (1980; 1984; 1985; 1989a) and Hodder (1982a; 1984; 1985; 1986) used sociological and historical critiques of archaeological work to demonstrate how embedded processual archaeology really is in specific cultural and historical contexts (Fawcett 1990:4). These archaeologists, and others who followed their lead, challenged a basic assumption of processual archaeology: that the scientific world view on which the work was based was ideologically pure. They demonstrated that all varieties of archaeology, including culture-historical, processual, and post-processual, must be understood within a social, political, cultural, and economic context.

Studies linking archaeological work to its socio-political context began to appear during the 1980s. Among these there were a few which addressed directly or indirectly the question of archaeology and nationalism. Hall (1984; 1990), for instance, discussed the influence of both white and black nationalism on archaeological interpretations in historic Rhodesia, and contemporary Zimbabwe and South Africa. Fowler (1987) analyzed how nationalist ideologies in Mexico, Great Britain, and the People's Republic of China have explicitly and implicitly affected cultural resource management and the presentation of archaeological information and materials. Both Silberman's *Between Past and Present* (1989) and Hobsbawm and Ranger's *The Invention of Tradition* (1983) clearly describe the relationship between history, archaeology, and nationalism in various parts of the world. Martínez Navarrete's (1993) timely presentation of the Spanish and Soviet/Russian "regional traditions" of archaeological research contextualizes their practice of archaeology and consciously attempts to create a "meta-nationalist" dialogue (see below) of understanding not only among Spanish and Russian archaeologists but also among a much broader international archaeological community.

Several articles in Gathercole and Lowenthal's *The Politics of the Past* (1990) and in an issue of the *Archaeological Review from Cambridge* entitled "Archaeology and Politics" touch on the issue of nationalism and archaeology. Price (1990), for instance, argued that site restoration is influenced by the values of the society doing the reconstruction which, in the case of modern nation-states, means that sites will be restored in accordance with national cultural world views and values. In a discussion of museum displays in the United States of America, Blakey (1990) noted that the archaeologists and museologists preparing the exhibits present American national identity as white Euro-American. O'Regan (1990), Butts (1990), Creamer (1990), and Olsen (1986) discussed the dilemmas that minority groups, particularly indigenous peoples, face when they assert their claims over the remains of a past used by the majority population to create an image of the nation's bi-cultural or multi-cultural identity. Willett (1990), MacKenzie (1990), Foanaota (1990), Ray (1986), and Sinclair (1986) examined the issue of archaeological materials as symbols of national or ethnic identity among peoples who are in the process of defining their national identity in colonial or post-colonial situations.

Although all of these studies touch on aspects of nationalist archaeology, few focus solely on this issue. In addition, many of the papers which deal with the influence of nationalism on the interpretation of the past do so either through analyses of the ways in which archaeology is presented to the public through museums, books, or historic monuments or through discussions of how state policies affect cultural resource management policies. Few deal with the ways that nationalism affects the works and the interpretations of the archaeologists themselves.

Detailed consideration of the relationship between nationalism and the practice of archaeology is needed, particularly given the current epidemic of nationalist conflicts. We suspect that one reason for the relative silence of investigation is recognition of the dangers of articulating the link between archaeology and nationalism: one's career – for a local scholar – or one's research program – for a foreign archaeologist – may hang in the balance. Obviously, in certain circumstances, circumspection and discretion may be a wiser and more effective means of calming objectionable nationalist practices; cautious responses certainly need not always be exercises of self-interest.

Yet it is also a basic premise of this volume that the positive and negative features of nationalist archaeology are better understood through explicit discussion; when distorted, nationalist archaeology must be confronted, not ignored. One major lesson that should be learned from the failure of the nationalist policies of the former Soviet Union and other Communist regimes is that ethnic issues are not resolved by declaring them non-existent or claiming that all peoples in the state live together harmoniously as fraternal brothers (when, in fact, many intensely hate each other, as well as "Big Brother"). Problems are not solved, but build up and are exacerbated by such refusals to address, resulting in the incredible and depressing explosions of hostilities that so pervasively infect contemporary events throughout the world. The case studies presented here are made in the spirit of initiating a long overdue consideration of politically sensitive issues affecting the practices of archaeologists throughout the world.

IV Archaeology and the construction of future identities

Nationalist identities are not the only ones in need of archaeological construction. Prehistorians, above all, should realize that nation-states are not natural or immutable entities but forms of political organization which have developed during a specific and, for that matter, fairly recent historical period. Today, particularly in Europe, such awareness has led to the creation of new journals, such as the *Journal of European Archaeology*, which consciously transcend the borders of nation-states and the analytical framework of nationalist archaeology. In expectation of the advent – however painful and punctuated – of the European community, Kristiansen (1990:828) eloquently argues that "we are in need of a European policy for archaeology to adjust the traditional national archaeologies to the needs of the future, and to prevent a revival of pre-war chauvinistic history and archaeology in the wake of the changes taking place in eastern, as well as western Europe."

What form will such a European archaeology take? At the end of her chapter on Portuguese archaeology, Lillios speculates that the coming unification of Europe will lead dialectically to a rise of nationalist archaeology in Portugal and presumably other countries. Alternatively, different European archaeologies can be envisioned, some possibly acceptable only to certain groups within the future European community; e.g., those focussing on a past shared Celtic identity (see Dietler 1994). For some, the new Europe will be synonymous with the West, its birth giving rise to civilization in the mythical sense dissected by Wailes and Zoll. Black Athena beware: it is Europe which witnessed the beginnings of metallurgy and monumental architecture; its precocious ancestors spread their languages and agriculture throughout the continent. Kristiansen apparently advocates a different "meta-nationalist" European archaeology. European union will, in a variety of ways, result in the creation of a new European identity. Archaeologists would do well to remember the lessons learned about the influence of nationalism on archaeological practice when embarking on the study of the pan-European past and proceed again through explicit recognition of the *limits* of the evidence they control for reconstructing shared ethnic, national, or now perhaps "meta-national" pasts.

The construction of new social identities, which necessarily use archaeological materials, will continue into the future, even into a world that may ultimately and painfully outgrow its national boundaries. At present, the opposite trend is more evident; nation-states are fissioning, not fusing together, and new nationalist archaeologies are, correspondingly, emerging.

Use of the archaeological record for nationalist or "meta-nationalist" purposes can be evaluated both scientifically and ethically. What should not be abandoned in any archaeological undertaking is the perspective that acknowledges our common humanity and views the history of humankind as a special case of natural history, rooted in our biological development as a unique culture-bearing species. Like any form of archaeology, a responsible nationalist archaeology refuses to blur the distinctions between race, language, and culture and denies the purity or biological superiority of any culture over any another. It documents the rich, unique features of past human cultures; locates them in specific social, economic, and historical contexts; and traces their emergence and transformation over time, detailing how each has contributed to a shared world historical tradition. From this perspective, future archaeologies – nationalist or not – remain anthropological.

Part II

Western Europe

2 Civilization, barbarism, and nationalism in European archaeology

Bernard Wailes and Amy L. Zoll

In Europe after World War II overt ethnic chauvinism became politically incorrect on both sides of the Iron Curtain, though for somewhat different reasons. More specifically, the discrediting of Nazi-style racist archaeology made ethnic archaeology (defined below) very subdued. Today, with progressive unification within the European Community, it may be more difficult for states to ignore or to minimize ethnic diversity within or across their borders,[1] while for many in eastern Europe ethnicity has now become a fundamental principle of political identity. In either situation, archaeology may be used as an important aspect of cultural identity and to support moral claims to territory.[2] Territorial claims are unlikely to be settled by archaeological debate, perhaps, but archaeologists and other scholars have provided much ammunition that might be used on the cultural identity front. This might seem odd, if overtly ethnic archaeology has been muted for several decades, and if – as is generally the case – scholars have not fostered ethnicity deliberately in their research or publications. Yet scholars, along with other Europeans, have deeply ingrained perceptions of ethnicity in the European past, perpetuated by traditional terminologies as much as by anything else. A hypothetical, yet characteristic, example may clarify this.

In the two imaginary European countries of Paphlagonia and Crim-Tartary (see Thackeray 1854) the later part of the archaeological record represents documented societies of the historic Paphlagonian and Crim-Tartarian peoples, so the labels "Paphlagonian" and "Crim-Tartarian" are applied to archaeological units. Archaeological units of the historic period are thus identified by ethnic labels which, by inference, are also extended backward in time, into the protohistoric and later prehistoric periods. Such ethnic terminology, it must be emphasized, does not necessarily imply any bias or prejudice on the part of those engaged in archaeological research. To elaborate, let us look at Paphlagonian Studies (for which read Celtic Studies, Italian Studies, etc.). "Paphlagonianists" are happily engaged in linguistic, literary, historical, archaeological, and other scholarly research. They are not preaching Paphlagonian racial superiority, nor advocating the political dominance of Paphlagonians over their neighbors. Yet these scholars are enthusiasts for and advocates of whatever may be labelled "Paphlagonian," even though many of them are not Paphlagonians by ancestry, native tongue, natal location, or citizenship: the roster of Paphlagonian scholars doubtless includes Finns, Germans, Portuguese, and so on. All of them are Paphlagonophiles and to that extent, however mildly and implicitly, they are partisan. But to say that Paphlagonian Studies is necessarily "nationalist" would be misleading.

There is another dimension to this issue, too. If Paphlagonia is a fairly typical European country, "Paphlagonian Archaeology" might mean one of four things, none necessarily "nationalist."

1. The Paphlagonian state (or state-sponsored, or state-subsidized) archaeological establishment: (a) civil service bodies responsible for recording and preserving field monuments; (b) the national and regional museums; and (c) university departments of archaeology.
2. The corps of professional archaeologists employed in the Paphlagonian archaeological establishment. Some will be specialists in ethnic Paphlagonian archaeology (4 below).
3. All material culture remains, from the Lower Palaeolithic to industrial archaeology, within the boundaries of the Paphlagonian state. Archaeologists in the civil service and museums are responsible for this. It could be called "national archaeology."
4. The material culture remains that are (or are claimed to be) those of the historic, protohistoric, and later prehistoric Paphlagonian people, folk, or (confusingly) nation. It begins in later prehistory at the earliest, and its spatial dimension (at any period) probably does not coincide exactly with the modern Paphlagonian state.[3]

This last is the "archaeology of cultural, or historical, identity," often called "nationalist." But since "nationalist archaeology" is not necessarily connected ideologically with either an existing or a proposed nation-state, and since "nation" and "state" are often used synonymously, it is far more appropriate and far less confusing to call it *ethnic archaeology*.

None of these four "Paphlagonian archaeologies" operates in a vacuum. All take some account of, and interact with, the equivalent archaeologies of neighboring countries, such as Crim-Tartary. But while the first three archaeologies are defined by the political boundaries of the state, ethnic archaeology can be defined only in relation to the archaeologies of other ethnic groups. This must involve comparisons, so ethnic archaeology contains very evident potential for re-playing, or inventing, competition (or rivalry, or hostility) between ethnic groups of the past.

Such comparisons and competition are usually set within the paradigm of "barbarism versus civilization." For example, the historic Paphlagonians and Crim-Tartarians, and their putative later prehistoric ancestors, both played some role in the development of European civilization. Like all other European peoples, both were once "barbarian" and both became "civilized." When and how this happened is an entirely legitimate subject for scholarly enquiry, of course. The terminology traditionally employed in such enquiries is ethnic terminology, however. We might hear of such questions as "when did the early Paphlagonian state emerge?" or "how did the first Crim-Tartarian towns develop?" Since ethnic archaeology invites competition, however, not only do ethnically defined archaeological units become subsumed into the broader paradigm of barbarism versus civilization, but they become competitively engaged. The question "when did the early Paphlagonian state emerge?" becomes "did the Paphlagonian state emerge before the Crim-Tartarian state and, if so, was the latter state-formation process dependent upon the former?" Once more, a legitimate question, but a question that invites ethnic partisanship. Archaeologists are knee-deep in this conceptual morass, along with their fellow-scholars.

I Different archaeologies and the barbarian vs. civilized paradigm

The culture-historical approach in Europe has emphasized both the history of European peoples and the development of European civilization. We read of Celtic art, Slavic pottery, Visigothic brooches, and Viking houses, etc. These are terms which have self-evident ethnic-cum-linguistic implications. In later prehistory, where such identities were not known, they have been sought: the regional facies of the expanding "Urnfield" complex of the later Bronze Age, for example, are thought to represent the expansion of several Indo-European language groups, such as proto-Italic, proto-Celtic, proto-Germanic, and proto-Illyrian.[4] These peoples were incorporated progressively into European civilization as it diffused, from ancient Greece to the Greek colonies, from the Greeks to the Etruscans and Romans, from the latter to much of Europe in the course of Roman imperial expansion. Eventually the rest of Europe became civilized, as Christianity spread and as medieval urbanism and states emerged.[5] Thus "influences," migration, trade, conquest, and diffusion could account comfortably for the development of European civilization.[6]

Processual archaeology is above all neo-evolutionary. It stresses economic and socio-political indicators of cultural evolution such as ranking, status differentiation, economic specialization, exchange systems, settlement hierarchy, monumental construction, and urbanism. In particular, it is highly critical of external agents (diffusion, migration, etc.) being invoked as the sole, or at least the major, causes of cultural change. Rather, it stresses the systematic interaction of indigenous components at local and regional scales, as for example in analyzing state formation in the Bronze Age Aegean (Renfrew 1972, see ch. 21 especially), Late Iron Age Gaul (e.g. Crumley 1974), and parts of the Balkans and central Europe (e.g. Champion *et al.* 1984:297, 315–21). Following the collapse of the western Roman Empire in the fifth century AD, the emergence of native states around the North Sea and the Baltic has also been argued as a primarily indigenous process (e.g. Randsborg 1980; Hodges 1982).[7] Although processualists have tried to avoid such quirky human things as ethnicity and language, as well as diffusion and migration,[8] ethnic-cum-linguistic labels are unavoidable in the protohistoric and historic periods when most state formation took place. Consequently, the labels (Greek, Roman, Frankish, Anglo-Saxon, etc.) employed by processualists in their analyses of cultural evolution are the ethnic-cum-linguistic labels inherited from the traditional culture-historians. Moreover, both culture-historians and processualists equate the State with Civilization, despite their different emphases on each.

Post-processual archaeology seems to be a flag of convenience flying over a rather motley crew. Of concern here are those who seek to regain intellectual respectability for several traditional interpretations that were declared illegal, immoral, and probably fattening, by the more rigid processualists. Notably, core and periphery analysis reintroduces diffusion; structural approaches reintroduce cultural or ethnic tradition; and contextualism reintroduces historical contingency.

Traditional culture-historians, processualists, and some post-processualists, then, may play by somewhat different rules. But, explicitly or implicitly (as the case may be) their board-pieces are still ethnic groups; the name of the game is still barbarism versus civilization; and one object of the game is still to record and to analyze the evolution of barbarians toward civilization. Ivory tower debates, whether of trait diffusion and population movement or of systemic processes, merge all too easily into arguments about the relative contributions made to European civilization by, say, the Paphlagonians as opposed to the Crim-Tartarians. From there, alas, it is but a short step to the schoolyard: Paphlagonians versus Crim-Tartarians. My People were civilized before your People. Or better still, my people *civilized your* people. Thus archaeologists provide potential ammunition for nationalists, however unwittingly, not only by employing ethnic *terms* of reference, but a *frame* of reference – the cultural types or stages of barbarism and civilization – that can be glossed all too easily (if all too simplistically) as "retarded," "inert," or "primitive" versus "progressive," "innovative," or "advanced." This in turn can translate readily into the even more simplistic, but emotionally even more satisfying, bad guys versus good guys.

II The example of Insular art

The example of "Insular art" will illustrate these issues in concrete form.[9] The Insular art style was developed during the seventh century AD in an area that included Ireland, western Scotland (the Irish kingdom of Dalriada), northern England (Anglo-Saxon Northumbria), and perhaps eastern Scotland (Pictland), all of which are conventionally regarded as more barbarian than civilized at this time. This art style is one of the more remarkable developments in earlier medieval Europe, for it combines "barbarian" elements derived from late La Tène (insular Celtic) and Germanic sources (notably animal ornament) with "civilized" elements derived from the contemporaneous Mediterranean culture of late antiquity, and perhaps the late provincial Roman world of the (then) recent past. The diversity of these elements has prompted, rightly, much debate over their relative importance to Insular art and to the historical implications of such interaction.

In the broader context, Insular art is important because of the books in this style. In these we find the precocious development of a new style of elaborate full-page illumination, of equally elaborate initial letters, and of the characteristic and elegant Insular script. This manuscript style was transmitted to continental Europe by emigrant insular churchmen. There, in the eighth century, the books became important exemplars, and can be seen as a material counterpart to the important role played by insular churchmen on the continent, most notably in the Carolingian renaissance of the late eighth century. The Insular manuscript style, then, was one manifestation of the "paradigmatic shift" (Wallace 1972) from the world of late antiquity to the Christian *ecumene* of medieval Europe. This is when it is possible, for the first time, to see indigenous temperate European contributions to an urban, literate society in which states were developing. For until this time any native European contributions to civilized life had been Greek or Roman.[10] Thus Insular-style manuscripts appear to have been an integral part of the process by which European medieval civilization developed. One might even say that they exemplify that process.

This being so, and since they are also magnificent works of art, it is no surprise that the origins and dating of the Insular manuscript tradition (and, more generally, of Insular art) have been debated in great detail by many scholars. This debate is all the more necessary not only because many Insular art objects are highly portable, e.g. books and reliquaries, but also because such artefacts are known from contemporary written sources to have been transported, often over great distances.[11] While this debate is entirely appropriate, its terminology is cast in the familiar ethnic terms (here Anglo-Saxon, Pictish, Irish, etc.), and its framework is the familiar development from barbarism to civilization. So although the numerous participating scholars cannot be accused of ethnic propaganda (as noted already), their writings sometimes do seem to imply that ethnic group X played a more substantial role in developing European civilization than did ethnic groups Y or Z.[12]

Viewed from another perspective, we seem to be in the very familiar archaeological territory of the Nuclear Area Hypothesis, with every cultural advance of note originating in Sumer, say, or Teotihuacan. The only difference here is that, for a short while at least, a peripheral area (Ireland and northern Britain) seems to have played a nuclear area role by developing Insular art. As elsewhere, the larger scale of the culture area may well be far more appropriate and profitable for debate and analysis, as for example, "the Middle East," or "the Mesoamerican interaction sphere." Thus Insular art developed within the relatively small area of Ireland and northern Britain, but that included several identifiable peoples, and so can be called a culture area. Moreover, since continental and Mediterranean elements contributed to this style, as well as insular ones, Insular art simply could not have developed in isolation, but must be seen in the context of the larger culture area of western Europe. The debate over dating and origins must now be outlined, a debate in which the Lindisfarne Gospels play a central role.

Unlike nearly all other Insular art items, the Lindisfarne Gospel Book can be assigned both a probable date and a probable location of manufactures – *c.* AD 700 in the monastery of Lindisfarne, Northumbria.[13] It displays a highly accomplished and intricate combination of Germanic and Celtic decorative elements, so is likely to be a product of "mature" rather than "developmental" Insular art. It also includes relatively naturalistic human figure representation based upon late antique Mediterranean models, which indicates a close, perhaps direct, connection. By contrast, in some other Insular manuscripts the human figure may be highly stylized and relatively non-naturalistic, i.e. non-classical; this feature is particularly marked in the Book of Durrow, on which more below. In short, the Lindisfarne evidence indicates that *c.* AD 700 was the approximate *terminus ante quem* for the developmental stages of Insular art, and that by this time at least Northumbria was capable of producing the highest-quality Insular art. The names of those stated to be responsible for the manufacture of the Lindisfarne Gospels, moreover, are Anglo-Saxon names. Thus a strong case can be made not only that this book was made in an Anglo-Saxon monastery in an Anglo-Saxon kingdom, but that it was actually made by Anglo-Saxons. (How ethnic can you get?) Since it is an example of mature Insular art, however, it demonstrates neither where the developmental stages may have occurred nor that the Anglo-Saxons played the dominant role in that development.

Historical background

In 597 Pope Gregory the Great sent Augustine to begin the conversion of the insular Anglo-Saxons. From the successful base established in Kent, one Paulinus was sent in 601 to convert Northumbria. The mission was initially successful, but a resurgence of paganism followed. Christianity in Northumbria was reestablished (or revitalized) in 635, this time by Irish churchmen from Iona (who were also in the process of converting the Picts). Thus Irish monasteries were established amongst both the Picts and the Northumbrians. The monastery of Lindisfarne, indeed, was one of these. Two factors, however, have placed the Irish at a disadvantage in historical debate.

First, many of the Irish in Northumbria rejected the decision (Synod of Whiby, AD 664) of the Northumbrian king and churchmen to change from "Celtic" to Roman usage in several matters – notably, calculating the date of Easter.[14] This was recorded in detail by Bede (born *c.* 673, died 735) in his *Ecclesiastical History of the English People*, written in the early eighth century, and the primary near-contemporary historical source for the period. Bede, a Northumbrian and a monk of the reformed (i.e. post-Whitby) Northumbrian church, wrote both as an Anglo-Saxon and as a partisan Romanist (e.g. Riché 1972:380). It was natural enough that he should identify the participants in ethnic terms, but it is unfortunate that the consequent Anglo-Saxon versus Irish tone of his account has colored much scholarly writing.[15]

Second, Northumbrian eagerness to establish close conformity with Rome is reflected in material culture (e.g. Alexander 1978:12), in a manner that could be called "classicizing" (see the "Anglo-Saxon Renaissance," below). Benedict Biscop (*c.* AD 629–90), a Northumbrian noble and churchman who spent many years on the continent, sent for masons and glaziers from Gaul to help in the construction of the twin monasteries that he founded on his return – Monkwearmouth in 674 and Jarrow in 681 or 682. Mortared masonry and glazed windows were thus reintroduced to the island of Britain for the first time since its opening night on the civilized stage centuries before, under Roman management. From Gaul and Rome Benedict Biscop also brought books and pictures, and it is argued plausibly that these had a profound effect on the subsequent development of

Northumbrian manuscripts and sculpture. The naturalistic representation of the human figure, as in the Lindisfarne Gospels (and in the Codex Amiatinus, see below), is an obvious case in point.

The Anglo-Saxons can be seen as more closely associated with Rome than were the other insular peoples; they brought continental building techniques to the islands; and they appear to have been the main conduit for late classical styles of illustration and decoration. To some scholars this seems to show that the Anglo-Saxons were more innovative and more civilized, or were at least more keen to become civilized, than their neighbors the Irish, the Picts, and the Britons. So archaeology seems to confirm Bede's disparagement of the Irish for not accepting Roman practice at the Synod of Whitby.

In this vein, Wormald (1982:75) writes of Biscop's monasteries as being, during the lifetime of Bede (later seventh and earlier eighth centuries), "an island of Mediterranean culture in a barbarian sea." While it is implicitly clear here that "Mediterranean culture" may be translated as "civilization," it is admittedly unclear whether the "barbarian sea" means the rest of Northumbria, including Lindisfarne, or everything outside Northumbria. He does not mean that the Lindisfarne Gospels were totally barbarian, though, for he links the book implicitly to this Mediterranean tradition by drawing attention to the relatively naturalistic late antique style of the human figure (Wormald 1982:93). As of course he recognizes, this poses a problem, for in itself this book shows islands of Mediterranean culture (the naturalistic human representations) in a barbarian sea (of Insular Celtic-Germanic abstract decoration). Thus one complex artefact is both barbarian and civilized at the same time.

If mature Insular art became a part of early medieval European civilization, however, then even its barbarian elements became civilized. So if people X are ascribed a larger role in the developmental stages of Insular art than people Y or people Z, it could be implied that people X are ascribed a larger role than peoples Y or Z in the development of medieval civilization in Europe. From this it could be implied further that people X were perhaps less barbarian than peoples Y and Z because they were more active in using and resynthesizing a series of barbarian art motifs. Such notions would be an entertaining paradox, but one might begin to wonder whether the ethnic classificatory system and the barbarian versus civilized paradigm are the most enlightening or useful analytical concepts that could be employed here.

The Book of Durrow[16]

The Book of Durrow, another Insular manuscript, sharpens the focus on such questions. In the Book of Durrow the Germanic and Celtic motifs of

Insular art are far less integrated than in Lindisfarne and human representation (as noted above) is markedly stylized and non-classical. Kendrick (1938:97), indeed, writes: "the Book of Durrow is in its ornament the only manuscript in the early Irish and English group that is wholly and relentlessly barbaric in concept from beginning to end [note Irish, English, barbaric]." On typological grounds, Durrow is widely regarded as the earliest illuminated Gospel Book in Insular style – that is, the earliest book to employ Insular art for full-page illuminated displays and for highly elaborated initial letters[17] – and so plays a critical role in scholarly assessments of how that art developed (see references in note 9). If it is typologically earlier than Lindisfarne, it presumably was made before *c.* AD 700. On this, most agree – but how long before 700, and where?

The earliest date proposed for Durrow is "shortly after AD 600" (Roth 1987:28), though most scholars in recent decades have inclined toward the mid- or later seventh century (usefully summarized by Roth 1987:25).[18] At this stage of the argument, its place of manufacture begins to become an issue. If the Book of Durrow was made in Northumbria, textual evidence indicates that the period 635–74 would be the most likely. The Celtic elements suggest a date after the arrival of Irish churchmen in 635. The stylized human figure, on the other hand, suggests a date before (or not too long after) Benedict Biscop's return from the continent in 674 because, as we have seen, it is inferred that this event opened the conduit through which late antique styles, such as the naturalistic human figure, began to flow from the Mediterranean to Northumbria. Following this logic, a date prior to 635 (e.g. Roth 1987, see above) would virtually preclude a Northumbrian origin, and a date later than the Lindisfarne Gospels would make such an origin unlikely. A date in between would permit, but certainly would not require, the interpretation that Northumbria was the region where Gospel Books illuminated in Insular style were first developed.[19]

We do not know in what monastic *scriptorium* Durrow was made, however (see note 16). It has no contemporary vernacular glosses, and palaeographic analysis is inconclusive. Therefore it should be regarded impartially as of unknown origin – any wealthy monastery[20] in Northumbria, Dalriada, Ireland, or even perhaps Pictland (note 16) could be a possibility. And, if we were to regard the Insular art zone as a culture area, the ethnicity of the Book of Durrow is not very important. If, though, the Book of Durrow is analyzed in terms that state or imply ethnic authorship, then ethnic initiative and inventiveness (if not outright superiority) is implied, even if not explicitly inferred. The discussion that follows is intended simply to provide a few examples of the positions sketched in above (see note 9), for Nordenfalk's succinct and pithy 1987 essay makes it redundant to pursue these at length. (Although his study was not written for this purpose, Nordenfalk, in reviewing the scholarship on Insular art, supplies a number of examples germane to the purpose of this paper.)

Nordenfalk makes it clear that Insular style manuscripts have been classified in ethnic terms since study of them began in earnest in the 1830s. Opinion has tended to polarize between those emphasizing Irish roots and those favoring a stronger Anglo-Saxon role, though these positions are complicated by the varying regard which different scholars appear to hold for the barbarian elements of Insular manuscript art. For example, as cited above, Kendrick (1938:37) commented on the "wholly and unrelentingly barbaric" nature of the Book of Durrow, which he argues was made in Ireland (pp. 94–105). While clearly he admired the art ("magnificent design and brilliant execution"), in the next chapter (ch. VI) he extolled the "Anglo-Saxon Renaissance" initiated by Biscop's Northumbrian monasteries. "Renaissance" he defined explicitly as the revival of classical styles that had been absent in Britain since the collapse of the western empire in the fifth century. In particular, he described the Codex Amiatinus, made at Jarrow not long after 700,[21] thus: "[It] is almost entirely Italian in style and shows no weakening whatsoever in the direction of a barbaric Celtic or English ornamental apparatus such as is seen in the Book of Durrow and the Lindisfarne Gospels" (p. 113). Despite his admiration for barbaric art, Kendrick quite clearly rates classical (civilized) art more highly. In a rather crasser vein, the palaeographer Lowe opined that Irish and Anglo-Saxon scribes were temperamentally distinct: the former were "guided by whim and fancy," the latter "balanced and disciplined" (cited in Nordenfalk 1987:2). As Nordenfalk comments caustically, this "virtually made all rough manuscripts Irish and all fine ones English." Needless to say, Lowe assigned to the Book of Durrow both Northumbrian manufacture and a later seventh-century date.

If scholarly works sometimes seem to show rather subjective opinions, we should not be surprised to find them in derivative popular syntheses too. In some ways these are more important, of course, for it is from them that the student and other non-experts learn of Insular art and manuscripts. To the Laings (1979:139), for example, the Book of Durrow is quite simply and baldly "the first major masterpiece of Northumbrian painting." Manufacture of this book by Anglo-Saxons may be understood from this, and, unsurprisingly, these authors favor a date *c.* 650. More judiciously, Wormald (1982:72) notes: "[it] has several Irish features . . . [b]ut the script and some 'Germanic' decoration suggest that it may have been produced in Northumbria under Irish influence . . . If so, this is not only the first of the great insular *codices de luxe*, but also one of the very first surviving English books." Note "English"; again, manufacture by Anglo-Saxons must be understood, even though here some more remote Irish "influence" is acknowledged. To others, though, such English appropriation "[deprives]

Ireland of the honour of having played an essential part in what has been considered its greatest national exploit" (Nordenfalk 1977:11).

Comment on the Insular art debate

It has been emphasized already that arguments over stylistic origins and places of manufacture are entirely legitimate scholarly business. As the quotations illustrate, however, these arguments are usually cast in an ethnic frame of reference, and this ethnic frame of reference is almost universally employed despite all the archaeological evidence that Insular art was multi-ethnic in distribution and multi-cultural in origin – that it was, in fact, a culture area phenomenon. What is more, there is ample historical evidence that there was much inter-ethnic contact and travel (e.g. see Hughes 1971) and that many insular monasteries were multi-ethnic. They were not founded as enclaves of ethnic purity but to foster the Christian life, and it was here that Insular manuscripts were produced. Under these circumstances, it seems positively perverse to attribute almost all important insular innovations to any one ethnic group in the islands, Anglo-Saxons or others. This perversity is compounded, moreover, by subsuming the ethnic frame of reference under the barbarian versus civilized paradigm to make that one ethnic group almost the sole insular link in the developing chain of European civilization, while reducing the contributions of the others to little better than a walk-on part, at best.

This brief discussion of Insular art has argued that because some of its components are conventionally identified in terms of barbarian ethnic groups (Celtic or Irish, and Germanic), much of the scholarly debate has focussed upon the relative importance of those groups in its manufacture. Further, it has been argued that because other components can be identified as late classical, the conceptual framework of debate has been that of barbarian and civilized. These analytical modes of thinking appear to promote some agonizing, as if such a combination were somehow "wrong." There are gleams of more productive thinking. Koehler's discussion of the human figure in Insular manuscripts is summarized thus by Nordenfalk: "dismissing the question Irish or English as of secondary importance, he treated the material as a single school, trying to show the inner logic of its development" (Nordenfalk 1987:4).[22]

This sounds like a big step in the right direction of recognizing, first and foremost, that we are dealing with a new phenomenon which should be treated in its own terms, rather than in terms of preconceived ideas about ethnicity, barbarism, and civilization. Those terms, surely, are that Insular art was part and parcel of the process by which a new civilization emerged in Europe in the early medieval period. As noted before, in archaeological terms it is a culture area phenomenon. Luckily, we have enough historical information from Europe at this time to see clearly that many of the clergy travelled widely, and that many monasteries were occupied by monks from several different ethnic groups. It is this cosmopolitanism that is important, not ethnicity, nor the question of who or what might be called barbarian or civilized. Two concluding examples underscore this point.

The Echternach Gospels (Gospels of St Willibrord) are named after the monastery of Echternach, founded by Willibrord *c*. 700. According to Bede (V.9–11), Willibrord was a Northumbrian who had spent twelve years in Ireland where Egbert, another Anglo-Saxon, had been his mentor. Egbert had intended to go to the continent to convert the Frisians, but Willibrord went instead, in 690. Backhouse (1981:37–9) claims that he left for the continent from Northumbria, and that this book was made in Lindisfarne, but it is perhaps more likely that he left from Ireland, and that the book was made there, as Nordenfalk (1977:48) implies. At all events, the book ended up in Echternach (and might even have been made there).

At Echternach, a Gospel Book was produced for the cathedral of nearby Trier – the Trier Gospels (see Nordenfalk 1977:88–93). Two scribes collaborated, one trained in a Merovingian Frankish monastery, the other in the Insular tradition. The latter signed two of his full-page illuminations: folio 5^{v} has "thoms scribsit" at the bottom, and folio 12 has "thomas" inscribed at the top. Folio 5^{v} is largely in "barbaric" style, with plenty of interlace; even the human face, though somewhat classicized, is a rather schematic full-face. Folio 12, on the other hand, is almost exclusively in late classical style, and the human head is slightly turned to the left, with the eyes looking further left still. The evidence is virtually indisputable that one man was responsible for these two very different pages. We should be fervently grateful that his name gives no clue as to his ethnicity, and so no opportunity for ethnic claims to be made on him. He might have been Irish, or Anglo-Saxon, or a Frank – conceivably a Copt or Armenian – but does it matter one whit? He was certainly versed in both barbarian and classical traditions, which is a far more important observation.

III Conclusion

"Ethnicity" (however defined, and with whatever supposed implications) may seem a fundamental way to classify groups and individuals. However, it is certainly not the only way, and certainly not always the most analytically useful. In the early medieval European contexts discussed above, for example, an individual's ethnicity was probably largely irrelevant compared to the far more important criteria of a Latin education, training in thus and such a monastery, pilgrimages or mission work undertaken, and so forth. If one must insist on employing the categories barbarian and civilized, such people would be defined as civilized – even though some of them, like Thomas, could and did produce barbarian art, and some might even have started life as barbarians.[23]

European concepts of ethnicity, of barbarism, and of civilization were born in antiquity, or at least first recorded in antiquity. They persisted through earlier medieval times, when barbarians were the pagans (often referred to as "gentiles" then) and Christians were civilized. They persisted through the later Middle Ages, for although Christianity spread right across Europe, religious backsliding or heresy could summon accusations of barbarism. Jones (1971), for example, has deftly summarized later medieval English attitudes toward their Celtic neighbors the Welsh, the Scots, and the Irish. The adjective "wild" was commonly used as a synonym for "barbarian." Thus, the civil Irish were those conforming to English ways, while the wild Irish were those who did not. These attitudes persisted into the sixteenth and seventeenth centuries, when the English finally managed to conquer the whole of Ireland, and to bring it under English administration. By then, the Reformation had provided added impetus. The Irish were not only wild but Catholic, and might obtain diplomatic or military aid from any Catholic power at odds with England. Consequently, the advance of Protestantism in Ireland would not only advance civilization, but reduce military threat. The plantations were intended as a main agency of this process, whereby Protestants from Britain were lured into taking up Irish land.

The last gasp of insular barbarism was the Jacobite rebellion of 1745–6. The majority of those who rallied to Prince Charles Stuart, the Young Pretender, were highland Scots to whom both the lowland Scots and the English attributed the full range of barbarian characteristics. Indeed, their descriptions of the highlanders echo classical accounts of the barbarians of antiquity remarkably closely. After the Jacobite defeat at Culloden and the subsequent Highland Clearances, the remaining highlanders were no longer a threat. But the "Real European Barbarian" had survived into the mid-eighteenth century, in an unbroken line from antiquity.[24]

The contrast between the civilized European and the barbarian European was inherited from antiquity and was periodically modified to changing circumstances. It still seemed both fresh and apposite in the eighteenth century. Small wonder that *it* moulded native European ideas of ethnic history and identity. Small wonder that this classification was employed in other parts of the world. And small wonder that it was used in European schemes of human evolution. This then is how the European thinks about the European past, and how European peoples are classified. This is how the European archaeologist thinks – the traditionalist, the processualist, and at least some post-processualists.

This is not to suggest that scholars are condoning, still less abetting, the abuse of historical and archaeological interpretations by those who seek dubious political justification from the past. Nor does it lead necessarily to the conclusion that there should be a politically inspired agenda for archaeologists. Simply, we should be aware that the "Real European Barbarian," usually ethnically defined, lives on as a very potent metaphor. As this paper has argued, these concepts may often distort archaeological analysis, but they probably do no great harm used in the purely scholarly context. But they enter public culture in even more simplified form. They can be used for political ends. If and when that happens, maybe scholars bear some responsibility.

NOTES

1 Despite considerable relaxation of inter-ethnic hostilities in western Europe, the Basque and the northern Irish situations are simply the most obtrusive of many such problems.

2 Such identity may include not only the ethnic past of a people, but the landscape they inhabit – note, for example, the common use of monuments in the more culturally redolent tourist literature. Wailes (1989) examines the case of a disputed site, which is now being developed as a "heritage center."

3 An attempt to make these several archaeologies coincide was made by the Nazis: the German state was extended; all historically ethnic Germans were to be incorporated into that state; early German society was claimed to have been the most advanced in Europe; and every effort was made to suborn the German archaeological establishment into providing scholarly justification for this ideology. This simplifies the actuality, but not we think the aims: the archaeology of the state was ethnic archaeology, and ethnic archaeology was cast in stage-evolutionary terms. The equation of ethnicity with biology provided a racially pure and culturally superior Aryan antiquity to support the racial purification and cultural superiority of the Nazi present. See Arnold 1990.

4 Attempts to correlate prehistoric archaeological groups with language groups begin with Kossinna (see Trigger 1989a:163–7), and were developed more cautiously by Childe (e.g. 1950 ch. X).

5 The work of Worsaae, Montelius, and others established regional sequences for later European prehistory, establishing synchronisms between regions that eventually reached to the "civilized" world of the Mediterranean, and its calendrical chronologies. This greatly strengthened the perception that innovations originated in the ancient Near East or Egypt (or, later, the Mediterranean), and were passed northward to the "barbarians" by diffusion.

6 Traditional, culture-historical archaeology in Europe was not replaced by processualism, or even driven into hiding. Many, probably most, European archaeologists remained staunch culture-historians. Further, it should be seen neither as intellectually outmoded nor as socially dangerous. For example, fusty old diffusionism has re-emerged more nattily dressed as core-and-periphery,

and the excavations of medieval York and Dublin have prompted multi-ethnic interpretations that are essentially inductive, not derived from processual models.

7 The second edition of Hodges' 1982 book was not available at the time of writing.

8 The negative reaction of processualists to diffusion and migration is complementary to their positive search for internal processes of change, though neither diffusion nor migration is inherently anti-evolutionary, as Childe realized.

9 The discussion below simply uses Insular art as an example of the arguments developed in this paper, and in no way should be taken as a reflection of authorial expertise in this field. In order to keep this discussion as brief as possible, further detail is provided in footnotes for those who wish for additional guidance. Readers are referred to Campbell *et al.* (1982, chs. 3 and 4), Megaw and Megaw (1989, Epilogue), Nordenfalk (1977, 1987), and M. Ryan (1991). These are four recent works which are authoritative, accessible, and illustrated; they are introductory, but provide more extensive treatments than space permits here.

10 This represents the conventional view. This is no place for a discussion on the pros and cons of whether or not transalpine "state formation" might or might not have taken place prior to Roman conquest.

11 Some of this might be ascribed to "prestige goods exchange," such as Ceolfrid's intended gift of the Codex Amiatinus to the Pope (see note 21 below). Some, on the other hand, may have been more commercial: Benedict Biscop purchased many books on the continent for eventual shipment to Northumbria.

12 This tendency is surely reinforced by the training of most of the scholars involved, and the scholarly structure within which they work. This encourages specialization into, for example, "Saxonists" and "Celticists" – terms which thus refer to scholarly specialities, of course, not to the ethnicity of the scholars (e.g. the Saxonist F. Masai and the Celticist F. Henry were, respectively, Belgian and French). For readers unfamiliar with the more arcane aspects of early European history and ethnic terminology the following may help. The term "Scotti" meant Irish. The kingdom(s) of Dalriada extended from northeast Ireland across to northwest Britain, so the inhabitants of both Ireland and northwest Britain were known indifferently as Scots or Irish. The Picts of northeast Britain, who spoke some form of Celtic language, are very poorly known historically. To judge by Irish and Northumbrian references, they were a considerable power until the ninth century, when they were incorporated into the Scottish kingdom of Dalriada. The whole of northern Britain has been known as Scotland ever since.

13 The Lindisfarne Gospel Book is usually regarded both as indisputably Northumbrian and as firmly dated to *c.* AD 700 because of its colophon, which states unequivocally that the book was written by Eadfrith, bound by Ethelwald, and decorated (with gems and precious metals) by Billfrith. This information is reiterated by Symeon of Durham. Eadfrith became Bishop of Lindisfarne in 698 and died in 721. The Lindisfarne colophon states that Eadfrith wrote the book to commemorate (*inter alia*) St Cuthbert, who died in 687. Eadfrith may have written the book before he became bishop, of course,

which gives a maximum range of 687–721 for the writing of Lindisfarne. Ethelwald succeeded Eadfrith as Bishop in 721, and died *c.* 740. If Billfrith, otherwise unknown, was the Billfrith mentioned in the Lindisfarne *Liber Vitae*, he probably died in the later eighth century. The colophon not only appears to be very specific and reliable, but seems to be confirmed by the independent source, Symeon of Durham. While there is no reason to doubt the veracity of this colophon, it does not provide absolutely unquestionable evidence for the date and source of Lindisfarne, for it was written in the mid- or later tenth century AD (by one Aldred, who also wrote the word-for-word translation of the Lindisfarne text from Latin into Anglo-Saxon), more than two centuries after the ascribed date for the manufacture of Lindisfarne. Symeon of Durham wrote in the early twelfth century, and could have been familiar with Aldred's account. (See Backhouse 1981: chs. 1 and 2 for details.)

14 Ironically, most of the Irish monasteries had conformed to Roman usage in the calculation of Easter not long after AD 630. The Iona *paruchia* (a confederation of monasteries) did not, however, and it was from Iona that most Irish churchmen in Northumbria came.

15 See Bede (III.25) for the Synod of Whitby. Bede gave the Irish churchmen full credit for their faith, their proselytizing zeal, and their role in the permanent establishment of Christianity in Northumbria. He states also that some Irish did accept Roman usage, staying in Northumbria, while some Anglo-Saxons did not, and went to Ireland. This, incidentally, is one of the many pieces of evidence for multi-ethnic monasteries. Bede's partisanship was by no means totally unbalanced, therefore, making the conscious or unconscious partisanship of modern scholars the more obviously over-simplified and misleading.

16 The Book of Durrow is so called because it was kept at the monastery of Durrow, Co. Offaly, from the late eleventh or early twelfth century until the dissolution of the monastery. It was later discovered nearby in the possession of a farmer, who cured his cattle of ailments by treating them with water into which the Book had been dipped. It was acquired in 1661 by Henry Jones, Vice-Chancellor of Trinity College Dublin and a former officer in Cromwell's army. Jones donated it to the TCD library, where it still remains. Its later and altered first colophon invokes St Columba, the sixth-century Irish founder of the famous monastery on Iona, in Dalriada. Neither its sojourn at Durrow nor its first colophon demonstrates its origin, however. As noted, some consider its origin to have been in Ireland, or an Irish foundation such as Iona; others argue for Northumbria. In the text above, a Pictish monastery was suggested (at least as a faint possibility), largely because (as noted by many) the Evangelists' animal symbols "are strikingly similar to animals found on a series of Pictish carved stones" (Alexander 1978:31).

17 There is another, technological, attribute of these manuscripts: the vellum was prepared by some new process that produced pages described as suede- or chamois-like, considerably superior to earlier vellum. See references in note 9.

18 The dating of the Book of Durrow is such a complex issue that a modest expansion on the sketch provided in the text is needed. Roth (1987) bases her argument for an early date on the documented presence of Irish clerics in continental Europe from the later sixth century. Notable amongst these was

Columbanus, who arrived in Frankia *c.* 590, and founded several monasteries. The last was Bobbio (founded *c.* 612) where he died in 615. Since Bobbio was in Lombard Italy, this exposed Irish churchmen directly to late classical culture. Specifically, Roth draws attention to two decorated manuscripts "belonging to the founding generation of the monastery of Bobbio," which have parallels with Durrow. The "founding generation" there implies the period between 612 and (say) 630. It is assumed by Roth and others, not unreasonably, that Bobbio became (or at least exemplified) the southern end of the channel by which Mediterranean motifs – notably ribbon interlace, as featured in the Book of Durrow – reached Ireland. Two large stone cross-slabs with ribbon interlace in Donegal clearly attest to the application of this motif in Ireland. One bears a formulaic inscription first recorded at the Council of Toledo in 633, so these cross-slabs may date as early as that time (Roth 1987:24). This does not demonstrate that the Book of Durrow was made in Ireland, of course, though it is one of the arguments used to support that position. It does supply independent evidence that ribbon interlace, of Mediterranean derivation, could indeed have been adopted in Ireland (and perhaps elsewhere) by, say, the 620s and very probably before 650.

Mediterranean motifs could have reached Ireland (and western Britain) well before the seventh century, however. Late Roman pottery – *terra sigillata* table-wares and amphorae – were arriving in both Ireland and western Britain in the earlier sixth century, apparently by direct sea route from their source of manufacture in North Africa and the eastern Mediterranean (Thomas 1981 summarizes these). While there are no grounds for dating the Book of Durrow as early as the sixth century, the evidence of this pottery does not harm Roth's case for an early date (Roth 1987:23).

19 This position is complicated by Durham Cathedral Library manuscript A.II.10 which shows interlace decoration of Mediterranean type also known on the two stone cross-slabs in the northwest of Ireland (see 18 above), and a relatively elaborate initial letter with "Celtic" motifs. Both these factors favor an Irish or a Dalriadic origin. It does not show combined "Germanic" and "Celtic" motifs, however. In typological terms, then, it should pre-date Durrow. Its location in Durham Cathedral Library suggests that it has been in Northumbria since earlier medieval times, but was it made there, or perhaps brought there from Dalriada by Irish monks during the period between their arrival in 635 and the Synod of Whitby in 664? Perhaps partly for these reasons, it is dated to *c.* 650. If it is to be argued that the Book of Durrow was made in Northumbria, then, this narrows the plausible chronological range somewhat (see Nordenfalk 1987:3).

20 One says "wealthy" here for two reasons: (a) It is a reasonable assumption that only the larger and wealthier monasteries could afford to train or to attract the highly skilled craft-workers (whether monks or not) so obviously necessary for such work. (b) The cost of vellum alone (never mind the cost of its preparation, inks and paints, and binding) was considerable. Ryan (1987) cites 150 calf-skins required for the Books of Kells, and calculates that a herd of 483 cattle (including 343 breeding cows) would be required to supply a *scriptorium* with the seventy calf-skins per year needed to supply one scribe for that year's work. To put this in another perspective, the honour-price of an Irish high king (whose

territory would be roughly equivalent to that of an Anglo-Saxon king) was (variously) forty-two or forty-eight milch-cows, so it is not wildly hyperbolic to suggest, then, that a Gospel Book approximated in worth to the proverbial king's ransom. If not quite a ransom, King Aldfrith of Northumbria (685–74) paid a stiff price for a book on travel (of "wonderful workmanship"): he gave in exchange land sufficient to support eight families. In monetary terms, a cow in seventh-century Frankia was worth 1 gold solidus, *c.* 3.9 grams. If a calf was valued at no more than one-eighth of a milch-cow, the vellum needed for one scribe/year was "worth" 34.125 grams of gold.

21 The Codex Amiatinus, as Kendrick states, shows no trace of Insular art and is stylistically late classical. It is identified as Northumbrian work only by its dedicatory verse. It was commissioned by Ceolfrid, first abbot of Jarrow, who died on the continent in 716 while taking this book as a present to the pope.

22 Unfortunately, Nordenfalk does not supply a full reference or date for this publication.

23 If this sounds faintly familiar to some readers, it is because that milieu was the forerunner of the modern university world, in which ethnicity is little more important than, say, height in assessing and categorizing an individual. One might go a step further to note that some scholars in modern universities, indeed, come from societies that would conventionally be classified as "barbarian" (if such an appallingly insensitive term – classificationist? – was permitted on today's campus). Again, this is not a fundamental trait by which such individuals are categorized in these contexts.

24 In the later eighteenth and early nineteenth century large numbers of highland Scots were evicted to make way for the more profitable rearing of sheep. The remaining highlanders, now harmless, were transformed conceptually by the Romantics into the quaint and picturesque. Indeed, the Hanoverians, no less, took the lead (starting with George IV, who died in 1830) in emphasizing their (part-) Scots ancestry by the wearing of kilts, highland holidays, and associated fashionable Caledomania. One might say that, rather than being coerced into civilization, the last "Real European Barbarian" was reconstituted as "Barbarian Lite" in a Hanoverian theme park.

3 Archaeology and nationalism in Spain[1]

Margarita Díaz-Andreu

The purpose of this chapter is to analyze the importance which the appearance of nationalism as a political doctrine had in the formation of archaeology as a scientific discipline in Spain. This question cannot be understood without first taking into account the complexity of the phenomenon of nationalism and the specificity of its development in Spain. Here a number of different nationalisms existed, and archaeological data were, therefore, interpreted from a nationalist perspective in a number of different and, to a certain extent, contradictory ways.

This article argues that in Spain, as in most of Europe, archaeology developed as the result of the need to find data which would permit the reconstruction of the remotest periods of the national past. The crystallization of the study of history for nationalist aims occurred in the nineteenth century, leading to the dramatic growth of historical studies in the universities, the creation of archives and libraries, and, finally, the funding of historical research, including archaeological excavations. However, one should not exaggerate the role of archaeology in the construction of national histories. Historical studies were centered fundamentally on the modern and medieval periods. The Romantic movement drew on medieval times for inspiration. Nevertheless, to a lesser degree during the nineteenth century, and to a greater extent in the twentieth, the growth of historical studies affected ancient history and prehistory and led to a greater recourse to archaeological data. In this way archaeology became politically charged. Archaeologists were fully aware of this situation, yet after World War II this politicization was systematically denied. Only recently have some archaeologists rediscovered the influence of nationalism on archaeology.

National histories were not elaborated without difficulties. This is clear in the case of Spain. Here, the construction of a national history was more complex than in many other parts of Europe, because Spanish nationalism was challenged by other peripheral nationalisms in Catalonia, the Basque country and, to a lesser extent, Galicia. Hence, four distinct nationalisms, which developed antagonistic versions of the national past, were found within the same nation-state.

How was it possible for a political ideology like nationalism to foster the appearance of different interpretations of history, and why did this occur from the middle of the eighteenth century and most notably at the end of the nineteenth century? The word "nation" was employed before the term "nationalism." As the word itself came from Latin, it continued to be used throughout the old territories of the Roman Empire. In the Middle Ages its meaning was more diffuse than today. "Nation" referred to sets of individuals related either because they lived in the same territory (a village, a town, or some more extensive area), or because they shared certain cultural traits. In some cases, the word "nation" was used to refer to people who were members of a concrete political unit.

The French Revolution of 1789 finally gave the term "nation" a political meaning, associating it with the concept of national sovereignty. A nation was conceived, in the words of Sièyes, as "a union of individuals governed by one law, and represented by the same law-giving assembly" (Kedourie 1988:5). Thus, this first political use of the term "nation," which some have referred to as political nationalism, did not consider its cultural origin. The French nation was simply seen as equivalent to the French state.

However, from the middle of the nineteenth century this politically based definition of nationalism was replaced by another definition which has become an integral part of what we now refer to as cultural or ethno-nationalism. This new definition of nation was based on two ideas: first, the world was divided naturally into cultures; and secondly, these cultures should ideally be political entities (Kedourie 1988). It was this essentialist interpretation of the nation which gave history an importance previously unknown. This enhanced importance stemmed from the fact that it now became necessary to justify the origin and formation of the nation from earliest times. Yet problems emerged when the attempt was made to delineate nations. As distinct from the French case where from the Parisian perspective the revolutionaries saw no problem in equating the nation with France, in other parts of Europe, like the German-speaking territories, a nation was not a political reality. The political potential that the term "nation" acquired in the French Revolution was then taken up by the supporters of this cultural definition of nation. The basis of the nation became cultural, and it was on the basis of this supposed cultural unity that the nationalists demanded political unity. But what did these people understand by culture? The emphasis on distinct factors – language, race, religion, or territory – made this term ambiguous. As in the case of Spain, these varying definitions were potential sources of bitter disputes on the identity and existence of a particular nation.

Together with France, Spain is one of the oldest political entities in Europe, given that the limits of its territory have varied little since the end of the fifteenth century. However, it only became a modern state in the eighteenth century, when several different kingdoms, which had until then only owed allegiance to the same king, were unified under Castilian law. Nevertheless, the concept of Spain[2] as a territory having a single history which differs from the histories of territories beyond the Pyrenees dates back at least to the Middle Ages (Maravall 1981). From the fifteenth century, when all the kingdoms of the Iberian peninsula, with the exception of Portugal,[3] were under the Habsburg Crown, the fact that individuals from different kingdoms fought in the same wars reinforced a consciousness of belonging to the same country.[4] This identification with Spain occurred despite the fact that most people also identified with their particular kingdoms or regions (Aragon, Castile, Catalonia, etc.).

The construction of a national history in Spain began in the mid-nineteenth century (Cirujano Marín *et al.* 1985). In contrast to developments in France, where there were few critics of the official version of the national history, in Spain dissident voices from the 1880s on were to be heard in Catalonia, the Basque country, and, to a lesser extent, Galicia. In the first two regions industrial growth resulted in the rise of a strong middle class which felt discriminated against by the Madrid central government. The fact that in both regions distinct languages were spoken, which the state's disastrous educational system was unable to undermine (as in France), intensified the consciousness of separate identities in these regions. Hence, they were also able to create national histories which justified the alternative nation's eternal existence. In all these cases archaeology contributed to the creation of the national myth.

I Spanish nationalism and archaeology

The appearance of nineteenth-century nationalism provoked a massive growth of interest in history, and therefore in archaeology. Yet it should be stressed that there existed, particularly from the Renaissance on, elements of nationalist sentiment and of the use of the past for pre-nationalist ends. In Spain some authors, such as Maravall (1981), detect already the existence of a consciousness of belonging to one single cultural unit, which sometimes corresponds with the desire to belong to one political unit, in the Middle Ages. One of the manifestations of this feeling, expressed after the fall of the Roman Empire, was remorse over the loss of Roman Hispania, when all the Iberian peninsula was united under the same rule.

In the sixteenth and seventeenth centuries the concept of Spain as a cultural and political unit was quite developed. It is significant that by the end of the sixteenth century the first *History of Spain*, written in 1598 by Father Mariana, had appeared. Likewise, literature reflected an interest in the past and a defense of Hispanic identity. A good example of this is the play, written by Cervantes in 1584, about Numantia, the Celtiberian town which heroically resisted the advances of the Romans in the second century BC.

From an archaeological perspective, what is important is that it was at this time that intellectuals began to look into the material culture of the past, especially that of the classical era. One reason for this was that possession of classical items and ruins reinforced the importance of a person or a locality. Therefore, the European intelligentsia, who had been fascinated since the fifteenth century by the classical period, proudly claimed ownership of the remains of the classical world located in their territories. In addition, Roman ruins were described by travellers and were included in engravings to emphasize the importance of cities. In Spain, ancient objects were systematically collected for the first time in the fifteenth century (Morán and Checa 1985:33). Roman sculptures and objects were used as decorations in noble houses. To cope with this new demand for antiquities, excavations of Roman sites began. Italica was one of the sites that were excavated at this time (Rodríguez Morales *et al.* 1991:95).

The new importance accorded the past also meant that it could become subject to manipulation. Forgeries of ancient objects provide clear examples of this tendency. It is worth emphasizing in this context the use of the past to try to resolve the ethnic conflict provoked by the presence of the *moriscos* (Moslems who had converted to Christianity) in Spain. One of the ways in which they fought for equality with the Old Christians was through the falsification of archaeological objects, such as the lead plates of Sacromonte in the sixteenth century.[5]

The appearance of political nationalism in the French Revolution at the end of the eighteenth century did not initially affect archaeology. This was because the main thrust of the movement toward political nationalism was not based on cultural identities. Consequently, although political nationalism was soon adopted in Spain, it was not this political philosophy which was behind the attention paid to the past by people such as King José I (Napoleon's brother). Bonaparte signed a decree which attempted to protect the Roman site of Italica (Rodríguez Hidalgo 1991:93). His intention was to protect an ancient site because of its antiquity, and not to save a symbol of the nation from destruction.

Ancient objects were not considered as part of the national heritage until the 1830s. As a result of the dissolution of the monasteries in these years the state acquired a vast quantity of works of art and archaeological objects, which were exhibited in newly created museums. These museums were no longer referred to as royal but, reflecting the new nationalist ideology, they were now called national or provincial. Provincial museums, which displayed archaeological remains, began to appear in the 1830s, and the National Museum, reserved for artistic objects, was opened in 1840 (Bouza Alvarez 1981). These museums needed curators. Therefore, from 1856 archaeology was taught in the *Escuela Superior de Diplomática* (Diplomatic School), where curators were trained (Pasamar Alzuría and Peiró Martín 1991:73). The last step in the creation of museums of archaeology was the opening of the National Archaeological Museum in 1867.

Nonetheless, one should not exaggerate the importance of nationalism at this time in Spain, nor of the study of archaeology in its elaboration. As against the powerful nationalist movements in France, Britain, or Germany, Spanish nationalism showed itself to be weak and hesitant. It should not be forgotten that at precisely the time when the major European powers were expanding their imperial possessions Spain was to lose the remnants of her Latin-American empire. Given her weakened position, Spain had difficulty constructing the image of a glorious nation. Hence, other ways were found to exalt the national spirit. These included the identification of Spain with Castile, the War of Independence against Napoleon, the creation of a national historiography, and the attempts to overcome political tensions within Spain through military campaigns aimed at fostering a national spirit (García Casado 1987:41). In this glorification of the national past the heroic defense of pre-Roman cities like Saguntum and Numantia against their invaders was used, and was associated with the defense of the Spanish nation and the invincibility of the Spanish national spirit.

Because of the weakness of Spanish nationalism there was only a limited interest in the archaeological past in the nineteenth century. Two examples illustrate this fact. First, in comparison with other European countries, Spain's popular archaeological literature was underdeveloped (Olmos 1992a and 1992b:52). Secondly, attempts to create a national consciousness through the excavation and glorification of sites of interest for the construction of the national past were minimal. Moreover, even when efforts were made in this direction, they had little impact. The history of the excavation of the Celtiberian town of Numantia is significant in this respect. Initial excavations of Numantia were conducted briefly in 1803. These excavations were not published, and the collections from the excavations were lost (Gómez Santacruz 1935). In 1842, a cultural association tried to build a commemorative monument on the site as a means of awakening the national consciousness. This attempt could be seen as an example of Hobsbawm's "invention of tradition" (Hobsbawm 1983a:7). But this commemorative monument was never finished, owing to a lack of funds. Some excavations were hurriedly carried out in 1853. In

1856 the Academy of History gave a subsidy for the excavations of the site, which were carried out between 1861 and 1867. However, at the end of the excavations, little use was made of the new data in terms of organizing a national mythical symbol. The results of the excavations were not presented as anything spectacular, and the site was not granted any special protection. Neither a monument identifying the site, nor a provincial or special museum to display its collections was provided. Numantia lay abandoned for two decades until, in 1882, it was declared a national monument, forty years after the first monument had been given this status.[6] Despite the scant importance given to archaeology, the ancient past, nevertheless, was used in nationalist art, as seen, for example, in the painting of Alejo Vera, *The surrender of Numantia*, and in Manuel Dominguez's *The death of Seneca* (Reyero 1989:55).

The loss of the last colonies in 1898 forced Spaniards into a period of self-examination and, as Carr (1982:473) points out, into a debate on whether the catastrophe was explicable in terms of the Spaniard's incapacity to operate institutions imported from abroad, or whether Spain "had been excluded from those currents of progress which swept other nations towards prosperity and power." Intellectuals in Spain realized more than ever the necessity to create a national identity, but it was perhaps too late. Spanish nationalism had become more difficult to maintain as alternative Catalan, Basque, and Galician nationalisms had appeared. These peripheral nationalisms presented alternative ways of understanding the meaning of Spain.

The upsurge of Spanish nationalism in the twentieth century was reflected in archaeology. Myths such as those about Numantia were finally taken seriously. A memorial monument was set up on the site in 1905 by private initiative, and the king, Alfonso XIII, agreed to inaugurate it. The fact that just a few days earlier a German archaeologist, Adolf Schulten, had begun to excavate the site was considered a scandal. Schulten was prevented from working further on the excavation, and a Spanish expedition was charged with continuing the work. To examine the growing maturity of Spanish nationalism at this time, it is useful to compare the work carried out by the prestigious archaeologist José Ramón Mélida in the nineteenth century as against his later work in the twentieth century. In the nineteenth century Mélida studied mainly Egyptian archaeology. Yet, by the twentieth century his nationalism had developed to the point that he mentioned it expressly in his work. In 1906, Mélida was included in the team that excavated Numantia. His publications had a clear nationalist aim. For example, he began the report on the first excavation with the following remark: "The discovery of the remains of the heroic town of Numantia was a national duty." After some pages written in a similar tone, he admitted that the site had been excavated not only for scientific reasons but "to satisfy this historical duty, to make explicit through these relics the historical event of which our Fatherland is proud" (Mélida 1908:3, 10). Finally, in 1919 the Museo Numantino (Numantian Museum) was opened to keep and display the materials collected in the excavation; King Alfonso XIII inaugurated this museum.

From the beginning of the twentieth century stories about places such as Numantia and Saguntum, and about historical characters such as Viriatus, Indibilis and Mandonius, were included more and more frequently in didactic literature for children. These stories were also displayed in other media such as the *cromos culturales* printed in the 1930s. *Cromos culturales* were educational postcards for children, decorated with a national historical picture on one side and an explanation on the other (Olmos 1992a:20). The upsurge of Spanish nationalism was also reflected in the archaeological literature, for example in the attempt by Joaquín Costa to write three National Novels based on archaeology (Costa 1917 [probably written in 1908–9]), or in the novel *La novela de España* (*The Novel of Spain*) written in 1928 by the archaeologist Manuel Gómez-Moreno.

The institutional basis of Spanish archaeology was being organized at this time. In 1907 the Junta de Ampliación de Estudios or JAE (Commission for Further Studies) was created. The purpose of this official institution was "to train the future teaching body and to give to the present one the means and facilities to follow closely the scientific and pedagogical movements of the most cultivated nations" (foundation decree, quoted in Sánchez Ron 1988:6). The JAE had a leading role in Spanish archaeology. Some archaeological institutions depended on it. These included the Centro de Estudios Históricos (Center for Historical Studies), which, since the 1920s, has had an Archaeology section; the Escuela Española (Spanish School) in Rome, which had a short life owing to the First World War; and the Comisión de Investigaciones Paleontológicas y Prehistóricas (Commission for Palaeontologic and Prehistoric Research). The JAE also gave grants to post-graduates to study abroad, and thus the majority of the country's future staff spent some time in foreign universities, mainly in Germany. The importance that archaeology had acquired was also reflected in the passage of laws, such as the 1911 Excavations Act, and the 1933 Heritage Act. Through the first act the Junta Superior de Excavaciones y Antigüedades (High Commission for Excavations and Antiquities) was created.

The Spanish Civil War (1936–9) was, in a sense, a fight over two ways of understanding Spain as a nation. Some saw Spain as a multi-cultural unit, as it had been seen during the Spanish Second Republic (1931–6/9). Others, such as General Francisco Franco, viewed the country as a single cultural unit. Franco imposed this latter view between 1936/9 and 1975.

At the end of the Civil War archaeology still had a clear political role (Alonso del Real 1946). Julio Martínez Santa-Olalla, a falangist (the *Falange* was the Spanish fascist party), was put in charge of the reorganization of Spanish archaeology. Spanish nationalism in the Franco era drew its inspiration from the glories of Imperial Spain in the sixteenth and seventeenth centuries, and in the defense of the country's Catholic identity. Consequently after the Civil War, research on Spain under the Romans and under the Visigoths was encouraged. The Roman era was studied because it was argued by scholars that this was the first time Spain had been united, and that it was during this period that Spain learned how to act as an empire. Furthermore, it was during this time that Christianity entered Spain. The Visigothic period had also seen Spain united under one rule. Moreover, in the early years of Franco's rule, the Francoist ideologues admired Nazi Germany, and Spanish archaeologists tried to demonstrate an Aryan presence in Spain. This affinity led to close collaboration with teams of German archaeologists in the excavation of Visigothic sites (Werner 1946).

The end of World War II resulted in a gradual lessening of these extreme measures. Previously banned topics were discussed more openly. An example of this increasing openness was a seminar on the multiple roots of Spain given by the Catalan archaeologist Luis Pericot in the 1950s (Pericot 1952, quoted in del Pino 1978:58). Archaeology, however, began to lose its previous political power because of the appearance of "modified positivism" or "pragmatic reformism," a theory of scientific knowledge which argued that reality could be discerned through impartial, meticulous, and exhaustive observation. The goal of archaeology became, first, to impose order on the data and then to describe it. Progress in knowledge was measured by the increase of information accumulated and catalogued (Vicent 1982:31–2). The transformation of archaeology into endless lists of described objects and chronologies took archaeological data further and further away from the general public. Official archaeology became isolated and gradually lost the interest of those advocating nationalism.

Franco's death in 1975 led to a process of democratization in Spain. Once the constitution of 1978 came into effect, all regions were able to ask for autonomy. Consequently, by 1985 Spain had been divided into seventeen self-governed autonomies. The new territorial composition of Spain has greatly affected archaeology since each autonomy now administers its own cultural heritage as specified by the 1985 Heritage Act. Archaeology has not again been used to legitimize a single cultural Spanish nation. Nor is the past often used in defense of a present multi-cultural concept of Spain. This is based not on notions of the past, but on the modern concept of Spain as a democratic and developed country, a concept frequently mentioned in King Juan Carlos I's discourses.

II Catalan nationalism and archaeology

Catalan nationalism appeared toward the middle of the nineteenth century. Its clearest expression was the cultural movement called Reinaixença*[7] (Renaissance). Catalan nationalism had little influence on archaeology during the nineteenth century, although intellectuals related to the Renaixença* movement, such as Joaquín Rubió i Ors and Francesc Martorell i Peña, included among their interests Catalan archaeology. These intellectuals, however, did not use archaeology to legitimize the Catalan nation.

Enric Prat de la Riba was one of the first to describe Catalan archaeology in nationalist terms. His book *La nacionalitat catalana** (The Catalan Nationality), written in 1906, was of great importance for the ulterior development of Catalan nationalism. Prat de la Riba based Catalan nationalism on the Catalan language (Prat de la Riba 1978:84). He believed that the roots of Catalonia were to be found in the pre-Roman Iberian "ethnos," as he saw it, the Iberian "nation" which extended from Murcia to the Rhône (p. 87). In this way he claimed as Catalan all the Catalan-speaking countries, i.e. apart from Catalonia itself, the French Roussillon, the Balearic islands, and Valencia. He even maintained from the study of Iberian-Roman coins that this area was characterized, even in the pre-Roman period, by a special phonetic system which seemed to be related to that of modern Catalan (p. 91). Prat de la Riba saw Roman conquest as a deep misfortune since, at this time, the Iberian nationality had disappeared. However, because the influence of the Roman culture on the population was only superficial, the Iberian "ethnos" – now transformed into the medieval Catalan "nation" – was revived once the Roman Empire came to an end (pp. 88–9). He saw the archaeological site of Empúries* (Emporion in Greek) as a kind of capital of the Iberian nation (p. 90). Prat de la Riba's aim, however, was not to gain political independence for Catalonia. He preferred the idea of Catalan self-government in a federal Spanish state (pp. 105–18).

In 1907 the Barcelona provincial government, directed by Prat de la Riba, created two institutions, the Institut d'Estudis Catalans* (Institute for Catalan Studies) and the Junta de Museus de Barcelona* (Commission of Barcelona Museums), both of which were important in the development of Catalan archaeology. The Institut d'Estudis Catalans,* an institution for the study of Catalan culture, was divided into several sections. One of these sections was devoted to archaeology. The excavation of Emporion began in 1908 under the direction of J. Puig i Cadafalch. In 1909 excavators uncovered two statues representing Venus and Aesculapius. Catalan nationalists were elated, and it was even argued that their finding had given Catalonia an ancient history and, therefore, consecrated the rebirth of the Catalan nation (d'Ors 1911:9).

Between 1909 and 1923 Catalonia achieved a very limited form of self-government called the Mancomunitat de Catalunya.* Prat de la Riba was the president until his death in 1917. He was succeeded by Puig i Cadafalch, the director of the Emporion excavation. In 1923 General Primo de Rivera imposed the first dictatorship of twentieth-century Spain and abolished the Mancomunitat. It is significant that no excavations were carried out in Emporion between 1924 and 1930.

The principal figure in Catalan archaeology during these years was Pere Bosch Gimpera. Between 1914 and 1939 he was able to organize in Catalonia the best infrastructure for archaeology in Spain. He was also the creator of what has been called the Catalan school of archaeology. Bosch Gimpera was a convinced Catalan nationalist. His thesis, written in 1915, dealt with the Iberian culture. This was, as we have seen in the case of Prat de la Riba, a subject of special interest for the elaboration of the Catalan national past. Bosch Gimpera saw the prehistory of the Iberian peninsula as the direct precursor of a multi-cultural Spain. This thesis was best expressed in his major work *Ethnology of the Iberian Peninsula* (1932). He intended to relate ancient "etnie" to modern cultures, and demonstrate that the cultural diversity of Spain had prehistoric roots. This finding allowed him to support a federal structure for the Spanish state, in which Catalonia had an autonomous status (Bosch Gimpera 1937).

However, Catalan archaeologists did not share a monolithic vision of the past. Some held a more Spanish nationalist position. For example, in 1934 Pericot, rather than emphasizing the cultural diversity of Spanish prehistory, maintained that the prehistoric period had been a time when all the races of the Iberian peninsula had intermingled and Spain had flourished as a center of European civilization. The evidence he cited to uphold such an argument was the cave art of the late Stone Age and the creation of the Beaker culture in the Iberian peninsula during the Copper Age, a culture later exported throughout Europe. Pericot did not see the Roman presence on the Iberian peninsula as a deep misfortune, as had Prat de la Riba. Rather, he believed that the Roman period was fundamental to Spanish history since it was at this time that Christianity arrived in Spain (Pericot 1934:14 and 18).

The end of the Civil War meant the exile of Bosch Gimpera. All his archaeological posts were taken over by Martín Almagro Basch. This intelligent, young non-Catalan archaeologist transformed Catalan archaeology into a discipline at the service of the Francoist state (Díaz-Andreu 1993). In the 1950s Almagro Basch moved to Madrid. Even though he was replaced by the Catalan Pericot, the Catalan School of Archaeology did not recover until the 1960s and 1970s (Marc-7 1986b:227) when, with the return of other Catalans such as J. Maluquer de Motes (in 1959), M. Tarradell (in 1970), and P. Palol (in 1970), it flourished once more (Marc-7 1986b:228). However, in the 1960s and 1970s when the Catalan school had begun to be reorganized, archaeology had lost much of its power to affect nationalist thought since Catalan archaeology had also been influenced by "modified positivism" or "pragmatic reformism."

In 1982 Catalonia became self-governed. What effect does Catalan nationalism have on archaeology at present in a country in which nationalism has a strong presence? First, in contrast to what might be expected, there is no marked tendency to subsidize research on any particular period, as the annual reports, the *Memòrias del Departament de Cultura** of the Generalitat clearly show. Secondly, nationalism in archaeology is demonstrated in other ways such as the language used to write scientific archaeological publications. These are written mostly in Catalan. Catalan is used to such a degree that papers written in Spanish, Castilian, English, or other languages are translated into Catalan (for example Shennan 1989 and Vicent 1990). However, this feature could be seen as consistent with a Spanish trend, given that foreign languages are also translated into Spanish in Spanish journals (Hodder 1987).

Catalan politicians rarely use archaeology to legitimize the Catalan nation. Nevertheless, Catalan symbols such as Emporion continue to have some power. One of the best examples was the arrival of the Olympic Torch at the port of Emporion at a time when there was an intense debate in Spain about the attempt to use the 1992 Olympic Games in Barcelona as a forum for Catalan propaganda to the world.

III Basque nationalism and archaeology

Basque identity and the use of the past to create it have a long tradition in the Basque country. Since the sixteenth century some intellectuals, such as Esteban de Garigay and the anonymous author of the Códice de Mieres, or, in the eighteenth century, the Jesuit Father Larramendi (Caro Baroja 1957 and Duplá and Emborujo 1991:107–8), had tried to explain the existence of the Basque language by linking it to the pre-Roman population. They saw Basque as one of the languages which had spread throughout the world after the fall of the Tower of Babel. Basque people were, therefore, considered to be the descendants of Tubal, who was himself a descendant of Noah.

The industrialization of the Basque country in the nineteenth century led to the immigration of large numbers of non-Basque speakers into the area. After this time, class differences were paralleled by linguistic differences; that is, there was a proletariat of non-Basque speakers (who were scornfully called *maketos***) and a Basque middle class and peasantry. Basque nationalism first emerged in Bilbao, the Basque industrial heartland. Sabino de Arana Goiri (1865–1903) was its main ideologue and organizer, although he had some precursors, such as the Frenchman Joseph Augustin Chaho (1811–58) (García de Cortázar and Azcona 1991:17). De Arana Goiri's nationalism was based on a condemnation of the industrialization of the Basque country and an exaltation of traditional society. He passionately believed in the need to maintain the purity of the Basque race. His nationalism was represented by the slogan "God and Old Laws." He defended the independence of the Basque country, including not only the three official Spanish Basque provinces, but also Navarra and the three French Basque provinces. After de Arana Goiri's early death, Basque nationalism continued to grow and gradually broadened its popular base. The conversion, mostly during the 1920s, of large numbers of the lower clergy to Basque nationalism was extremely important.

Basque nationalism affected archaeological research in various ways. First, there was a debate between the opponents and the followers of the Basque-Cantabrist theory. This theory maintained that the Basque country had never been ruled by the Romans and that, therefore, the Basque race and language had been able to survive. The actual presence of Roman remains in the Basque country led to different interpretations of the same data. Nevertheless, Basque archaeologists maintained there was a racial and cultural division between Basques and Romans, and, in this way, they defended the purity of the Basque race and explained the survival of the Basque language (Duplá and Emborujo 1991; Ortiz de Urbina Montoya and Pérez Olmedo 1991). Secondly, the analysis of physical human remains became very important for scholars who wanted to study the relationship between the prehistoric and the modern Basque populations. This goal sometimes became the primary aim of excavations. Important work on physical anthropology was done at the end of the nineteenth century by Telesforo de Aranzadi. His thesis, written in the late 1880s on *El pueblo Euskalduna*/** (the Basque people), tried to prove the racial uniqueness of the Basques. Later, in the first years of the twentieth century, he was to work in the field of archaeology.

Basque archaeology was highly nationalistic during the first three decades of the twentieth century. It seems to have been no accident that two of the three main representatives of Basque archaeology before the Civil War – Aranzadi and Eguren – were physical anthropologists, and that the other – Barandiarán – was a priest. The collaboration of these three men began in 1917. From 1918 on their works were subsidized by the nationalist institution Sociedad de Estudios Vascos, called in Basque Eusko Ikaskuntza** (Society of Basque Studies).

Father José Miguel de Barandiarán was the crucial figure of Basque archaeology in the twentieth century. He began his training in archaeology (and in ethnology) as a pupil of Aranzadi. Unlike Aranzadi and Eguren, Barandiarán lived in the Basque country and, therefore, was the person who organized the infrastructure of Basque archaeology from 1916 onwards. He founded the Laboratorio de Ethnología y Folklore Euskera/** (Laboratory of Ethnology and Basque Folklore) (1916), and the Seminario de Prehistoria Ikuska/** (Seminar of Ikuska Prehistory) (1921), later replaced by the Centro de Investigaciones Prehistóricas (Center of Prehistoric Research) (1925), which was dependent on the Sociedad de Estudios Vascos (Barandiarán 1988:44). He also promoted the reviews *Euskalarriaren Alde*** on prehistory and mythology from the First World War (del Pino 1978:72), and the *Anuario de Eusko-Folklore*/** (Annual Journal of Basque Folklore) (1921), which from 1927 included a section on prehistory. Like Bosch Gimpera in Catalonia, Barandiarán stressed a straightforward relationship between prehistoric and modern Basque culture (Barandiarán 1917, 1932 and 1934).

After the Civil War Barandiarán fled to the French Basque country and lived there until the 1950s. In his absence little archaeological work was done. However, some of the archaeological research carried out manifested signs of Spanish nationalism. An example of this was the excavation of a site located just 9 km from Guernica, a town of fundamental historical importance for Basque nationalism, and which was bombed by the Nazis during the Spanish Civil War. This excavation was used to document the presence of Celtic/Indo-European invasions of the Basque country. In this way the prehistory of the Basque people was equated with that of the rest of northern Spain (Taracena Aguirre and Fernández de Avilés 1945).

Barandiarán was allowed to return to the Basque territory in 1953. Basque archaeology was again institutionalized. The Servicio de Investigaciones Arqueológicas de la Diputación de Vizcaya (Department of Archaeological Research of the Vizcaya provincial government) (1958), Instituto de Investigaciones Arqueológicas Aranzadi (the Aranzadi Institute of Archaeological Research) (1962), and the Instituto Alavés de Arqueología (the Archaeological Institute of the Province of Alava) (1966) were created (Barandiarán 1988). Archaeology began to be taught in a Basque university in 1964.

The Basque country achieved autonomous self-government in 1981. At present, Basque archaeology is quite similar to Catalan archaeology and, in fact, to the archaeology of the other Spanish autonomous regions with regard to the periods and subjects which archaeologists choose to study and for which they can get funding. There is no special attention paid to any period. The nationalist ideology adhered to by archaeologists is reflected, as in Catalonia, in the language used in archaeological scientific publications. A great quantity of the publications are written in both Basque and Spanish. Basque is rarely chosen as the only language for publication, because not all Basques are able to read it and these articles would be absolutely incomprehensible to non-Basque speakers, as Basque is a non-Indo-European language. Nationalist ideology is also reflected in the decision made by some archaeologists to choose as an area of study the three French provinces, Navarra, and the three Spanish Basque provinces (for example Barandiarán 1988). Nationalist feelings are also seen in exhibitions such as *Gure herriaren lehen urratsak*** or *Ciento cincuenta mil años de prehistoria vasca* (*One Hundred and Fifty Thousand Years of Basque Prehistory*) (1982). The aim seems to be to root the present Basque country in an endless past.

IV Galician nationalism and archaeology

There was an upsurge of Galician identity around the middle of the nineteenth century. Before the 1840s the teaching of the Galician language had been supported by Fr. Martín Sarmiento, and, by 1843, the journalist and revolutionary Antolín Faraldo de Malvar saw Galicia as a nation (Beramendi 1981a:37). In his *History of Galicia*, published in 1838, José Verea y Aguiar, a liberal activist, stated that Galician history began with the Celts and Suebians (Beramendi 1981a:35, 42, 182 note 10). The Suebians had been among the Germanic invaders who entered Hispania at the end of the Roman Empire during the early Middle Ages. They settled in a territory broadly coincident with Galicia. José Verea y Aguiar was the first president of the Diputación Arqueológica Gallega (Provincial Galician Archaeological Institute) created in Santiago de Compostela in 1843 (*Enciclopedia* 1924 (67):1477).

The "Renaissance" movement in Galicia was called Rexurdimento*** or Rexeneración*** (1861–85), transformed later on into a nationalist movement called Rexioinalismo*** (1885–97) (the exact dates of these movements are still disputed). Although the cultural development of this movement was similar to that of Catalonia, the political implications neither were felt as early nor were as important. This contrast can partially be explained by the underdevelopment of Galician industry and the resultant unimportance of the bourgeoisie. This situation limited nationalist aspirations to a small circle of intellectuals. Furthermore, Galician nationalism was poorly organized. There were constant disputes between nationalist leaders, Lamas Carvajal against Murguia, and later Murguia against Alfredo Brañas (Castelos Paredes 1990:41).

During the nineteenth century Galician nationalism was based on a belief in the Galician race, language, character, customs, and geography, as expressed by Manuel Murguia (Beramendi 1981a:50). The Celts were seen as being at the origin of the Galician race. This race was thought to have been renewed later on by Suebian blood (Murguia 1865 in Beramendi 1981a:51). The impact of these ideas on archaeology could be seen in the importance given to Celtic remains by archaeologists such as Leandro Saralegui y Medina (who in 1867 published *Studies on the Celtic Period in Galicia*), Pondal, Verea and Martínez Padín (Máiz 1984:46). The growing importance of archaeology in Galician life was shown by the creation of archaeological associations, such as the Sociedad Arqueológica de Pontevedra (the Pontevedra Archaeological Society) in the province of Pontevedra, which in 1895 promoted a provincial museum.

Nationalist cultural life at the beginning of the twentieth century included the *tertulias*, cultural meetings with friends, usually held once a week to debate subjects specially relevant for the participants. It seems significant that one of the best known of these *tertulias* adopted the name *La Cova céltica**** (the Celtic Cave), which had archaeological connotations.

In 1920 a group of Galician nationalist intellectuals created *Nós****. The activities of this group included ethnography (Vicente Risco) and archaeology (Florentino López Cuevillas). The head of the group was Vicente Risco y Agüero, who actively participated in nationalist political life throughout the whole period. He carried on the myths formulated in the nineteenth century which described the origin of Galicia. According to these myths, Galicia was one of the seven Celtic nations which included the Highlands of Scotland, Isle of Man, Ireland, Wales, Cornwall, Brittany, and Galicia (in which he included Portugal) (Beramendi 1981a:141–2). Only in this context can it be understood why some Galician archaeologists used their JAE grants not to go to Germany, as was usual, but to visit any of the previously mentioned seven "Celtic nations." Fermín Bouza Brey, for example, went to Portugal (1929) and Brittany (1933) (*Gran Enciclopedia* 1984 (4):31–2).

Galician cultural life was institutionalized in 1923 by the Seminario de Estudos Galegos*** (Seminar of Galician Studies) (*Gran Enciclopedia* 1984 (28):115–18), although there existed some previous associations, such as in archaeology the Xuntanza de Estudos e Investigacións Históricas e Arqueolóxicas*** (Commission of Historical and Archaeological Studies and Research) of Pontevedra. Anthropologists/archaeologists, such as Fermín Bouza Brey and José Filgueira Valverde, were among its creators.

In 1926, it opened sections on "Prehistory" and "Archaeology and the History of Art," directed by Florentino López Cuevillas and Carro García respectively. After the Civil War the Seminario de Estudos Galegos*** was replaced by the Instituto Padre Sarmiento (Father Sarmiento Institute) (*Gran Enciclopedia* 1984 (28):115–18), which did not include archaeology until 1967. In that year the Institute established its Department of Prehistory and Archaeology.

Galicia obtained its autonomy in 1983. As in Catalonia and the Basque country, nationalism is reflected mainly through the use of the Galician language in publications. Nevertheless, Galician is not as widely used in archaeological works as is Catalan in Catalonia.

V Conclusions

This chapter has analyzed the relationship between nationalism and archaeology in Spain. A number of points have been stressed. First, it has been emphasized that the development of archaeology as a scientific discipline in the nineteenth century can only be understood in the context of the creation of a national history; that is to say a history directed at legitimizing the existence of a nation and, therefore, its right to constitute an independent state. Thus, in the case of Spain, the past was used in this way by all the nationalist movements – Spanish, Catalan, Basque, and Galician – without exception. This does not mean that archaeological interpretations were monolithic within each nationalism. Indeed a more detailed study would reveal different tendencies and nuances amongst the supporters of each nationalist movement.

Secondly, it seems clear that the relationship between archaeology and nationalism became most explicit in the first half of the twentieth century. It was also at this time that archaeologists laid down the basis for the institutionalization of their profession. Hence, new laws were passed; archaeologists were given a niche within the universities; and new institutions and associations were created. This institutionalization cannot be separated from the interest produced by archaeological discoveries, and, in particular, by the interpretations archaeologists made of these discoveries. In other words, archaeology attained an importance heretofore not experienced, allowing the discipline to become institutionalized because the data it produced were politically useful to elites dominated by a nationalist discourse. This explains why the study of archaeology grew most rapidly in Madrid, Catalonia, and the Basque country and, to a lesser extent, in Galicia.

Thirdly, after the Spanish Civil War, and particularly from the end of the Second World War, the academic work of intellectuals who attempted to pursue a scientific method slowly became depoliticized. Archaeology was no exception to this rule. This coincided with a decline in the social and political impact of nationalism. However, despite the current resurgence of nationalism, the type of discourse developed by archaeologists in the early twentieth century has not reappeared. Today few archaeologists would dare to write that they can see a relationship between the culture and identity of their own society and that of the prehistoric peoples they are studying, although it is true that on the margins of academic work, in the presentations and prologues of some publications, such a connection is still sometimes made. It is perhaps because of this lack of interest of archaeologists in nationalist interpretations that politicians have become less interested in archaeological research. This situation is reflected in the growing difficulties archaeologists have in getting their work subsidized by the autonomous governments which had at first heavily subsidized their labours.

NOTES

1 I would like to thank Andrés de Blas Guerrero, Vicente Cacho Viu, Timothy Champion, Manuel Fernández-Miranda, Ricardo Olmos, and Angel Smith for their comments on this work; Mike Rowlands for reading earlier drafts of this paper; and Sian Jones for helping in the correction of the English version of the paper. This paper was written in December 1992 during my post-doctoral stay in the Department of Archaeology, University of Southampton, thanks to a Fleming fellowship from the British Council.

2 This concept of Spain was the heir of Roman and Visigothic Hispania; i.e., it included Portugal.

3 Navarra was integrated only in 1512. Portugal only belonged to the Habsburg Crown between 1580 and 1640.

4 Some scholars even say that numerous examples show that wars transform a people into a nation (Shafer 1964:44).

5 It is in this context of ethnic conflict that the well-known falsification of the lead plates of Sacromonte should be placed. In 1588, when the old minaret of the Granada mosque was knocked down, a lead box was found on St Gabriel's day (Gabriel is the most important angel in Islam) with a statue of the Virgin Mary, a bone of St Esteban, and a parchment written in Arabic, Latin, and Castilian. The text contained a prophecy by St John, announcing the coming of Muhammad and Luther, with comments by St Cecilio, bishop of Iliberri. The forgers identified the ancient city of Iliberri with Granada. This identification was rejected by contemporary opinion, and was one of the arguments later used to deny the find's authenticity. Aware that the forgery had not been discovered, the forgers in 1595 went further and left a series of lead plates, inscribed with religious texts, on the Granada Sacromonte (Sacred Mount). These texts linked both Arabs and Christians to the origins of Christianity. The aim of these forgeries was to try to convince the Old Christians that Islam had played a key

role in the preservation of Christianity. Thus, the forgers were attempting to resolve the ethnic conflict between the *moriscos* and the Old Christians and to integrate the *moriscos* into the dominant Christian society (Alvarez Barrientos and Mora Rodríguez 1985 and Caro Baroja 1992).

6 Reflecting the greater importance given to the medieval past in the creation of national sentiment, the first heritage monument to be protected as a national monument was the medieval León cathedral in 1844 (Hernández-Gil 1983:27).

7 The asterisks indicate the following languages: * Catalan, ** Basque (/** where the Basque name has been Hispanicized), and *** Galician.

4 Nationalism and Copper Age research in Portugal during the Salazar regime (1932–1974)[1]

Katina T. Lillios

> Shame on the child that is not proud of his parents. Shame on whomever is not proud of his fatherland. Yes, I am proud. I am proud of being a Portuguese, and the primary cause of my pride is the history of my country . . . Admirable history of a heroic race that has no match in the world. My chest expands, my heart beats with pride. Yes, blessed mother that raised me, blessed this passionate race, supreme and magnificent, of our beloved Portugal.
>
> (Sampaio 1926:13, 33)

> We were a great people, therefore we are a great people.
>
> (Aragão 1985:291)

That archaeology can be informed by nationalist ideologies is assumed. Specifying precisely how nationalism articulates with interpretations of the past, however, presents a formidable challenge to the historiographer. Archaeologists rarely make explicit, either in published form or in correspondence, their political, social, or psychological agendas. The historiographer is forced, therefore, to make associations from often meager documentation. Furthermore, many archaeological historiographers are archaeologists who have been trained to deal with long-extinct societies. When considering the individual, who may still be alive, they must employ a new scale of analysis and exercise a higher degree of political awareness and sensitivity. But, to pursue the issue of nationalism in archaeology, to understand the link between the mind of a political leader and the archaeological record, the historiographer must assume these responsibilities.

In this paper, I explore the articulation between the politics of António de Oliveira Salazar, Prime Minister of Portugal between 1932 and 1968, and the Portuguese Copper Age (3000–2000 BC) and suggest that the dominant interpretation of Copper Age society between the 1930s and 1970s was a prehistoric mirror image of Salazar's vision for an ideal Portugal. Colonialism, religiosity, and artistry were as integral to Salazar's vision of a future Portugal as they were to characterizations of the third millennium BC. This parallelism resulted from the interplay of three trends.

1. The Copper Age of Portugal had been interpreted by European prehistorians, since its recognition in the late 1800s, as a "golden age" of the country's prehistoric past. The architecture (settlement walls with semi-circular towers, corbel-vaulted tombs) and artefacts (anthropomorphic figurines) of the period were viewed as evidence of colonization from or trading contacts with the civilized centers of the eastern Mediterranean.

2. During Salazar's regime (1932–74), archaeology had not yet been professionalized in Portugal. Prehistorians generally had other occupations and often had close ties to the government and the Catholic Church. Such was the case for Manuel Afonso de Paço, an official in the Portuguese army, and Eugénio dos Anjos Jalhay, a Jesuit priest. In addition to their positions in organizations closely tied to Salazar's regime, Paço and Jalhay were also very active in Copper Age research in Portugal.

3. Salazar promoted a form of nationalism which drew inspiration from the Age of Discoveries, the country's "golden age" of missionizing, trade, and colonization. The glorification of Portugal's past role in bringing Christianity and civilization to Africa, South America, and Asia served to legitimize contemporary colonial claims in Goa, Angola, and Mozambique. In a similar way, glorification of the Copper Age, as a period during which Portugal was colonized by more "civilized" peoples from the eastern Mediterranean, reinforced the idea that colonization was justifiable and, in fact, desirable when carried out by a more civilized nation on to a less "civilized" people. Similarities between the Copper Age and the Age of Discoveries were, consciously or unconsciously, highlighted by Paço and Jalhay and further served to legitimize Salazar's territorial policies.

The methodology employed in this study is avowedly particularistic. I have chosen a narrow topic – two prehistorians and one cultural period. A broad-sweeping analysis of Portuguese politics and archaeology spanning forty years or its comparison with the contemporary situation in Spain during Franco's rule might produce insights into general trends, but would not help us to understand the specific mechanism for the influence of nationalism on archaeology. At the opposite analytical end, there is no attempt to engage in psycho-history or to identify the individual motives of Paço or Jalhay. Neither the available data nor my training allow me to take on these forms of analyses.

Both primary and secondary sources have been utilized. A multi-volume collection of Salazar's speeches, *Discursos e Notas Políticas* (Salazar 1946), was available, as was a compilation of his political thoughts, organized thematically and entitled *The Road for the Future* (Salazar 1963). Among the secondary sources, *Salazar and Modern Portugal* (Kay 1970), notable for its wealth of information and relatively balanced treatment of the man, was particularly helpful. The published site reports of Paço and Jalhay illustrate their views of the Copper Age, and it is also illuminating to consult the recently published entries by prominent European prehistorians in the guestbook for the Museu Conde de Castro Guimarães. This museum in the Lisbon suburb of Cascais was, and continues to be, the repository of material from many of Paço's and Jalhay's excavations (Carvalho 1989, 1991). From these entries, it is clear that Paço and Jalhay accompanied many of these visitors on their tours and supplemented whatever text existed in the exhibits with their own interpretations. These entries, which provide personal views by contemporary European archaeologists, including V.G. Childe,[2] Stuart Piggott, and Glyn Daniel, of Paço and Jalhay and their research on the Portuguese Copper Age, demonstrate several points. First, Paço and Jalhay were well respected by and well connected to the European prehistorian community. More importantly, it is clear from these entries that the Copper Age was not a neutral archaeological landscape; rather, it was charged with emotions and, at times, clearly nationalistic sentiments. What is less apparent from these entries and the published literature is the actual relationship of Paço and Jalhay to Salazar himself. What can be assumed, however, is that they supported or at least did not openly defy Salazar; Salazar had very little tolerance for dissidents.

I The nationalist ideology of António de Oliveira Salazar

Dr. António de Oliveira Salazar was Prime Minister of Portugal from 1932 until 1968, when he suffered a coma resulting from injuries sustained in a fall. Although not in control of his nation after his incapacitation (he died in 1970), his regime can be said to have lasted until April 25, 1974, when rising opposition from within the military over the colonial wars in Africa led to a *coup d'état*.

Salazar's formative years as a seminarian, lawyer, and economist made an indelible mark on his political career. While a teenager, he entered a seminary in Viseu, in northern Portugal. After eight years in the seminary, he decided against entering the priesthood and enrolled in the law school at the University of Coimbra. He received his law degree in 1914, and later served as lecturer and professor of economics in the University. He was Finance Minister in 1928, before becoming Prime Minister. Religiosity, respect for authority and order, and economic austerity, virtues cultivated in his youth, were the pillars of his regime and, from these values, articulated his agendas.

When Salazar assumed the position of Finance Minister, Portugal was a nation in economic and political chaos. Between 1910 (the first year of the Republic) and 1926, the cost of living had increased twenty-five-fold. In that same time, the country underwent eight presidents and forty-four ministries (Fryer and Pinheiro 1961:113). Not surprisingly, the Portuguese turned outward, particularly to France, for philosophical and political inspiration. Salazar, however, railed against this preference for things and ideas non-Portuguese: "The root of this is the notion that everything which is foreign to the Nation as a whole is admirable and everything which has been assimilated or created by the Portuguese is to be ignored or looked down upon. All of this is either a shortcoming or is positively wrong!" (Salazar 1963:93).[3]

Salazar's brand of nationalism was isolationist. He fought against any ideology which he perceived to threaten the integrity of the Portuguese nation, such as Communism. As a reaction against the internationalism of the Boy Scout movement in Portugal, for example, he founded the Mocidade Portuguesa (Portuguese Youth). The Mocidade was a youth group controlled by the state which participated in physical recreation, religious instruction, paramilitary exercises, and even archaeological excavations, such as that at the Copper Age settlement of Parede, excavated by Paço, Eduardo da Cunha Serrão, and Eduardo Prescott Vicente (E. Serrão 1983:123–5).[4] Membership was compulsory for all Portuguese youth of the middle and upper classes and between the ages of seven and fourteen. Their uniforms were inspired by the German and Italian fascist youth movements and included belts bearing a metal buckle with the letter S (for Salazar) (Fryer and Pinheiro 1961:127–8; M. Martins, personal communication).

Of Salazar's accomplishments, he is credited for the economic and infrastructural reforms which he initiated within a few years of taking office, such as balancing the budget, restoring the Portuguese currency, creating a modern army, and building thousands of homes (Kay 1970:7). He is also "credited" for his infamous secret police force, the PIDE (Polícia Internacional e de Defesa do Estado – the International Police and State Defense), which was responsible for the censorship, brutal torture, imprisonment, and killing of political dissidents.[5]

The most coherent expression of Salazar's nationalist agendas was in his vision of the "Estado Novo" (New State). It was an authoritarian, corporative,[6] and pro-Catholic regime. Salazar wanted each Portuguese to have "a clear-cut conception of his country and national unity; of the family as the social nucleus par excellence; of authority and those in authority; of spiritual values and the respect due to every individual; of the right to work, the excellence of virtue, and the sacred nature of religious belief . . ." (Kay 1970:68).

Salazar willingly accepted a label of dictator and authoritarian (Kay 1970:3).[7] Indeed, he argued that:

> Our great problem is how to form elites, capable of uplifting and leading the nation. The absence and insufficiency of proper leaders is Portugal's greatest problem . . . The subversive tempest which is shaking the world and threatening the very foundation of society imposes on us the very first duty of taking the power to uphold the State and to defend uncompromisingly the lines of order. To every man who loves his country and the very origins of our civilization this must be the first step of all. To save the Nation from ruin and anarchy it is necessary to be master of the State . . . (Salazar 1963:92)

Closely tied to Salazar's belief in authority and order, was the importance he placed on beauty and art: "I am interested in Art because I prize beauty, that indispensable food for the mind" (Salazar 1963:138).

To Salazar, strong religious sentiments (Catholic) and missionizing values were of the utmost importance. He believed that religion was

> virtually priceless to the scientist or the peasant, the man of action or the thinker, in every latitude or era. Religion is potentially the sole – but intrinsically higher – cultural attainment of unlearned persons, and can be compared to a star that, shining above, gives orientation and sets bounds to our course. (Salazar 1963:139)

Salazar saw the Portuguese nation as the traditional defender of Christianity. The country's successful expulsion of the Moors from her territory in the twelfth century (the "Reconquista"), and the "discovery" and Christianization of the "uncivilized" parts of the world, such as Brazil, Angola, Mozambique, etc., in the fifteenth and sixteenth centuries marked the apogees of Portuguese Christian virtue. Portugal was, to Salazar, a nation chosen by God for the expansion and defense of the faith in the world (Aragão 1985:354).

II Salazar, history, and prehistory

A critical element of Salazar's ideology was the importance of history and the past glories of Portugal. "Central to Salazar's mind was an all-pervading, transcendent sense of history. Portugal was once a major power, commanding a far-flung empire of lands her sailors discovered . . . He believed the spirit of endurance of the days of exploration was not dead" (Kay 1970:4–5). Salazar aimed to return Portugal to a glory last enjoyed during the Age of Discoveries. It was during the fifteenth and sixteenth centuries that Portugal was perceived to be at her historical "height" – discovering, colonizing, and establishing trading posts in South America, Africa, and Asia.

One way Salazar and his government hoped to "resurrect" the former glories of Portugal was by sponsoring conferences and founding historical societies whose explicit aims were to glorify Portugal's past and validate her territorial integrity (particularly in the colonies). In 1940, as a celebration of 800 years since the nation's independence, the Congresso do Mundo Português (the Congress of the Portuguese World) was held. In attendance were representatives from North American and European governments and universities (Comissão Executiva dos Centenários 1940).

An important instrument of Salazar's historical interests, and sponsor of the Congresso do Mundo Português, was the Academia Portuguesa da História (Portuguese Academy of History). The Academia was founded by Salazar in 1936 and had, as its first honorary president, General António Oscar de Fragoso Carmona, President of Portugal. The Academia was envisioned as

> a specialized society of scholars who devote themselves to the investigation and critical reconstitution of the past, which has, as its primary objectives, the stimulation and coordination of the revisionist efforts for the reintegration of the historical truth and the enrichment of the documentation of the inalienable rights of Portugal. (Academia Portuguesa da História 1937–8:91)

The Academia also saw its mission to publish works in Portuguese and other languages on the civilizing expansion of Portugal in the world (Academia Portuguesa da História 1937–8:197).

The Academia counted as its members the most prominent Portuguese prehistorians and historians of the day. Among the early members of the Academia were Manuel Afonso do Paço and Eugénio dos Anjos Jalhay, both investigators in Copper Age research. Manuel Afonso do Paço (1895–1968) was one of the most active prehistorians working during Salazar's regime. Paço received a degree in Philology of Romance Languages at the University of Lisbon and later attended military school. At the time he was an official in the Portuguese army (he attained the rank of colonel), he was co-directing the excavations of the Copper Age type-site, Vila Nova de São Pedro, with his colleague from the Academia and Jesuit priest, Eugénio dos Anjos Jalhay (1891–1950) (Paço 1947, 1957; Jalhay and Paço 1945; Paço and Arthur 1952; Paço and Sangmeister 1956). Paço and Jalhay worked at and published the material from numerous other, now classic, Copper Age sites, including the settlements of Parede (Paço, Serrão, and Vicente 1957; Paço 1964) and Pedro do Ouro (Paço 1966), the rock-cut tombs at Alapraia (Paço and Jalhay 1935; Paço 1954), and the cave burials at Estoril (Paço and Vaultier 1943) and Cascais (Paço 1941). That Paço and Jalhay were not trained as archaeologists was not unusual at the time they lived. The "licenciatura" (rough equivalent of a Master's degree) was not offered in

Portugal until after the 1974 Revolution (*Diário de Lisboa*, May 31, 1974).

Another institutional link between the government and archaeology was the Centro Piloto de Arqueologia (Pilot Center of Archaeology, "CPA"). The CPA organized the participation of youths in archaeological investigations and was sympathetic to Salazar's government, so much so that, after the Revolution, it was disbanded.[8]

The ideology and personnel of the Academia and CPA illustrate how, during Salazar's rule, history, particularly Copper Age research, and politics were inextricably linked in Portugal.[9]

III Copper Age research during Salazar's regime

Research on the Portuguese Copper Age (3000–2000 BC) underwent a florescence during Salazar's rule. Most active in this research were Paço and Jalhay, who excavated dozens of sites, including the type-site, Vila Nova de São Pedro, and received generous government funding.[10] I suggest the excavators were so well supported because they had close ties with the government and with that institution most closely tied with the government, the Church. Furthermore, the picture they presented of the Copper Age was consistent with Salazar's vision of an idealized past and future Portugal.

The most well known of these sites is Vila Nova, excavated for nearly twenty years by Paço and Jalhay. The site is a walled hilltop settlement located along the Tagus river, approximately 60 km inland from the Atlantic coast, and is dated to the Copper and Bronze Ages. The inhabitants of the settlement were herders and farmers, who smelted copper and engaged in pottery and textile production at the site. An abundance of artefacts was recovered, including thousands of flint arrowheads, groundstone tools, and ceramics. While Vila Nova was not the first Copper Age site discovered, it was, until the excavations at Zambujal conducted by the German Archaeological Institute during the 1960s and 1970s (Sangmeister and Schubart 1981), the most thoroughly excavated Copper Age site in Portugal. Reports of the finds were regularly published in the scholarly archaeological journals of the time and presented at national and international conferences. Today, it is one of the few Portuguese sites regularly included in syntheses of European prehistory (e.g., Phillips 1980:184).

Excavations at Vila Nova received generous funding from the Instituto para a Alta Cultura (a branch of the Ministry of National Education) and the Direcção dos Monumentos Nacionais (a branch of the Ministry of Public Works and Communications) which Paço gratefully acknowledged:

"Only in this way has it been possible to disinter from the silence of so many centuries one of the most wonderful pages of Portuguese prehistory" (Jalhay and Paço 1945:91). This view of the site was not that of Paço alone, but was shared by prominent European prehistorians of the day. Julio Martínez Santa-Olalla, the eminent Spanish prehistorian, General Commissioner of Archaeological Excavations in Spain, and Nazi sympathizer (Gilman in press), affirmed that "the work at Vila Nova de São Pedro had transcendent importance for the history of the Peninsula and Europe" (*Diário de Manhã*, April 4, 1944, p. 5).[11]

The rock-cut tombs at Alapraia, excavated by Paço and Jalhay in the 1930s and 1940s, similarly received a good deal of attention and public exposure. These four tombs were found with an abundance of Beaker ceramics, groundstone tools, flint tools, and stone beads, as well as an assortment of Copper Age "ritualia," such as limestone idols and lunulae. Martínez Santa-Olalla thought the site to be "one of the most interesting in the world" (*Diário de Manhã*, April 4, 1944, p. 5) and "one of the most brilliant chapters of Portuguese archaeology" (*Diãrio de Manhã*, April 22, 1944, p. 5). After visiting the collections in the Museu Conde de Castro Guimarães, Joaquim Fontes, the President of the Associação dos Arqueólogos Portugueses, wrote "the magnificent finds of Alapraia and S. Pedro do Estoril [another Copper Age burial site] are documents that honor, through the assistance of the Tourism Board, the persons that directed the excavations" (Carvalho 1989:6). Paço's contribution to the culture history of Cascais, the district in which Alapraia is located, was considered by local officials so important that a square near the caves was named after him in a ceremony on November 6, 1969, when Alapraia was visited by attendants of the First Archaeological Congress of Lisbon (d'Encarnação 1979:9).

This splendor evoked by Copper Age sites in general inspired both Portuguese and non-Portuguese prehistorians. Alberto del Castillo Yurrita, Professor of Ancient and Medieval History of the University of Barcelona, remarked: "The Portuguese can be proud of the richness of their past. Few countries can present archaeological material of such interest" (Carvalho 1989:10). Mendes Correia, a physical anthropologist and deputy in the Assembleia Nacional (legislative body of the government) (*Grande Enciclopédia Portuguesa e Brasileira* 1935:56), beamed:

> I feel happy as an archaeologist and proud as a Portuguese at the end of my visit to the sites and the material of the Copper Age, whose understanding is indebted to the illustrious Lusitanians that found, in the Tourism Board of Cascais, the most intelligent and praiseworthy of support. How scientific investigation and culture in Portugal would progress if in many other sectors were found such lucid understanding, of great national and human interest, as these studies! (Carvalho 1989:5)

Finally, Martínez Santa-Olalla, in another visit to the museum in 1945, proclaimed:

> The moment of cultural apogee of the Peninsula took place at 2000 BC . . . The symbols of this splendor are the ceramics of Ciempozuelos and Palmella (Copper Age ceramic types). The best examples, the most sumptuous and rich assemblage, is the discovery in Cascais – Estoril that is housed in the Museum of Cascais and with reason one could consider as the genuine symbol of the great Peninsular civilization that brought metallurgy and civilization to all of Europe. (Carvalho 1989:5)

These quotes demonstrate, quite clearly, that the Copper Age – the sites and their material – satisfied more than pure intellectual curiosity for Portuguese and non-Portuguese prehistorians. What was it about the Copper Age or, more precisely, what was it about how the Copper Age was presented by Paço and Jalhay that inspired such emotion which, at times, had such overt nationalistic overtones? To answer this, it is necessary briefly to consider that the Portuguese Copper Age had been consistently glorified, since its recognition in Iberia in the late 1800s by the Belgian brothers and mining engineers, Louis and Henri Siret. The rich tombs, filled with decorated ceramics, gold jewelry, and engraved schist plaques, suggested wealth and opulence. The decorations on the ceramics and the stone idols were thought to reflect Aegean, Egyptian, or Near Eastern influences. The fortified hilltop settlements were evocative of trading outposts. To the Swede Nils Åberg, the Copper Age of Portugal "attained a rich flourishment" (Åberg 1921:112). Louis Siret wrote: "There is not, in the history of Iberia, a period whose study presents such a strong attraction as the Copper Age, not only in terms of Iberia, but in the history of the entire ancient world" (Siret 1913:27–9).

Thus, when Paço and Jalhay studied the Copper Age decades later, there had already been a tradition of viewing the period as a prehistoric "golden age." What differentiated Paço's and Jalhay's vision of the Copper Age was that it had become somewhat more personalized. The past glories of the Copper Age buttressed the greatness of contemporary Portugal. This case was strengthened by the physical and cultural continuity that was thought to have existed between the third millennium BC and the mid-twentieth century AD. Mendes Correia argued that Copper Age peoples were the first Portuguese peoples:

> the Eira Pedrinha series [a Copper Age site] appears to us to confirm . . . that it was in the neo-eneolithic of the country . . . that is found that substrate of which, with some small modifications, by revolution or influences of other elements, arose the principal mass of the Portuguese population of today. (Anonymous 1950:14)[12]

The manner in which Paço and Jalhay described the Portuguese Copper Age was so strikingly similar to popular perceptions of Portugal's role in the Age of the Discoveries or the vision of Portugal that Salazar maintained that one could argue that the delineation between the prehistoric past, the historic past, and the ideal future had become somewhat blurred in the minds of Paço and Jalhay, as well as contemporary European prehistorians who were influenced by Paço's and Jalhay's work.

The Portuguese Copper Age represented, to Paço and Jalhay, a period of active colonizing and trading activities. This was a vision consistent with the position of Portugal in the Age of the Discoveries, during which the country had intensive trading contacts with, and colonized portions of, Asia (e.g., Macau, Goa, Timor), Africa (e.g., Morocco, Angola, Mozambique, Cape Verde), and South America (Brazil). Copper Age populations in Portugal were believed to represent colonizers and traders from the eastern Mediterranean who had contacts with the Atlantic, Oriental, and Mediterranean world. "They were populations that came in search of metals, and because of this they are principally traders" (Paço 1942 [1970]:299). It was this aspect of the Copper Age that gave it some of its splendor. Julio Martínez Santa-Olalla believed Alapraia to be "one of the most brilliant chapters of Portuguese archaeology in its relations with the Oriental world, the Mediterranean, and the Atlantic" (*Diário de Manhã*, April 22, 1944, p. 5). The parallel between past and present was clearly articulated in his reference to the "prehistoric navigations" of the "most brilliant world" of the Copper Age (*Diário de Manhã*, April 22, 1944, p. 5).[13] Finally, the struggles Portugal had undergone, and was experiencing, to maintain her overseas territories were echoed in the vision of Copper Age populations "fighting for possession" of their copper mines (Paço 1942 [1970]:299).

Paço and Jalhay suggested that the eastern Mediterranean traders and colonizers brought to Portugal religious beliefs – a vision not unlike the colonization and Christianization of Portugal's overseas territories: "And were the successive inhabitants of the 'castelo' [Vila Nova] endowed with religious sentiments? It will not be difficult to respond affirmatively" (Paço 1942 [1970]:300). The "religious ritualia" of Copper Age sites, such as stone vases, cylindrical idols, and bone anthropomorphic statues, were viewed as evidence of these eastern beliefs. One can only speculate on Jalhay's contribution, as a Jesuit priest, to this treatment of the Copper Age.

Finally, Copper Age populations had, to Paço and Jalhay, marked aesthetic sensibilities; similarly, art and beauty had been actively promoted by Salazar as manifestations of order. To Paço, the Copper Age represented "a rich and artistic civilization" (Paço and Jalhay 1935 [1970]:170). Evidence of this could be found in their production and use of decorated ceramics (Beakers), engraved slate plaques, finely flaked flints, and carved limestone idols.

The glorification of the Copper Age by Paço and Jalhay served two related purposes. First, it subtly legitimized colonial and missionizing activities that were actively being promoted by Salazar's regime, the thinking being "so it was done in the past, so it should be in the future." Secondly, reminding the Portuguese of their splendid past, marked by wealth and beauty, and reminiscent of the nation during the Age of the Discoveries, served to bolster Portuguese nationalism.

Salazar strove to restore the confidence and nationalistic pride of the Portuguese by reminding them of their historic "golden ages." He founded and supported projects, such as the Academia Portuguesa de História and the Congresso do Mundo Português, that promoted "positive" images of Portugal's historic past, particularly those that affirmed the nation's role as colonizer, trader, and missionizer during the Age of the Discoveries. His regime also supported, in terms of funding and publicity, the investigations of Afonso do Paço and Eugénio Jalhay at numerous Copper Age sites. These individuals had close institutional and ideological ties with the Salazar regime and, not surprisingly, their interpretations reflected this. Like Salazar's ideal Portuguese society, the Copper Age was portrayed by Paço and Jalhay as the "golden age" of Portugal's prehistoric past. As Salazar strongly believed in Portugal's colonizing role and the nation's "civilizing mission," so prehistorians saw the Copper Age as the result of colonization by traders from the eastern Mediterranean, who brought distinctive religious practices which were adopted. Finally, as art and beauty as manifestations of order were extolled by Salazar, so were the "elegant" artefacts found in Copper Age sites, such as the decorated ceramics, finely flaked flints, limestone idols, and engraved schist plaques.

The April 25 revolution dealt a decisive blow to the intimate relationship between government and archaeology in Portugal. One month after the Revolution, approximately fifty archaeologists, who were generally young and leftist in leaning, formally petitioned the Ministry of Education and Culture to create the "licenciatura" in Archaeology. They were also the group responsible for the disbanding of the CPA. This request and the archaeologists' desire "to guarantee veracity to archaeological research" were described in an illuminating newspaper article, entitled "Archaeology in the Service of Fascism" (*Diário de Lisboa*, May 31, 1974).

Given the currently looser, although still extant, ties between government and archaeology in Portugal, it would be expected that current models of the Copper Age would be less reflective of a national ideology than during Salazar's rule. The "Copper Age" chapter in the guide to the new permanent exhibit at the Museu Nacional de Arqueologia in Lisbon entitled "Portugal from its Origins to the Roman Epoch" (MNAE and IPPC 1989:40–7) suggests that this is, in fact, the case. The tone is distinctly post-Salazarian, that is, Marxian. The Copper Age is viewed in terms of class conflict, territorial control, and agricultural surpluses. Nowhere is found the glorification of the riches of the tombs.

The disarticulation of archaeology as an instrument of the Portuguese government and subsequent professionalization after the Revolution has served to diminish the impact of nationalism on the archaeological record. Nevertheless, nationalistic sentiments still inform the archaeological record in Portugal. For example, the idea that Copper Age society represents a formative Portuguese society is still in evidence. In a popular series sold at street news-stands, *Historia de Portugal*, the section entitled "the foundations of nationality" begins with the Copper Age (Silva 1983).

With the economic and political unification of Europe, it is likely that Portuguese nationalism will increase, although its particular form is difficult to predict. As union provokes individualism, so internationalism breeds nationalism. These seem to be universal dialectics of human nature. It will, therefore, not be at all surprising also to see, within the near future, a heightened nationalist tenor of archaeological research in Portugal and throughout Europe. What role can archaeologists and archaeology assume in these global movements? This is a highly individual and, ultimately, personal decision. It is important to recognize, however, that although we, as archaeologists, are not politicians, our work is always political.

NOTES

1 This paper benefited from the critical comments offered by Margarita Díaz-Andreu, Clare Fawcett, Antonio Gilman, Philip Kohl, João Ludgero Marques Gonçalves, and João Zilhão. I especially wish to thank Miguel Martins for sharing with me much obscure and unpublished bibliographic material. In undertaking this work, I have become acutely aware that, although there are many valid ways of interpreting the past, it is, nevertheless, still possible to err in fact. I bear full responsibility for any such inaccuracies that remain in this paper.

2 According to Carvalho (1991:270), Childe's work did not have much impact in Portugal, despite his visit in 1949 and the fact that his book was translated into Portuguese. The fact that he was a Marxist might have affected archaeologists who feared punishment from the dominant regime. The exception was E. da Cunha Serrão, who familiarized himself with the work of Childe. Curiously, although the political climates in Portugal and Spain were similar during the mid-twentieth century, Childe was very influential in Spanish prehistory, and his ideas were widely quoted by such prehistorians as Julio Martínez Santa-Olalla (M. Díaz-Andreu, personal communication).

3 Nevertheless, a major component of Salazar's Second Republic was the philosophical and political movement developed in the First, known as "Integralismo Lusitano," a philosophy inspired by Charles Maurras' *L'Action française* (M. Martins, personal communication).

4 According to Cunha Serrão, Paço allowed the Mocidade Portuguesa to

participate in the excavations "because in this way we would obtain better support, in all aspects, on the part of the entities who had the capacity to concede this support" (Serrão 1983:123–5).

5 A prominent Portuguese archaeologist was known to be a PIDE informant (*Diário de Lisboa*, Feb. 24, 1975).

6 By corporative, Salazar meant that society was to be organized, not along class lines, but through corporations, or people engaged in a similar trade (Kay 1970:52).

7 In fact, many public buildings built during his government bear the inscription "Construído sob o governo da Ditadura Nacional" (constructed under the government of the National Dictatorship) (M. Martins, personal communication).

8 The CPA was responsible for preventing four Portuguese archaeologists from conducting fieldwork in Portugal because their "attitudes did not conform to the spirit that characterized the objectives of the Center" (read "leftist tendencies . . .") (unpublished letter, Dr. João Filipe Salvado to the Director of the Museu Nacional de Arqueologia, June 30, 1972).

9 The Academia still functions today in much the same way. Its president, Joaquim Veríssimo Serrão, is a Salazarist. Correspondence between Serrão and Marcello Caetano (Prime Minister of Portugal between 1968 and 1974), while Caetano was in exile in Portugal, records Caetano encouraging Serrão "to revive the call of a common ideal" in the Academia (Serrão 1985:129).

10 Many of these, now "classic" sites, are (perhaps not coincidentally) located in the exclusive Lisbon suburbs where government officials, including Salazar, lived.

11 The *Diário de Manhã* was the newspaper of the União Nacional, which was the official, and only recognized, party during Salazar's rule.

12 Mendes Correia's statement was originally published in 1949 in a scholarly journal, the *Memoirias dos Serviços Geológicos de Portugal*. He was quoted a year later in *Noticias de Portugal*, a highly propagandist weekly newsletter put out by Salazar's Office of Information Services. The lines of communication between the archaeological community and Salazar seemed to be quite direct.

13 Such a personalized vision of the Copper Age has been remarkably persistent. In a popular guide to the caves of Alapraia, published in 1979, the inhabitants of the caves were described as follows:

> Devoting themselves to a busy life of trade, or leading the more peaceful life of farmers and fishermen, the men of 4000 years ago would have appreciated as we do today, the tranquility of the countryside, the almost daily presence of the bright sun radiating in the blue sky, the amenable climate seemingly without winter . . . (d'Encarnação 1979:42–3)

5 Archaeology in Nazi Germany: the legacy of the Faustian bargain

Bettina Arnold and Henning Hassmann

The systematic and institutionalized abuse of archaeology for ideological and political ends during the Third Reich has contributed significantly to developments in post-war German archaeology. The legacy left by the Nazi system has manifested itself as a theoretical void in West German archaeology and the exclusively Marxist perspective of East German archaeology since 1945 (Härke 1989a, 1989b, 1991). German reunification poses urgent questions regarding future developments in German archaeology, both in academia and in state-funded research. It remains to be seen how this future will be determined. The post-World War II histories of these two modern nation-states have been very different politically but very similar with regard to the identity crisis now faced by archaeology as a discipline. The much-needed theoretical debate in German archaeological research, which seems now to be developing actively for the first time since 1945 (Hassmann n.d.), should contribute to a better understanding of the symbiotic relationship between archaeology, politics, and nationalism in other national contexts as well.

Just as Faust struck a bargain with Mephistopheles, German archaeology had a relationship with the Nazis that has continued to affect developments within the discipline. The legacy of the "Faustian bargain" entered into by German archaeologists during the Third Reich has several components, which can be subdivided as follows.

Causes:

1. The awkward debt, in the form of research institutes, museums, university chairs and funding sources established between 1933 and 1945, owed to the National Socialist regime by the current archaeological establishment.
2. An historical emphasis in German archaeological research on typological classification, what Jankuhn has called "stamp collecting" (Härke 1991:204).
3. The loss of a whole generation of potentially innovative archaeological

thinkers to war fatalities, denazification procedures, and post-war economic conditions.

4. The denazification and restructuring of German universities after 1945 by Allied Occupation Forces.

Effects:

1. The "Kossinna Syndrome" (Smolla 1980).
2. An allergic response to theoretical developments in archaeology in the US and Great Britain, especially the search for universal laws of human evolution and behavior (Härke 1991). The current defensive rejection by German archaeologists of processual archaeology (and subsequent theoretical approaches to archaeological research) is due primarily to the racial and nationalistic deformation of theory and interpretation by the National Socialist regime.
3. An unwillingness on the part of German archaeologists to examine and analyze the role played by their discipline in the creation and justification of the policies of the Third Reich, and a tendency to whitewash or play down that role. This defensive attitude continues today, as exemplified by a recent publication purporting to recount the history of German archaeology which glosses over and minimizes the contributions of archaeologists to the political system of the Third Reich (Kossack 1992).

In order to understand the state of archaeological research in Germany today, it is necessary to examine developments in the discipline in the early twentieth century, a time when German archaeologists were active in the field of developing a theoretical approach for prehistoric archaeology. Scandinavian and German researchers together laid the foundations of archaeology as a discipline by developing methods of chronology, artefact analysis, and excavation. Paul Reinecke and Carl Schuchhardt, well known for their contributions to chronological studies and settlement excavation techniques respectively, come immediately to mind (Härke 1991:188).

Perhaps most closely associated with pre-war German contributions to archaeological theory is the linguist-turned-prehistorian Gustav Kossinna, who laid the groundwork for a nationalist German prehistory, although he died about a year before Hitler's rise to power. Kossinna's approach also had a profound influence on a number of important non-German archaeologists. Gordon Childe, in particular, developed and elaborated upon Kossinna's concept of "cultural provinces" as defined by artefact distributions. Childe's independent contribution was the emphasis on material assemblages rather than individual artefact types and a focus on the social rather than ethnic or racial interpretation of archaeological cultures (Härke 1991:189; Veit 1984).

Several researchers have discussed the cooption of Kossinna's theories by the National Socialists and the subsequent post-war backlash against this approach (Evans 1989; Härke 1991; Klejn 1974; Smolla 1980, 1984/85; Veit 1984, 1989; von Krosigk 1982). There has even been a recent attempt to resuscitate Kossinna's explicitly nationalistic, racist, and ethnocentric approach to German prehistory (Korell 1989). Smolla (1980), Veit (1984), and Härke (1991) have specifically identified the need for the present generation of German archaeologists to unravel the complex mass of assumptions and misconceptions from the constructive contributions to archaeological theory which constitute the "Kossinna syndrome."

There is a continuing tendency to set Kossinna up as a sort of straw man, whose scholarly work is presented as the primary basis of later archaeological research under the Nazis. This approach is flawed for two reasons. First, it lumps all of Kossinna's work into an indistinguishably negative and ideologically tainted mass while ignoring his potentially valuable theoretical contributions. Secondly, it minimizes the contributions, both positive and negative, made by German archaeologists working after Kossinna's death. Until this aspect of the legacy of the Faustian bargain has been confronted, the "Kossinna syndrome" will continue to act as an obstacle to the development of a theoretical debate in German archaeology.

It is evident from recent developments at the graduate student level in some universities (Hassmann 1990, n.d.; Arnold 1990:476) that such a reexamination of the role of theory in the cooption of archaeological research in the Third Reich is beginning to pick up momentum again after a hiatus of more than two decades. In the mid-1960s students at some universities agitated for a curriculum which would include seminars and lectures on the role of prehistoric archaeology under the Nazis. For a brief time a number of departments paid lip service to this demand. These seminars generally structured their explanation of events during the 1930s and 40s according to the following list of contributing or motivating factors: 1. the humiliation of defeat after World War I and the shameful terms of the Treaty of Versailles, which produced a need for a program rehabilitating national self-respect; 2. the desperate economic situation; 3. the weak structure of the German political system, still a relatively new construct; 4. the influence of eighteenth-century Romanticism on the interpretation of the past; and 5. the German "tendency" toward totalitarian institutions (Rothfels 1965:91–2).

Post-war academics have represented the response of universities and other institutions to National Socialist aims and programs before 1933 as "cautiously optimistic," which was probably the attitude of most of the German population during this time. From 1933 to 1945, on the other hand, the attitude of academia is described as "loyal but distant" (Hunger

1984:17), implying that many archaeologists had recognized the ethical dilemma of acting as handmaidens to the National Socialist regime but were unwilling or unable to do anything about it.

In addition, the widespread acceptance of racial and imperialistic policies in archaeological research under the Nazis was rationalized in the 1960s and continues to be rationalized by establishment researchers today as a necessary departure from pre-1933 models which looked to external catalysts as explanations of prehistoric culture change. This phase of self-evaluation on the part of academic archaeologists, more apologetic than critical, was short lived, and until recently the subject of "Nazi archaeology" has been very little discussed in academic circles.

A by-product of the unwillingness to confront the National Socialist abuse and exploitation of archaeology has been a general suspicion of developments in archaeological theory in the United States, Great Britain, and more recently Scandinavia (Härke 1991:191–2). The German archaeological community was slow to respond to the theoretical debate surrounding the New Archaeology in the 1960s and later, and the few publications which addressed the issue (Bayard 1978; Eggert 1978; Wolfram 1986) had little impact on the discipline as a whole. As Härke has pointed out, one of the primary objections of German traditional archaeologists to the New Archaeology is its neglect of the role of the individual in prehistory (1991:199). The emphasis in German prehistoric archaeology continues to be on chronological and typological artefact studies (p. 197). The classification of archaeology as a scientific rather than a historic discipline by the New Archaeology may have contributed to this defensive and uncompromising rejection of its basic tenets by most German archaeologists. The creation of a "scientific" theory of Germanic dominance was one of the ultimate aims of the Ahnenerbe (Kater 1974) and of the Amt Rosenberg (Reinerth 1936a), and the association between prehistoric archaeology and science came to have distinctly negative associations.

Many promising and potentially original young archaeologists were killed on the front lines between 1939 and 1945; the loss of a generation of gifted researchers and teachers is one of the contributing factors in the present vacuum of innovative archaeological scholarship. The emigration of a great number of established and often innovative scholars who were either Jewish, or openly critical of the regime, or both, exacerbated this situation. The elimination, owing to death or emigration, of hundreds of researchers from the job pool after 1945 had a major impact on archaeology as a discipline. In part as a result of the scarcity of trained professionals after 1945, many prehistoric archaeologists who had been active party members and operatives during the Third Reich were reinstated in their old or related departments after denazification had removed them from their posts for a brief interlude.

The SS-Ahnenerbe scholars, in particular, managed to maneuver themselves into higher positions after the war, whereas the Amt Rosenberg archaeologists found life after 1945 much more difficult (Hassmann n.d.). This reflects the fact that the SS-Ahnenerbe was the winning side in the power struggle between Himmler's organization and the Amt Rosenberg in the mid-1930s (Bollmus 1970). There was general condemnation of Hans Reinerth, Rosenberg's operative in charge of prehistoric research and excavation, and of his campaign to purge the discipline of "undesirable elements." Before 1945 this condemnation was largely covert, but after the end of the war it became overt and had a direct impact on the careers of a number of German archaeologists. Probably one of the best examples of a high-ranking Nazi official who parlayed his SS-Ahnenerbe connections into a successful post-war archaeological career is Herbert Jankuhn, excavator of Haithabu, and mentor of an impressive number of well-respected post-war archaeologists.

Another legacy of the Nazi regime was the rapid and disorganized expansion of the West German university system in the late 1960s and 1970s. This resulted in the occupation of a large number of teaching posts by "less qualified candidates than would have been the case under ordinary circumstances" (Härke 1991:207). Härke argues that this at least partially explains the present stagnation of German archaeological research. The organizational structure of the German universities themselves, particularly the hierarchical nature of the system and its tendency to produce over-specialized researchers who owe their positions to senior scholars, has also contributed to the problems of the current system.

Denazification procedures, which varied considerably from one part of Germany to another depending on which of the Allied powers was in control, were initially overly stringent, and subsequently overly lenient. Directive 1067, which went into effect immediately after the surrender in April of 1945, dictated that any individuals formerly employed in higher education who had voluntarily joined the Nazi party prior to 1937, among other qualifying characteristics, were to be summarily removed from positions which involved more than "ordinary labor." This characterization was so inclusive that the guilty, the less implicated, and the innocent were affected equally. In December 1945 the denazification selection process was turned over to the German authorities in the various occupation zones, mainly due to the logistical difficulties of processing the thousands of cases with the limited Allied military personnel available.

The burden of proof was on the individual being accused of collaboration; he or she was assumed guilty until proven innocent. Five degrees of implication were defined: 1. major offenders; 2. politically incriminated offenders; 3. less politically incriminated offenders; 4. fellow-travellers; and 5. persons cleared of all charges. This last category in the American zone was dependent on the accused bringing evidence of active resistance and resulting hardship. The proceedings dealt with the lesser offenders first and were supposed to progress to more implicated persons, which led to problems when most of the proceedings were eventually terminated without having actually tried the more culpable offenders.

The reasons for these uneven prosecution procedures are easily identified. In 1948 American denazification policies experienced a sudden and radical change, owing in part to changes in the global political climate. All denazification proceedings were to cease by May 8, 1948, and any still outstanding at that date were to be terminated. This decision was made at a time in the process when the proceedings against the majority of the fellow-travellers had just been concluded. Proceedings against the more deeply implicated party operatives had only just begun, with the result that most of the charges against these persons were dropped. There was a general feeling that "The little guys were hanged, and the big guys got off scot-free" (Bachof 1965:203).

Needless to say, this situation had long-term repercussions in the academic arena, including departments of pre- and proto-history. There is no doubt that if denazification proceedings had continued, many high-ranking Nazi archaeologists would have been unable to continue their activities in prehistoric research after 1945. Oswald Menghin, for example, who was Austrian Minister of Education and Culture under the Nazi regime, was a prominent figure in the German archaeological establishment. Denazification proceedings were much more thorough in Austria. As a result, Menghin ended up spending the rest of his life in South America, where he continued to excavate and publish (Arnold 1990).

The ineffectiveness of the denazification process in German academia certainly contributed to the unwillingness of prehistorians and archaeologists after 1948 to point the guilty finger at fellow academics, having in many cases only narrowly escaped prosecution themselves. Unfortunately, it also contributed to the conspiracy of silence regarding this time which still dominates the archaeological discipline today. The critical attitude of the archaeological establishment toward a theoretical debate is an outgrowth of the more general suspicion of anything which might raise the specter of pre-1945 archaeological research.

The debt prehistoric archaeology owes to the patronage of the National Socialists is a further factor in the unwillingness of many researchers to confront directly the legacy of the Faustian bargain struck by German archaeologists with the Nazi regime. Prehistoric archaeology was not a prestigious and well-endowed academic discipline before the rise of National Socialism. The first chair in prehistory was not established until 1928 (Sklenar 1983:160), and the subject was taught by lecturers whose economic and social status was considerably lower than that of classical and Near Eastern archaeologists or art historians. Prehistoric archaeologists seemed, in 1933, to have everything to gain by an association with the rising Nazi party.

Between 1933 and 1935, eight new chairs were endowed in German prehistory, and funding became available for prehistoric excavations across Germany and eastern Europe on an unprecedented scale (Arnold 1990; Hassmann n.d.; Veit 1984:333). By 1939, prehistory was being taught at more than twenty-five universities, and the number of academically qualified prehistorians had doubled by 1941 (Härke 1991:206; Veit 1984:333). Numerous new institutes and museums were established, and archaeological journals, films, and open-air museums proliferated (Arnold 1990; 1992). There was, of course, a price to be paid for this generous financial and institutional support. Prehistoric archaeology was to become the handmaiden of the National Socialist platform of territorial expansion and racialist dogma (Reinerth 1936b). Its importance to the political machine was evident in the attempts, first by the Amt Rosenberg and later by the Ahnenerbe, to take control of archaeological institutions (Härke 1991:205).

The control of archaeological research institutions by the propaganda centers of the Third Reich was eventually extended to countries occupied during the war as well. Anders Hagen has eloquently described the SS takeover of the Oldsaksamling (Antiquities Museum) in Oslo in September 1941. On September 10, the terror of the German occupation began in earnest with the imposition of martial law; there were numerous arrests and executions in Oslo after this date. On September 11 the president of the University was arrested and imprisoned by the Nazis. Three other leading professors were imprisoned, among them A.W. Brogger, director of the Oldsaksamling and active in the intellectual resistance to the Nazi occupation.

According to Hagen, Brogger's pro-Norwegian nationalism and anti-German attitude in print and in public speaking had brought him to the attention of Herbert Jankuhn, then a high-ranking SS officer and a prominent member of Himmler's research and cultural propaganda organization, the SS-Ahnenerbe. Jankuhn apparently reported Brogger some time in November 1940, which led to a public-speaking ban for the Norwegian scholar and might have contributed to his arrest a few months later (Hagen 1985/6:269). In view of the role played by German archaeologists in "occupied" countries with German "archaeological branch offices," it is no coincidence that since 1945 most of the publications by archaeologists which deal with the subject of the abuse and exploitation of archaeology by the Nazis have been written by non-Germans (Blindheim 1984; Hagen 1985/6; Schnapp 1977; McCann 1988; Evans 1989; van der Waals 1969).

The official Nazi party attitude toward prehistoric archaeology in Germany and those countries earmarked for invasion or annexation was ambivalent at best and openly cynical at worst. Himmler and Rosenberg were both ridiculed and criticized by Hitler and other high-ranking party officials for taking all of their "homemade Germanic myths" seriously (Arnold 1990:469). On the other hand, the propaganda value of an academic discipline which advertised its ability to identify ethnic boundaries on the basis of material culture remains could not be denied. This inconsistent attitude toward prehistoric research was partly due to the absence of a centralized organizational structure within the Nazi party, and partly due to the lack of a unified party ideology.

The resulting grab-bag ideological approach attracted many researchers who were active on the "lunatic fringes" of the various disciplines like archaeology which were useful to the party machine. Hermann Rauschning, president of the Danzig Senate in 1940, described this situation as follows:

> All the little stunted wanna-be's who haven't been able to find real satisfaction anywhere else: nudists, vegetarians, natural foods enthusiasts, opponents of vaccination practices, atheists, biosophists, lifestyle reformers, who have been trying to reify their hobby horses and turn them into religion: they all are injecting their secret desires into the gas cells of the giant balloon of the party. (1973:208)

The National Socialist system has been described as a polycratic form of bureaucratic Darwinism whose activities and motives are extremely hard to interpret in the absence of adequate documentation, which is rarely accessible, even after almost fifty years (Hunger 1984:42). This situation complicates any analysis of the actual significance of archaeological research to the party platform and its inner circle.

One of the contributions of prehistoric research to the Nazi propaganda machine was in the realm of symbolism and iconography. Rune research became a legitimate academic discipline with the help of party support during this time. Most of the party emblems, including the swastika, were derived from prehistoric symbols. Hitler designed the swastika flag of the National Socialists himself in 1920, and he was involved in the design of all other party badges and emblems. The swastika is not, of course, a rune, although it is still often mistakenly interpreted as one. It dates back at least five thousand years, and is much older than the futhark, or runic alphabet.

Hitler chose the swastika as the party symbol because it was supposed to represent good luck and protection against evil. Its origins were thought to be in central Europe, and it was supposed to be unknown to Semitic peoples (Hunger 1984:98).

The Nazi party had as one of its goals the gradual replacement of Christian religious practices with a centrally organized pseudo-pagan religion based on an amalgam of real and fantastic prehistoric Germanic cults and mythological constructs. Christian symbolism was to be replaced by Germanic runes and symbols. The SS symbol was actually designed by an out-of-work illustrator named Walter Heck in 1929, and was chosen less for its symbolic or magical significance than for its graphic impact. The SS-Ahnenerbe subsequently expended a considerable amount of time and energy to tracking down runes and markings on prehistoric pottery which vaguely resembled the SS symbol in a futile attempt to verify its "authentic" Germanic origins (Hunger 1984).

There was little or no open opposition to the attempted "Gleichschaltung" (ideological coordination) of prehistoric archaeology as a discipline in Germany itself, although there was covert resistance, especially in response to Hans Reinerth's plans for a centralized umbrella organization which would have controlled all archaeological research in "Greater Germany." The Amt Rosenberg and the SS-Ahnenerbe were involved in a power struggle from 1933 to 1937, which has been documented by Bollmus (1970) and Kater (1974). Eventually the Ahnenerbe prevailed, but not until a number of respected scholars had been caught in the webs of intrigue spun by Hans Reinerth and his operatives.

This in-fighting was turned to good use after 1945 by some archaeologists attempting to justify their party connections. A particularly good example is the explanation given for the SS-funded excavations at the Iron Age burial mound known as the Hohmichele in Baden-Württemberg. According to apologists for Gustav Riek, the excavator, who was a member of the SS-Ahnenerbe and later a "Schulungsleiter" at an SS "reeducation" camp near Luxembourg, Riek only took on the job of excavating the burial mound with SS funds in order to prevent Reinerth from excavating the site. Riek's membership in the SS is presented as a noble and self-sacrificing act, a pact he entered into under protest for the greater good of the profession and in the interests of prehistoric preservation. Unfortunately, it is often convenient to confuse the quality of an individual's scholarship or the significance of their contributions to the field with their personal integrity, particularly (as in this case) when there is the possibility of collaboration or conformity.

As noted above, the denial of responsibility on the part of German prehistoric archaeology with regard to the role played by the discipline in the events of 1933–45 has had as a by-product the suspicion of advances in archaeological theory. The following rationalizations are typically offered by members of the German archaeological establishment to explain post-war developments in German archaeology and their reluctance to confront the role of the discipline in the Third Reich.

1. Hindsight is always clearer than foresight. It is impossible to judge the actions of prehistorians who lived through the Third Reich out of context, and it is just as impossible for anyone who was not a witness to those times to reconstruct or second guess the motives or intentions of the participants.

2. German archaeology, in particular classical and Near Eastern archaeology, had traditionally been apolitical prior to 1933, and politically oriented scholarship was considered inappropriate by the archaeological establishment at German universities. Accordingly, the vast majority of German archaeologists, with a "few" exceptions, perceived the role of prehistory as an academic discipline during the Third Reich as an embarrassing incident which was only too gladly swept under the rug and forgotten. According to some German archaeologists, archaeology today should continue to distance itself from political debate, and should present itself as politically neutral regardless of the practical difficulties of maintaining this illusion.

3. Even if German prehistorians after the war had wanted to "make a clean breast of it," they were living in a defeated, occupied country. They were never free to engage in open debate regarding the part played by prehistory in the political developments between 1933 and 1945, for fear of compromising individual researchers as well as the future of the country as a whole.

4. German academics have traditionally been viewed not only as paragons of scholarship and culture, but also as role models for their students and by extension for society in the aggregate. When the majority of German university professors voted for Hitler in 1933, the message which was received by the general public was unmistakable – and the consequences fatal. In view of this failure of academics in their role as leaders and guides for society in political matters, most German university professors today tend to distance themselves from taking a stand on political developments, including those of the past.

5. German academics are locked into an extremely hierarchical system of mentorship and mutual obligation which makes it difficult, if not impossible, for a student to criticize his or her professor openly without fear of repercussions. The generation of graduate students who were in Ph.D. programs just after the war had advisors who were all implicated to a greater or lesser degree in events between 1933 and 1945. These students are now of retirement age, and it would no sooner occur to them to "expose"

their Ph.D. advisors (the German term "Doktorvater" indicates the nature of the relationship very clearly) than it would occur to a son to accuse his father of embezzlement, fraud, or even murder. A recent whistle-blower in a prehistory department at a major German university was treated like a parricide by his colleagues when it was revealed that he had given information to the press regarding his dissertation advisor's role in the SS during the war (Kleeman 1986). As long as the personal integrity of the scholar was beyond question, it would not have occurred to most German archaeologists of the post-war generation to venture exposure on ideological grounds alone. On the other hand, where there was clear evidence of abuse, as in the case of Hans Reinerth, there seems to have been no hesitation in warning against reinstatement after 1945.

It is often very difficult if not impossible to categorize the German archaeologists who were actively involved in their profession between 1933 and 1945. Did they volunteer for leading roles within the system, were they reluctant participants, or were they simply exploited by the party machine? Was their research cannibalized and manipulated for propaganda purposes without their active consent? If so, by whom, and in what way?

One of the few well-documented examples of manipulation of archaeological research by the party without the consent of the researcher is the work of the archaeologist and documentary filmmaker, Lothar Zotz. Zotz produced his films to be used as educational aids. They were intended to promote public awareness of and active participation in prehistoric preservation (Zotz 1933). A number of his films have survived, and several of them include footage which can only be described as Nazi party propaganda: in one case, a swastika etched on the bottom of a prehistoric ceramic vessel fades to the Nazi flag waving at a rally in Nürnberg. Subsequent frames document the party rally, followed by film credits. According to Thomas Zotz, the archaeologist's son, his father frequently complained about the dubbing and splicing of several of his films for propaganda purposes by the party; the implication is that these changes were made without his consent after he submitted his films for review by the party (Zotz 1986).

There are other problems in evaluating the available documentary materials. To what extent can written documents, which invariably pay lip service to party dogma, be considered "evidence" for actual complicity or degree of active involvement? There is no question that using the appropriate language was essential to obtaining funding. Under the circumstances, is it even possible for a researcher to differentiate between the motives and intentions of the confirmed party liner and the cynical, expedient opportunist? Is such a distinction significant when viewed from a historical perspective?

None of these considerations adequately explains the continuing reluctance of the German archaeological establishment to confront the legacy of the Faustian bargain long after repercussions might have negative consequences for the living. This is a problem that will solve itself eventually. One by one, the generation of archaeologists who were active during the 1930s and 40s are dying off, and their graduate students are beginning to follow suit as well. The questions need to be asked now if they are going to be asked at all. Why the violent reaction against developments in archaeological theory in America, in Great Britain, and to some extent in Scandinavia? Why the refusal to consider a departure from traditional archaeology, inductive reasoning, and the exclusively descriptive approach to interpretation?

It is almost as though the old adage "Once bitten, twice shy" can be applied to a whole generation of German archaeologists, with a few notable exceptions who are coming forward too late to do much to redress the situation. It will be up to the current generation to make sense of the scraps that remain in the archives and the personal libraries of a few venerable deceased professors, and to try to find a path out of the maze of self-delusion and self-denial that constitutes the legacy of the Faustian bargain in German prehistory. It is discouraging, however, that as recently as the summer of 1992 a prominent German archaeologist, who has in fact been teaching some of the few seminars offered at any German university on the subject of archaeology under the Nazis, backed out of a television interview on this subject the day before he had agreed to meet with the film crew (M. Edmunds, pers. comm.). One can only hope that the continuing atmosphere of threat, retribution, and oppression will eventually pass and make it possible for German scholars to pursue their investigations into this subject without fear of reprisal.

There are some positive signs. Several student groups and a series of seminars taught at the Universities of Freiburg, Kiel, and Berlin are beginning to address this situation (Hassmann n.d.). There is reason to expect that organizations such as the Unkel Circle (Härke 1989a; 1990) will further advance the gradual dawning of an interest in theoretical debate among German archaeologists. In all likelihood the next generation of German prehistorians will bring the profession into the twentieth century, at least with regard to developments in archaeological theory. Unfortunately, by the time that happens, it will be too late to undertake an in-depth study of German archaeology's last infamous experiment in cultural evolutionary theory. The paper trail is cold and fragmentary, and the living, breathing participants of those twelve years will have gone, taking their insights and experiences with them.

6 Nazi and eco-feminist prehistories: ideology and empiricism in Indo-European archaeology

David W. Anthony

This study presents a case of interpretive abuse. One unfortunate archaeological data set has been forced to yield two diametrically opposed interpretations in the service of two ideological movements, one heinous (the Nazis) and one innocent (eco-feminism). Oddly, both interpretations share the same theoretical and logical form; it is only a politically motivated reversal of the "good" and the "bad" that separates them. Neither interpretation can be empirically justified. Sadly, the archaeological and linguistic matter lying quietly at the root of this disagreement – the archaeological identity of the ancient speakers of Proto-Indo-European – offers unprecedented access to the ideals, beliefs, and symbolic structures of a truly remote prehistoric society. A robust body of linguistic research on Proto-Indo-European language, social organization, and comparative mythology presents to archaeologists what is probably the richest collection of knowledge of its kind anywhere in the world. But the history attached to the subject has prompted many scholars to avoid it out of suspicion, a situation which has bred ignorance and indifference within most of the archaeological community.

Indo-European linguistics and archaeology have been exploited to support openly ideological agendas for so long that a brief history of the issue quickly becomes entangled with the intellectual history of western Europe. The search for Indo-European origins began in the nineteenth century within the same intellectual circles that spawned today's hermeneutic and ideologically based doubts about rationality and objective understanding. In fact, the growing discipline of linguistics nourished all of these seedlings at once in the chaotic soil of German Romanticism. J.G. Herder and A. von Humboldt studied language both as a window into the Indo-European past and as a vehicle of symbolic expression that defined particular ways of thinking, separating nations and making inter-cultural understanding possible only through the hermeneutic spiritual quest.

Because these problems are so deeply intertwined, I propose to address the broad philosophical issues first. My approach to unraveling the ideological threads that have imprisoned Indo-European archaeology is itself situated in history, while the very idea that I can identify one interpretation as adequate and another as inadequate is, in some circles, unjustifiable.

I The peril in paralysis

They spoke in paradoxes, for they were afraid of uttering half-truths.
Kakuzo Okakura, *The Book of Tea*

Objectivity in interpretation is a goal that most archaeologists once hoped to achieve. That hope has faded as hermeneutic and critical approaches have taken hold in modern archaeological theory. Both of these approaches emphasize the contingency of archaeological knowledge: hermeneutic theory asserts that cultural objects or behaviors, including the behaviors of the archaeologist, can be interpreted profitably only in terms of their meaning, which is so contingent on local history, habit, and symbolic structures that objectivity itself ceases to be meaningful; while critical theory proposes that all cultural objects and acts, including archaeological interpretation, are motivated or controlled by implicit ideological forces and agendas that make objectivity impossible (Hodder 1982b, 1990, 1991a; Miller and Tilley 1984; Shanks and Tilley 1988; Leone, Potter, and Shackel 1987; Hill 1992; etc.). Neither approach has yet matured sufficiently to provide firm guidelines that define how any particular archaeological interpretation should be evaluated, in the absence of claims to objectivity. It is in this ambiguous space recently vacated by objectivism that nationalism, bigotry, and even silliness are now freer to flourish than ever before in archaeological interpretation.

The lack of clear evaluative standards is particularly acute in the interpretation of those non-literate, prehistoric societies whose material remains constitute the focus of the majority of archaeological research, but whose ideological and symbolic systems remain difficult to reconstruct with any confidence. The critical approach to prehistory seems to recommend the production by archaeologists of a "poetic counterdiscourse to the reality of domination," explicitly recognizing that local prehistories must be recomposed in terms that are relevant to contemporary social processes (Hill 1992:811). Relevance is, however, a notoriously elusive standard by which to judge scholarship; in a world of competing ideologies, relevance is entirely relative. The criteria of adequacy for judging a hermeneutic explanation are even more uncertain – indeed, uncertainty is displayed proudly as a badge of wisdom – but many would accept Geertz's (1973:16) opinion of 20 years ago: "we must measure the cogency of our explications . . . not against a body of uninterpreted data . . . but against the power of the scientific imagination to bring us into touch with the lives of strangers." Again we are enjoined to become poets.

Of course all really good science *is* poetry, in a way. The dichotomy between the white-coated Enlightenment empiricist, whose bloodless generalizations are vacant of human meaning, and the creative Romantic ethnographer, whose imagination and powers of observation permit access to the core of experience, is itself an ideological contrivance. Both empirical science and thick description depend upon a recursive and creative hermeneutic between data, thought, experiment, experience, intuition, more data, more experiment, and so on, as Kosso (1991) has noted in relation to archaeology. Thoughtful empiricists are fully aware of the importance of experience and intuition even in a physics laboratory, and consequently couch their explanations in terms of probability, not Truth. All explanations are admitted to be contingent, by both sides. The two do not even really differ in the scale of their analyses: the generalist must be aware of the particular, or risk falsification; and the particularist must ultimately rise above his/her scented minutiae, or risk irrelevance.

The difference lies in the standards by which their accounts are judged to be adequate. It is a difference that has both academic and social consequences. In purely academic terms it is not at all clear how the critical and hermeneutic approaches to adequacy are or should be applied in the evaluation of any particular archaeological narrative. Although evaluation, like any other activity, depends to some degree on personal experience and frame of reference, we should all be troubled when a major hermeneutic/symbolic/structuralist book, Ian Hodder's *The Domestication of Europe*, is evaluated by two prominent, accomplished archaeologists as, on the one hand, "an important and original book . . . consistently produces illuminating insights . . . these are productive lines of argument . . . a decisive step" (Sherratt 1991); and, on the other, "300 pages of the most unfounded use of archaeological data recently seen between hard covers . . . preposterous . . . snake oil . . . fiction" (O'Shea 1992). It is even more troubling that many serious hermeneutic archaeologists would shrug off this disagreement, noting that book reviews are themselves absurd, since "Any text contains not only what the 'author' puts in but also what the 'readers' put in. Each of these readings makes a new text" (Potter 1992:556).

Perhaps some can dismiss the Sherratt–O'Shea reviews as mere idealist–materialist polemic. However, a serious social problem is raised when such a fundamental lack of agreement exists within what purports to be our discipline. Having lost its former objectivist guideposts, prehistoric archaeology has opened itself to innumerable popular reinterpretations of the past, ranging from nationalist bigotry to fantasies of spiritual roots-seeking. If we cannot agree among ourselves on how to distinguish the adequate from the inadequate, are we not responsible for encouraging the kinds of popular social abuses represented by the myth of the Aryan super-race? Nationalist or racist agendas are only encouraged in an intellectual environment where the "real" world is visualized as a web of competing ideologies, all of which are equally true and all of which are equally false.

The oddest aspect of the current paralysis is that it has issued from an intellectual tradition that seems on its face to be applicable to archaeological data only in special cases. The acceptance by archaeologists of the hermeneutic search for meaning and the cognitive search for mind has in most cases been translated into a variety of structuralist/symbolic studies (Shanks and Tilley 1982; Leone, Potter, and Shackel 1987; Hodder 1990). These can be optimistic about the possibility of discovering a past, as opposed to creating one, when parts of that past are already documented historically. Access to a prehistoric past, however, lies in recovering the meanings and symbols that gave shape to the lives of undocumented people, and it remains difficult if not impossible to determine how likely it is that the researcher has accomplished that goal. Why have we accepted a form of scholarly practice that is in effect impossible to evaluate?

Let us glance briefly at one example. Fotiadis (Watson and Fotiadis 1990:625–6) has praised a study by Shanks and Tilley (1982) of Neolithic burial practices, recommending it as an example of a cognitive/symbolic study that penetrated prehistoric meaning without compromising established standards of rigor. If this were true, it would be a study that all archaeologists should examine closely for guidance. What "structuring principles" did Shanks and Tilley (1982:150) find operating in the distribution of human skeletal remains within Neolithic megalithic tombs?

1. The fact that the bones of several different individuals were combined in bone piles within tombs indicated "an assertion of the collective, a denial . . . of differences between individuals." This interpretation assumes that human bones retained identities as individual persons. It is of course possible that individual identity was extinguished with death, and that bones were not perceived as representations of individual personalities. A second assumption is that the mixing of bones represented a denial of individual differences. Neither assumption is supported or even closely examined.

2. The fact that several bone piles were in some cases found together in one part of the tomb, and that these locations were in some cases "symbolically bounded" by deposits of pottery and animal bone, indicated "an expression of boundedness and thus the . . . solidarity of the local social group using the tomb." This interpretation was potentially contradicted by

tombs where bone piles were found in separate chambers. Pottery and animal bone deposits were interpreted as marking symbolic boundaries when they might as well have represented a linear sequence of ritual acts having nothing to do with boundary marking. Again, alternative explanations and counter-evidence were not examined.

3. The fact that disarticulated bones were regrouped into piles that maintained approximately (but not exactly) natural ratios between left- and right-side body parts indicated, "in the expression of symmetry between body parts, a denial of asymmetrical [social] relationships in life." A simpler and therefore more probable explanation is that the approximately symmetrical ratios derived from the fact that the human body is symmetrical! No symbolism need be implied. Departures from symmetry were examined statistically, then were assumed to be small enough to be meaningless. This conclusion again was simply an assertion.

4. The fact that bone piles in some tombs seemed to be sorted according to sex (though not always) or that some separated adult bones from immature bones (again not always) indicated that Neolithic society was characterized by social inequality. The first three "structuring principles" were being directly contradicted by the fourth, revealing the first three as a misrepresentation of social reality (1982:151):

> the principles according to which the human remains were placed within the tombs formed part and parcel of the reproduction of power relations, designed to secure the misrecognition of the arbitrary nature of these relations, and . . . to mystify the contradictions existing between the two major structuring principles upon which these societies were ordered, the symmetry of kin relations and the asymmetry of power/political relations.

This interpretation was achieved without any discussion of supporting archaeological evidence (other than the bone distributions) for power inequalities in Neolithic northern Europe. Instead there was an extensive review of general social theory that suggested that all Neolithic-level societies should have been characterized by power inequalities. Of course if we are going to accept general social theory without testing it against particular cases then we need not dig at all. The principal interpretations presented in the study were based on assumptions that were not questioned or defended. Alternate explanations for the observed data, and there were at least a few (see Thomas and Whittle 1986), were not explored. As an exemplar for symbolic archaeology, this study is unconvincing.

The point of this digression into megalithic Europe is not to suggest that symbolic/structuralist approaches should be abandoned by prehistoric archaeologists. It is rather to plead for a more disciplined archaeology. The search for "meaning" in the past is a search for an ungraspable infinity, because "meaning" has an infinite number of possible meanings. "What did it mean?" is a question that has an infinite number of answers, which is to say no answer.

Among the most basic requirements of a disciplined archaeology is the requirement that questions about the past be framed in terms that have a finite number of possible answers. An adequate question should be situated within an explicit frame of reference, or what van Fraassen (1980: ch. 5) calls a "contrast class" – we should specify which aspects of the data are of interest to us ("why did X happen *rather than Y*?"), where our specification of Y tells us exactly which kinds of causal connections we are exploring. If the question has been adequately framed, it is valid to seek a "best explanation" within that frame of reference, meaning by that not the Truth, but an explanation that is both empirically adequate (is not contradicted by the data *as they stand*) and that most economically accounts for the widest range of apparently disparate empirical observations (Gasper 1990; O'Meara 1989).

A wide range of supporting observations protects against relying too much on a single, theory-laden interpretation, a key element in the convergent realism of Hardin and Rosenberg (1982), espoused by Wylie (1989:99, 1992:28) and indirectly by Kosso (1991). Explanatory power is defined on the basis of evidence, but all evidence is subject to multiple interpretations or to misinterpretation. When the "facts" that are consistent with a particular explanation derive from many different sources, however, it becomes increasingly unlikely that *all* the evidence is tainted in the same way. This guard against the plasticity of "facts" has been summarized by Wylie (1989:99):

> circularity and arbitrariness of inference . . . is decisively broken when researchers exploit a concatenation of inferences that are based on principles drawn from a range of collateral (independent) fields. Interpretive inferences based on quite different interpretive principles can be counted on to be mutually constraining, even self-correcting, i.e., error in one is unlikely to be replicated by parallel errors in all the others; the likelihood that they will all converge on a single test hypothesis dwindles very quickly as the range of sources on which they are based is expanded.

A similar defense was presented by Gasper (1990), who argued strongly that this is the manner in which all empirically based science normally proceeds. Science is a search for more or less probable explanations, not Truths. Probability is initially defined within a particular frame of reference, or within a specific contrast class. A frame of reference defines those aspects of empirical reality that are relevant. However, empirical reality is always interpreted, measured, or deduced by humans whose biases affect their observations. Therefore, the most probable explanations are those that most efficiently subsume or account for the widest range of relevant observations, derived from observers whose biases differ.

This is not a prescription for political hegemony. It is a description of a disciplined approach to asking questions about the world, from any frame of reference. If we abandon our standards for choosing between alternate explanations, we abdicate any right to exclude explanations that promote bigotry, nationalism, and chicanery. Our abdication need not extend to ethics – we retain our ability and right to protest a racist explanation on ethical grounds – but we lose our right to protest on the grounds of accuracy and conformity with "the facts." One could argue that the primary value of the Academy for society at large lies in our willingness to correct inaccurate or counter-factual claims made by public figures, including scholars. If we declare ourselves no longer able to perform this function, society might well wonder why we exist.

II Romanticism, nationalism, and the Aryans

The relativist/idealist approaches to the past that are now current in the West have developed from the same intellectual tradition that gave birth to Indo-European linguistics, and, through that window, to the search for the material remains of the Indo-European past. That tradition is derived from European, and particularly Germanic, Romanticism, as it was articulated during the nineteenth century by figures such as J.G. Fichte and G.W.F. Hegel (Palmer 1969; Schnädelbach 1984), and revived during the early years of this century by others, notably L. Wittgenstein and M. Heidegger. Heidegger was, in turn, a (if not the) major influence on the thought of M. Foucault and J. Derrida (Murray 1978; McFarlane and Murrell 1988; Gellner 1988; Johnsen and Olsen 1992). The nineteenth-century German Romantics explicitly rejected the rationalist, empiricist traditions of the Enlightenment, and instead embraced a commitment to a humanist, spiritual interpretation of the world. Thomas Mann once said of a fellow Romantic philosopher (Schlegel) that his thought was contaminated too much by reason, and that he was therefore but a poor Romantic (Poliakov 1974:205). In the 1780s J.G. Herder proposed a view, later developed by A. von Humboldt and elaborated in this century by Wittgenstein, that *language* creates the categories and distinctions through which humans give meaning to the symbolic world they inhabit, and that language therefore generates and is enmeshed in a closed social community or "folk" that is at its core meaningless to an outsider. Meaning was created within the community and made the community possible. Universalist or uniformitarian interpretations of human communities were not only impossible, they were part of a capitalist, imperialist, or Jewish conspiracy

(Gellner 1988). Formal logic was a seductive delusion. Authentic experience and even ethics were grounded not in a bloodless rationality, but in a spiritual union with the symbols and essences through which humans gave meaning to their traditions; and these essences were to be found in harmony with ancient myths, folktales, wilderness spirits, and pagan traditions rather than in the tricks of technological formalism (Palmer 1969; Schnädelbach 1984; Gellner 1988).

It was for this reason that the brothers Grimm set out to gather authentic folktales before they were forgotten, and to investigate the prehistoric origins of the Germanic languages; in the process Jacob Grimm helped to create the discipline of comparative linguistics. It was for this reason that J.J. Bachofen began his investigations of mythology, mother-goddesses, and matriarchy that ended with the publication in 1861 of the influential *Mother Right*, a work that proposed primitive matriarchy as a fundamental stage in the evolution of human society, and that is still cited by writers in the eco-feminist movement (Gadon 1989:227). Bachofen's evolutionist interpretations have long since been discredited in the academic community, but his methods sound surprisingly familiar. As he wrote in 1854, a full century before Collingwood (Campbell 1967:xxvii):

> There are two roads to knowledge – the longer, slower, more arduous road of rational combination and the shorter path of the imagination, traversed with the force and swiftness of electricity. Aroused by direct contact with ancient remains, the imagination grasps the truth at one stroke, without intermediary links. The knowledge acquired in this second way is infinitely more living and colorful than the products of the rational understanding.

Colorful indeed; but there are no rules by which one might evaluate an interpretation arrived at in this way. That has not kept modern hermeneutic philosophers from following the same trail. Heidegger's notion that mere rules of correct procedure are transcended by understanding achieved through preunderstanding ("Vorverständnis"), foresight ("Vorsicht"), fore-conception ("Vorgriff"), and the anticipation of meaning ("Vorhabe") through Being-in-the-World is drawn from the same set of ideas. He has been followed into the current era by Gadamer, who is still recommended to us as a source of archaeological understanding (Johnsen and Olsen 1992:429). If we follow this spiritual-humanistic lead, however, we abandon any pretensions to objectivity or empiricism.

The study of the prehistory of Indo-European speakers has unfortunately developed in a similar manner. Sir William Jones discovered in 1796 that Latin, Greek, and Sanskrit were linguistic cousins, descended from an ancient and forgotten mother tongue. European scholars, German linguists being prominent among them, soon produced a brilliant flurry of linguistic comparisons that expanded the family to include most of the European languages, Armenian, Persian, and eventually such surprising relatives as Hittite and Tocharian. So far so good. But the search for the prehistoric origins of the Indo-European language family quickly became entangled with two other notions: first, Romantic theories that made language a defining factor in the formation of a particular culture type and world view; and second, a mistaken equation between language and race.

As a result, the popular mid-nineteenth-century conception of the speakers of prehistoric Proto-Indo-European was of a noble race of civilized, brilliant warriors and priests who marched out of the great mountains north of India and brought a culture described as Aryan to a primitive world still largely sunk in barbarism (Poliakov 1974:188–214). The location of the homeland became a matter of scholarly and popular debate, but the basic idea remained that of a "slim, tall, light-complexioned, blonde race, superior to all other peoples, calm and firm in character, constantly striving, intellectually brilliant, with an almost ideal attitude towards the world and life in general" (Veit 1989:38).

The politically volatile nature of this kind of interpretation of culture prehistory began to become apparent after the Franco-Prussian war (1870–1). In 1872 the great philologist Max Müller appealed for scientific caution, observing that the notion of an Aryan skull was not just unscientific but anti-scientific, as ludicrous as the notion of a dolichocephalic language (Poliakov 1974:214). But the confusion of race, culture, and language had already entered the currents of popular and scholarly thought. Madison Grant's *The Passing of the Great Race* (1916), a virulently racist warning against the thinning of superior Aryan blood through interbreeding with inferior races, was a best-seller in the US and was avidly read by Hitler's advisors (Arnold 1990). Related concepts entered the neo-Romantic philosophies of Wittgenstein and of Heidegger, who was himself a Nazi (read Heidegger 1959 [1935]:37–51). These figures, through their effect on Foucault and Derrida, have influenced (post-) modern post-processualism (Miller and Tilley 1984) and eco-feminism (Spretnak 1990:5).

III Eco-feminism, Old Europe, and the Great Mother

Eco-feminism is a recent movement that weaves together three conceptual threads: 1. environmental or "Green" politics; 2. a distrust, based partially on the ideas of Foucault, of hierarchical power structures (so often organized against both women and the environment); and 3. a celebration of spiritual, nurturing qualities that are thought to be distinctively feminine (Diamond and Orenstein 1990; Plaskow and Christ 1989). The movement is widely popular and has spawned a vast array of books and journals, including an article in the *Harvard Business Review* that promoted a nurturing, non-hierarchical management style associated specifically with women (Rosener 1990).

A central element in the mythological charter for eco-feminism has been the study of ancient and non-Western nature-based religions, usually associated with the Goddess (Stone 1976; Eisler 1987; Gadon 1989). Goddess-centered rituals, often held out of doors, have allowed eco-feminists to experience deep feelings of spirituality infused with ecological wisdom and wholeness. The Copper Age societies of southeastern Europe provide one of the most important eco-feminist models for Goddess-oriented religion; these societies are said by the eco-feminists to have been destroyed by patriarchal Indo-Europeans at the end of the Copper Age. On its surface, eco-feminism would seem to share little with the history of Aryan racism. Through their common attachment to prehistoric Aryans, however, the two movements share a common archaeological mythology.

The concept of a central European (German) homeland for the prehistoric Aryans was encouraged and disseminated by Nazi propagandists, largely on the basis of the research of Gustaf Kossinna (McCann 1990; Arnold 1990). Kossinna developed perhaps the first systematic archaeological methodology for identifying ethnic groups in the archaeological record (Kossinna 1911; Veit 1989), then used it to argue for a central European origin for many of the innovations of the European Neolithic and Bronze Age – even the prehistoric Greeks were ultimately perceived to be transplanted Germans (Arnold 1990). Kossinna's empirical data were: early historic maps showing the locations and distributions of tribes or "nations" at the time they first emerged into history (itself difficult to document reliably); artefact type distributions mapped within those tribal regions at successively deeper chronological phases; and linguistic reconstructions that suggested that Proto-Indo-European, the language of the homeland, might have included a few words that referred to northern European flora and fauna, such as "salmon" and "beech." His theoretical support was a mixture of diffusionist "Kulturkreise" theory and nationalist Romantic philosophy. Prehistoric ethnic migrations were represented on Kossinna's maps as arrows that thrust outward from north-central Europe to the south, east, and west, using the symbols of a military offensive . . . an offensive that actually followed the pen of the prehistorian some decades later.

Although some linguists continued to argue for a northern European Indo-European homeland after World War II (Thieme 1958), archaeologists who remained interested in the problem were drawn increasingly to the views of V. Gordon Childe, who borrowed Kossinna's method for identifying prehistoric ethnic groups, but stripped it of its nationalist rhetoric. Childe (1926:183–204) reviewed the conflicting arguments over the location of the Indo-European homeland and tentatively identified the "South Russian" or Ukrainian homeland as the most probable one. Since the 1926 publication of Childe's *The Aryans*, the Indo-European homeland has been sought by many west European archaeologists (Hencken 1955; Piggott 1965:80–91: Gimbutas 1970, 1977) in the steppes of Ukraine, north of the Black Sea. Also beginning at least as early as the 1920s, archaeologists had suggested that Indo-European-speaking steppe pastoralists invaded and destroyed the stable agricultural village societies of the southeast European Copper Age, the "Old European" societies now mythologized by eco-feminists (Childe 1926:196; Fuchs 1937; Gaul 1948:213–17).

Childe, Kossinna, and Gimbutas agreed in that they presented a vision of migrating Aryans who imposed their will and languages upon non-Indo-European indigenes. All three used combinations of archaeological and philological data to support their views. Childe and Kossinna disagreed over the location of the homeland, a disagreement that was based on both archaeological data and nationalist politics (McNairn 1980:13–16). Gimbutas disagreed with Kossinna over the nature of the invading Aryan and indigenous non-Aryan societies: for the latter the invading Indo-Europeans were interpreted as heroic crusaders bringing culture to the primitives, and for the former as uncivilized herders bringing patriarchal violence to a world of peace and equality. It is this second dispute that resonates today among eco-feminists.

If this were a paper on critical theory, I might at this point present Kossinna and Gimbutas as purveyors of ideologically motivated interpretations of the past, and draw the conclusion that all interpretation is ideological and therefore suspect. But it is more productive, in my opinion, to point out that both views are demonstrably wrong.

Kossinna's theories have now been rejected, not just because they were associated with Fascism, but because they were empirically inadequate. The idea that artefact types equate easily with ethnic groups can no longer be defended on empirical grounds; migration is only one possible explanation among many for the geographic diffusion of an artefact type or custom; Kossinna was empirically incorrect in his description of how migration worked as a social process; and the chronological and typological data published by archaeologists since the 1930s do not support the notion that any major cultural complex originated in north-central Europe and subsequently diffused southward into the Balkans and Greece during the Neolithic, Copper Age, or Early Bronze Age.

The eco-feminist characterization of the Aryans grew out of Gimbutas' elaboration of Childe's theories (Anthony 1986). Gimbutas (1970, 1977) accepted and greatly developed the argument that the speakers of Proto-Indo-European could be identified with the Yamna or Pit-Grave culture of the Ukrainian and Caspian steppes. But this culture was clearly *less* complex and, in terms of material remains, *less* sophisticated than those of southeastern Europe. That realization planted the empirical seed that led to the reinterpretation of the Indo-European spread as a process in which barbaric Indo-European invaders destroyed what had been higher cultures, particularly in southeast Europe. Gimbutas presented this view with increasingly fanciful elaboration from the 1970s (Gimbutas 1974, 1980, 1989a, 1989b). It is an interpretation that would have been largely ignored – indeed, it has been, within most professional circles (but see Sherratt 1989 and Tringham 1991) – except for the fact that it was discovered by eco-feminism. Eco-feminists have constructed a complex mythology around Gimbutas' image of Copper Age southeast European societies (Stone 1976; Eisler 1987, 1990; Gadon 1989).

In this mythology these societies are seen as gynocentric, peaceful, artistic, egalitarian communities where weapons – particularly male-associated thrusting weapons – were largely absent; where women, through the various guises of the Goddess, were ritually and spiritually dominant but in a non-hierarchical manner; where the earth and its creatures were regarded as holy; where female artistic creations in clay and textiles attained exquisite levels of beauty; and where the essential skills of a civilized way of life – agriculture, animal breeding, art, architecture, creativity – were nurtured into being by and through female-centered activities. This utopia was destroyed at the end of the Copper Age by invading Indo-Europeans who established hierarchical power systems based on violence, warfare, and the patriarchal domination of women. Their triumph laid the foundation for the evolution of those male-dominated Western societies that now rule the world, and that threaten to destroy it unless the lessons of the Copper Age can be relearned as a guide to how to remake our social and political order (Eisler 1987, 1990).

This powerful message, like the earlier myth of the Aryan master race, is familiar to and believed by many more people than have been reached by any mainstream academic interpretation of the southeast European Copper Age (e.g. Tringham and Krstic 1990). Yet professional archaeologists, whose manner of discourse has left them increasingly detached from the public, have ignored it, perhaps because it is merely "popular." No professional prestige can be gained by discussing it. Social responsibility should require that we discuss and publicize the empirical inadequacies in popular or utopian views of the past.

For example, the gynocentric societies of Copper Age "Old Europe" are described in the accepted mythology as peaceful and non-violent. Why is it, then, that many Copper Age settlements, particularly in the east Balkans, were heavily fortified throughout the late Copper Age (the Karanovo VI period, the culmination of "Old Europe")? Fortifications appear in the bottom levels and appear to have been rebuilt and elaborated throughout the late Copper Age sequence at sites such as Ovcharovo and Polyanitsa, implying substantial and continuous inter-village warfare (Florescu 1966; Todorova 1978:48). Some east Balkan fortifications – ditches dug around the village 2–3 m deep, backed by multiple lines of palisade walls with elaborate gate-like constructions – have been interpreted as peaceful flood-control devices, but it is difficult to see how a palisade wall could repel water. Deep ditches and banks also guard Tripolye villages built on high promontories in the Carpathian foothills, and these ditches could not possibly have been meant for flood control.

In addition, status weapons such as mace heads made of exotic porphyry were symbols of authority in the Copper Age (Georgiev 1961:74–5; Todorova 1978:69). A mace, unlike an axe, is a specialized anti-personnel weapon; it has no other functional purpose. Gimbutas' assertion that weapons were elevated to symbols of status only after the invasion of the patriarchal Indo-Europeans might actually be reversed. The mace heads in the steppe cemeteries of Nikol'skoe and Mariupol appear to have been imports, probably from the "Old European" area (Anthony 1986).

Was "Old Europe" organized on egalitarian social principles? The cemeteries at Varna, Durankulak, and other east Balkan sites contain clear evidence of hierarchical status differences, and the richest sexable graves are of males (Renfrew 1986; Lichardus 1988). Valuable prestige goods, such as copper ornaments and exotic stone hammer-axes, have been found concentrated in hoards rather than distributed evenly across settlements (Tringham 1971:202–5). Settlement sizes in the Tripolye region, northeast of the Carpathians, exhibit a markedly hierarchical distribution, with a few regional centers that attained sizes of 300 ha and supported specialized craft centers for ceramic production (Shmagli and Videiko 1987; Anthony 1991b). In at least some parts of "Old Europe" hierarchical social principles (an admittedly vague label) seem to have been operative.

Was "Old European" religion centered on the Goddess, in her many guises, and on nurturing, life-giving values? Infant and juvenile burials, arguably human sacrifices, are found beneath the floors of Karanovo VI and Tripolye structures that might have had ritual functions, so it is at least possible that child sacrifice was included in Old European rituals (Dumitrescu 1958; Comsa 1960). Female figurines do seem to have been very important in "Old European" domestic rituals, but Gimbutas has presented only impressionistic interpretations of their meanings. Todorova

(1980) and Pogozheva (1983) have published much more systematic analyses. Pogozheva presented a quantitative correlation of decorative motifs with position on the figurine body to investigate the possibility that specific decorative motifs might have had meaning in relation to body symbolism. Gimbutas did not make use of these studies.

Gimbutas' broad comparisons often remove the figurines from their proper settings, obscuring important regional and chronological differences in their contexts, typological development, and potential uses. It is simply misleading to compare Upper Paleolithic figurines of western Europe, Copper Age figurines of southeastern Europe, and Minoan figurines of the Aegean Bronze Age as if they were representatives of a single cultural tradition (e.g., Gimbutas 1989b:100–1). These periods did not overlap chronologically or geographically; the closest they came was the 1000-to-1500-year gap between the Copper Age and Bronze Age traditions. Gimbutas' notions of a spiritual unity transcending time and place would fit well in the thoughts of Heidegger or Bachofen. As for the connection between the figurines and the actual social position of Copper Age women, the role of women in these societies is just beginning to be responsibly investigated and is far from clearly understood (Tringham 1991).

Finally, was "Old Europe" destroyed by invading Indo-Europeans? Geomorphological data suggest deforestation and environmental degradation, rather than invading Indo-Europeans, as causes for the transformation of at least some of these societies (Dennell and Webley 1975). Sherratt (1981) and Bankoff and Greenfield (1984) have suggested that the adoption of horses, wheeled vehicles, and the herding of sheep for their wool at about 3000 BC could have caused many societal changes. Gilman (1981) has pointed to processes of agricultural intensification, and Shennan (1984) to changes in the ideological expression of social competition as possible causes of the same period of change. Other internal mechanisms of change are being investigated. Outside invaders need not be invoked. The best archaeological evidence for an incursion from the steppes into southeast Europe is associated with the late Baden-Ezero period, long after the stable villages of the Copper Age had disappeared (Anthony 1990, 1991a). In short, the "Old European" world of the southeast European Copper Age does not seem to have been a gynocentric utopia; it is not likely that it was destroyed by Indo-Europeans; and the lessons it teaches include lessons on Copper Age environmental degradation.

Perhaps the greatest loser in all of this is the field of Indo-European studies. If comparative philology can be enlisted to support interpretations as diverse as those of Gimbutas and Kossinna, it might seem that "the clues afforded by linguistic paleontology were either so general that they accommodated both centres without much difficulty, or they were so hypothetical that they could be easily ignored if unsuitable" (McNairn 1980:14). This widely shared sentiment has only been amplified by the mythologizing of the eco-feminists. It is nevertheless inaccurate.

Much of historical linguistics rests upon a theoretical and methodological foundation that is more secure than that of prehistoric archaeology. Historical linguists have been able to make *predictive* statements specifying that a given trait must have existed in an undocumented phase of a prehistoric language (such as the labiovelar in archaic Greek) prior to its actual discovery in ancient texts (Bynon 1977:72). No descriptive method or theory of culture change would permit an archaeologist to predict accurately the shape or decoration of the pots belonging to an as-yet-undiscovered phase of a prehistoric culture. Language change is a more rule-bound and predictable process than change in material culture. In the case of Indo-European, the rules of language change permit the reconstruction of aspects of a prehistoric language – Proto-Indo-European – and of the world view encoded in those language fragments.

Archaeological data are particularly weak when it comes to exploring the meaning and content of prehistoric symbolic systems. Indo-European comparative mythology and linguistics really do hold out the possibility of reconstructing the ideologies and symbolic systems of an entirely prehistoric European society, a possibility of unparalleled potential because there is no prehistoric linguistic and mythological tradition anywhere that has been so intensively studied by linguists over the course of the last two centuries. The very real reward of using that information to enrich our interpretation of ancient Europe should attract substantial attention. Perhaps when we agree on evaluative standards that can maintain intellectual rigor in the field, it will.

Part III

Eastern Europe and Eurasia

7 Archaeology and ideology in southeast Europe

Timothy Kaiser

> History, after all, is nothing more than a pack of tricks we play on the dead.
> Voltaire

Nowhere has it been made more horrifyingly clear that the past is a prize, a resource to covet and for which to contend, than in the west Balkans today.[1] When the towers and walls of ancient towns are shelled for no military purpose, when medieval churches and mosques become targets, and when the calls to arms unfurl histories like banners, then it is starkly apparent to what extent the past can intertwine with the present – and to what effect. Memories, real and imagined, ancient and new, sustain the civil conflict in Croatia and Bosnia and Hercegovina as much as any weapon. The wars of the Balkans unequivocally show that possession of the past is no trifling matter, and that the construction of the past is fraught with consequence. One need look no further than the ranges, valleys, and fields of the Dinaric Mountains to see that the past and the present are inextricably bound together.

As the papers in this volume demonstrate, archaeologists have recently exhibited a growing concern about two aspects of the relationship between past and present. First, it is coming to be appreciated that many of the notions about the past held by archaeologists are derived from present conditions. Secondly, it appears that, often, archaeological efforts are geared overtly or covertly toward serving a political agenda of the present.

This chapter focusses on archaeological interpretations of the prehistory, protohistory, and history of southeast Europe, and the practice of archaeology in the Balkans, to provide vivid, concrete illustrations of both these points. It is the contention of this chapter that, in the Balkans, the relationship between past and present has been a reflexive one conditioned by several factors: ethnicity, nationalism, and (until 1989) Marxism. Each of these must be taken into account when considering the influence that the "present" has on interpretations of the "past," or the contemporary political significance that the "past" frequently takes on in southeast European contexts.

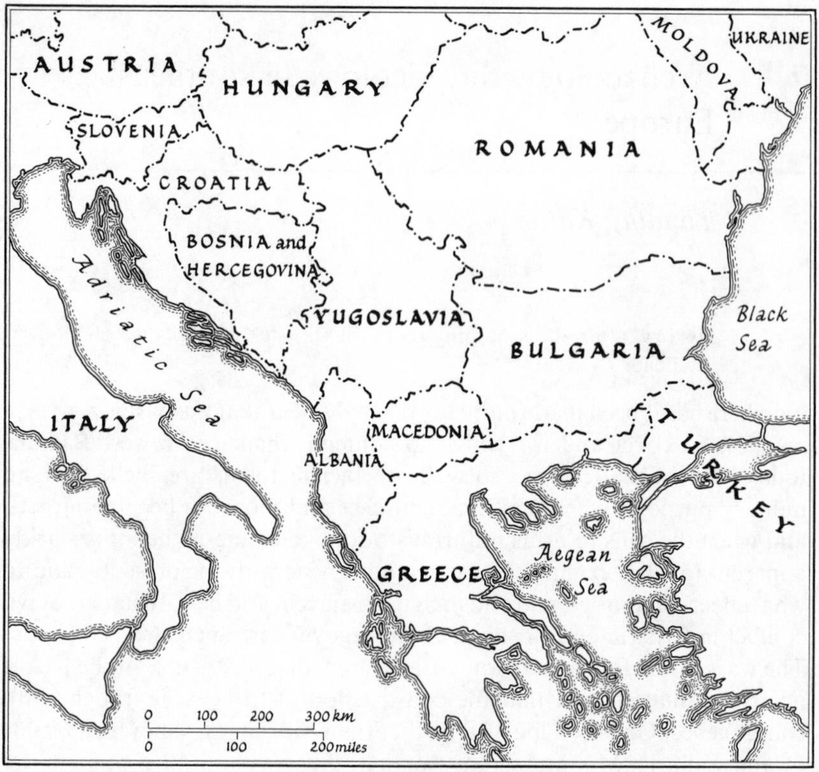

1 New and old states of southeast Europe

While in the discussion that follows each of these factors is considered more or less separately, it is recognized that in reality they are all bound together. For example, sometimes ethnic and nationalist ideologies merge, making the former indistinguishable from the latter; Marxist ideology habitually incorporated nationalist ideology. Yet to say that the factors which influence archaeological practice in southeast Europe are bound together does not necessarily mean that they have always acted in harmony. To the contrary, they sometimes have been in conflict with one another – a situation which, if historically understandable (as I hope to show), has occasionally led to internally inconsistent presentations of the archaeological past.

This chapter deals with an archaeological tradition which is unfamiliar to most Anglo-American readers. The focus here is on the archaeology of the former Yugoslavia, especially Serbia and Croatia, and Romania, with additional examples from neighboring countries. However, the following discussion is not the result of any formal ethnographic fieldwork, but rather derives from more than fifteen years' experience of doing archaeology in southeast Europe. So while I do not know, for example, what the class interests of specific Balkan archaeologists might entail or how those interests affect the work they do, nonetheless I feel I can demonstrate some aspects of the ways in which, in the Balkans, as elsewhere, the relationship between the past and the present has clearly influenced both archaeological interpretation and archaeology's socio-political role.

I The lens of the present

A Ethnicity and archaeological interpretation

Since its inception in the late nineteenth century, archaeological research in the various states of the Balkans has undergone major changes in field methodology, bureaucratic organization, and overall scope. Much, however, remains relatively unchanged, especially in the area of archaeological interpretation. Most notably, changes in the archaeological record have been, and continue to be, explained as the products of migrations and invasions which saw the displacement of one ethnic group by another. Thus, the origins of agriculture, metal-working, and urbanism have all been explained with reference to the arrival of new groups. In archaeological texts these processes have been rendered as a series of curving arrows which thrust into, through, and out of southeast Europe in a way that could do credit to any general staff's operational plans. In this respect, the Balkan approach to archaeological explanation differs little from that of traditional practice throughout most of Europe.

Elsewhere in Europe, the popularity of stories about the prehistorical past which invoke large-scale movements of people and/or ideas can be attributed to the social Darwinist and imperialist notions of "progress" and "civilization" so characteristic of the Victorian and later periods (Tringham 1974). It may be argued that these notions were such central elements of the bourgeois ideologies of England, France, and Germany that they were readily adopted by the archaeologists of the time. To a certain extent, Balkan approaches to the archaeological past of southeast Europe were influenced by those of western Europe, principally those of Germany and Austria, since many of the earliest Balkan excavations were carried out by foreign archaeologists such as the Austrians Radimsky, Hoernes, and Fiala in Bosnia, the Duchess of Mecklenburg in Slovenia, and the French Jérôme, Séure, and Degrand in Thrace. Furthermore, the major university centers in Vienna and Berlin attracted young scholars, such as the Romanians Tocilescu and Pârvan, who then returned to

UNIVERSITY COLLEGE LIBRARY SWANSEA

Bucharest to become patriarchs of the Romanian archaeological establishment.

However, the reasons for the appeal of diffusionist explanations are somewhat different in the Balkans. The first of these reasons has to do with the history of the Balkans, which has been dominated by ethnic struggle and displacement. The first inhabitants of the peninsula north of Greece about whom there is historic information were the Iron Age Illyrians, Thracians, and Geto-Dacians. Following the period of Roman rule, during the time of the Byzantine Empire, the Balkans witnessed a millennium of destruction at the hands of successive waves of invading tribes. The Goths swept through in the third, fourth, and fifth centuries AD; the Huns, also of the fourth and fifth centuries, were followed by the Avars, Slavs, and Bulgars in the sixth and seventh centuries. Next came the Magyars in the ninth and tenth centuries, the Pechenegs in the tenth and eleventh, the Cumans in the twelfth, and, finally, the Mongols in the thirteenth century. Of these various invaders, only the Slavs stayed to settle south of the Danube.

Despite the periodic invasions, and repeated Byzantine attempts to subjugate the entire peninsula, the six centuries from *c.* 800 to 1400 saw the florescence of a variety of short-lived principalities and kingdoms in Serbia, Croatia, Bosnia, Bulgaria, Wallachia, and Moldavia whose territories often fluctuated – at times growing larger at the expense of their neighbors and at other times almost vanishing. Competition between these polities was vigorous, and if territorial encroachments of neighbors did not result in the dissolution of a dynasty or the dismemberment of a kingdom, then an invasion by a wider-ranging group could usually be counted on to achieve that result. The ultimate encroachments, dominating the whole of the Balkans from the fourteenth to the nineteenth centuries, were those of the Ottoman and Habsburg Empires, which brought a conclusive end to the autonomous feudal states of southeast Europe. These two empires carved the Balkans in half, occupying the now-annexed peninsula, and establishing two radically different, mutually antagonistic systems.

Under Habsburg and Ottoman rule, the Balkans continued to be characterized by ethnic differences. Each empire was a socially heterogeneous entity, in which the imperial rulers or their agents were at odds with the local ethnic elites. In the Balkans, the Ottoman and Habsburg empires subsumed many ethnic groups, including the Slavic Slovenians, Croats, Serbs, Montenegrins, Macedonians, and Bulgarians, the Magyars of Hungary and Transylvania, the Romanians, the Greeks, the Albanians, the Gypsies, the Jews, the Vlachs, and the Muslim Slavs. Internally, the socio-political situation of the empires was fluid, with shifting patterns of alliance and opposition between the imperia and certain ethnic groups as the state-builders tried to consolidate their positions. Indeed, although there were no more migrations on the scale of those of the Avars, Huns, and their successors, imperial policy frequently called for the forced resettlement of ethnic groups, especially in the area of the military frontier. The eventual stalemate which developed between the Habsburg and Ottoman Empires did sometimes afford ethnic groups (or segments thereof) great latitude of action: the Magyar nobility of Transylvania, for example, enjoyed virtual autonomy in the eighteenth century.

It can be argued that the very attempts of the two states to strengthen themselves through the direct mobilization of the local citizenry, circumventing the established, regional ethnic elites, had a galvanizing effect on those elites, spurring them to separatist and nationalist action. Then, too, the increasing importance of the state as a source of scarce valuables, such as jobs and education, meant that ethnic conflict continued as ethnic groups were forced to organize themselves in order to compete with one another for access to those state-controlled resources. Verdery (1983:352) believes that these processes account for the perpetuated conflicts among regionally differentiated groups in the Balkans. As a consequence, in the aftermath of the nationalist revolts of the nineteenth century and the final dismemberment of the two empires following the First World War, the nations of the Balkans found themselves to be of multi-ethnic composition.

The effect of ethnic heterogeneity on modern politics in southeast Europe has been profound, but varied in that ethnicity has been institutionalized in different ways. In Europe, ethnic groups are often referred to as "nationalities," and sometimes as "nations." In the former Yugoslavia, "nations" constituted the federal republics of Yugoslavia: Serbia, Croatia, Slovenia, Bosnia, and Macedonia. "Nationalities" were ethnic groups that were officially recognized but had less political autonomy; they included Hungarians, Romanians, and Albanians. In Yugoslavia, under Tito, political decentralization was pursued to the extent that multiple centers of power at the level of the republic competed for scarce resources. The tensions thus engendered simmered until Slovenia, Croatia, Bosnia and Hercegovina, and Macedonia seceded from federal Yugoslavia in 1991 and 1992. At this writing, of course, ethnicity in the former Yugoslavia is now institutionalized from the level of states and smaller polities (e.g., Bosnian Croats, Bosnian Serbs), down to the murderously personal.

The degree to which plural interests were once formally expressed in ex-Yugoslavia was not shared elsewhere. For example, in Ceauşescu's Romania only one ethnic group – the Romanians – was fully institutionalized. A number of more or less uninstitutionalized ethnic groups exist there of course, e.g., Hungarians, Saxons, and Gypsies, but these groups lack the political organization and economic power of the dominant national ethnic groups. Consequently, nationalist ideology in Romania has been and is ethnic ideology, as will be seen below; part of the nationalist ideologies is to deny ethnic heterogeneity.

In each of these countries ethnicity is an extremely salient aspect of contemporary politics. However, what it is about ethnicity that is salient differs. In former Yugoslavia, ethnicity is the basis for political-military hyper-mobilization and economic organization pervading many levels of society (cf. Hammel 1992 and Denich 1993 for penetrating discussions of ethnic politics in the former Yugoslavia). In Romania, ethnicity is part of the basis for the political mobilization of the majority group; assimilation to the majority group was until recently (perhaps) the only avenue for social/economic advancement for members of the ethnic minorities (cf. Verdery 1983).

Clearly, then, ethnicity as an organizing principle is one of the most salient features of Balkan history, both recent and remote. Beneath an overlay of waxing and waning imperial domination, Balkan history is largely ethnic history, a history of ethnic movements and ethnic conflicts. This being the case, it should hardly come as a surprise that archaeologists in southeast Europe who deal with the prehistoric past think of that past in terms of ethnic groups, their movements, their territories, and their customs; that archaeologists working in protohistoric and historic periods do the same scarcely merits comment (for examples of such interpretations, cf. Korošec 1957; Čović 1959; Georgiev 1965; Jovanović 1972; Benac 1972).

The archaeological remains which are found sandwiched between *brandthorizonten* and other features supposedly diagnostic of abrupt change introduced from abroad are typically analyzed in terms of inter-assemblage similarities and interpreted as the emblems of particular ethnic groups. There are many examples in the archaeology of the Balkans of the tendency of researchers there to divide up the landscape in terms of ceramic style zones inhabited by "ethnic groups." Three major examples of the use of the concepts of ethnicity (as organizing principle) and ethnic migration in archaeological interpretation may be cited.

The first example comes from the early Neolithic, the period which saw the introduction of agriculture in the Balkans. The settlements, material culture, and land-use patterns of the first farmers in southeast Europe bear little resemblance to those of the Mesolithic hunter-gatherers, but are reminiscent of features first seen in western Turkey and Greece. Attention has focussed on the cultural affinities between the Balkans and the Aegean/Anatolian areas, and in particular on the similarities between the respective pottery and figurine assemblages. Almost universally, the early

Neolithic sites of southeast Europe are interpreted as the settlements of migrating farmers who found their way from the Mediterranean basin, and settled in and along the major rivers of the Balkans. Upon their arrival in the Balkans, these early food producers are thought to have separated out as five territorial groups whose distinctive ceramics symbolize their different ethnic identities (for discussion, cf. M. Garašanin 1979; Dumitrescu 1970; Georgiev 1961).

Somewhat later, at the end of the Chalcolithic, a second major ethnic upheaval has been perceived. At this time, it is argued, a large-scale movement of people out of the south Russian steppe into eastern, southeastern and central Europe took place (Gimbutas 1973). The stereotypic trait of the last Neolithic inhabitants of south Russia is the placement of dismembered corpses, sprinkled with red ochre, in grave pits under earthen mounds (*kurgans*). Thus when tumuli containing these features are found in eastern Europe in the Chalcolithic and early Bronze Age, it is assumed that the people responsible for these barrow constructions were descended from the Neolithic inhabitants of the Russian steppe. Gimbutas (1973) identified these people as speakers of Proto-Indo-European, and maintains that their invasion ushered in new forms of social organization, technology, and culture; in this she has been followed by many Balkan archaeologists (e.g., Comşa 1975; D. Garašanin 1972; for an extended critical discussion of these interpretations see Anthony 1986 and this volume; Renfrew 1987).

The third example is from the Iron Age. Classical sources permit the rather precise identification of many Celtic tribes throughout Europe and attest to their wide-ranging movements, most notably the "Celtic migrations" of the fourth and third centuries BC. In many instances it has been possible to observe cultural spheres, or distinctive archaeological groupings, which encompass several documented tribes. These distributions are suggestive of ethnic groupings, and some European archaeologists prefer to use the term "ethnos" to refer to this phenomenon of cultural uniformity subsuming multiple centers of authority (Nash 1978; Snodgrass 1980). In southeast Europe, late La Tène invasions of Celts in the fourth century BC were quickly consolidated to the point where a Celtic "dominance" of the north Balkans may be seen by 290 BC (Alexander 1980). Ethnic groupings such as the union of the Scordisci tribes in the middle Danube basin (Jovanović 1974a), and the Geto-Dacian confederation of Romania (Crişan 1969; Daicoviciu 1979), are documented historically by classical commentaries and archaeologically by distributions of diagnostic pottery, fortified settlements, fibulae, weaponry, and the like.

In none of the examples just cited is the notion of ethnicity very well elaborated, if western anthropological standards are to be used. Instead, ethnicity appears as a term whose meaning is expected to be shared by writer and reader alike, based no doubt upon shared knowledge of the Balkans' past and present. Anthropologists are accustomed to regard ethnicity as a fluid form of social organization among groups which interact within a society. Thus, ethnicity involves interactions across social boundaries and a set of categories which define those boundaries (Barth 1969). These categories tend to regulate social exchanges by defining contrastive identities, designating "them" and "us," and specifying how each is to be treated (Verdery 1983; Cole and Wolf 1974). However, ethnic identity and boundaries are not necessarily permanent, nor are they universally salient. They are variables that are socially and historically conditioned. Folk notions of ethnicity (at least in Europe and North America) regard ethnicity as unambiguous, based on real differences and real origins. As Verdery (1983:15) remarks, ethnicity is commonly thought of as if it were state citizenship. In many respects, the notions of ethnicity which obtain in eastern Europe are similar to those of western Europe, but the salience of the concept differs. In eastern Europe, ethnicity played a larger role in nation-building than it did in the West, and so it looms even larger (Halpern and Hammel 1969).

B *Ideologies of nationalism and ethnicity*

Just as the ethnic history of the Balkans has suggested models for the interpretation of the region's archaeology, so too has that history provided powerful ideologies which have influenced the development and current practice of archaeology in southeast Europe. Two of the most important kinds of ideologies in this respect are nationalist and ethnic ideologies. In the past, the two have sometimes been difficult to distinguish from one another; today it is virtually impossible.

One well-known view of ethnic and nationalist ideologies is that they are attempts at mystification, a means by which class differences within an ethnic group or nation are blurred to the advantage of the elite. However, Verdery (1983:353) suggests that nationalism in southeast Europe grew initially out of local elites' struggles against the centralizing tendencies of Vienna and out of irredentist movements against the Sublime Porte: it was principally a way of discussing those struggles among the members of the local elites and between those elites and representatives of the empires. Nationalist ideologies in the Balkans thus may be seen as a new idiom of political discourse employed by regional elites in their disputes with those at the imperial courts whose efforts at state-building put the regional elites at risk. Nationalist ideology was at first a language spoken and understood by the upper and intellectual strata of the Balkans.

The rise of nationalism in southeast Europe is intimately associated with the development of archaeology there. As was the case in western Europe, the early nationalist ideologies of the Balkans emphasized a rediscovery of indigenous pasts; the pursuit of history and prehistory was integral to the nascent nationalist program (Jelavich 1982:174–9). To the nationalists of the nineteenth century, individuals were joined in one group, one nation, by virtue of certain shared traits, such as language, religion, customs, and long historical association: *Volksgeist* (Jelavich 1982:172). From state to state, the motivations behind an attempted revival and celebration of the past varied, but a consideration of the history of the period suggests that two reasons were paramount.

In the national movements of the nineteenth century, while a common language was regarded as the most important determinant of which people should form a nation-state, their history was seen as the prime determinant of the territory they should occupy. In Balkan historiography of the eighteenth and nineteenth centuries the sharpest controversies occurred as the pre-Ottoman and pre-Habsburg eras were sifted, revealing not only past glories but also the conflicting boundaries of the medieval kingdoms (Jelavich 1982:178). Thus, historical research became extremely important in defining which territories could be claimed by a particular nation-state.

Another problem was one of legitimacy. The creation of new political entities required that the loyalties of the citizenry also be newly created. As d'Azeglio remarked, "We have made Italy: now we must make Italians" (cited in Hobsbawm 1983b:267). Similarly, in the Second German Empire of Wilhelm II, which brought together a plethora of German polities under Prussian hegemony, a major effort was made to stress those historical experiences which linked Prussia with the rest of Germany, to merge the two by rewriting history (Hobsbawm 1983b:274).

All of these processes were also to be found in southeast Europe, where problems of national boundaries and political legitimacy abounded, vexing Serbia and Croatia, Romania, and Bulgaria. Thus was sparked a renewed interest in the past of the Balkans. While many old Balkan traditions and some of the indigenous history had been preserved by the Orthodox Church, by certain dioceses of the Catholic Church, and by the oral epic poetry and songs of the villages, far more was unknown. It was in this context that indigenous Balkan archaeology began; it was a logical progression from the revival of historical research, tapping a vast, unexplored domain of the past.

In Romania, Alexandru Odobescu introduced courses in archaeology at the University of Bucharest in 1874, having already devoted considerable attention to the country's antiquities (Condurachi 1964). By the 1890s local archaeologists (most of them trained in Vienna or Berlin) were at work in

Bulgaria, Bosnia, Serbia, and Croatia. There was a growing interest in prehistory, in addition to the well-established interest in classical antiquities, and in the following forty years a systematic method for classifying artefactual remains, based on Montelian precepts, was worked out (Sterud and Ivey 1973).

Besides making certain junctures of space and time seem more interesting than others, the nationalist motivation of many of the early Balkan archaeologists and their successors also influenced interpretation. In many cases, modern geo-political boundaries acted as unstated criteria for classifying artefactual material. If an artefact was found on one side of a modern frontier then it belonged to one "culture"; if found on the other side then it belonged to another "culture." These different cultures were identified by different names, a tendency still very much alive. Two examples may be cited.

As noted above, the early Neolithic of the Balkans is characterized by widespread similarities in material culture (especially the presence of diagnostic painted pottery), subsistence strategies, and settlement patterns (Tringham 1971). Nevertheless, in Serbia the early Neolithic is called Starčevo; in Hungary it is called Körös; in Romania it is called Criş, and in Bulgaria it is called Karanovo. The early Bronze Age of the Carpathian Mountains/northern Hungarian plain area provides another example of modern political geography's influence on archaeological classification. Here, hillfort settlements are found in an arc following the flanks of the Carpathians; in the adjacent lowlands of the northern Hungarian plain we find *tell* settlements, some fortified. All share a common ceramic inventory as well as other aspects of material culture, and yet those sites on Hungarian territory are distinguished by the name Füzesabony; those in Romania are called Otomani; and those in Slovakia are known as Nitra. Balkan archaeologists vociferously maintain that these distinctions are more than terminological, that real socio-cultural differences are being reflected (Marinescu-Bîlcu 1982). Such assertions bring occasional expressions of dismay from foreign archaeologists (e.g., Ehrich 1965:404; Tringham 1971).

Another consequence of the nationalist-inspired historical revival in the Balkans has been the adoption of essentially historical methods in archaeology. Chief among these methods is the use of artefact typology as a means of chronology-building and of delimiting cultural boundaries. With their typologies and analyses of artefact style, archaeologists have sought to construct a history of the Balkan past in the absence of written records. While a preoccupation with artefact typology is hardly unique to southeast Europe, it does seem that the enterprise is widely regarded as the most serious and important aspect of archaeology. Careers and reputations stand or fall on questions of chronology and typology. Even a cursory inspection of bibliographic compilations (e.g., Comşa 1976, 1977), conference proceedings (e.g., Novak 1971), or regional syntheses (e.g., M. Garašanin 1979) will show that concern over accuracy in "periodization" continues to dominate the contemporary archaeological literature of southeast Europe.

As mentioned above, one of the most important criteria used by early nationalists in defining who precisely belonged to a nation was that of shared ethnicity. Consequently, throughout most of southeast Europe, nationalist ideology coopted ethnic ideology to the point where there remained few differences between the two. Thus in Bosnia, Croatia, Serbia, and Romania ethnic identity has come to be equated with national identity in the dominant nationalist ideology. Although ethnic minorities do exist in those countries, and do themselves possess distinct ideologies, expressions of minority ethnic ideology remain muted in the face of attempts orchestrated by the state to emphasize national social homogeneity. In the case of the former Yugoslavia's successor states, chilling campaigns directed at engineering such homogeneity are at the heart of the current fighting.

In Yugoslavia of the Tito era a more decentralized federal structure allowed freer rein to the various ethnic ideologies as long as they did not propose to subvert the spirit of cooperative unity posited by pan-Yugoslav ideology. For the writing of archaeology, this relaxation permitted ethnic prehistories to be composed under the guise of regional prehistories (e.g., M. Garašanin 1974). Then, as the breakup of the country began to occur, the insistent fusing of nationalism and a notion of ethnicity allowed the guise to be dropped and made prehistories of this or that people more or less standard in the professional literature (e.g., Srejović 1988).

In summary, the rise of nationalist ideology in southeast Europe has affected profoundly the direction of archaeological research and interpretation there. Nationalist ideology attached a high value to the writing of indigenous history, and, by extension, indigenous prehistory. Balkan archaeology developed as an historical science devoted to the investigation of historic and prehistoric questions made relevant by nationalist ideological programs: issues of settlement continuity, territoriality, and cultural affinity. Much interpretation of the archaeological past appears to bear an imprint from the nationalist present and recent past with, for example, modern national boundaries being perceived as having some sort of prehistoric reality.

C Marxist ideology

Nationalism, of course, is not the only modern ideology to have influenced archaeological interpretation in the Balkans. Not surprisingly, in southeast

Europe from 1945 to 1989, Marxist ideology also figured prominently in theories of the prehistoric and protohistoric past. Marxism's impact on Balkan archaeology was felt mostly in three areas.

The first area of impact was in the domain of theory. As is well known, historical materialism is a theory of society and social change which is concerned with the ways in which contradictions between forces and relations of production come about and lead dialectically to transformations of society. Using this materialist framework, Marx undertook to analyze the origins and dynamics of capitalist society, tracing aspects of social change in the historic periods preceding it; his treatment of prehistoric societies, however, was sketchy at best. In the course of his analysis, Marx (1954:200) observed:

> [r]elics of by-gone instruments of labour possess the same importance for the investigation of extinct economical forms of society, as do fossil bones for the determination of extinct species of animals. It is not the articles made, but how they are made, and by what instruments, that enables us to distinguish different economical epochs. Instruments of labour not only supply a standard of the degree of development to which human labour has attained, but they are also indicators of the social conditions under which that labour is carried on.

Taking their cue from this orientation, Marxist archaeologists accordingly were disposed to give careful attention to artefacts of all kinds, considering material culture to be the most informative – even "objective" – category of evidence available. Put into practice, this emphasis on material culture provided further reinforcement for the typological bent already well established in the discipline of Balkan archaeology. (Interestingly, other approaches to the study of prehistoric artefacts, such as archaeometry, which directly address the issues raised by Marx, were less common but not altogether unknown (e.g., Todorova *et al.* 1977; Todorova and Nacheva 1971).)

Among the avowed aims of archaeological research in the Balkans in the years 1945–89 was the reconstruction of "the economic and social conditions which engendered the different cultures and their transformations" (Condurachi 1964:51). While certain Western observers (e.g., Harding 1983:12; Milisauskas 1986:782) once expressed doubt as to whether statements such as the above reflect anything more than lip service to the principles of historical materialism on the part of most east European archaeologists, there were many counter-examples of research which were thoroughly informed by Marxist tenets. Todorova, for instance, brought together research into a wide range of topics (material culture, technology, settlement, subsistence, demography, and exchange) in a synthesis of the Chalcolithic period in Bulgaria (Todorova 1978). Her assessment of the period is worth quoting at length:

> The Eneolithic is one of the most remarkable periods in the prehistory of South-eastern Europe. Its distinctive feature was that it created the requisite conditions for taking the first step towards a second division of labour, i.e. the rise of production (crafts) specialisation of individual groups of people and the development of barter trade between them. It was during this period that socio-economic conditions made their appearance, which led to inequality in property status with all the ensuing consequences . . . [T]he Eneolithic . . . is characterised by the development of a number of new spheres of human activity, leading to profound changes and transformations in tribal community relations. (Todorova 1978:7)

Todorova then goes on to show how recent fieldwork supports these contentions. A discussion, couched in similar terms, of the socio-economic development of Bronze Age communities in Serbia may be found in Garašanin (1972). Examples such as these demonstrate that Marxist theory was often interwoven in the interpretation of Balkan prehistory, even if highly theoretical considerations of the relationship between archaeology and historical materialism were rare.

Marxism's impact on Balkan archaeology was more keenly felt in a second area, the periodization of history. Following the works of Morgan and Tylor, Marx and Engels envisioned the history and prehistory of society before capitalism as being composed of evolutionary stages which reflected the hypothetical development of social relations prior to the emergence of class divisions and the nation-state (Engels 1884). Within each of these stages, groups all shared certain material and social characteristics; their historical role was to be transformed and replaced by a higher stage. Engels' work was routinely cited in the archaeological literature of pre-revolutionary eastern Europe, and his (borrowed) concepts were often adopted and discussed. Terms such as "primitive community," "tribal aristocracy," and "emerging class divisions" were frequently encountered in the literature of the time (e.g., Condurachi 1964; Garašanin 1972; Peikov 1973).

Soffer (1985:10) has noted that the widespread acceptance of Engels' formulation of the socio-economic stages of prehistory had, for a time, a stultifying effect on archaeology in the Soviet Union. "Because what happened in the past was known, what was needed, in effect, were just illustrations." By and large this effect was less felt in the Balkans, although archaeological research was by no means free of the occasional hubristic assumption that what lay in the ground was already known.

Perhaps the most telling example of recent years is the case of Lepenski Vir. When, in the 1960s, the Danube Gorges were to be surveyed and sites there excavated prior to the area's flooding by the Yugoslav-Romanian hydroelectric dam at Kladovo, the job of digging below an unprepossessing scatter of early Neolithic (Starčevo) sherds was given to a then-junior archaeologist, Dragoslav Srejović, precisely because everyone "knew" what a Starčevo site would contain. Srejović subsequently made his reputation when he found that beneath the sherds were the remains of a remarkable and unique Mesolithic settlement of hunter-gatherers containing trapezoidal houses, burials, and monumental sculpture. For Srejović, and indeed for those who joined debate with him, the most interesting aspect of the Lepenski Vir site concerned the relationship between the apparently complex organization of hunter-gatherer life there and the origins of farming in southeast Europe: could it be that experiments in domestication began independently in the Balkans, or were creative developments of the Mesolithic hunter-gatherers superseded by the arrival of immigrant farmers (Srejović 1972, 1974; Jovanović 1972)?

Indeed, rather than only provide illustrative materials for some Engels-inspired ethnography of the past, Balkan archaeologists also delved into the transformations by which one stage replaced another. This concern was translated into action in the form of a vigorous program of field research beginning in the 1950s. Throughout the Balkans, excavations concentrated on the large, stratified sites whose multiple levels spanned long stretches of the Holocene. Large exposures were excavated at now famous sites such as Karanovo, Gomolava, Vučedol, and Ezero in order to refine the chronological picture and thereby come to grips with the dynamics of social change.

One major contention of the evolutionary-Marxist theory of the past is that any given stage is genetically and dialectically related to its predecessors, that is to say, there is a continuous aspect to change. This was the third major contribution of Marxist theory to southeast European archaeology: an assertion of a degree of cultural continuity through prehistory up to the emergence of class divisions in the Iron Age (Peikov 1973), and sometimes beyond (Miclea and Florescu 1980). This emphasis is one which is in line with the nationalist ideologies of the nineteenth-century and contemporary Balkan governments, but it runs counter to another major trend in Balkan archaeological explanation; namely, the view of change brought about by migrations and invasions. The contradiction has often been happily resolved through compromise: the migrations and invasions are still accepted as having happened, but processes of assimilation and acculturation allowed an autochthonous element to remain.

The resulting view of the Balkan past may be summarized as follows. During the Pleistocene and the early Holocene, hunter-gatherers worked out a series of highly successful and often complex adaptations to the ecologically diverse Balkans. These hunter-gatherers were overwhelmed (but not exterminated) by a wave of immigrant farmers from the Near East and Greece; their assimilation by the newcomers explains the regional differences observed in the early Neolithic (Srejović 1974, 1988). Similarly, a second wave of migrations during the late Neolithic (Garašanin 1954), the arrival of the Indo-Europeans in the early Bronze Age (Garašanin 1972), the appearance of Celtic warrior tribes in the Iron Age (Tasić 1974; Jovanović 1974a), and even the establishment of Greek colonies and Roman provinces – all incorporated the previous inhabitants and elements of their cultures. Moreover, each successive type of social organization, whether the result of a migration or not, can be seen to have been distinguished by "corresponding developments" in the mode of production (Jovanović 1974b).

II Projecting the past

Just as the present constrains interpretations of past events, so too can present interests select certain aspects of the past to serve purely contemporary ends, and, in fact, to *interpret* the present. Fowler (1987), Trigger (1989a), and Gathercole and Lowenthal (1990), among others, have all recently discussed the ways in which archaeology, and, more generally, the past, can be brought into the service of the state. Primarily, authorized versions of the past – historic or prehistoric – can be used to lend legitimacy to the current order. This can take a number of forms, such as: (a) the establishment of a link between present governors and ultimate sources of power and legitimacy which reside in the past; (b) the advancement of claims to the effect that a nation's population is in some way superior to all others, on the basis of past achievements; or (c) to glorify the present by casting the past in an unfavorable light. In the endeavor to legitimize state policies and ideologies, the past constitutes a symbolic resource. The control of that resource is as important to a state's legitimacy as control over any of the more tangible and traditionally cited resources which prop up state power (Edelman 1964).

In the Balkans, archaeology is one of the means of uncovering and presenting the symbolic resource of the past and, as such, it is used in the quest for political legitimacy; perhaps more than in many places, archaeology here has an unambiguous contemporary relevance. Below, it is suggested that the Balkan past has been made to serve a number of mutually reinforcing goals: (a) the establishment of political and territorial legitimacy; (b) the buttressing of political ideology; (c) the maintenance of cultural identity; and (d) the invention of tradition.

Ever since the late nineteenth century, when the post-imperial political boundaries of the Balkan nation-states began to be established, there have been conflicting territorial claims. Since at one time or another in each of their territories the medieval polities of southeast Europe encompassed vast tracts of land, it has always been possible to claim bits of neighboring countries on the basis of historical precedent. Neither the arrival nor the disappearance of socialist regimes did anything to make these rival claims disappear. Romania and Hungary, for example, still dispute their present boundary, which gives Transylvania to Romania. Bulgaria, Greece, and Serbia all sometimes dispute Macedonian territory. Albania sometimes presses its claim to Kosovo. Today, of course, the border disputes between Serbian, Croatian, and Bosnian Moslem forces are of the most violent kind. And in each case, the dispute has swirled around the extent to which available historical and archaeological evidence supports the claim of continuous occupation, or prior presence, of either group, in a particular territory.[2]

For the archaeology of the region conflicting claims have encouraged a resurgence in medieval archaeology in the disputed areas, since the origins of most of the present territorial disputes are to be found in the Middle Ages. For example, in the Kosovo region of Yugoslavia, which is hailed as the heart of Old Serbia, and which has been the scene of nationalist ferment on the part of the Albanian ethnic majority since 1981, the tempo of archaeological excavation and survey increased dramatically in the 1980s. The not surprising finding of much of this research was that Slavs have long occupied Kosovo.

It is important to place all this in historical context. In the middle 1980s, as post-Tito Yugoslavia began to fall apart, one of the competing political visions to re-emerge was that of Greater Serbia. This vision was advocated by, among others, the Serbian Academy of Science and Art. In 1986, the Academy developed a policy formulation (leaked and subsequently disavowed) which critiqued the Communist system. Special vitriol was directed at the system which, the Academy claimed, had given political privileges to minority groups, but not to Serbs, in areas always claimed by Serbia: the Vojvodina, Krajina, and, most especially, Kosovo. This document is now regarded as one of the key historical documents of the current war since it helped provide the intellectual justification for Slobodan Milošević's policies, including his harsh repression of Albanians in Kosovo.

Interestingly, the same year as it was building the intellectual case for a Greater Serbia, the Academy sponsored a symposium in Belgrade on the archaeology and history of the Illyrians and the Albanians. The timing was hardly accidental. The purpose of the symposium, as A. Isaković observed, was to "set straight" the "facts" about the genetic relationship between Illyrians and Albanians (Isaković 1988:5–6).

In Albania, it is widely believed that the Illyrians were the ancestors of modern Albanians. The argument begins with the stratified site of Maliq, where cultural continuity is allegedly to be seen from the Neolithic through to the late Bronze Age (by which time an Illyrian people arguably can be recognized), and then to Iron Age, thus "proving" that the Illyrians of classical times were indigenous (Prendi 1966; Buda 1984; see Stipčević 1991:1–14 and Wilkes 1992:1–13 for overviews of the development of Illyrian studies). Thus, ran the Albanian logic, whatever was once Illyrian could be claimed today by Albania.

The specific issue with respect to Kosovo has to do with the status of the Dardanians, a group which occupied Kosovo, northern Macedonia, and southern Serbia from at least the first millennium BC onward. Albanians take the view that the Dardanians were an Illyrian tribe, while the Serbian view is that the Dardanians reflect a fusion of Thracian and Illyrian elements (Wilkes 1992:12). The implications for political legitimacy in Kosovo are obvious (Stipčević 1986). Papers presented in the Belgrade symposium by M. Garašanin (1988), Popović (1988), and Cirković (1988) attacked the Albanian claims and took pains to review the evidence of late prehistoric, classical, and early medieval archaeology in Kosovo. They found little evidence to support any direct link between Illyrians and Albanians; they emphasized the "mixed" character of the Dardanians; and, for good measure, the participants in the symposium also noted the prevalence of Slavic finds and Slavic toponyms within modern Albania.

Conflicting political and territorial claims have also led archaeologists to attempt to demonstrate still longer term continuity of cultures in the Balkans. The most extreme example is that of Romania, which claims to have an unbroken record of human habitation dating back one million years. Of especial importance to the Romanians is the assertion of cultural continuity from the Iron Age through the Roman and medieval periods. What is at stake here are the notions that Romania has never been fundamentally changed by its non-Latin neighbors and that Romanian claims to all of present-day Romania are founded in historical priority. This theme is repeated in every museum display and textbook dealing with the country's past, serving to distinguish Romania and Romanians from the surrounding parvenus – Slavs and Magyars.

In Romania before the revolution, the issues of settlement continuity and territorial legitimacy were taken so seriously, and the contribution of archaeology validating national claims was regarded so highly, that the President, Nicolae Ceauşescu, was moved to contribute to a popularization of Romanian prehistory. He commented: "with every excavation, the archaeologists are bringing to light more evidence, proving that it is here, in this land, and not elsewhere, that the bones of the forefathers of our forefathers' forefathers are to be found" (Ceauşescu in Miclea and Florescu 1980: Supplement 4).

Also at issue, albeit covertly so, is the implied claim that Romania's connection with that which was Roman and Dacian in its past somehow establishes the Romanian people as superior to their neighbors in much the same way that the Romans were superior to the barbarians on their borders. Of course, it is never put quite so baldly:

> Depuis . . . [le] Ier siècle avant nôtre ère . . . notre peuple a dû mener de durs combats pour constituer et défendre son propre être, son identité nationale . . . Descendant "des plus justes et des plus braves entre les Thraces" – comme Hérodote nommait les Géto-Daces – ainsi que des fiers Romains, le peuple roumain s'est toujours fait distinguer par . . . sa volonté d'être de ses destinées . . .(Ceaušescu, cited in Dobrescu 1979: x)

It is clear that the past has played, and continues to play, a role in the construction of Balkan cultural identities. The present war in the west Balkans is starkly revelatory. Who are the combatants? To say that the conflict pits "Serbs" against "Croats" and "Moslems" is uninformative: who are they? Customarily, religion and dialect are used to distinguish one from the other, but, as Hammel (1992:5) points out, "Ethnic identification [in former Yugoslavia] is . . . essentially fluid, and the characteristics used in description are often not necessary and seldom sufficient." What people who identify a commonality among themselves most often have is a past they regard as shared. So, people whose relatives suffered atrocities in the Second World War at the hands of the Ustše (Croatian fascists) become Serbs, Moslems are related to those massacred by Četniks (royalist Serbs), and so on into ever more remote pasts.

The war today has been built upon historical falsehoods (see Halpern 1993). Using first selective readings and misreadings of history to mobilize support, leaders in the conflict then offered up a version of the past as a blueprint for the future. In effect, each side saw the contested parts of Croatia, Bosnia, and Hercegovina as having once been ethnically unmixed and sought to restore that condition. Of course, nothing of the sort ever existed. However, since micro-regional ethnic homogeneity was the goal, and since what is determinative of ethnicity is history, it follows that history, or rather specific parts of the past *as they exist in the present*, must be eradicated. And that means, as Chapman (1994) points out, that places intimately associated with another group's past – a minaret, a bridge, a hillfort – become important targets marked for destruction.

Since 1991, the nationalist-ethnic war that has enveloped regions of Croatia has had a very specific impact on the practice of archaeology there. In eastern Slavonia, Krajina, and Dalmatia, heavy damage was done to a vast range of cultural monuments. In some cases, the damage was "collateral," an accidental consequence of location (hilltops were strategic places in antiquity as much as in the present), but more often the destruction of the past was carried out as a deliberate act. Consequently, archaeological efforts have been geared towards damage assessment. Rescue and reconstruction are likely to dominate archaeologists' field efforts in Croatia and Bosnia for the foreseeable future. The journal of Croatia's archaeological society, *Obavijesti*, has carried regular articles detailing the loss of or damage to Croatia's cultural heritage (e.g., Žile 1992; Kirigin 1992; Zekan 1992; for a comprehensive review, see Chapman 1994). This publicity campaign has had an unmistakable ideological component. It seeks to portray Croatia's cultural monuments as the innocent victims of barbaric enemies, and it has the effect of fueling *revanchiste* flames.

Finally, in surveying the role of the past in the present, we may note that archaeology in southeast Europe has been of active assistance in the invention of Balkan traditions, a process which, in Europe, has been in high gear since the third quarter of the nineteenth century. The object of invented tradition is to cloak the present with the respectability of antiquity (Hobsbawm 1983a). What are invented are, in the language of political science, *condensation symbols* which fuse "into one symbolic event, sign, or act patriotic pride, anxieties, remembrances of past glories or humiliations . . ." (Edelman 1964:6). The term "invented tradition" is used broadly here, following Hobsbawm (1983a:1), to refer to traditions actually invented (such as the wearing of clan kilts in Scotland) and those emerging quickly but in a less traceable manner (such as the practices associated with fraternity recruitment drives on American college campuses). Invented traditions can be ritual practices, formally or informally governed, memorializing a past which is quite simply made up, or they can be celebrations of a "real" past which was not previously valued. Invented traditions can also take the form of constructions, such as monuments and buildings, which make an overt link to the past.

On the landscape of the Balkans, archaeological excavations often stand as national monuments, scooped out rather than erected. Just as tall statues, columns, and arches propose to remind one of past events or figures and thus symbolize a common identity, so too do archaeological excavations (especially preserved ones such as Lepenski Vir, Karanovo, and Gamzigrad) serve to concretize a connection to a remote antiquity which is claimed as an important part of a national identity. That the strength of this connection is perhaps open to question is beside the point: enough "scientific" archaeological evidence can be mustered to convince non-archaeologists of the solid basis for such claims.

In Romania, archaeological research into the late Iron Age proved invaluable for the invention of tradition, providing a wealth of detail about armaments and ornaments, costumes and customs – all of which could be re-created in the massive parades and spectacles which celebrated Romania's past and present national identity in the Ceauşescu era. The year 1980, for example, was the 2050th anniversary of the creation of the "Dacian state" under Burebista, the Dacian king. Prior to the anniversary an impressive collection of Geto-Dacian artefacts was assembled and toured the museums of Europe before coming home to rest as the center-piece of the National Museum's contribution to the anniversary. Dacocentrism was so prevalent in Romania through the 1980s that even the official calendar of the Romanian Orthodox Church sported pictures of the Dacian kings Burebista and Decebal (Verdery 1983:70). As with so many other modern traditions in Europe, the celebration of Romania's Dacian heritage goes back to the nationalist movement of the late nineteenth century and no further. Archaeology's role has been, effectively, to provide new fuel for that celebration.

In Croatia, the past is presently being mined for symbols that can be deployed in support of the nation-building campaign that the Tudjman regime has begun. Part of this nation-building involves a rejection of forms too closely identified with Tito's Yugoslavia. In this vein, in mid-1994 a new currency was introduced, the *kuna*, to replace the old *dinar*. Each *kuna* banknote sports the portrait of some famous Croat on one side, and a place or object of historical note on the other. For example, on one side of the new 20 *kuna* note we find juxtaposed two images from Vukovar, the eastern Slavonian town which fell to Serb forces at the end of 1991 after a long, bloody siege. The note is graced by an eighteenth-century palace, now destroyed. Next to the palace sits a Copper Age pot, an elaborate ornithomorphic vessel from the site of Vučedol. (The pot has survived, but Vučedol has not: it was used by Yugoslav army tanks and artillery as a position from which to flatten Vukovar.) Together, the images spell out the message that Vukovar is a Croatian place, integral to Croatian cultural identity, and has been so for a very long time. (The banknote takes the trouble to date both pot and palace.) The past, presented in the form of invented tradition, can thus be used to symbolize national identity or to legitimize present policy. The past can also be used to lend support for current political ideology.

Obviously, the basic premise of this chapter, and of this volume as well, does not constitute a new idea in the sociology of intellectual life. It has long been evident that the social, political, and economic contexts within which any discipline operates wield both overt and covert influences on that discipline (Mannheim 1936; Habermas 1973). This kind of analysis, which situates intellectual traditions in particular historical moments, is no longer new to archaeology (cf., however, Trigger 1984, 1989a; Gero 1985; Fowler 1987; Gathercole and Lowenthal 1990; Mikolajczyk 1990). Critical examination of archaeology attempts to reveal the influences of tacit, culturally conditioned presuppositions on archaeological interpretation, with the ultimate goal of making those interpretations more valid through explicit qualification.

Such attempts benefit from the widest possible comparative perspective, and it is in this spirit that the present chapter has been offered. Archaeology in southeast Europe provides an interesting case study in this respect precisely because it has emerged from historical/socio-political contexts quite different from those of western Europe or North America. In the Balkans, ideologies of ethnicity, nationalism, and Marxism have interacted in a unique fashion. Together, they have cast archaeology in a politically active role, and induced Balkan archaeologists to perceive particular patterns in their past. As a consequence of the predisposition of archaeologists in southeast Europe to think about prehistory and history in terms of the categories suggested by these ideologies, it has also become possible for advocates of these ideologies to make overt use of archaeological evidence.

Clearly, historically situated analyses of archaeology have a long way to go. This study, for example, has tended to treat the last hundred years or so of Balkan archaeology as if it were framed in the context of one or two historical moments. The reality is doubtless more complex. Here, as elsewhere, our understanding of archaeology will improve as critical analysis becomes ever more sensitive to the relationships which exist between particular constellations of social, political, and economic trends and the kinds of archaeological interpretations and methodologies that are formulated under these conditions.

NOTES

1 This chapter was written in 1993, and revised in 1994, at which time a war, starting first in Slovenia in 1991, was still being fought in Croatia and Bosnia and Hercegovina.

2 Serb claims to territory are founded on a rather peculiar logic. Seeking to unite all Serbs in a single polity, they draw their intended borders so as to encompass the territory that was Serbia's at the zenith of the thirteenth-century Nemanjić dynasty's power *and* all the territory settled by refugee Serbs fleeing the Turks in subsequent centuries. As Hammel (1992:5) observes, this is an attempt to turn "both victory and defeat into territory." The Croatian claims to huge tracts of Bosnia and Hercegovina are based on where in medieval times certain linguistic forms and Catholic worshippers were to be found.

8 From internationalism to nationalism: forgotten pages of Soviet archaeology in the 1930s and 1940s[1]

Victor A. Shnirelman

Studies of ethnogenesis (or "the formation of peoples") played a prominent role in the USSR for many years. Western scholars often are genuinely surprised at the development (if not overdevelopment) of such studies relative to other research programs. Why was the question of ethnogenesis so important for Soviets, especially for the intellectuals? Was this a response to purely academic challenges or stimulated by external forces? Also, were the ethnogenetic studies always emphasized in Soviet scholarship or were they introduced at a certain period of its development? Probably, only a few people remember now that Soviet scholars only began to study questions of ethnogenesis in the late 1930s. What happened then? What forced scholars to revise almost completely their former concepts and methodologies? In this respect, it is worth mentioning that many ideas, approaches, and theories that continued to dominate Soviet academic research until very recently were deeply rooted in developments during the late 1930s and 1940s. Thus, what happened at that time in the USSR greatly affected subsequent Soviet scholarship.

I The intellectual climate and political background of early Soviet times

To answer these questions one needs to return to a somewhat earlier period and to explore the ideological climate in Soviet scholarship from 1920 through the early 1930s. At that time the so-called "Pokrovski school" was dominant in the historical disciplines, and the field of linguistics was involved in a critical transformation initiated by academician Nikolai Ya. Marr. Mikhail N. Pokrovski, an old Bolshevik and a companion of Lenin, was a prominent Soviet historian and an indefatigable fighter against pre-revolutionary Russian historiography. Grounded in Social-Democratic Party ideology, Pokrovski's works were sharply opposed to the Tsarist monarchy. Consequently, he treated Old Russia only as an imperialist police state, "a prison of the peoples," and occupied himself with unmasking her colonial conquests. At the same time, he attempted to defend the rights of the non-Russian peoples that were suppressed by the tsar's regime. Accordingly, Pokrovski rejected the term "Russian history" as a counter-revolutionary one that paid no attention to the multi-ethnic composition of the population of imperial Russia. In brief, Pokrovski was a convinced internationalist opposing the very nature of a national state regime (Neretina 1990:32–5).

Nikolai Ya. Marr was also an internationalist. A well-trained Orientalist, he made valuable contributions to Armenian and Georgian philology (Alpatov 1991). In time, he became more and more interested in comparative-historical linguistics and prehistory. He occupied himself primarily with the development of these disciplines from the 1920s through the early 1930s. Marr was not satisfied with the backwardness of Caucasian linguistics, and he first attempted to demonstrate close relationships among the Caucasian languages and to confirm their deep antiquity. Thus, on the one hand, he (1915:287) constructed the so-called Japhetic family of languages and identified it with a certain "entity in blood" or a racial type, initially using a migration model to explain the extension of the Japhetic area in time in accordance with the ideas then characteristic for contemporary comparative linguistics and archaeology.

On the other hand, he put forward the idea that the principal factor in linguistic development was the mixture and "interbreeding" of languages rather than their split or disintegration, as advocated by orthodox Indo-European linguists. This approach became a focus of Marr's later works and led to several important conclusions. First, according to Marr's theory, all the modern languages, as well as the peoples themselves, were of mixed ancestry, i.e., they emerged from close interrelations among various populations in the deep past. Secondly, autochthonous development was claimed to be of primary importance, and it took place locally and continuously from one stage to the next through the integration of adjacent groups. According to this perspective, migrations played a lesser role or were altogether rejected. Thirdly, Marr pointed out that language, race, culture, religion, and the like were historical phenomena and, thus, under a state of permanent change, a condition which meant that it made no sense to look for any rigid correlations among them. Fourthly, cultures and languages, including the most ancient ones, were not only mixed, but also structured according to social class differentiation. In other words, Marr treated ethnicity as a result of ethnic stratification that emerged from inter-group or inter-tribal integration. Different populations obtained specific social positions in a newly born cultural entity and turned into particular social strata. This idea was developed by Marr (1915:293) already in 1915 and accompanied all his later works. Moreover, a class principle of cultural structure became universally operative in Marr's speculations, and Marr attempted to trace this principle from the time when prehistoric "magicians" invented the very language itself, thus raising themselves above the rest of the population.

In contrast, ethnicity was treated by Marr as something non-permanent and ephemeral. He argued:

> There are no ethnic cultures in genesis as such; in this sense there are no tribal cultures that differ from each other in genesis, but there is a uniform human culture at particular stages of development that is partly or separately maintained by various tribes, often by the whole group or groups of backward tribes and peoples. A culture as such is uniform in its ancestry; and all its varieties originated from a uniform creative process at different stages of its development. Thus, there are varieties, aren't there? Certainly, but these varieties are of a real class nature rather than of a mysterious ethnic one. (1933:236)

Thus, one had to study universal stages of cultural evolution rather than particular lines of development of certain unique or peculiar cultures, "language systems" rather than particular "families of languages." "Homelands" and "proto-languages" were discredited as non-existent. What really took place, according to Marr, was a continuous process of endless cultural change. The theory in question agreed well with the main idea of the "Pokrovski school" that main attention should be given to stages common to all nations regardless of any differences among them (Kushner 1927).

What occasioned cultural and linguistic changes? Marr answered that they resulted from socio-economic shifts. Thus, he argued (1935:325–6) that it was the discovery and expansion of metallurgy that forced Japhetic languages to turn into Indo-European ones. This idea was put forward by Marr in 1924 in a paper entitled "Indo-European languages of the Mediterranean basin"; it was considered a turning point in his development of the Japhetic theory (Meshchaninov 1935:24). At this time Marr emphatically insisted on the organization of combined interdisciplinary researches including, especially, linguistics and archaeology. In brief, Marr's later works were characterized by anti-racism and anti-colonialism and emphasized the inherent value of the cultures of small non-Indo-European peoples. At the same time, he called ethnicity "a transitory stage in human evolution," thus rejecting ethnos as a permanent natural category. However, he also considered class structure inherent in humanity because of the continuous process of inter-group mixing. All of Marr's later speculations corresponded to Bolshevik ideology in the 1920s, especially the simplified version produced by Stalin and his followers.

To evaluate the high esteem accorded Pokrovski and Marr from 1920 through the early 1930s – their ideas being supported and protected by the highest authorities – one has to consider the peculiar features of the socio-political atmosphere of that period. The discussion in the twenties on the character of the future Soviet national state culminated in Stalin's victorious insistence on building a rigid, uniform administrative structure, in contrast to the development of a confederation or new type of federation which was advanced by Lenin and many Bolsheviks of non-Russian origin (the so-called ethnic Bolsheviks). A conference of the Central Committee of the Russian Communist Party in June 1923 was a turning point in the discussion when Stalin charged his opponents with nationalism and attempts to split the country (Nenarokov 1992). As a result, an imperial political-administrative system was recreated under the USSR umbrella that was ideologically masked with the slogans of internationalism. The ethnic Bolsheviks' positions remained sufficiently strong during the first decade of Soviet power, and the central authorities were not powerful enough to impose their will by force. Thus, while combating the nationalism that was an inherent feature of Soviet internationalist ideology and practice, the officials emphasized primarily "Great Power chauvinism" and only after that "local nationalism."

It was just this strategy that was chosen by Stalin (1936:422–8) for his talk at the 16th Communist Party Congress in 1930. While treating the so-called "national question," Stalin argued that the cultures that were developing in a multi-ethnic state under the dictatorship of the proletariat were "national in form and socialist in content." This was his vision of internationalism. He added that this trend will result in the merging of various cultures into a uniform socialist culture with the same language when the proletariat will win its victory over the entire world. Before that time, he insisted, one has to fight permanently against two different enemies: Great Russian chauvinism and local nationalism. At that time, he stressed only the struggle against Great Russian chauvinism.

II Internationalism: its influence on Soviet archaeology

Does it make any sense to treat such political events and ideas in respect to archaeology? Formerly, it was impossible in Russia even to think in these terms, and some scholars (Gening 1982; Pryakhin 1986) pretended that Soviet archaeology developed as a purely academic discipline. Unfortunately, this was not the case. In the 1920s, when Soviet power was still emerging, state interests were not focussed on scholarly concerns, and a very intensive internal struggle was being waged within the Communist Party. At that time, approaches and concepts were developing in various disciplines that had appeared already in pre-revolutionary Russia with their own peculiar ideas and methodologies (Formozov 1993:72–7). For example, ideas on the close relationships between culture, race, and language were still alive in archaeology. Some scholars (Efimenko 1923; Zhukov 1929a:33; 1929b:59) attempted to identify particular archaeological assemblages with ethnic groups; some (Bogoraz-Tan 1928) shared Kulturkreis school approaches, and, in general, migration and diffusion models were commonly invoked to explain cultural change. In this respect, Soviet archaeology resembled Western archaeology in the 1920s.

The situation changed drastically at the very end of the 1920s and beginning of the 1930s as a result of the introduction of Marxism into archaeology, especially its Stalinist version. The discipline was violently transformed through purges and reorganizations demanded by the party bureaucracy (Graham 1967:120 ff.; Formozov 1993:74–81). People of the new generation, who now received leading academic positions, had grown up sincerely believing in world revolution and the imminent victory of Communism all over the globe. Their ideology was based on an internationalism that required scholars to study only global universal regularities that confirmed the non-unique character of the Russian experience or, in other words, the inevitability of socialist revolutions in other countries.

S.N. Bykovski and V.B. Aptekar' played especially important roles among this new generation. Both were faithful followers of Marr who believed that the exploitation of "true" methodologies could compensate for one's poor knowledge of the discipline or its subject matter. Indeed, both had no systematic training in archaeology, ethnography, or linguistics. S.N. Bykovski began his career during the Civil War as a Red Army commissary where he became known for his cruelty. In the 1920s he worked first as a teacher in history at Viatka Pedagogical College. V.B. Aptekar' graduated from a medical institute and was employed in a publishing house for some time (Alpatov 1991:55). Nevertheless, both played decisive roles in the extirpation of old archaeological and ethnological schools and the introduction of Marxism into Soviet scholarship in its Marrist guise. This is, of course, paradoxical, since Marr himself was poorly familiar with Marxism before 1927–8 (Alpatov 1991:68).

S.N. Bykovski was especially diligent in the Marxist transformation of Soviet archaeology; he was generally successful in his attempts to combine Stalin's instructions with certain ideas borrowed from Pokrovski and Marr. Following Marr, he (1931c) insisted on the uniform ancestry of peoples all over the world. At that time, the process in question was called "ethnogeny." Bykovski treated it as the endless interbreeding of various cultural groups in the course of a socio-economic evolution which was represented everywhere by the same stages. The size of newly formed groups increased permanently from stage to stage as a result of intercultural integration. Bykovski (1931c:4) represented this process schematically as a transition of small economic "totemic" groups to clans, then to tribes, further to peoples, and, finally, after the world socialist revolution, to the world communist society that included all mankind (cf. Carneiro 1978). In other words, Bykovski (1931c:99) postulated that: "a uniform sociological scheme of historical process among various societies all over the world confirms the inevitability of a proletarian revolution and the dictatorship of the proletariat in the West and all over the world and rejects the idea of any peculiarity or uniqueness of the revolution in our country." Simultaneously, this scheme pretended to give a historical justification for the building of the USSR and its further integration with new entities. That is why Bykovski (1931c:2) followed Pokrowski in his rejection of the term "Russian history" and claimed that it had died out as an independent discipline.

It is worth mentioning that Bykovski (1931c:2–3) was quite conscious of the political significance of his position: "Consciously or unconsciously, a historian performs a political task expressing his political interests and inclinations in his choice of a particular topic, in his methodological tools, and in his representation of historical data." He understood that a political position could affect a solution in the case of a complicated issue: "In these cases a politician speaks with the historian's lips who blindly discovers in historical sources only what is pleasant to his heart." In fact, he (1931c:5) was genuinely proud of his voluntary political tendentiousness. It is interesting that this idea was recently still alive in the USSR, although then with quite a different political climate and, correspondingly, a different message. Thus, one famous Soviet archaeologist used to repeat that, if archaeological data allowed for several different interpretations, one had to choose the more patriotic version.

However, in the early thirties one would have to wait for the emergence of this "patriotic" trend, and Bykovski appealed for the rejection of "nationalist history" and "racist archaeology," which he defined as any attempts to reveal any peculiar lines of development of particular peoples. This criticism was made to combat the migrationist theories of western, especially German, scholars who considered mechanical resettlements of people as a universal explanation for cultural change. While rejecting migrationist concepts as inherently vulnerable, especially in methodological terms, the Soviet archaeologists of the late 1920s–early 1930s stressed the close relationships between these concepts and racism, imperialism, militarism, and territorial expansionism (Meshchaninov 1928, 1931a; Bogaevski 1931; Krichevski 1931; Bykovski 1931a, 1932; Boriskovski 1934). Such criticism went far beyond purely abstract reasoning. The scholars were genuinely anxious over the future of their country in the face of fascist and expansionist threats on the western borders of the USSR. It is worth noting that such an expansionism was looking for ideological justification and sometimes exploited certain historical, archaeological, ethnological, and linguistic theories for this end (Khudyakov 1931; Palvadre 1933; Ravdonikas 1932a, b, 1935), although more often than not Soviet scholars, following Stalin and his functionaries, overstated the real danger (Nezhinskij 1990).

What could Soviet scholars propose in place of the migrationist concepts? It was here that Marr's theory stressing autochthonous development played an important role. While basing himself on Marr's ideas, Bykovski (1931b:5–6) argued that the Japhetic theory precluded the transfer of modern political/ethnographic situations deep into the past, when there were neither "proto-peoples" nor "homelands," Aptekar' (1928:264) adding that there were also no "ethnoses," "tribes," nor "proto-languages." Consequently, it made no sense to look for the roots of modern peoples in the remote past. Indeed according to Marr (1927:38; 1935:405), one could observe only small groups in prehistory that were permanently involved in economic-social relationships and, thus, were under endless changes in terms of their composition, language, and culture. Correspondingly, at that time there were no tribes, peoples, nor national or ethnic groups with their modern territorial borders. What is called a tribe, Marr (1933:241) stated, is always a result of a mixture of several different groups rather than a biological entity with any inherent characteristics. Various language families are not entities that differ in racial features, but rather are "families of economically and socially recently created language types that emerged in the course of the formation and development of public economies and the mixtures and interbreedings of various tribal languages that resulted from the process in question" (Marr 1935:331).

Thus, since ethnic entities continuously changed over time, it made no sense to identify past archaeological cultures with more recent linguistic entities; e.g., the Fat'janovo archaeological culture with the Aryans (Marr 1935:345). Moreover, in principle it made no sense to identify any ethnic or linguistic group with any culture at all. Marr (1935:314) insisted: "for us, any Finnish, Iranian, or Turkic uniform tribal nature and natural cultures produced by them cannot exist at all; there also is no Indo-European tribal culture of this kind and also no Japhetic culture, no Japhetic language without any tribal mixture or without interbreeding." Language, culture, religion and the like – all change through time. That is why it is impossible, for instance, to look for rigid links between Turks and nomadism (Marr 1927:50), or Arabs and Islam (p. 24).

It is worth noting once again that all these ideas were not developed from purely academic discussions but were founded on certain political positions. Bykovski (1931a:2–3) explained this feature in the following way:

While persistently seeking ethnic or national characteristics of this or that culture and proceeding from a modern political and ethnographic map, a student-archaeologist who shares principles of racial theory confirms "scientifically" an imperialist right to conquer specific territory, arguing that it originally belonged to the corresponding nation.

Thus, he (1931b:4–5; 1931c:57), as well as some other Soviet archaeologists (Krichevski 1931) of the early 1930s, emphatically supported Marr in his rejection of identifying archaeological cultures with ethnic groups or races (Mongait 1963:80–1). One of the most prominent archaeologists of the time, V.I. Ravdonikas (1930:81), declared: "Old concepts on the specific cultures characteristic for particular peoples, I believe, have to be consigned to the archive of the history of science." The logic of this politicized reasoning led Bykovski (1933) to a complete rejection of the term "archaeological culture," as well as to a refusal to utilize any specific archaeological terminology in general that seemed to him to be overloaded with a "bourgeois" spirit.

Given the high degree of politicization and the ideology of Soviet scholarship at that time, it is not surprising that Soviet students identified particular disciplines with corresponding academic theories. For instance, some scholars believed in the early 1930s that migrationist and racial theories were inherent in both archaeology and ethnology. That is why Marr himself (1931), as well as his students (K predstoyashchemu sezdu 1931), demanded the abolishment of "bourgeois" archaeology and ethnology, replacing them with "the history of material culture." This task was at least partly fulfilled by the Pan-Russian Archaeological-Ethnographic Conference held in Leningrad on May 7–11, 1932 (Mongait 1963:84). Since that time, an evaluation of specific academic concepts has proceeded from the ideological dogmas of Soviet scholarship, rather than from methodological approaches. That is the reason why for many years Soviet scholars wasted considerable energy in devising and improving terminology rather than methodology.

By rejecting the ethnic identification of archaeological cultures and by replacing it primarily with the "class principle" embedded in human societies, Marr articulated a theory of universal social and economic stages that, in his view, corresponded to particular language systems. He (1927:58) treated language as a superstructure and insisted that languages changed directly in conjunction with shifts in economic and social forms. Bykovski (1931c:12–13) added that not only languages, but also racial types, varied in this fashion, taking the theory down a path of total absurdity. The approach advocated by I.I. Meshchaninov (1928) was more fruitful in that it stressed the effect of socio-economic shifts principally on cultural changes, making the theory of socio-economic stages more relevant and productive for archaeology.

In the Soviet publications of the early 1930s, all these stages were decorated with the embroidery of Marr's phraseology. Marr (1935:306, 340) himself introduced the concept of a Japhetic stage that functioned as a foundation for all the world languages. In particular, he was convinced that a "Slavic-Russian" entity formed itself on the foundation of the "Scythian-Japhetic" one. Following Marr, I.I. Meshchaninov (1931b) attempted to reveal archaeologically the transformation of the "Scythian stage" into a "Slavic-Finnish" one. Bykovski (1931c:98) believed in Scythian, Cimmerian, and Japhetic stages and stated that they developed out of each other. For him, this theory meant the unity of all humankind in terms of origin and, thus, the purity of the internationalist principle.

V.I. Ravdonikas' (1932c) monograph dealing with the problem of the Goths was one of the most influential publications of the early 1930s made by a professional archaeologist. This study was based on archaeological studies in the Crimea that had been conducted by a Leningrad team since 1928. According to the prevailing ideas of the time, Ravdonikas argued against an identification of the Goths with the ancient Germans coming from the north. He insisted that one could not trace such a migration archaeologically. That is why he attempted to reconstruct the process of an autochthonous evolution through the course of several socio-economic stages from the Cimmerian through the Scythian and the Sarmatian up to the Gothic stage. It is worth noting that he was well informed on the German language of the Goths that survived in the Crimea even during the Middle Ages. Nevertheless, there were no problems here for the Marrists: languages emerged autochthonously like any cultural element, i.e., the same languages could come into being independently in different areas providing there were the same socio-economic conditions. This was the key point of the "ethnogeny" theory that was defended and propagandized by Marr and his students (Bykovski 1932). According to Marr (1933:236), each ethnic population was nothing more than a "survival of a particular evolutionary stage in the history of humankind." Thus, he identified the origin of each ethnic culture with the origin of this or that stage of cultural evolution. There was no place in Marr's scheme for particular ethnic cultures (Mongait 1963:82).

A.N. Bernshtam (1935) also followed this line of reasoning to reconstruct a cultural evolution in the Asian steppes and deserts from the Scythian stage to the Huns and further to the Turks. All the investigations in question focussed their analysis on the socio-economic variables that affected the local processes of cultural and social change. Utilization of labels, such as Scythian, Sarmatian, Gothic, and Turkic, for the reconstructed stages played a formal role in the works of professional archaeologists and can be attributed to the dominant ideology. All these studies had almost nothing to do with the origins of the particular peoples concerned. A famous Soviet archaeologist M.I. Artamonov (1949:4–5) confessed later that Soviet archaeologists did not occupy themselves with ethnogenetic problems before the late 1930s and had no corresponding methodology. Ye. Yu. Krichevski's (1933) research, which was opposed to G. Kossinna's concept of migrations, is worth mentioning in this respect. He argued that the cultural evolution in the southern Rhine, Danube, and Dnieper areas took place locally in an autochthonous fashion from the Neolithic through the early Bronze Age, and that serious cultural changes occurred because of socio-economic reasons rather than because of any migrations or influences from the outside. It is interesting that Krichevski used sociological terms to define particular stages rather than linguistic or ethnic ones.

All these trends were not fortuitous since it was practically impossible to study ethnogenesis, i.e., the particular evolutionary path leading to the emergence of a specific people, under Stalin's internationalism. A scholar who was brave enough to do this risked being charged with "Great Power chauvinism" or "local nationalism," charges that were perceived as quite close to fascism (Palvadre 1933:55). For instance, Bykovski (1932:6) treated the identification of the Scythians with modern language entities like Slavs, Turks, or Finns as "Great Russian chauvinism" that should be combated. Such was the socio-political and academic atmosphere in Soviet archaeology during the short period of Stalin's internationalism.

III A change in paradigms: from internationalism to nationalism

The period in question came to an end in 1934. Experts (Avtorkhanov 1964; 1991:25, 43; Carrière d'Encausse 1978:50, 51; Graham 1987:19–20; Fedotov 1992:60; Artizov 1992:102) explain this turning point in different ways; evidently it was a result of various trends. First, a totalitarian national state had been built in the USSR by that time that required special ideological confirmation and support for its further development. Now it had to survive by itself since all its hopes for the world revolution had not materialized. Secondly, new ethnic intellectuals grew up in the republics as a result of the cultural revolution, who began to claim their particular ethnic-cultural requirements and the like. A Russian philosopher, G.P. Fedotov (1992:60), who had already emigrated at that time, pointed out that many peoples in Russia awoke to their national life for the first time: "their young self-respect was very scrupulous. They could hardly tolerate their dependency on Moscow." This situation was wrought with future tensions and conflicts. Stalin obviously thought the same, and, not accidentally at the 17th Congress of the Communist Party in 1934, he declared "local nationalism" to be the main enemy. Thirdly, in the face of an increased military threat, he understood clearly that the Russian people were the only real force that could defend the Empire. However, Russian ethnic self-consciousness and Russian patriotism had been deeply weakened as a result of the internationalist propaganda of the previous decade. Slavic studies had suffered heavy losses by the 1930s when the Slavic Studies Commission of the Academy of Sciences had been eliminated and many scholars arrested (Graham 1967:155; Bernstein 1989; Goryainov 1990; Aksenova 1990).

Thus, beginning in 1934, Russian history and culture were rehabilitated. History faculties were once again opened at the universities, and various kinds of national symbols were reintroduced and the like. The term "Great Power chauvinism" died out. As Neretina (1990:41) noted, the Lord of the World Revolution was replaced by the Lord of Russian History. A discussion on history textbooks arranged by Josef V. Stalin, Sergei M. Kirov, and Andrei A. Zhdanov in 1934 was seminal (Artizov 1992). Their remarks and a special decision of the Central Committee of the Communist Party on historical education were published in 1936. The "Pokrovski school" was destroyed so that historians would realize the ideological changes better and begin to fulfil more expeditiously their new political tasks. This campaign was inspired by several decisions of the Central Committee of the Communist Party in 1934–8. Besides other accusations, Pokrovski was charged with a "distortion" of the concept of Russian history; with "slander" of the best representatives of the Russian people; with "mockery" of Russian patriotism; and with – most terribly and symptomatically – "contempt for the Motherland" (Rubinstein 1939; Protiv 1939).

Simultaneously arrests began among Pokrovski's colleagues and students (Artizov 1992), as well as among Marr's followers. Bykovski and Aptekar' were first imprisoned and later shot; in particular, they were charged with scholastic pseudo-academic reasonings that turned scholars away from concrete research and destroyed archaeology as a discipline (O vreditelstve 1937; Artamonov 1939:122–3; Tolstov 1947a:13). All these events forced historians to change direction. A meeting of famous historians took place in Moscow on May 5, 1937 (Institut 1992). One of the main decisions was that one should not produce abstract sociological schemes but publish more data on the concrete history of peoples. The meaning of this message was explained by several speakers who exhorted the participants to combat actively the fascist falsifications of history, to unmask German predatory politics toward the Slavs, and to demonstrate the real nature of the ancient Germans and their culture. From then on, these ideas became a leitmotif of Soviet ethnogenetic studies (Aksenova and Vasil'jev 1993:88).

Historians responded to the new situation with the preparation of a multi-volume series entitled "Ancient History of the Peoples of the USSR," initiated in 1936 by academician Yu. V. Got'je. As already emphasized, archaeologists, disarmed by Marrism, were unprepared for these changes. Nevertheless, by the late 1930s they initiated extensive studies on the past of several non-literate peoples of the USSR, e.g., the Turkic populations of the Altai Mountains, the peoples of the north, Buryats, Mordovians and the like. Interestingly enough, this activity was still conducted by the proponents of Marr's ideas and was heralded as a continuation of Marr's works, a scholar who supposedly had paid much attention to ethnogenetic studies (Artamonov 1940a). At first glance, such studies of the remote past of the different peoples of the USSR looked like a continuation of the former internationalist politics. As A.D. Udaltsov (1944:252) observed, ethnogenetic researches in the USSR aimed to struggle against fascist theories of the peoples' origins. In fact, the main focus of research was only on the Slavs' or eastern Slavs' prehistory; the best Soviet archaeologists were involved in tackling this problem, and this focus, of course, corresponded well with the new patriotic nationalist directions of Stalin's politics, which were defined as "USSR nationalist" by Efirov (1989).

It is worth noting that Marr himself was ready for such a crucial change and was quite conscious of its political background. Thus, during his later years, he attempted (1927) to argue that the Turks originated in the Mediterranean area, a position obviously discrepant with his "theory of stages." Moreover, he pointed out (1934:59–61) that this was "in accordance with the main point of Turkish national politics stressing the recognition of the Turks' historical rights." According to the theory in question, Medians, Chaldeans, Elamites, Sumerians, and probably many other ancient peoples of the Near East were closely related to the Turks and the Turkish languages. In short, Marr (1936:97) included the Turks among the ancient builders of European civilization. What were the reasons? It was simply due to the fact that Turkish experts, including the President of the Turkish Republic, Mustafa Kemal Gazi, had broken away from the school of European comparative-historical linguistics that Marr himself so detested. Thus, Marr enriched Soviet scholarship with one more characteristic feature – impassioned emotionalism and intolerance toward opponents.

A specific character of the archaeology of the late 1930s through the early 1950s was that many scholars tried to exploit the Marrist methodology to solve ethnogenetic problems. In this respect M.I. Artamonov's (1947) paper dealing with the prehistory of the Indo-Europeans is of great interest. Its author was one of the most prominent archaeologists of the period who attempted to combine Marrism with Kossinnism. While still rejecting

Kossinna's conclusions on the northern homeland of the Indo-Europeans and their conquests, Artamonov now recognized the ethnic appearance of some archaeological assemblages. On the one hand, following Krichevski, he based himself on the theory of stages and stated that all changes in ceramics, dwellings, and the like were the direct consequences of economic and subsistence transformations, in particular of the further development of pastoralism. On the other hand, he was now inclined to identify archaeological entities defining them through ceramic analysis (just as Kossinna did) and to recognize their relationships with ethnographic traits. Artamonov pointed out that an entity characteristic of any stage always expresses itself in some ethnic form. Thus, he attempted to construct "stage-ethnic entities" that in fact corresponded to well-known archaeological cultures – Corded Ware culture, Bell Beaker culture and the like.

Thus, the very term "archaeological culture" began to be rehabilitated, although the Soviet experts first tried to avoid the simplified treatment of the concept that was characteristic of Kossinna's works. A.Ya. Briusov (1940:8–16) was probably the first to analyze this problem. He recognized relationships between an archaeological culture and any type of social system, but also stressed the methodological difficulties for revealing and interpreting the former. First, it was not easy to trace any precise geographical limits for archaeological cultures. Secondly, their various elements typically consisted of many different features. Thirdly, the richest elements, or so-called "diagnostic types," were frequently reflections of inter-group exchange rather than kinship ties. Thus, the archaeological culture could mask very different types of contacts between people, and an *a priori* simple interpretation was impossible. In brief, "an archaeological culture expressed a unity of domestic life and by no means a racial unit or people" (Briusov 1940:16). However, during the 1940s to early 1950s ethnogenetic studies were recognized as one of the most important fields for Soviet scholars (Artamonov 1939:128–9; Tolstov 1947a:22; 1950:9; Znachenie . . . 1950:6; Zadachi . . . 1953:14–15), and Soviet archaeologists shifted to Kossinnism, i.e., to the dominantly ethnic interpretation of the archaeological culture. The discussions took another direction now and became more specific: for instance, how to identify an archaeological culture, i.e., an ethnic entity, through a set of various traits (Artamonov 1949:13; Briusov 1952:20; Udaltsov 1953:14–15) or with the help of some specific variables such as pottery decoration (Foss 1952:64–77).

IV The Slavs are coming

During the period in question, Soviet ethnogenetic studies as such were stimulated by the ideology of "Soviet patriotism," i.e., nationalism. The role of methodology was of less importance, and these studies combined elements of both Marrism and Kossinnism in a very strange way. Nationalism affected the choice of problem and strategy of investigation. Slavic-Russian archaeology turned into the main field of ethnogenetic studies from the late 1930s. The problems of the origins and early development of the Slavs, their homeland, the formation of the eastern Slavs, the evolution of early Slavic culture and the beginnings of their state were considered most important. The goals of these investigations were to prove an independent local formation of a rich and unique early Slavic culture, while demonstrating the backwardness of early Germanic tribes and their negative influence on adjacent peoples.

From the very late 1930s Soviet archaeologists insisted on the exceptionally autochthonous evolution of the early Slavs and traced it from the Bronze Age, i.e., from Pre-Scythian or even Tripolje times. They were convinced that one could reveal uninterrupted continuity between the Tripolje culture, the Scythian assemblages, the Urnfield culture, and the Ants' antiquities up to the formation of Kievan Rus (Tretyakov 1939, 1940, 1941a, 1941b; Artamonov 1940b; Levenok 1941; Rybakov 1943; Passek 1945; Grekov 1953). As summarized by A.D. Udaltsov (1943:72), one could observe an exceptionally autochthonous evolution in eastern Europe, and demonstrate that the "Great Russian people" with its original, highly developed culture was a direct heir of Tripolje, Hellenistic-Scythian, Sarmatian-Alanian, and Antian traditions. Academician N.S. Derzhavin (1944:3–4) went so far as to speculate on the roots of the Russians in the Upper Palaeolithic culture of the Middle Dnieper River area. He considered this culture to be the most evolved among other European (i.e., world) cultures of the time. In his view, they were already demonstrably familiar with incipient farming and pastoralism. It is quite obvious that he consciously challenged the long-deceased G. Kossinna, who looked for the ancestors of the Germans among the Mesolithic inhabitants of northern Europe, and treated the Slavs as savages who appeared rather late in prehistory. Derzhavin (1944:7) insisted:

> From the Palaeolithic times up to the Early Iron Age . . . basically one and the same people lived here [in southwestern USSR], who traversed a long path of material and cultural development during the course of centuries . . . We have no reasons to ignore here . . . a substratum of the later Slavic population of the area in question, who occupied the same territory from the very beginning, which is now inhabited by the eastern Slavs.

It is worth noting that some Soviet archaeologists (Udaltsov 1944:264; Artamonov 1949:5) did not share Derzhavin's most extreme views, though many of his ideas were quite popular in the 1940s. A core of proto-Slavic territory was identified with the Middle Dnieper River region where its population "interbred" with their neighbors, later resulting in the formation of the southern and western Slavs. The Middle Dnieper area always surpassed adjacent regions in the level of its cultural manifestations and benefited from this "hegemony" – as B.A. Rybakov (1943:75) called it. Udaltsov (1943; 1947a, b) used to point out that it was the eastern Slavs or "the Great Russian people" who were the direct heirs of the most ancient Slavic core and its original territory.

Another idea that was argued simultaneously by the same scholars concerned the formation of the autochthonous Slavic entity over a much larger territory of central and eastern Europe. It was formulated originally by Marr's true follower, Academician Derzhavin (1944:46; 1946:23), who defined a Slavic realm between the Don River and the Upper Oka and Upper Volga Rivers in the east and the Elbe and Saale Rivers in the west and also between the Aegean and Black Seas in the south and the Baltic shore and Lake Ladoga in the north during the first centuries AD. He argued (1946:28–9) that Slavic colonies spread to the west up the Rhine during the second half of the first millennium AD, and that Hamburg was an ancient Slavic town. While founding himself on the methods of Marr, Derzhavin (1944:52, 53; 1946:11) stated that Scythians, Cimmerians, Thracians, Sarmatians, Etruscans, and even Goths and Huns were among the ancestors of the Slavs. Many Soviet scholars sympathized with these ideas in the 1940s. They were emphatically developed by S.P. Tolstov (1946; 1947b), whose original contribution was to include the Thracian-Illyrian population (the Hallstatt culture) among the Slavic ancestors rather than only the Scythians and Sarmatians, as earlier considered. This was an important argument (1946:20) for him to explain the sudden penetration of the Slavs throughout the Balkans.

At the same time Derzhavin (1946:50–1) stated that the Bulgarians received their name from Slavic [sic!] troops headed by Asparukh. This ignorance of the Turkic core of the Asparukh army is not surprising if one considers Tolstov's (1947b:55) belief in the "Scythian-Sarmatian" character of early Bulgarian unity and the large number of Slavs among the Khazars and along the lower Volga in "Sarmatia."

In other words, the Soviet scholars of the 1940s attempted to look for the ancient Slavs almost everywhere in response to the Germans' "ethnogenetic" expansion. The D'jakovo culture was included among the Slavs' ancestors in the north (Tret'jakov 1941a; Rybakov 1943; Derzhavin 1944:102; Udaltsov 1947a:97; Mongait 1948; Fedorov 1948), and even the famous Estonian archaeologist H. Moora (1950:29–31) had to recognize at that time that Slavic tribes were the autochthonous population of the territories adjacent to the east Baltic region. Derzhavin (1944:102) emphatically rejected the idea that the early eastern Slavs had resettled in the northern areas that had been occupied formerly by Finnish-Ugrian inhabitants. In his view, the Slavs and the Finns "grew up" from the same "Japhetic stage." These beliefs were partly based on the early archaeological investigations of P.N. Tret'jakov (1939; 1940; 1941a; 1941b) who insisted that northern groups of eastern Slavs emerged locally in the course of their autochthonous evolution.

One can reveal the same trends in the treatment of the archaeological data from southern Russia, taking into consideration also that a new political reason came into being to look for Slavic antiquities in the Crimean peninsula after the Crimean Tatars had been forcibly deported from there in 1944. Few could be surprised at that time with Tolstov's (1946:121) ridiculous hypothesis on the early "Slavic-Alanian-Cherkessian" state in Taman' under the leadership of the Russian princes. Rybakov argued seriously at the time that the Slavs could inhabit Taman' and the lower Don River area before the tenth century (Mongait 1948; Fedorov 1948). Archaeological excavations were generously supported in the late 1940s, and the best scholars had to prove a Slavic or Russian historical priority in the Crimea. Archaeologists tried to do their best. P. N. Shul'ts (1950:147) resumed the excavations in Scythian Neapoli, Chersonese, and the like; this work made the Crimea "closer to the Russian heart." It became clear that "the Crimea was our native Russian land rather than a strange one, be it of the Tatars, Genoa, Gothic or Greek-Roman." Like many others, Shul'ts believed in the genetic relationship between the Scythians and the Slavs. P.N. Nadinski (1951), who was a Party boss in the Crimea at the time, went so far as to argue that the Crimean lands were originally owned by the Slavs and their Scythian ancestors, that Tatars had illegally encroached on these Russian lands, and that only Russians had unquestionable historical rights to the Crimea as their native territory. It is worth mentioning that the state encouraged a huge migration of Russians and Ukrainians to the Crimea at this time.

The problem of Slavic antiquities in the Crimea was intensively debated among Soviet scholars (Tolstov 1946:121; Mongait 1948:138; Vejmarn and Strzheletskii 1952; Reshenije 1952; Grekov and Bromlej 1952; Rybakov 1954; Smirnov 1953) during the late 1940s and early 1950s, a subject that was stimulated by the preparations to celebrate the 300th anniversary of the unification of Ukraine with Russia in 1954. Later, this research ended, partly because of an absence of true facts (Gadlo 1968) and partly because N.S. Krushchev gave the Crimean peninsula to Ukraine in 1954 as a gift for this anniversary (Isklyuchitelno zamechatelnyj akt 1992).

Thus, Soviet scholars responded to a German "ethnogenetic expansion" with a Slavic one. In this respect, a reinterpretation of the antiquities of the western borderlands is worth noting. In 1932 Ravdonikas (1932a) could remain neutral on the German-Polish discussion of the ethnic identification of the famous Lausitzer culture, and treat it as pursuing political rather than academic goals. However, in the 1940s Soviet scholars (Artamonov 1940b; Udaltsov 1947a:98), following Polish archaeologists, insisted on the Slavic identification of the Lugeans and the Lausitzer culture. Artamonov (1950:16) identified the Przeworsk and Aksywie cultures with the Slavs rather than with the Germans (Vandals). And Tolstov (1946:30) went so far as to include the Vandals and Langobardians among the Slavs and proclaimed territories beyond the Elbe as ancient Slavic.

In the light of the previously mentioned views one can easily understand the post-war Soviet archaeological attitude toward the Goths who were treated by the German scholars as the most gifted and powerful of all the early Germanic tribes. According to Udaltsov (1947a:99; 1947b:12), the Goths were small, odd tribal groups with a very poor culture that quickly adopted the local culture and dissolved among the indigenous population when they came to the north Black Sea area. Similarly, Derzhavin (1944:38–40) treated Jordan's evidence for the Goths as a myth. He considered the Goths as a local Japhetic population and insisted that their core consisted of the "Russian Slavs [sic!]." The Soviet scholars (Udaltsov 1947a:99; Tolstov 1946:119; Shul'ts 1950:154; Nadinskij 1951:43) unanimously treated the "early Gothic state" as an obvious legend. The early medieval antiquities of the forest steppe and steppe zone of Ukraine, represented by the Urnfield culture, were claimed to be of Slavic origin (Artamonov 1940b, 1950; Rybakov 1943:77–8; 1952:54). Thus, the problem of the Goths was deprived of its archaeological factual foundation, and experts (Tikhanova 1958; Merpert 1958:156 ff.) had to analyze it only with the written sources at hand.

While taking away considerable lands and the cultural heritage of the ancient Germans, the Soviet archaeologists allotted them the same unenviable place in the ethnogenetic map of Europe that the German authors of the 1920s to 1930s allotted to the early Slavs. S.P. Tolstov (1946:31) stated that a sparse German population lived in savagery on the margins of a prosperous Europe before the first century BC. They were backward hunters, fishermen, and primitive cultivators who had no linguistic achievements and occupied a "transitional stage" between the Japhetic and Indo-European languages (Udaltsov 1944:261). As Tolstov (1946:31) commented, they were "superficially Indo-Europeanized through the influence from neighboring Celts and proto-Slavs." In contrast to German archaeologists, the Soviets insisted that the German people began to be formed only from the tenth century AD with a heterogeneous racial and ethnic foundation (Cheboksarov 1944).

All the Soviet speculations mentioned above had to destroy "the myth of the German cultural expansion," as determined, for example, at the Conference on the Ethnography of the Baltic Peoples in 1950 (KSIE 1950). The speakers emphasized the deep roots of friendship and relations among the Baltic peoples and the Russians, even during those times when they shared no common borders! Relations with the Germans, on the other hand, were described as permanently hostile, and any positive results of these relations were completely denied. In contrast, during the 1940s and early 1950s the Russian people had to be mentioned with the epithet "Great," and it was a common practice to point out their salutary influence on their neighbors.

It is obviously reasonable to evaluate all these ideas while considering the international political situation of the 1940s; Russia's role in the victory against fascist Germany; and Stalin's speech on May 25, 1945 when he pointed out the special merit of the Russian people. His idea was that the economically destroyed and politically disintegrated Germany should be finished ideologically as well. One not only had to unmask the myth of the gifted powerful German warriors who brought culture and wisdom to their savage neighbors, but also had to prove the backwardness of ancient German culture which was far behind that of the "highly developed" Slavs.

Simultaneously, this concept had a wider ideological implication which elevated Russia high above the western world in general. Finally, the concept in question had to justify historically the Soviet Empire headed by the Russian people. This was proclaimed by S.P. Tolstov (1947b:49):

> a political history of our country is rooted not in separate widely dispersed political centers that emerged in different areas but in a more complex and powerful political system that opposed, on the one hand, Western political unity – the Roman Empire . . . and, on the other hand, the third Eastern political center of the ancient world – the Chinese Han Empire . . .

And further:

> One has to consider the ancient history of our country not as a history of spontaneously interacting particular tribes, but as a history of a complex system of political interactions among ancient powerful states that were closely connected culturally and politically both among themselves and also with related northern tribes that were deeply affected by them in terms of their economy, politics, and culture.

In other words, the author insisted that the prerequisites for the formation of the USSR had emerged by the beginnings of the Christian period, if not earlier.

Indeed Tolstov (1947b:53) believed that the Russian people and the "brother" peoples of the East originated from the same genetic foundation

– from the Scythian/Massagetean and Sarmatian/Alanian environment! These ideas are worth comparing with a leaflet of today's Russian nationalist group "Pamiat'" that declares: "the territories that belonged traditionally to various ethnic groups should remain a Motherland for living together – with necessary priority accorded the nation that combined these different peoples in this uniform state." It is not an accident that a head of one section of "Pamiat'", Dmitrij D. Vasil'ev, gave advice recently to President Boris N. Yeltsin to occupy all the territories within the former borders of the Russian Empire. During the parliamentary elections in fall 1993 one could observe how effectively this very idea was exploited by another nationalist leader, V. Zhirinovsky.

Nationalist myth-building has accelerated very rapidly in Russia during the last few years. As we have shown, however, this is not a new development. The growth of nationalism was intentionally encouraged by Russian authorities from the late 1930s on, and, over time, non-Russian intellectuals, as well as ethnic Russians, were involved in this process (see Chernykh this volume). During the last few decades, this growing struggle for the past among various ethnic "academic schools" in the Middle Volga area, the Caucasus, and the like has played an important role in the sharpening of inter-ethnic tensions throughout the former Soviet Union.

Probably while anticipating this exploitation of his concepts, Tolstov (1946:122) noted: "We are certainly far from a primitive nationalism that exalts everything that is its own and despises everything that is strange . . ." However, such disclaimers could not neutralize the powerful message of the nationalism that was contained in the Soviet ethnogenetic publications of the 1940s on Slavic-Russian problems. The latter unquestionably have played their role in the formation of the contemporary nationalist mood in Russia.

NOTE

1 This work was supported by a grant from the Cultural Initiative Foundation in Moscow, 1993.

9 Postscript: Russian archaeology after the collapse of the USSR – infrastructural crisis and the resurgence of old and new nationalisms[1]

E.N. Chernykh

Archaeology's dependence upon political and economic circumstances is graphically illustrated by recent developments affecting its practice in the former Soviet Union. This brief postscript to Shnirelman's longer historical study first describes the breakdown of state-sponsored support for archaeology and then attempts to explain the recent outbreak of various nationalist archaeologies throughout the former USSR through a consideration of the disguised Russian nationalism of Soviet "Marxist" archaeology. Since the current situation is so volatile, it is worth recording that these remarks were prepared in winter 1994.

I The current crisis

The whole centralized system of Soviet (now Russian) science quickly and inexorably began to unravel simultaneously with the advent of *perestroika* in 1985–6. This disastrous process occurred so suddenly that by 1993–4 only one important question was left for discussion: has the whole infrastructure of the former global Soviet scientific organization already collapsed or is the final *dénouement* still to come? Obviously, political and economic factors explain this ongoing tragedy. New realities, associated with the break-up of the Soviet empire, have erected severe and sometimes nearly insuperable political barriers among different parts of the huge state-sponsored Academy of Sciences, the organization which for decades provided the complex infrastructure for nearly all scientific research.

Economic factors, however, were far more important. State financing of scientific research, which had been in fact the main source of support for scientific organizations, was cut drastically and, in many cases, completely. Consequently, numerous large scientific projects were implemented slowly or were completely frozen. By 1989 the hard currency resources for buying foreign literature for the scientific institutions and their special libraries were exhausted, cutting off one of the main channels of information about world science. Tremendously increased oil costs caused an "explosion" of prices in transportation and communication (telephone, postal service, etc.), restricting scientific travel both domestically and abroad. Some scientific teams were physically isolated and deprived of valuable information about research in related fields done elsewhere. The volume of scientific publications decreased dramatically. By the end of 1993, this near total collapse had even reached the point where several scientific institutes of the Russian Academy of Sciences did not have enough money to pay for electricity, water, and other utilities. At the same time, the salary of a newspaper vendor or delivery person was 2–3 times that of a professor of an academic institution. Whereas a professor's salary was very close to the official poverty line, scientists with lower degrees had salaries below it. The flight of scientists from the institutes of the Academy of Sciences and the universities sometimes led to a complete break-up of fully functioning scientific teams. Fields like physics, chemistry, and mathematics were particularly affected.

The general state of archaeology, especially those branches of it that actively use natural scientific methods, resembles that of the other "hard" sciences. The number of expeditions has decreased drastically, by far more than half, and the control over the quality and legal safeguards for field work have weakened considerably. Laboratory research has been dealt an even heavier blow. The unbelievably rapid increase in prices has made it difficult to purchase nearly all analytical materials and has made it almost impossible to obtain new, more advanced laboratory equipment, the only exception being the more active use of computer technology for routine archaeological research. Sometimes, paradoxically, this deprivation occasioned positive results: some researchers concentrated their attention on the creation of huge data bases by systematizing their earlier analyses. One example of this was the systematic processing of a gigantic range of materials from the vast Circumpontic metallurgical province of the early and middle Bronze Ages (Chernij *et al.* 1990; Cernyh *et al.* 1991).

Archaeological institutes and groups of archaeologists had actively to seek new sources to finance their work outside the state organizations, the former sole source of support. Sometimes, this search was successful, although always shaky and unreliable. Some domestic and foreign sponsors appeared, and more programs of collaboration with Western and Japanese archaeological institutions were established. Sometimes, local regional departments of culture also contributed monies. Thus despite the immense difficulties, these sources kept a number of research programs going, making it possible to obtain some interesting and even important results.

II The legacy of Russian chauvinism and the rise of nationalist archaeologies

One cannot imagine, of course, that the current nationalist movements raging throughout the former Soviet Union began *de novo* as a product of the events unfolding since the beginnings of the Gorbachev *perestroika* period. Although such movements, out of necessity, were somewhat disguised during Soviet times, they have a long pedigree extending back into the pre-Revolutionary Russian Empire. In order to understand their origins and current intensity, one must, in fact, view them as responses to Russian chauvinist accounts of the Great Russian past and its special historical mission. Beneath the veneer of trite Marxist slogans praising "internationalism," "the friendship of peoples," "the effacement of borders among separate nationalities," and, most dubious of all, "the formation of a single Soviet people," lurked the reality of more telling and real phrases, such as "immersion in the origins of a people's spirit and the wisdom of its ancestors" or "nestling against the glorious graves of one's earliest forebears – the creators of this spirit." Today nearly everyone from the Super Star of Russian chauvinism V. Zhirinovsky to the humblest native bard makes use of the latter phrases, dipping, when convenient, into the archaeological literature to document their claims. Thus, for example, in late Brezhnev times, the literary figure V. Chivilikhin (1982) devoted his book – significantly entitled *Memory* (*Pamyat'*) – to "penetrating into the deep bosom of history and the spirit of the truly Russian people."

Such dangerous mysticism cannot be discounted as gross vulgarization of a responsible and scientific Marxist archaeological literature. Rather, as exemplified by the many contemporary leading figures of radical nationalist movements throughout the former Soviet Union, who began their careers as archaeologists, ethnographers, folklorists, and historians, such statements represent a logical popularization of what could actually be found in this literature. There one could easily uncover references to "the strikingly high level of development of the material and spiritual culture" of a specific people or to the deep antiquity of a people and its nearly timeless origin on the lands that it currently occupies. Neighboring peoples were seen as newcomers, mostly unwanted and unbidden, and were dismissed as inferior, mixed peoples. If the archaeological or historical record documented the movement of one's people into a specific territory, then their arrival could be viewed as exceptionally fortuitous for the benighted aborigines vegetating in blissful, primordial ignorance. Such arguments were particularly favored by Great Russian chauvinist archaeologists during Soviet times.

The roots of Russian chauvinism can be traced far beyond the Soviet period to the millennium-and-a-half-long confrontations among Slavic-Germanic and Slavic-Turkic peoples across the great expanse of northern Eurasia, the latter uneasy association being historically expressed in crueler forms. Again despite perfunctory obeisances to Marxist internationalism, Russian archaeology during Soviet times reflected a double standard that can be related to this troubled history. On the one hand, the Ugro-Finnic, Turkic, and Caucasian peoples to the north, east, and south were treated condescendingly. Their cultures were considered vestigial, if not savage, and their so-called "voluntary" entrance into the Russian state was deemed indisputably progressive, despite the readily admitted predations of various Tsarist officials, Orthodox priests, and greedy merchants in pre-Revolutionary times.

Germanic-speaking peoples (and others lying farther west), on the other hand, received a different treatment. It was necessary continually to emphasize the evil, aggressive advances of these ethnic groups and the absence of any long or, at least, fruitful contacts with the Slavs. In both Soviet and contemporary Russian and Ukrainian archaeology, two themes have dominated this discussion: first, the well-known battle against any participation of Germanic peoples in the formation of the early Slavs and ancient Rus or the painful problem of the rise of the "pristine" Russian state; and secondly, documentation for the Slavic affinity of the Chernyakhovsky culture (dated to the second–third centuries AD) and its localization in Ukraine, despite obvious material similarities with Gothic, pre-Baltic archaeological cultures. Participants in this latter dispute vividly recall the harshness of the attacks during the sixties waged against them by official archaeologists, such as B.A. Rybakov, which included dangerously branding their opponents as Germanophiles. At present, these "German themes" have not yet resurfaced in Russian archaeology, but there can be little doubt that a new outbreak of such hostilities lies in the not distant future.

If battles on the "Western front" have momentarily quieted, much sharper and more bitter conflicts today are being waged across the vast eastern steppes. Russian chauvinists have long attributed the backwardness of Tsarist Russia to their more than 300-year-long subjugation under "the Tatar-Mongol yoke." The necessary recognition of this painful historical burden meant that even seemingly politically correct assertions of the primordial, centuries-old solidarity and friendship among Turkish and Russian peoples, such as enthusiastically proposed by the Kazakh activist and scholar O. Suleimenov in his seminal popular study *Az i Ya* (Suleimenov 1975), assumed a somewhat artificial, strained tone. They correspondingly were greeted rather skeptically both by academics suspicious of their questionable palaeolinguistic reconstructions and by high Party functionaries unhappy with their deviation from the conventional line and emphasis on Russian subjugation during medieval times.

Although it is unquestionable that the fury of Turkish nationalists is primarily a reaction to this Russian chauvinism and its officially condoned version of the past, one can still scarcely comprehend, much less justify, the current distortions of the past promulgated by pan-Turkic activists who find it necessary to claim a staggering primeval antiquity for Turkish-speakers in Eurasia. The playful attempt of Suleimenov to demonstrate a close historical affinity between Turkish and Sumerian is taken seriously by his disciples and developed to absurd heights. Thus, the north Caucasian archaeologist I. Miziev (1986; 1990)[2] has proposed that the builders of all the so-called burial mound (*kurgan*) cultures from the early Bronze Age through Scythian times, whose material remains have been documented throughout eastern Europe and across the Eurasian steppes, were Turkic-speakers. One of the earliest and most famous of these, the Maikop culture of the northern Caucasus, migrated farther south into Transcaucasia and the ancient Near East, bringing their Turkish with them and bequeathing the world the earliest form of writing, Sumerian, the southernmost lateral branch of Turkish. For Miziev, the bearers of the Maikop culture did not only speak Turkish but conversed in his own Karachai-Balkar dialect! A less comprehensible and, in a sense, even more bizarre theme currently complicating Russian–Tatar relations is the strongly expressed desire of Tatar intellectuals (above all, archaeologists and historians) to change the name of their people to a different Turkic ethnos – the Bulgars (Karimullin 1988; Khalikov 1992). Such a simple transformation apparently will somehow remove the complex burden of faults associated with "the Tatar–Mongol yoke" since the Bulgars themselves cruelly suffered from the Mongol invasion of Batu-khan in the thirteenth century AD.

I cannot consider here that most complicated knot of national energies, the Caucasus (see Kohl and Tsetkhladze, this volume). Suffice it to say that nearly all the "hot" conflicts currently burning throughout this area are directly supported, if not headed, by archaeologists and historians of antiquity, who have taken Marx's famous XIth Thesis on Feuerbach seriously and are not only interpreting the world through their chauvinist readings of the remote past but attempting to change it through violent political action. Many of the leaders of nationalist movements in the Caucasus are trained scholars of antiquity. Thus, for example, the official leader of Abkhazia, the new republic that seceded from Georgia in fall 1993 after a protracted and exceptionally bloody struggle, V. Ardzinba, is a trained specialist in ethnology and oriental studies; the philosopher historian M. Shanibov is one of the leaders of the Confederation of the

Mountain Peoples of the Caucasus; the archaeologist Yu. Boronov heads the "Slavonic house" in Abkhazia and is now the Vice-Prime Minister of this new "Republic"; and the archaeologist V.E. Oganesian is one of the most important leaders of the Dashnaktsutiun nationalist party in Armenia, a party which, among its other activities, has been stoking the fires burning over Nagorno-Karabagh. He is now in prison for anti-government activities. In addition, the archaeologist G.E. Areshian was formerly a government minister and ideologist for the Armenian President, L. Ter-Petrosian, himself a trained orientalist.

The phenonomenon of archaeologists and ancient historians leading aggressive political movements is not limited to the Caucasus but can be detected throughout the former Soviet Union. To cite just one more example, the archaeologist Z. Poznyak is the leader of the opposition National Front in the Belarus Parliament and an outspoken critic of the Great Russians' "imperial mentality." Recently, in a Belarus newspaper, he evaluated Russians in the following terms:

> as a mosaic patchwork people, without any defined territory completely mixed together with Finno-Ugrian, Turkic, Mongol, and other ethnic enclaves and dispersed in colonies throughout Siberia and Asia. The ideology and fundamental mentality of the majority of Russians is based on an imperial consciousness. And this consciousness is destructive. (Cited in *Izvestiya*)

It is scarcely possible to find a more explicit, essentially racist example of a chauvinist reaction to Russian chauvinism. It is worth emphasizing that these are the views of a politically active *archaeologist.*

As recently as 1986 the late Director of the Institute of Ethnography in Moscow and Party ideologue, Yu. V. Bromlei, could write:

> A narrow outlook and insufficient knowledge of the past and present of other peoples are . . . frequently nurtured by the prejudices of less well-educated circles of society and by people of older age. Broad educative activity and explanatory ideological work by the mass media significantly help to overcome national narrowness. (Bromlei 1990:71)

In other words, nationalist tendencies in the late Soviet Union were survivals or vestiges from the past, perpetuated only by ignorant, poorly educated peoples who had not yet received sufficient indoctrination in Marxist international consciousness.[3] Exactly the reverse is true.

III The appearance of new or the reemergence of hallowed forms of ethnic prejudice in post-Soviet archaeology

The openness fostered by *glasnost* gave expression to many antagonisms and problems that had been suppressed, at least officially, during the stable years of Soviet rule. Here we cite only three problems that have recently appeared in archaeological writings during post-Soviet times: 1. friction among Slavs, as illustrated by the work of Z. Poznyak cited above; 2. the rewriting of the pre- and early history of Finno-Ugrian peoples and their relations with Slavic-Russian colonizers; and 3. that old – though not uniquely Russian – favorite, anti-Semitism.

For brevity's sake, we will concentrate only on the last frightening phenomenon, the rise of anti-Semitism and its reflection in archaeological and early historical writings, but just to get a flavor of the recently kindled Finno-Ugrian chauvinist readings of the past, we cite the work of the well-respected archaeologist V. Patrushev. He writes:

> After having attained a millennia-long history of extraordinary accomplishments in cultural development, the Finno-Ugrian world was essentially destroyed by the colonization of Slavic-Russian tribes. Arriving on Finno-Ugrian lands without women, the enemies either killed the local men or forcibly recruited them into their detachments, selecting the native females "as their concubines." This was only the beginning of a destructive process, the tragic completion of which we see occurring now when the urban Russian speakers [. . . occupy all the best social positions] and live in far better conditions than the representatives of the indigenous nationality. (Patrushev 1992:183–8)

Needless to say, cultural purity is the desired state, and, for Mr Patrushev, archaeology is hardly an idle academic pursuit.

The recent anti-Semitic writings of L.N. Gumilev, an extremely well-known Russian savant and man of letters – well-versed in history, archaeology, ethnology, geography – and the author of numerous popular scientific works (1960, 1967, 1992, 1993a, 1993b, etc.) are possibly even more impassioned and inflammatory, as well as dangerously mystical. Such works appear unexpected in a veteran inmate of Stalin's gulag and the son of the highly respected poets N. Gumilev and Anna Akhmatova, both of whom also suffered greatly at various times under Soviet persecution. Yet the present times in Russia yield such surprises . . .

Earlier, with respect to ethnic relations, L.N. Gumilev was renowned as a tireless literary champion of the prowess of nomadic Mongol and Turkic-speaking peoples and of hatred of the Chinese from whom all Eurasian misfortunes derive (Gumilev 1960; 1967); today one must add to them the Jews (Gumilev 1993a:366–478; 1993b:95–217). Parenthetically, one can note that his earlier love for the Mongols was difficult to explain and was sharply criticized by Russophiles (Chivilikhin 1982, no. 17:57–68). According to Gumilev, the "Tatar–Mongol yoke" simply did not exist but was an evil fiction developed by enemies; in reality, there was always a lively, creative friendship between the Russians and the Mongols, as well as a close military union when Mongol warriors defended the

Russians from their external foes (Gumilev 1992:515–77; 1993b).

Gumilev's concern with the Jewish question relates to his historical understanding of the expulsion of Jews from Persia in the seventh and eighth centuries AD and their arrival on the steppes of eastern Europe, then occupied by the simple-spirited Turkic-speaking Khazars. As formulated by Gumilev, their arrival led to the appearance first of an ethnic, then of a socio-political fantastic entity or "chimera" known as the Khazar khanate. The clever Jews concocted very complicated biological and social relations within this socio-ethnic chimera; namely,

> Turks rewarded Khazar women with children, who developed into Khazar men with heightened states of passion [in Russian, *passionarnost'* – an extraordinary favored term of Gumilev]. The Jews extracted children from the Khazars either as fully valued Jews with Jewish mothers or as bastards with Jewish fathers. By doing this they impoverished the entire ethnic system, further simplifying it. (Gumilev 1993a:397)

Moreover, they captured the entire Great Silk Road from China to France and then seized control over the whole web of Eurasian geopolitics. For example, "In the middle of the ninth century AD the Jewish Khazars concluded an agreement with the Normans for the division of Eastern Europe . . . and by the beginning of the tenth century they had completely captured it . . ." (Gumilev 1993a: 428). For the conquered peoples

> it was always known that the war was burdensome and unpleasant. But there were still worse things than war: their forced conversion into slavery; the outrages to their sacred relics; the plundering of their wealth; and, finally, abusive neglect. All this became the burden of the peoples of Eastern Europe after they had fallen under the sphere of influence of the Jewish Khazars. (Gumilev 1993a:433)

Gumilev's violent fantasy of the "chimera" Khazar khanate resembles nothing so much as a very evil and poisonous fairy tale. The chimera or fantasy here, of course, is not the khanate, but the pseudo-facts which the author himself has conjured up to appeal to readers of a certain persuasion, to those for whom the Jews were always if not the only, then the chief source of human misfortune. In this respect, L.N. Gumilev cannot be distinguished from his audience. But it is less understandable, why such an original "thinker" should attempt to elucidate the secret role of the Jews in world history in some special form, not unpretentiously and efficiently, but through appeal to higher mystical spheres. Thus, he crowned the final work of his life with an amazingly – to use his own gem-like term – "strange learned doctrine" which he named the "Apocrypha." In it, there is the following point listed under the mystical number 13: "The best friend of Satan – the fiery demon Yahweh, who spoke on Mt Sinai; the highest holy Satan – Judah, who betrayed his Master; he who follows the principles of

Judah is free from sin and everything he does may be considered a blessing. These people are beyond good and evil. For them, everything is permitted, except truthfulness and mercy" (Gumilev 1993a:480; it is revealing to compare this version of his "Apocrypha," which makes different points, with another version published a year earlier, see Gumilev 1992:592–5). Comment would be superfluous.

How to conclude? Certainly, there is much in the rise of these nationalist ideologies that is specific to the Soviet experience. To list just a few: the incredibly heavy historical burden of millennia-old confrontations between Russians and Germanic-speaking, Turkic-speaking peoples and countless other natives, and among the more than 100 recognized Soviet peoples themselves; the imperial embrace of the Russian bear and the preexisting, rich tradition of Great Russian chauvinism; the inadequate "Marxist" disguise of the latter during the Soviet period, a fact that may actually have intensified the contempt and resentment felt by the colonized peoples; the rise of Russian nationalism associated with events leading up and subsequent to the defeat of Nazi fascism; and the entire legacy of the federal administrative structure of the Soviet Union, the names and borders of which were structured along ethnic lines and which were blatantly manipulated "for reasons of State."

Soviet archaeology never overcame the nationalist tendencies of the countless peoples that lived within its borders – not only because seventy-four years was simply too short a period to overcome the prejudices built up over millennia, but also because the internationalism it espoused all too often was not genuine. The empty mouthings of Party officials and Russian chauvinists were perceived accurately by non-Russians and quietly but fiercely resisted. Real internationalists were either silenced and/or too few numerically to resist the stronger historical forces of nationalism and counter-nationalisms arrayed against them.

It is perhaps more useful, however, to focus not on what is unique but on what is common with the Soviet experience and with the archaeologies of the colonizers and the colonized in other times and places. Specifically, the archaeological and historical consciousnesses of other colonized peoples often also emerged within similar contexts of long, pre-existing traditions of ethnic prejudices, as well as confrontations with and similar resistances to imperial powers. This simple reality should alert one to the dangers of being fuzzy-headed, of uncritically romanticizing these colonized peoples, or of uncritically facilitating their empowerment by supporting their often questionable "readings" of their own pasts. That is, the nationalist crazies out there are not uniquely restricted to eastern Europe and the former Soviet Union. Rather, little fascists eager to distort their pasts to further their own, often violent political ends are capable of sprouting up like weeds everywhere, and one must recognize them for what they are and not excuse them away on the basis of some slippery relativist standard.

NOTES

1 Part I of this postscript initially was written to update a volume of translated Russian articles tentatively titled *Soviet Archaeology: Theoretical Perspectives and Current Approaches* (ed. P.L. Kohl, Cambridge University Press, in preparation); it has been edited for inclusion here. Parts II and III represent a reworked and condensed version of the paper "Chauvinist Archaeologies of the Colonizers and the Colonized: Lessons from the Soviet Marxist Historical Experience," which was presented with P.L. Kohl for the "Archaeology as a Colonial Endeavor" symposium organized by R. McGuire at the Society for American Archaeology meetings in Anaheim, CA, April 1994. Part I was initially translated by Ms. M. Alexandrovich, and Parts II and III by P.L. Kohl. Both sections were reworked and slightly modified and elaborated upon by Kohl for this volume. The concluding paragraphs were also written by Kohl.

2 Miziev's 1990 article has been translated into English as "On the Creators of the Maikop Culture" and appears in a recent issue of *Soviet Anthropology and Archaeology*, entitled *Turmoil in the Northern Caucasus: The Maikop Archaeology Debate*, ed. Marjorie M. Balzer (30 (3), 1991–2) which is entirely devoted to the various controversial interpretations of this culture.

3 It is only fair to point out that Bromlei's successor as Director of the now recently renamed Institute of Ethnology and Anthropology in Moscow, V.A. Tishkov (1992:378–9), does not share his predecessor's ridiculous, out-of-touch illusions.

10 Nationalism, politics, and the practice of archaeology in the Caucasus[1]

Philip L. Kohl and Gocha R. Tsetskhladze

This chapter examines the politics of archaeology in an area that can justly be viewed either as part of the northern frontier of the modern Middle East (and ancient Near East) or the southeastern boundary of Europe (Map 2). One of the fascinations of Caucasia – both Ciscaucasia and Transcaucasia[2] – is that it is a region where European (Christian) and Oriental (here Islamic) traditions meet or, more appropriately today, collide. It is also characterized by exceptional, almost unparalleled ethnic and linguistic diversity, making it – depending upon one's temperament – either an ethnographer's dream or nightmare.

In addition to sectarian, linguistic, and ethnic diversity, the Caucasus is characterized by a very long and vivid historical consciousness, extending back with rich historical and then archaeological documentation for millennia. Archaeology and ancient history are exceptionally alive and meaningful for all the myriad peoples of the Caucasus. Today, given the collapse of the former Soviet Union, it is a very volatile region replete with numerous territorial disputes and several exceptionally bloody and explosive ethnic conflicts. Given all these conditions, it is an area where one would not expect the practice of archaeology to be an idle academic pursuit, unrelated to contemporary politics. One is not disappointed.

This paper will demonstrate the political nature of archaeology in the Caucasus by relating several examples illustrating this fact, proceeding first regionally, considering interpretations of the prehistoric record in Azerbaijan, Georgia, Armenia, and the northern Caucasus, and then chronologically with an evaluation of Caucasian archaeological evidence for the classical period, particularly as it relates to Greek colonization in western Georgia, beginning in the mid-sixth century BC. As it proceeds, it will also attempt to establish criteria for distinguishing acceptable "readings" of Caucasian prehistory from serious "misreadings" or distortions of that past that may result in the systematic suppression, if not slaughter, of one people by another.

At the outset, we wish to emphasize that, while we are being critical of the practices of many local Caucasian archaeologists, this does not mean that

2 The Caucasus: political and administrative boundaries in 1991

we are not appreciative of their many substantive achievements in reconstructing their incredibly rich remote past; while we generalize critically about the behaviors of entire peoples (and as generalizations, there are, of course, numerous exceptions), this does not mean that we are at all demeaning or holding suspect the proud and distinctive cultural traditions that make the area so fascinating and intellectually stimulating. If we spend more time illustrating the questionable practices of archaeologists of one culture and fail to mention those of another, it is not a political statement of support for the latter on our part. Sadly, no group is above criticism. Current ethnic conflicts, based on territorial political disputes in the Caucasus and all too often justified by archaeological "readings" of an always deficient, never satisfactory record, are extremely complex and, unfortunately, lack simple solution.

We argue against an "essentialist" conception of culture, particularly as applied to the archaeological record. This view maintains that cultures are like minerals that have crystallized; once formed, they assume a distinctive shape that characterizes them "from time immemorial" to the present. An essentialist (or primordialist) view holds that Azeris, Armenians, Georgians, Ossetians, Abkhazians, Chechens, etc. have "always" existed in a manner that blurs necessary distinctions between culture, language, and race. This conception of culture, which is adopted consciously or not by most Caucasian archaeologists, is opposed to the view of cultures as constantly "in the making," historically rooted, open-ended systems which are continuously transforming themselves, borrowing from their neighbors, and being inextricably caught up in historical processes much larger than themselves (Wolf 1984; Kohl 1992:173–4).

Although one cannot try to reconstruct the past by ignoring the real and important phenomenon of ethnicity (itself a grossly underconceptualized causative factor in cultural evolution), one must be extremely circumspect in attempting to identify specific ethnic groups solely on their material culture remains. Sometimes, of course, such identifications – however tentatively – can be made, but even then one must examine critically what problems one is solving through such identifications and not fall into the trap of conceptualizing cultures with long historic and prehistoric traditions as crystallized Platonic essences, exhibiting all their current distinguishing features in remote antiquity. As sensible anthropologists, like E. Wolf (1982) and R. Fox (1985), and sensible historians, like E.P. Thompson (1966) and R.G. Suny (1988, 1993a), have reminded us: cultures are always in the process of changing and reconstituting themselves, sometimes in almost unrecognizable, qualitatively different ways. There is no culture that has existed "since time immemorial" and no people that is aboriginal in terms of their contemporary culture with a specific piece of real estate; ethnogenesis is a fact, but it does not imply that cultures exhibit forever the characteristics present at their birth.

I Contradictory "readings" of Caucasian prehistory

A Azerbaijan

Most accounts written in the Soviet period that summarize the prehistory and early history of Azerbaijan adopt a rather straightforward evolutionary perspective, stressing local indigenous development from Lower Palaeolithic times onwards (e.g., Geyushev 1986; Guseinov 1985; Muradova 1979). Although they minimize external influences, there is nothing inherently suspect in such accounts – until one is politically attuned to what may be omitted or implied, a practice that occurs in both scholarly reports and more popular accounts. The latter are more problematic, particularly in so far as they reach a broader, less discriminating audience. Thus, for example, a widely disseminated tourist guide to Baku (Agaev 1987:13) begins with the following assertion:

> The tribes who inhabited this land in antiquity, the fore-runners of the Azerbaijani people, occupied a vast territory which included both Northern (now Soviet) and Southern (Iranian) Azerbaijan. Various parts of it became known after the tribes as Caspian, Mannai, Media, and Caucasian Albania. Some of the states which emerged in the area from the third millennium BC were powerful and relatively advanced, particularly Mannai and Media, the latter subjugating Assyria and Urartu among others.

Seemingly straightforward, this passage deserves critical scrutiny, particularly the phrase "fore-runners of the Azerbaijani people" and the implied cultural uniformity from Bronze Age times onwards of the entire area occupied today by Azeri peoples. The early historical cultures that are mentioned were certainly not directly related to the Turkic-speaking Azeris, and, while material cultural connections dating back at least to the third millennium BC (a much earlier time than the known period of existence for any of the specified cultures) link the area encompassing the Republic of Azerbaijan with that of northwestern Iran (what is called Iranian or southern Azerbaijan), it is debatable that such north–south connections were stronger or formed a greater unity than those, say, stretching east–west across Transcaucasia. In other words, the implication of this passage is that the area dominantly inhabited by Azeris, which today is politically divided into northern and southern parts, was originally united, that it naturally forms a coherent cultural whole. The political implications of the passage become clear when one considers recent history: one of the first confrontations of the Cold War, the slow withdrawal of Red Army troops from northwestern Iran in the wake of the Second World War; the demographic dominance of southern Azerbaijan; and, even more, certain inflammatory statements of the former President of Azerbaijan, A. Elchibey,[3] regarding Azerbaijan's right to control areas populated dominantly by Azeris (i.e., northwestern Iran).

More precisely, what is a relatively innocuous statement in one political context may become charged with political significance in a different context or as that context changes. A foreign archaeologist traversing this minefield of subtle political nuances must also be aware of what may be *omitted* from reviews of the prehistoric and historic record. Thus, for example, a popular overview to the development of the Autonomous Republic of Nakhichevan (Guliev *et al.* 1984) reviews the history of this region from prehistoric times to the present without once mentioning the Armenians despite the numerous cultural monuments that still silently testify to their millennia-old presence in, if not always political control over, the region (for documentation of the Armenian monuments from Nakhichevan, see Ayvazian 1990).[4]

The nominally Marxist evolutionary accounts that stress internal developments and minimize change wrought by incursions of different ethnic groups are, of course, not necessarily incorrect; the archaeological record frequently is ambiguous concerning the relative historical significance to be accorded internal and external factors, allowing more than one reasonable "reading" of that record. Nevertheless, the non-local archaeologist is better able to evaluate specific interpretations if he/she is conscious of the possible political implications of a specific "reading."

In a given context, emphasis on internal evolutionary development accords well with what we have termed the "essentialist" view of culture. Some Azeri archaeologists, who adopt this conception of culture, are excessively patriotic or chauvinistic of the land they today control. They are confronted with the uncomfortable historic fact that Turkic-speaking peoples, who became today's self-conscious Azeri ethnos,[5] migrated into the area during historic times as part of the centuries-long movement of Turkish peoples from central Asia across Anatolia and into southeastern Europe. Other cultures, such as the Christian Albanian state of the early medieval period, are known to have occupied Azerbaijan prior to the arrival of the Turkic-speaking pastoral nomads. This great east–west movement which had profound consequences for world history is, of course, well documented historically and can be attested archaeologically (e.g., by the fields of pre-Islamic *baba* stone "idols" or stylized anthropomorphic statues over graves which serve as a marker for the movement of Turkic-speaking peoples east to west and which can be traced like a perfect sloping horizon from southern Siberia and eastern central Asia across the Eurasian steppes all the way to the borders of Azerbaijan (e.g., Burney 1979; Stronach 1981)).[6] Nevertheless, some Azeri scholars adopt an extreme version of the essentialist view of Azeri culture by either denying the presence of non-Turkic cultures or seeing them all as Turkic-speaking; others more plausibly regard today's Azeris as an assimilated population with both "Albanian" and Turkic ancestors. Either view, however, can be slanted for nationalist purposes.

Why deny a history of physical and cultural assimilation that is at least centuries, if not millennia, old? In more pacific times, such denial could be excused as perhaps excessive attachment to the naturally rich region of eastern Transcaucasia. Assertion that the homeland of the Azeri nation, indeed of all Turkic peoples,[7] was the area immediately east and south of the Caspian Sea can be just a harmless statement of faith reflecting considerable pride in and devotion to the land they now occupy.

Apparently innocuous were other contradictory and/or incredible myths related by professional archaeologists that claimed that the Scythians were Turkic-speaking and that the script of the early first millennium AD Albanian state – under whose sway real history first dawns in eastern Transcaucasia – was written in Turkish.

A more critical evaluation of this misplaced pride in cultural origins, however, is warranted, as subsequent developments leading up to the outbreak of hostilities illustrate. Thus, for example, at an all-Soviet Union archaeological congress which was held in Baku, Azerbaijan in 1985, a young Azeri archaeologist (Akhundov 1985:77–8) read a paper that attempted to show that the carved stone crosses found in Azerbaijan were Albanian; that is, the products of the pre-Islamic Christian state of eastern Transcaucasia. He purported to distinguish these stone crosses from the Armenian *khach'k'ar*, the latter being one of the most potent symbols of the Armenian people with literally thousands of uniquely carved examples found throughout today's Republic of Armenia. Since the Republic of Armenia only occupies a fraction[8] of historic Armenia, it is reasonable to assume that such Armenian *khach'k'ar* exist or once existed throughout areas where Armenians once constituted a major, if not the dominant, population. The young Azeri's seemingly innocuous, abstract archaeological paper was a deliberate political provocation: all the crosses on today's territory of Azerbaijan, including significantly Nagorno-Karabagh and Nakhichevan, were defined as Albanian, a people who in turn were seen as the direct ancestors of today's Azeris.

The rest, as they say, is history. The Armenian archaeologists were upset and threatened to walk out *en bloc*. Protests were filed, and even Russian scholars from Leningrad objected to this blatantly political appropriation, posing as scholarship. No participant in this debate would have predicted that within two years the contest over ancestral claims to Nagorno-Karabagh would flare up into one of the bloodiest and most significant ethnic conflicts raging within the former Soviet Union. Yet it cannot be forgotten that agitation over the status of Nagorno-Karabagh in Armenia was initiated by intellectuals, including archaeologists, familiar with and incensed by this specific insult to their cultural heritage.

Thus, minimally, two points must be made. Patently false cultural origin myths are not always harmless. The political context within which such myths are articulated is critical, and this context continually changes: given the events of the last nine years, assertion that today's Azerbaijan was the original homeland of Turkic-speaking peoples is charged with political significance. Secondly, it is incumbent upon the external observer or, in this case, foreign archaeologist, to understand this constantly unfolding political context. For one unaware of the conflicting land claims and of the historical tension, even antagonism, between Armenians and Azeris, one would have listened to the 1985 presentation on the stone crosses quite innocently as a legitimate attempt to distinguish Albanian from Armenian material culture. Even the most fanatical Armenian nationalist could not pretend that wherever stone crosses appear, they necessarily were carved by Armenians, a claim that would be tantamount to identifying greater historic Armenia with all of Christendom. Objectively speaking, it should be possible to examine critically the specific attributes of these crosses to define regional variants and even, with certain supportive evidence (especially inscriptions), to distinguish Georgian from Albanian from Armenian *khach'k'ar*. In reality, however, such a legitimate, scholarly archaeological/art historical analysis minimally requires a political environment far less impassioned than what existed in 1985, much less today.

One should not discuss the Nagorno-Karabagh issue without mentioning the deplorable practice of the actual destruction of cultural monuments (not to imply, of course, that this practice only occurs in Transcaucasia or in relation to this particular conflict; the destruction of the Islamic legacy of Bosnia represents another particularly dreadful current example of this practice (see Kaiser, this volume and MESA Newsletter 1993)). An official publication of the Academy of Sciences of Armenia (1988:21–2) claims that dozens of ancient Armenian settlements, cemeteries, *khach'k'ar*, and inscriptions have been destroyed during the last few decades in Nagorno-Karabagh and that at least thirty such monuments, including churches, have been destroyed in Nakhichevan, the detached area of Azerbaijan that physiographically forms part of the fertile Ararat valley where more than half of today's population of the Republic of Armenia is concentrated.

Before one gets too irate at the Azeris, however, one must note the paucity of surviving Islamic remains in Armenia, including the capital of Yerevan.[9] To put this in historical perspective, in 1826, before the signing of the Treaty of Turkmenchai and the ethnic movements that followed in its wake, roughly 90,000 of a total population of 110,000 in the Khanate of Yerevan were Muslims – Persians, Kurds, and "Turko-Tatar" nomads (the last being the peoples who later became self-conscious Azeris) (Bournoutian 1983:78; and also, however, his critical review 1992:67–8). No matter what demographic statistics one consults, it is simply unquestionable that considerable material remains of Islam must once have existed in this area. Their near total absence today cannot be fortuitous.

B *Armenia*

The nationalist tenor of much Armenian archaeology is intimately associated with the recent history of the Armenians, particularly their loss of significant ancestral territories and massacre during World War I, events inextricably tied to the dissolution of the Ottoman Empire and the creation of the modern nation-state of Turkey (see note 4); one might even argue that the more exaggerated claims of past grandeur by Armenian nationalists are themselves a reaction to unsupportable age-old ethnic links to Anatolian prehistory by Turkish nationalists (for the latter, see McConnell 1989:109–10).

However unjustifiable, Turkey's refusal to acknowledge the state-sponsored massacre of Armenians is undoubtedly fueled by Armenia's irredentist claims on large portions of eastern Anatolia, collectively referred to as western "historic Armenia." Visitors to the State Museum in Yerevan or the Armenian Ethnographic Museum in Sadarabat are greeted with large physical maps of the Armenian Highland depicting the maximal extent of the Armenian kingdom under King Tigran II (the Great) prior to their defeat by the Romans in 69 BC. Series of maps in these and other museums or for sale in local bookstores depict the inexorable, millennia-old retraction of Armenian-controlled territory over time, poignantly illustrating the tragic history of this proud ancient culture. That events in this century have significantly altered the traditional cultural geography of this area is beyond doubt; what is relevant here, however, is to determine, if possible, the proper and improper roles for archaeology in the documentation and evaluation of that history. What is the appropriate relationship between an archaeological demonstration of cultural origins and/or chronological priority in an area and territorial aspirations, including consequent state policies?

There is no easy answer, particularly since exclusive, historically justified claims to any territory, when examined critically, are nearly always questionable. When, for example, does Constantinople become Istanbul? Never; as soon as it is conquered; after 500 years (i.e., 1953 AD); after 1000 years; etc.? In other words, at what point does present cultural occupation of an area override historical claims to it? The contemporary world is replete with such examples (e.g., biblical justifications for the existence of the State of Israel; historical claims for a Muslim "Bosnian" presence in the heart of the Balkans; or even the unquestioned acceptance of the foreign occupation of the western hemisphere at the expense of its indigenous peoples). Should the maximal extent of the Armenian kingdom, which existed for less than fifty years during the first half of the first century BC, be used as the relevant yardstick for what properly constitutes "historic Armenia"? Unfortunately, Armenian oft-expressed dreams of a *Reconquista*, based upon sometimes selective "readings" of the prehistoric and historic record, adversely affect relations with even potentially friendly neighbors, such as the Georgians.

In reality, each example is so unique and distinct as to preclude generalization. Moreover, it is unclear which criterion is more appropriate: chronological priority; duration of control; or present occupation. Archaeologists, particularly prehistorians, must be extremely careful if they attempt to enter such disputes, stating explicitly the limitations of the evidence they control.

It is not surprising that essentialist interpretations of Armenian culture and history abound. A particularly infamous "scholarly" example is S.A. Sardarian's *Pervobytnoe obshchestvo v Armenii* (1967), which, besides its numerous mistakes and plagiarisms, postulates a separate Armenian race that originated on the Armenian plateau; attributes the invention of metallurgy to the Armenians; and demonstrates that the widespread Kura-Araxes culture emerged initially in the Ararat valley of Armenia. The standard of scholarship is so low and the argumentation so tendentious as to raise the question as to how the book was even published (see the devastating critique by Martirosian and Munchaev 1968:262). An even more ludicrous popular example is provided by a widely distributed publication (MESHAG n.d.) from the Armenian-American diaspora on the evolution of the Armenian alphabet, tracing its development from Palaeolithic petroglyphs through the divinely inspired invention by Meshrob Mashtots of the currently used Mesrobian script in 406 AD. Fanciful internal evolutionary development here is taken to an extreme.[10]

No less problematic are heavily slanted interpretations of the Urartian kingdom, the first historically attested state in Transcaucasia (ninth to seventh centuries BC). Armenian chauvinists must explain why this state, a worthy adversary of the neo-Assyrian Empire of northern Mesopotamia and one that expanded over much of "historic Armenia," composed its royal cuneiform inscriptions in Urartian, a non Indo-European (i.e., non-Armenian) language, related to Hurrian and ancestral to the Northeastern Caucasian family of languages spoken today by different peoples in Daghestan, Chechenia, and Ingushetia (see Jankowska 1991:231). Reasonable historical hypotheses can be advanced for a Proto-Armenian component to this kingdom, and there is a real sense in which the Armenians are the cultural heirs of Urartu,[11] but an essentialist view of Armenian culture which equates it precisely with the Urartian kingdom cannot be sustained.

One must distinguish between popular and professional Armenian interpretations of Urartu, the latter being subtler and more difficult to evaluate. Thus, popular reference to the "Piotrovskii problem" is based on the fact that B.B. Piotrovskii, the late Director of the Hermitage in Leningrad (now St. Petersburg) and former head of the excavations at Karmir Blur (the ancient Urartian capital of Teishebaine now located within the city of Yerevan), had quite reasonably maintained that the mighty Urartian Iron Age kingdom did not constitute the first Armenian state for the reasons stated above; the "problem" only existed for those who wanted Armenians always to have lived in and controlled "historic Armenia" until the later ravages wrought by Romans, Persians, Arabs, and Turks. More discriminating professional archaeologists, who may accept the reasonable theory that the ethnogenesis or formation of Armenian culture occurred during post-Urartian Achaemenid times, extol the might of the Urartians and see them exercising political control over most of eastern Anatolia, western Iran, and Transcaucasia; in this respect they remain the direct precursors of the Armenian kingdom under Tigran II.[12]

Certain words and theories are laden with political significance. Thus, the controversial linguistic theory of T. Gamkrelidze and V. Ivanov (1984), which sees the original Proto-Indo-European developing in direct association with the Proto-Kartvelian (West Caucasian) and ancient Semitic families of languages in an eastern Anatolian homeland, receives an extremely warm reception not on its linguistic merits, but on its locating Proto-Indo-European speakers in the historic Armenian heartland. Proto-Indo-European thus becomes a buzzword for Proto-Armenian. This questionable identification is transparent in tendentious interpretations of Bronze Age and later prehistoric materials from Transcaucasia, as exemplified by V.E. Oganesian's (1992)[13] implausible ethnic interpretation of the fantastically suggestive iconography on a silver goblet recently excavated in the Karashamb cemetery north of Yerevan; or by G.E. Areshian's (1992:27) detailed and ingenious, albeit strained, attempt to weave together historical, mythological, and archaeological materials to demonstrate that "Armeno-Aryans" constituted "the population living in the basins of the Araxes and Kura from the end of the third millennium BC" and "continuously carried out rituals connected with Indo-European cosmogonic mythology."

Ironically, chauvinistic Azeri and Armenian archaeologists alike share a need to see their people as always present in the greater eastern Anatolian/northwest Iranian/Transcaucasian region.

C *Georgia*

During the late Soviet period, Georgia was blessed (or afflicted) with more practicing professional archaeologists than almost any comparably sized area in the world (see Lordkipanidze 1982). The works produced by these hundreds of Georgian archaeologists varied tremendously in quality with the best being exceptionally good by any standard. Even some of the most senior and responsible Georgian archaeologists were not immune to the ubiquitous temptation to identify prehistoric ethnic groups on the basis of their material remains and selectively to utilize incomplete linguistic and problematic physical anthropological evidence. For example, O. Dzhaparidze's recent, significantly entitled *Na zare etnokul'turnoi istorii Kavkaza* (*At the Dawn of the Ethnocultural History of the Caucasus*, 1989) represents not so much an implausible, as an unascertainable attempt to identify the ethnicity and linguistic affinities of archaeologically documented cultures extending back to late Palaeolithic times. Similarly, T. Gamkrelidze's substantial linguistic reconstructions of indigenous Kartvelian (i.e., Georgian) speakers in Transcaucasia during the Bronze Age and even earlier prehistoric periods are not without political significance.

Not surprisingly, more nationalistically disposed Georgian archaeologists provide essentialist accounts of their history and culture that duplicate the same constellation of features of their like-inspired Azeri and Armenian colleagues and culminate, of course, in claims to territories that are identified as having been Georgian since time immemorial.

One significant example of this regrettable tendency concerns the history of the archaeological documentation for the tremendous florescence of Caucasian metallurgy during the late Bronze and early Iron Ages. This impressive record of metallurgical achievements first attracted the attention of the scholarly world in the late nineteenth century from discoveries made in the small village of Koban located north of the Great Caucasus range in today's North Ossetia, today a separate administrative area within Russia (Virchow 1883; Uvarova 1900). Probably the best-documented and most fully published contemporary discoveries of "Koban culture" or "Koban culture-like" materials come from the Tli cemetery, located significantly south of the Great Caucasus and made by the South Ossetian archaeologist, B.V. Tekhov, who also was very active politically for Ossetian rights and autonomy within southern Ossetia. The most complete up-to-date synthesis of Georgian archaeology, *Nasledie Drevnei Gruzii* (Lordkipanidze 1989:194, 196; translated into German as *Archäologie in Georgien: von der Altsteinzeit zum Mittelalter* (1991), see pp. 95–102 and corresponding notes), rejects in a footnote even the term "Koban culture" as a kind of archaeological misnomer due to its accidental early discovery in northern Ossetia and dismisses its rich and distinctive artistic engravings on bronze axes as a minor variant of the "Colchidean (i.e., west Georgian) culture." The marvellous materials from the Tli cemetery are scarcely mentioned in this synthesis.

That such rejection has political significance is clear when one observes that the book's basic map of the historical regions of Georgia (1989: map 1, p. 6; 1991: fig. 1, p. 3) subsumes southern Ossetia completely within Shida or Inner Kartli (central Georgia), an intentional oversight that took on new meaning with the abolishment of the Autonomous Region of South Ossetia by the democratically elected nationalist regime of Z. Gamsakhurdia in December 1990. As a reaction to this Georgian "reading" of the archaeological record, Ossetian scholars today are at pains to point out similarities between Koban materials and those from Hallstadt in central Europe, thus demonstrating that the Aryans (i.e., Indo-Europeans – now a buzzword for Ossetians)) were always present in the central Caucasus (Shnirelman, personal communication). An outsider cannot even begin to understand Caucasian prehistory and appreciate the richness of its late Bronze/Iron Age metallurgical florescence without being hyper-attuned to the political realities of even naming archaeological cultures, much less defining the area they encompassed.[14]

The conflict over southern Ossetia still simmers with archaeologists occasionally having functioned as "expert witnesses" on the behalf of the nationalists' debatable claim (Gamsakhurdia 1991) that the Ossetians are not aboriginal inhabitants of the Caucasus[15] since they were only first pushed into northern Caucasia in the wake of the Mongol and Timurid invasions of the thirteenth and fourteenth centuries and then migrated south across the Caucasus range into historic Georgia first during the seventeenth and eighteenth centuries. Phrased politely, this revisionist historical account is open to serious criticism (see, for example, the much more balanced archaeological reconstruction of the ethnogenesis of the Ossetians by E.I. Krupnov (1960:390–3)). Even if true – and this is perhaps an even more important point – this revisionist dismissal of the Johnny-come-lately Ossetians begs the question of how many centuries, how many human generations, are necessary to have a legitimate ancestral claim to a piece of property. The point is not to belittle a complex issue, but to illustrate that archaeology can be knowingly manipulated to provide a politically correct "reading" of the past that then serves as a pretext to uproot and kill people living in an area minimally for several centuries.

The Djavakheti (or Djavakheti/Meskheti) region of southern Georgia (see Map 2) provides an almost textbook illustration of the complexities of historical/archaeological claims to a specific territory. The region is filled with beautiful Georgian medieval monuments, such as the Wardzhia cave monastery complex, most of which date to the tenth to twelfth centuries but some of which go back even earlier to the fifth and sixth centuries. Today's population is dominantly Armenian, probably exceeding 80 per cent of the total in eastern Djavakheti which borders northwestern Armenia. The recent history of the area is reasonably well known: Turks ruled southern Georgia from 1578 to 1828 and the Georgians who had been living there either left or were Turkicized.[16] With the signing of the same treaties that affected the ethnic composition of today's Republic of Armenia, Armenians from eastern Anatolia moved into this underpopulated area, preferring to live under the Christian tsar than under the Ottoman sultan.

Archaeologically, these events can be well documented, particularly by the construction of nineteenth-century Armenian churches on top of or next to the much earlier medieval Georgian churches. A history that only stretches back to medieval times, however, is insufficient for the local inhabitants, who ask, as soon as one enters one of their villages (Armenian or Georgian), who was there first, the Armenians or the Georgians. The practice of archaeology in southern Georgia cannot be divorced from this tense political context.

One must also distinguish an archaeological or historical identification of a people from current *state policies* affecting that people. What happened in the distant past is not the only, nor typically the most important, factor to consider in trying to understand, much less resolve, difficult territorially based ethnic disputes. Consideration of the historical archaeology of southern Georgia documents clearly that a legitimate historical claim[17] to this territory can be maintained by the Georgians. The ethnicity of the people who dominantly occupied this territory during Iron Age and classical times (including under the undoubtedly multi-ethnic reign of Tigran the Great) is unknown, and even the hypothetical (and improbable) discovery someday of inscriptions proving that most peoples in the area then spoke an Indo-European, Proto-Armenian, or Armenian-related language would not erase the Georgian historical claim to the area. This conclusion follows directly from the point made earlier about the ever-developing nature of cultures and the fact that Christianity has been an integral component of both Georgian and Armenian cultures for centuries; one simply cannot ignore those beautiful monastery complexes and churches with their Georgian inscriptions.

Admitting this, however, does not provide an excuse for the current Georgian *state policy* of deliberately underdeveloping the area and hindering communications and transportation between the local Armenian populations and their ethnic relatives to the south. Surely many generations of Armenians have lived and died on this soil since arriving *en masse* after 1828, and this fact alone is obviously relevant to their just treatment and the rights that they deserve.[18] The Bible or even biblical archaeology may be invoked to legitimize an historical claim to the West Bank, but such a claim does not provide justification for a specific *state policy* of uprooting Palestinian orchards and olive groves or demolishing their homes. These issues must be kept separate, and any honest archaeologist should be capable of distinguishing between them.

D *Northern Caucasus*

The bewildering array of peoples in northern Caucasia coupled with their relatively short historical record means that prehistory here is once more implicated in questions of ethnogenesis and claims to specific territories (for a recent historical introduction to this poorly known area, see Broxup 1992). The region today is characterized by ethnic tensions, occasionally breaking out into open hostilities (e.g., the conflict between the northern Ossetians and the neighboring Ingush, who, in turn, find themselves divorced from the Chechen to their east), and it is unclear at this writing whether further Balkanization of the region will continue or whether an effective federation of north Caucasian peoples will emerge (Ormrod 1993).

As to be expected, essentialist cultural interpretations abound which often are coupled with selective presentations of dubious linguistic evidence to "prove" diametrically opposed "readings" of the prehistoric record. Thus, we learn that the creators of the Maikop culture wrote in a previously unrecognized Abkhazian script (Turchaninov 1971) or that this same archaeologically documented culture bears material witness to supposed linguistic convergences and hence genetic relationships between Sumerian and Karachai-Balkar, that is, early Turkic (Miziev 1986; for devastating critiques of these unbelievable "readings" see particularly the reviews by Chechenov and Markovin in Balzer 1992). Periodically, "archaeologists" or "philologists" of Lezghin ethnic background or of one of the linguistically related smaller peoples of southern Daghestan and northern Azerbaijan (e.g., Udi) report the discovery of new or hitherto unreadable inscriptions which purportedly demonstrate that their ethnic group is the direct descendant of the Albanians and/or Urartians, peoples who once controlled extensive lands to the south; such claims are either fabricated wholesale or remain essentially unsubstantiated, despite the fact that most objective linguists would concede the historical likelihood that there were such genetic links to one or more of these peoples. The archaeological record is further complicated and politicized by documentable relations with steppe cultures to the north, including those elusive Proto-Indo-European speakers (for new evidence possibly documenting such connections, see Rezepkin 1992). In short, archaeology in the northern Caucasus occasionally exhibits on a smaller scale the same distortions and politically motivated features that characterize its practice farther south in Azerbaijan, Armenia, and Georgia and should be criticized along the same lines.

II Nationalism in the classical archaeology of the Caucasus: Greeks and "Georgians" in ancient Colchis

The interpretation of the later archaeological record in the Caucasus is also suffused with nationalist sentiments. The second part of this paper presents a detailed example of this practice: the denial of significant Greek influences on the local archaeologically attested cultures of western Georgia (ancient Colchis). Despite their historically checkered relations, Georgians and Greeks are not currently killing each other over conflicting ancestral claims. This case study represents neither the only, nor the most invidious example of nationalist archaeology in the later historical archaeology of the Caucasus. It does, however, nicely illustrate the pervasive extent of nationalist prejudice: implausible archaeological reconstructions, extolling the glory of all things indigenous while disparaging the influence of external contacts, dominate less partial, more sober and objective "readings" of the same rich body of archaeological and written sources.

In the West the term "classical archaeology" refers to Greek and Roman antiquities; in the former Soviet Union, the Russian word *antichnaya* is used for this period. Although use of this term typically is clear and unproblematic, it recently was suggested that the term *antichnaya arkheologiya* is inappropriate for the archaeology of Georgia and ought to be replaced by the term "Iberian-Colchian period" which extended in three sub-periods from the seventh century BC through the fourth century AD. According to the author, the reason for this substitution was that the term *antichnaya arkheologiya* is used in relation to Graeco-Roman sites, while in the territory of ancient Georgia only Greek and Roman trading *colonies* are to be found – there never having been a permanent Graeco-Roman population (G. Gamkrelidze 1985:123–6). This article did not elicit responses or commentaries from Georgian specialists in the field, though their lack of response does not mean that they did not agree with the author. Questions as to the presence of *the* Greeks in ancient Colchis, the Greek colonization of this region, and the influence of Greek culture on the indigenous inhabitants of Colchis are fiercely debated among Georgian archaeologists, and the only convincing explanation for controversy over what should be non-problematic is national pride.

Similarly, nationalist emotions predominate in the writings of local historians. In July 1991 an article appeared in a district newspaper in the town of Kobuleti about the name of the fortified settlement of Petra (Kontselidze 1991), one of the most significant archaeological sites in western Georgia. In the sixth to second centuries BC a Colchian/Greek settlement existed there; in the first centuries AD there was a Roman military settlement; and in the middle of the sixth century AD the Byzantines fortified the previously existing settlement and named it Petra. Kontselidze believes that this fortress should be renamed, since the name Petra is Greek and it had been built not by Georgians but by the Byzantines for themselves. He is distraught that professional archaeologists and historians are unable to find the Georgian name of this fortress.

The vast majority of Georgian (and some Abkhazian) archaeologists do not want to accept the Greek colonization of Colchis or the influence of Greek culture on Colchis. Some scholars even place the term colonization in quotes (e.g., Kaukhchishvili 1979:274). According to them, the Greeks did not found independent Greek colonies (*poleis*), but *factoria* for trade which did not have a *chora* (or agricultural hinterland). These *factoria* were under the control of the local Colchian rulers and either were small settlements or constituted districts of local towns. In order to substantiate these conclusions, it is argued that there existed a strong local state with a king in Colchis and that this state stood in the way of the emergence of independent Greek cities. Greek influence on the material and non-material culture of Colchis is also denied (at least in the sixth to fourth centuries BC) by reference to the fact that Colchian culture was highly developed and did not need to accept anything from Hellenic culture which was alien to it (Lordkipanidze 1989:256–72).[19] We shall not examine in detail the question of the Greek colonization of Colchis but attempt to paint a general picture of the eastern part of the Black Sea region in the sixth to fourth centuries BC (for more information, see Tsetskhladze 1994).

A The problems of the Colchian state and royal power in Colchis

Most Georgian scholars consider that a strong local state had emerged in Colchis at least by the end of the sixth century BC. Herodotus' account seemingly supports this opinion:

> The Persians live right up as far as the Southern Sea, known as the Red Sea [i.e. the Persian Gulf]; beyond them to the North live the Medes, beyond them the Saspiri, beyond the Saspiri are the Colchians, whose land reaches as far as the Northern Sea [Black Sea], into which flows the River Phasis. These are the four peoples whose lands stretch from one sea to the other. (IV.37)

From this passage, the following conclusion is drawn:

> Within this extensive territory the "father of History" [Herodotus] places only four peoples: the Persians; the Medes; the Saspiri; and the Colchians. It is well known that the states of the Medes and the Persians at that time were powerful, and the fact that the Colchians are mentioned in the same breath can probably be seen as an indirect indication of the fact that there also then existed a state of Colchis that was a large political entity. (Lordkipanidze 1989:220–1)

Such wishful thinking, however, is not really plausible. Mention of the Colchians alongside the Persians and the Medes need not indicate that the Colchians had a strong state-structured polity. If the same logic were to be followed further, one would be forced to assume that the Saspiri also had a strong state. More revealing is the note by the same scholar which refers to the Saspiri as "East Georgian [*sic!*] tribes" (Lordkipanidze 1989:221, note 20). In reality, Herodotus was simply listing these peoples according to their geographical location and not according to the extent of their population, nor to their control of large political states. Ancient authors are not cited for documenting royal power in Colchis; instead, we are informed that the descendants of King Aeetes ruled in Colchis and that later rulers inherited his throne (Lordkipanidze 1989:223–4). Scholarship here devolves into mythology.

Greek and Roman authors always showed an interest in Colchis, above all as the Land of the Golden Fleece and the home of Medea, and, for this reason, kept retelling parts of the myth of the Argonauts. There simply is very little reliable and concrete historical information about Colchis in the Greek literary tradition. One cannot reconstruct the social structure of the "erstwhile mighty Colchian Kingdom," as based, for example, on the *Argonautica* of Apollonius Rhodius (Lordkipanidze 1989:229), but only evaluate as critically and as objectively as possible the archaeological record and the more reliable historical sources.

Archaeological materials, primarily mortuary evidence, reveal marked social differentiation and the emergence of a local Colchian elite in the late sixth and early fifth century BC, and it is probable that a Colchian state, ruled by a king, existed at that time. The question then becomes: how centralized and powerful was this state? Written sources are helpful and indicate that Colchis was not a centralized state. Strabo, whose information on Colchis is always reliable, wrote that "the kings, ruling over a land divided up into *skeptouchs*, enjoyed a moderate degree of power" (XI.2.18). This passage testifies to the fact that Colchis was divided up into administrative/territorial units (*skeptouchs*) headed by *skeptouchoi* (a title based on the ancient Greek word meaning "scepterholder"), who were representatives of the local clan-based aristocracy. "Colchis" itself was not an ethnic but a political term; it was an alliance of numerous Colchian tribes and not a unified, centralized kingdom.

B *The question of Greek colonization*

According to the classical authors, three cities were founded by the Greeks in the region known as Colchis: Phasis, Gyenos, and Dioscuria. Admittedly, the archaeological evidence is problematic: Phasis has not been found; part of Dioscuria lies under the Black Sea and the rest is under the modern, now war-ravaged city of Sukhumi; and Gyenos has not been systematically investigated. Nevertheless, consideration of the relatively unambiguous and substantial historical record reveals that one cannot seriously question the existence of these *poleis* in Colchis, nor pretend that the Greeks only traded there.

We know that Phasis was founded by Milesians (Heraclides Ponticus, XVIII; Pomponius Mela, I.108; Anon. PPE, 44; Stephen of Byzantium s.v. Ethnika). Written sources provide the founder's name – Phemistagoras of Miletus (Pomponius Mela, I.108), the leader of the colonists. Pseudo-Scylax refers to it as an Hellenic city (81). A fragment of an "Aristotelian Constitution of the Phasians" (FGr Hist. II, p. 218) is a particularly important Greek source. Although the interpretation of this text and the translation of certain words are controversial, one fact is incontrovertible: the city of Phasis was a Milesian colony that had its own constitution, which attracted the attention of Aristotle, whose writings include descriptions of the constitutions of such *poleis* as Athens, Sparta, and Miletus. In Phasis the colonists were responsible for introducing the cult of Apollo, and a temple dedicated to that Greek god existed in the city. The city also minted its own silver coins – the so-called Kolkhidki (Dundua 1987:9–33).

Gyenos was also an Hellenic *polis* (Pseudo-Scylax, 81). The archaeological materials reveal that it too was founded by the Milesians. That same Greek city also founded Dioscuria, whose *chora* also has been documented. Appian (101), Charax of Pergamum (Frg. 36, 37 v), Pliny (Natural History, VI.61), Pomponius Mela (I, III) and Ammianus Marcellinus (XXII.8.24) link the name of the city "Dioscuria" with the name of the Dioscuri – Castor and Pollux – and are of the opinion that it had been founded in their honor. All the above-mentioned Greek cities were established in the middle of the sixth century BC, and they functioned as trading centers for the local tribes. Apart from these cities, there were also Hellenic settlements at Tsikhisdziri and Pichvnari (Tsetskhladze 1994).

It is difficult to understand why the local royal power in Colchis would have impeded the emergence of independent Greek *poleis*. The king and the local elite had every reason to be on good terms with the Greeks. The Hellenization of the elite began immediately, a process clearly reflected in the archaeological materials, most of which are found in Vani, a city-site inhabited by many nobles. It was precisely in centers such as these that craft production was concentrated, particularly in those spheres of production that provided for the needs of the ruling elite of Colchian society, such as, above all, the production of seal-rings as distinctive emblems of the elite. Greeks were working in the workshops – a fact universally accepted, even by nationalist-minded Georgian archaeologists. Although at present it is impossible to trace precisely and consistently the development of Georgian glyptics or to speak of a definite "Colchian" or "Graeco-Colchian" style in glyptics, systematic study of certain characteristic groups of intaglios has made it possible to pick out certain features and to distinguish preliminarily between Colchian and Graeco-Colchian seals.

The next "elite" branch of artistic craftsmanship that catered to the local rulers was goldsmithing. The written and archaeological sources together confirm that this type of craft production was not imported. It is difficult to say who was engaged in these gold workshops. The typology of the gold articles (e.g., earrings, diadems) shows that local craftsmen played the dominant role, but Greek influence is also evident. Granulation was widespread both in the classical world and farther east, and artistic analysis reveals Oriental influences (e.g., the depictions of fighting animals on diadems). The predilection of the ruling elite with regard to gold jewelry was the same everywhere. Some gold articles were gifts from the Achaemenid kings, and it is clear that others had been received by the local rulers as gifts from Greek merchants, a pattern also seen in the ornamental metal reliefs. Furthermore, the elite immediately began to use the Greek language; study of the graffiti reveals that the elite wrote in Greek (Tsetskhladze 1994; for more details on problems with the interpretation of Achaemenid materials, see Tsetskhladze 1992).

C The influence of Greek culture on Colchian culture

Some Georgian authorities have maintained that there was no *significant* Greek influence on the material culture of Colchis in the sixth to fourth centuries BC, such as in craft production, building techniques, funerary rites, domestic life, and the like (Lordkipanidze 1989:261). Rather than considering all these manifestations of material culture, let us turn our attention to just one aspect: the funerary rituals practiced by the local population. This phenomenon is most revealing in that ideology and religion are always conservative forms of material and non-material culture; if the influence of Greek culture made itself felt here, then this strongly suggests that the Greek presence in Colchis was significant.

Interesting materials have been brought to light by excavations of a Colchian cemetery dating from the fifth century BC which was discovered at Kobuleti-Pichvnari. The orientation of 103 of the 160 published burials has been established, and forty-two of these exhibit an orientation towards the east as was typical for the Greeks. We also encounter the "Charon's obol" ritual: forty-nine coins were found in nineteen of the 160 burials, one of them being from Sinope while the remainder were Colchian. Hellenic influence also serves to explain the presence of amphorae in six burials. The amphorae are from Chios and Phasos, apart from one which is proto-Phasian. One also must emphasize that similar materials from Tsikhisdziri show that the cemetery of Pichvnari is not the only place documenting the actual physical presence of the Greeks in Colchis.

Finally, while nothing is known about the local language, it has already been established that the *official* language for religious ceremonies and state administration in Colchis was Greek. This has been demonstrated by the find of official political and religious decrees written in impeccable Greek on bronze sheets in Eshera and Vani (Tsetskhladze 1994).

In short, what for all other people and states is seen as a source of pride – namely, direct contact between their culture and Graeco-Roman civilization – is unacceptable for certain Georgian archaeologists. Facts, however, should prevail over nationalist emotions. Scholars, who should serve Clio and not contemporary politics, must free themselves from prejudices that reflect nationalist feelings and current events. Today no-one doubts that a highly developed civilization existed in the first millennium BC within the territory of what is now western Georgia, a culture which at the same time enjoyed close political, economic, and cultural links with both the Mediterranean and the Eastern (particularly the Achaemenid Empire) worlds. Like any other highly developed culture, Colchis absorbed and refashioned the achievements of the Greek and Achaemenid civilizations. This should be seen as progress, not the opposite.

III Conclusion: the preferred "reading"

The prehistoric and early historic archaeological record of the Caucasus is consistently distorted for nationalist reasons. Thus, the earliest evidence for domestication, for full-scale metallurgy, for monumental architecture, etc. – all find their origins in that remarkably creative cradle nestled along the western shore of the Caspian (for an Azeri), in the lush foothills of the Great Caucasus and along the Black Sea coast (for a Georgian), or in the fertile Ararat valley of southern Transcaucasia (for an Armenian). Hyperbole, of course, is a trait not unknown to archaeologists and does not always illustrate the politicization of the discipline. But it happens so consistently throughout the Caucasus that one is tempted to despair of ever sifting through these claims and counterclaims to determine "objectively" from the known record the earliest or most complex manifestation of specific archaeological cultures. Nationalist-inspired interpretations of the archaeological record greatly complicate any attempt to understand or synthesize the prehistory and early history of the Caucasus.

Consideration of the extremely politicized nature of Caucasian archaeology, however, reveals far more serious problems than simply trying to determine more objectively prehistoric and early historic developments throughout the area. The recurrent, blatantly political interpretations of archaeological materials illustrate clearly why one should abandon the dangerously naïve position, advocated by some post-processual archaeologists, that one's or one people's "reading of the past" is as valid and justifiable as another's. Such "readings" of the Caucasian evidence have been used to destroy the cultural legacy of others or to uproot and kill local peoples who have been living in specific areas for centuries. Archaeologists must adopt more universal criteria which emphasize the common cultural heritage of the area in which they work, if not the common cultural evolutionary history of humankind in general.

The "story" that needs to be written about Caucasian archaeology is one that emphasizes the eminently documentable sharing of material culture traits throughout the region at least since the beginnings of the Bronze Age. Such sharing reveals a common historical legacy that defines a very rich Caucasian culture area. However imperceptibly, such a "story" and others like it might help bring together the numerous peoples of the Caucasus so that they can face together a very uncertain but exciting political future and confront together the ecological problems that will continue to beset their beautiful environment well into the next century.

NOTES

1 This article is an expanded version of the paper "Nationalism, Politics, and the Practice of Archaeology in Transcaucasia" presented by Philip L. Kohl at the American Anthropological Association meetings in Chicago, Illinois in November 1991 and published in the *Journal of European Archaeology* 2 (1993), 179–86. Several individuals read earlier versions of this paper and made many useful comments and provided additional references. We thank them all and particularly wish to acknowledge the thoughtful suggestions of V. Shnirelman and M.I. Martínez Navarrete. Andrea Finn drew Map 1. The prehistoric section of this paper (part I) was written by P.L. Kohl, while the treatment of classical archaeology in Georgian archaeology (part II) was written by G.R. Tsetskhladze.

2 Since one of the principal points of this paper is that archaeologists must be aware of the political implications of their work, including the connotations of even the terms they employ, we must note that the geographical designations Ciscaucasia and Transcaucasia have as their referent Russia (if not Moscow) which is located, of course, north of the Great Caucasus range. Although problematic, these terms occasionally are used here for convenience and because they are so enshrined in the Russian literature.

3 At the time of the basic revision of this article (spring 1993), such claims were not being articulated for the reason that Azerbaijan seeks Iranian assistance in its conflict with the Armenians. Such silence, of course, does not imply a renunciation of "northern Azerbaijan's" territorial aspirations in "southern Azerbaijan." Like many of the nationalist leaders that have emerged in the post-Soviet period, including President L. Ter-Petrosian of Armenia, the former

Azerbaijani leader maintains a keen interest in his "reading" of history (and prehistory).

Many very scholarly works on Azerbaijan (e.g., Altstadt 1992) are misleading in their almost exclusive focus on "northern Azerbaijan." Reading them, one would never appreciate that Azeris living in Iran are far more numerous than their northern relations (upwards of 10,000,000 people), form the second largest ethnic group after the Persians in the country, and have during many periods, such as under the Qajar dynasty, dominated the internal affairs of Iran.

4 The denial of Armenian history is not an exclusively Azeri practice. Armenian cultural remains in neighboring eastern Turkey are frequently dismissed or referred to as "Ottoman period" monuments. The continued denial of the wholesale state-sponsored massacre of at the least several hundreds of thousands of Armenians earlier this century (the Armenian genocide of 1915) and their forced expulsion from ancestral homes in eastern Anatolia is, of course, related to these practices. It is doubtful that the practice of archaeology in Azerbaijan, Armenia, or Turkey will ever be de-politicized without some official acknowledgement of this horrible historical tragedy inflicted on the Armenians by the then Turkish government. While one should not justify this refusal to acknowledge a terrible past, admission of these events in Turkey apparently is complicated by the fact that many historical figures still important in the construction of Turkish national identity are implicated in the 1915 slaughter of the Armenians.

5 The date for the emergence of the Azeris as a distinct, conscious ethnic group is variously set by different authors, some of whose political agendas are manifest (e.g., compare the contrasting views of Alekperov and Alijarov in Balzer and Paksoy 1990). Western scholars, such as T. Swietochowski (1983) and A. Altstadt (1992), associate this development with Azeri intellectuals' aspirations for modern nationhood, placing it either at the end of the nineteenth or the beginning of the twentieth century (i.e., quite late), the latter specialist even preferring the term Azerbaijani Turk to Azeri or Azerbaijani (p. xix). Swietochowski (1983:231) writes:

> In 1905 Azerbaijan was still merely a geographical name for a stretch of land inhabited by a people whose group identity consisted of being Muslims. The period between this date and the fall of the independent Republic in 1920 witnessed the rise of, for the Muslims, a novel type of community, the nation . . . Against this backdrop [the cataclysmic events of the early twentieth century], the universalistic *umma* consciousness was giving way at least among the intelligentsia to Turkism, and the next stage in the evolution was Azerbaijani nationalism.

To utilize the Soviet anthropological parlance, the ethnogenesis of the Azeri people effectively has only occurred during the last 100 years.

6 Of course, not all anthropomorphic stones set over graves represent remains recording the movement of Turkish peoples. As with most material markers, the archaeological record is more complicated. Stylized human-shaped gravestones are found even in early Bronze Age contexts in the Caucasus, and, in the absence of supporting materials, questions naturally arise as to the date of specific monuments. This problem, which is similar to that of interpreting carved cross-shaped stones (see below), can be reasonably solved through traditional art historical and archaeological analysis.

7 Upon querying the date for the initial appearance of Turkic peoples in Transcaucasia, one of the authors of this article (PLK) was informed by two archaeologists from the Institute of History in Baku in 1986 that many scholars in Azerbaijan thought that Turkic-speaking peoples had always lived there, that, in short, the *Urheimat* of Turkish-speakers was contemporary Azerbaijan, a belief that contradicts all historical and archaeological evidence.

8 Some Armenian irredentists insist that today's Armenia is only one tenth of "historic Armenia," a claim which also deserves critical scrutiny (see note 17 below).

9 One surviving mosque in Yerevan functions today as the city museum of Yerevan. Plans were developed for the Iranians to restore this mosque as part of a cultural/economic agreement between the two countries. In return, the Armenians were supposed to restore an Armenian church in Iran. It is unknown whether this agreement will be actualized, particularly given the current deterioration of relations between the countries which is associated with the war in Nagorno-Karabagh and the Armenian offensive into western Azerbaijan.

10 One of the authors (PLK) recalls his guided tour of the rich, handsomely displayed Ethnographic Museum at Sadarabat (which is located on the western edge of the fertile Ararat valley at the place where the Armenians defeated a Turkish army in 1918, preventing further catastrophe and an even greater Armenian diaspora). The overly enthusiastic guide explained that all the crafts and materials on display, such as carpets and even the fez or hat worn by males throughout the Ottoman Empire, were invented by Armenians. This essentialist interpretation of Armenian culture not only posits a separate evolution for the Armenian "race," but also grants them chronological priority in most significant cultural achievements which throughout history they then passed on to the less civilized barbarians surrounding them. Needless to say, their neighbors resent such claims, regardless of whether or not they can be historically verified.

Debates between Armenians and Georgians, for example, over who was responsible for innovations in early medieval Christian architecture seem absolutely puerile to an outsider but, unfortunately, sometimes have tragic consequences. (See Yakobson's sensible review [1968] of the Georgian chauvinistic study by G.N. Chubinashvili *Searches for Armenian Architecture* [1967]. We thank Dr. S. Aslanian for providing this reference and that of the previously mentioned review by Martirosian and Munchaev.) One wonders whether the early Christian communities in the Caucasus were as obsessed with ethnicity as their twentieth-century descendants; the "scholarly" debate among contemporary Armenians and Georgians over priorities in Christian architecture recalls the competing ethnic claims for the origins of Insular art in northwestern Europe (and the sensible criticisms of them by Wailes and Zoll, this volume).

One must avoid any temptation to ridicule the exaggerated, sometimes patently false claims to great antiquity associated with the essentialist vision of Armenian culture. As R.G. Suny (1993a:4–5) sensitively observes:

> An essentialist view of Armenians . . . has been for political nationalists the basis for their political ideology: the continuous existence of the Armenians as a historic people, their

origins in the Armenian plateau, arms them with the right of self-determination, nationhood, and a historically sanctified claim to the territories that constitute Armenia. Because this view of Armenian history plays such an important role for Armenians (as homologous views play for Georgians, Azerbaijanis, Turks, and other peoples), any attempt to dispute it, to decompose the collection of beliefs that make up this reading, must be done with care and sensitivity, with full awareness that such an investigation may be perceived as an attack on the very soul of the nation.

This entire critique of essentialist accounts of Azeri, Armenian, Georgian, and north Caucasian archaeology is made with this awareness and, hopefully, with the care and sensitivity that Suny rightly recommends.

11 And in the same sense, of course, the Azeris can be considered the cultural heirs of the Albanians, as well as of the other peoples who once occupied today's territory of Azerbaijan. I.M. Diakonoff concludes his brilliant linguistic study on *The Pre-History of the Armenian People* (1984:129–30) with the following observation:

it is evident that the history of the Armenian people is a direct continuation of the history not only of the Proto-Armenians [prior to the formation of the Armenian ethnos proper, probably in the sixth century BC], but also (and to no lesser degree) of the Hurrians, the Urartians, and the Luwians. The main mass of the Armenian nation consists of their descendants; there was a historical moment when a person might speak Old Armenian, his father, grandfather, or great-grandfather was more likely to have been bilingual, while his forefather was a pure Hurrian or Urartian . . . There is no question but that ancient Armenian history can correctly be understood only as the continuation of the more ancient history of the Hurrians and the Urartians, as well as that of the Luwians.

But he also emphasizes (p. 128):

the enormous cultural impact the Urartian state and culture . . . had beyond the confines of the Urartian linguistic territory proper. In this sense the cultural heritage of Urartu is *the property of all the peoples of Transcaucasia and not of the Armenian nation alone*. (italics added)

His study convincingly refutes various chauvinist attempts to equate the Proto-Armenians with various mentioned peoples in cuneiform and classical sources (e.g., Kavoukjian 1987) and postulates, on the basis of linguistic affinity between Proto- and Old Armenian and Thracian and Phrygian, a movement of Proto-Armenian speakers west to east across the Anatolian plateau during the second millennium BC.

12 An Armenian archaeologist specializing in the late Iron Age and classical periods informed one of us (PLK) that the Urartian state had extended as far north as the southern banks of the Middle Kura river (a belief not confirmed by Urartian inscriptions or, indeed, by even less certain material evidence); a politically attuned – if skeptical – interpretation of this claim would view it as a possible subconscious justification for Armenian dominance in Tiflis, which actually was the case for much of the nineteenth century but which was not true centuries earlier, nor today when Tbilisi is the capital of Georgia. Another Iron Age specialist claimed that the Urartian rule had extended at least as far north as the Tli cemetery in southern Ossetia (or Inner Kartli, see below), since Urartian or Urartian-inspired materials, such as figured bronze belts, had been excavated in this cemetery. A less chauvinistic "reading" of this same evidence would consider such items as imports or imitations from the Urartian world, since the

Urartian connections are relatively rare in the rich, clearly local assemblage of materials from this cemetery (see Tekhov 1980, 1981, 1985, 1988 and below).

13 Another indication of the politicized nature and importance of archaeology in many countries throughout the world (though not in the United States) is the recurrent fact that archaeologists often assume major political roles. Examples (e.g., Y. Yadin in Israel) of this phenomenon are too numerous to recount; suffice it to say that archaeologists, ancient historians, linguists, ethnographers, folklorists, etc. are playing a major role in current political developments throughout the Caucasus (and indeed the former Soviet Union), particularly those associated with various nationalist movements (Chernykh, this volume). That V.E. Oganesian today is one of the leaders of the Dashnaktsutiun nationalist party in Armenia is not irrelevant to his Indo-European "reading" of the Karashamb silver goblet. To paraphrase E.H. Carr's famous maxim, study the archaeologist before you begin to study his/her presentation of the archaeological record.

14 Similarly, given the incredibly tense political context of ethnic conflicts ranging throughout Georgia, including most tragically at the moment the Georgian/Abkhazian conflict, one must not ridicule or lampoon what appear to be ludicrous evaluations of the prehistoric record; rather one must appreciate them sensitively and sympathetically in light of this context.

15 Extreme Georgian nationalists distinguish the non-aboriginal Ossetians from the aboriginal Abkhazians of today's northwestern Georgia; current territorial conflict with the latter cannot be justified on the same ideological grounds, making this conflict more theoretically complicated and ambiguous.

16 Many of these Meskheti in turn were deported by Stalin to central Asia in 1944, illustrating vividly "the making" of the contemporary Meskheti ethnos; forced deportations, of course, constitute one of history's best-documented means for increasing a culture's sense of group self-identity and consciousness. Today tens of thousands of Meskheti, some of whom have Georgian surnames but profess Islam and speak Turkish, aspire to return to their "homeland," creating yet another serious ethnic problem for the nascent Republic of Georgia (Lomsadze 1989).

17 By the same token, of course, the Armenians have a legitimate historical claim to a core or heartland area of "historic Armenia" stretching at least from Van to Erzerum and north to include their medieval capital of Ani. The great difference, of course, is that this heartland was effectively "cleansed" of Armenians in 1915 and has been both *de facto* and *de jure* controlled by Turkey since the signing of the Treaty of Lausanne in July 1923. This difference in political control and the historically shaped realities of population distributions and the like that ensued create a different dynamic, far less tractable to a "just" solution. Nevertheless, one can maintain that the legitimate historical claim of Armenia to a core or heartland area in eastern Anatolia is one factor – among many others – that must be considered in trying to temper or resolve the long-standing enmity between the Armenians and the Turks.

18 Under the nationalist government of Z. Gamsakhurdia, the attempt was made to deny rights of citizenship to those inhabitants of Georgia who could not demonstrate their existence on Georgian soil as Georgian speakers before 1801,

a particularly insidious *state policy*.

19 One should mention that some Georgian archaeologists refer to a Bronze Age Colchian *state*, making it the earliest complex society in Transcaucasia. Here the competition once again is with the Armenians and their claims for this distinction: i.e., Urartu or even pre-Urartian states in the Ararat valley (Shnirelman, personal communication).

Part IV

East Asia

11 Thirty years of Chinese archaeology (1949–1979)[1]

Enzheng Tong

Science is a cause fighting for truth.
One must be free of fear, even of offending God. Li Shu (1985:25)

Chinese archaeology was characterized by numerous discoveries and significant research during the thirty years from 1949, the year of the founding of the People's Republic of China, to 1979, the year the Chinese Communist Party held its Third Plenary Session of the Eleventh Central Committee and began to correct the "leftist" errors of Mao Zedong. Compared to the period prior to 1949, many achievements are evident: archaeological excavations expanded into every area of the country, compiling abundant new data that filled in many historical gaps; the adoption of new techniques, such as C 14 dating, provided invaluable new insights into the prehistoric record; the training of younger archaeologists and the establishment of archaeological museums and institutes in each province provided proper conditions for the storage and study of newly unearthed antiquities; and the opening of a special publishing facility (Wenwu Publishing House) and the printing of several archaeological periodicals guaranteed the publication of important data. In addition, being a socialist country in which all the land belongs to the state, China owns all the antiquities and ancient remains on or under the ground. During the period under discussion, the Antiquity law, which prohibited the export of antiquities, was very strict and efficiently enforced by the police and customs offices. This virtually eliminated the smuggling of antiquities, which is a serious problem encountered by all countries that have a rich record of ancient civilization. For all these reasons, new archaeological finds in China frequently attracted worldwide attention, and archaeology was one of the few sciences of which the Chinese government could be proud (Xia Nai 1979a).

From 1949 to 1979, however, the country was under the absolute control of Mao Zedong. China carried out a thorough closed-door policy, and Chinese social science was deeply influenced by dogmatism and nationalism. In this thirty-year period, the guiding ideology of Chinese social science can be divided into two stages. From 1949 to 1959, the ruling principle was "follow the examples of the Soviet Union." At that time, the dogmatism, the nationalism, and the personality cult of Stalin in the Soviet Union exerted a negative influence on the Chinese. After 1959, the year which saw the dissolution of the relationship between these two countries, Chinese academics shifted to "hold high the great banner of Mao Zedong's thought." A series of political slogans – such as "take class struggle as the key link"; "eliminate bourgeois ideology and foster proletarian ideology"; "stress the present, not the past"; and "make the past serve the present" – guided Chinese scholarship for more than twenty years.[2] Under these circumstances, the purported theories of some scholars merely repeated a few key sentences from the works of Marx, Engels, Lenin, Stalin, and Mao Zedong, and their study of ancient societies merely used new data to certify their pre-existing conclusions. During the "unprecedented" Cultural Revolution (1966–76), the supposedly academic research conducted in China did not constitute true scholarship, but rather merely served the political power struggle, reaffirming political authority.

In 1983, when summarizing the experience of the study of history in China, the late famous historian Li Shu observed:

> In reviewing the historical study of the past thirty years, I believe that we did not use the advantages of the new society to accomplish more. On the contrary, due to the obstruction of ultra-"Leftist" ideology, especially the disruption of the counter-revolutionary cohort of Jian Qing, Kang Sheng, and Chen Boda,[3] the historical sciences suffered numerous setbacks, one after another. These successive damages caused severe confusion in ideology and left profound lessons. (Li Shu 1983:16)

According to the definition of Xia Nai, the late director of the Institute of Archaeology and the most authoritative scholar in China, archaeology is "a science which studies the past of humanity in terms of the materials left by human activities," and "it is a branch of historical science" (Xia Nai 1984:931). That is to say, archaeology and history have a close relationship. Although the materials for their studies are different, the object of the study, namely human society, is the same for both disciplines. Consequently their ruling principles and theories also should be the same: they both seek to understand the development and operation of human society. If the study of history was disrupted by ultra-"Leftist" ideology during this thirty-year period, could archaeology, which also deals with ancient Chinese history, be immune from the influence of contemporary political circumstances and the rigid control of ideology? Could it have developed unfettered, independent from general academic circles?

After careful introspection, including the examination of the study of archaeology in China as a whole and my own works, I believe that during this thirty-year period archaeology, like other social sciences in China, suffered from some shortcomings and errors, which today can provide many lessons and experiences. The main problems were the dogmatism and the rigidity of theory; the improper interference in academic matters by politics; the nationalistic priorities revealed by some studies; and the conservative leading thought of upper-level administrators. Although these problems were the common failings of Chinese social science at that time, they still have their particular characteristics in the field of archaeology.

I The Marxist/Maoist evolutionary model in Chinese archaeology and ideological dogmatism

The salient feature of Chinese archaeology is that it is guided by Marxism and the thought of Mao Zedong, a characteristic that defines its "new stage" of development after 1949 (Xia Nai 1979b:194). Comments on Chinese archaeology must begin by addressing this problem. The guiding thought and theory of any academic discipline are very important. Based on the same materials, different scholars can derive varying results by implementing different theoretical frameworks. Although always influenced by the prevailing philosophy and political viewpoints, the concrete theory of each discipline nonetheless can be distinguished. The dialectical materialism proposed by Marx and the class struggle theory required by Mao Zedong is not and cannot be the underlying theory of archaeology, no matter how strongly advocated by some Chinese authorities as universally applicable. In China, to the present day, we still have Marxist/Maoist economic theory, Marxist/Maoist literary theory, Marxist/Maoist philosophical theory, and Marxist/Maoist political theory. Curiously, although some authoritative Chinese scholars emphasized the importance of Marxist/Maoist thought to extremes, even now there is no book or paper published in China that systematically expounds what exactly constitutes Marxist/Maoist archaeological theory, or details its methodology. In addition, during this period Chinese scholars did not even recognize or use the developments in Marxist archaeology which were made in foreign countries (e.g., McGuire 1992). A large country like China, with so many magnificent archaeological finds, completely ignored theory for a period of more than thirty years. Even acknowledging the persistence of Marxist/Maoist guidance, it is difficult to excuse such narrow-mindedness.

Owing to the lack of theoretical works, we can only attempt to define what constitutes Marxist/Maoist archaeology by examining certain objective pronouncements of some of the authoritative scholars in China. In terms of the study of prehistory, an important component of Marxist/

Maoist archaeology is the unilineal evolutionary theory, originally proposed by the American anthropologist Lewis Henry Morgan (1877) and later expounded by Friedrich Engels (1884) in the nineteenth century. According to this theory, human prehistory evolved, without exception, along a unilineal sequence from primitive band through matrilineal clan to patrilineal clan. Xia Nai (1962:455) stated:

> For the study of the history of primitive society, we rely mainly on archaeological and ethnological data . . . the known Paleolithic sites were sparse and their remains poor, indicating that their social institutions were primitive bands and later evolved into early tribal societies. During the Neolithic period, the arrangement of the houses into villages and the graves into cemeteries of the agricultural tribes revealed that at first they were flourishing matriarchal clans and afterwards developed into patriarchal societies.

This passage is very synthetic, but for that time it was the only model for the study of prehistoric archaeology in China. Thus the culture of *Homo erectus pekinensis* (Peking Man), the Yangshao culture and the Longshan culture were labeled as "primitive band," "matriarchal society," and "patriarchal society," respectively. The statuses of social development of other regional cultures within China were determined by comparison with this sequence. Debate may have arisen concerning the particular placement of a certain culture within this time-frame, but no one dared challenge the validity of the whole model.

The classic evolutionism which prevailed in the nineteenth century certainly had its historical value. But as with other scientific theories in their infancy, this model also contained imperfections and errors. In the twentieth century, many scholars from various countries have discussed the pros and cons of Morgan's evolutionism, altering tenets to conform to new data, rejecting erroneous assumptions, and generally refining the underlying theory (see Sanderson 1990). Although some of the issues are still debated, the following points are generally recognized as valid by the majority of anthropologists: the evolution of human society did not follow one fixed unilineal model; matrilineal and patrilineal societies were not necessarily successive; and matrilineal society did not always denote matriarchy (Tong 1989). Some Chinese academic authorities may oppose these opinions or persist in their own conclusions, which they regard as correct, but it is not compatible with academic freedom to demand that all the archaeologists in China adhere to an old, outdated model, or to prohibit the expression of contrary opinions. The underlying value of any scientific theory, its efficacy as well as its failings, can only be determined after extensive testing, after open discussion. It is regrettable that during this thirty-year period, some Chinese scholars never acknowledged the necessity of discussing theoretical questions, or of introducing the theoretical developments occurring in foreign countries. Consequently, their adherence to Morgan's model lacked a scientific basis. This phenomenon cannot be explained except as an example of adherence to an antiquated and repudiated dogmatism.

Political motivation, rather than scientific reason, caused these Chinese academic authorities to persist in this classic evolutionism and refuse to allow any open discussion. Xia Nai (1958:3–4) considered the following as ideal examples of archaeology and anthropology:

> The archaeological studies of Guo Moruo,[4] using inscriptions on oracle bones and bronzes as data, proved that ancient Chinese history followed Marxist social developmental theory. His work refuted the counter-Marxist fallacies of Hu Shi and his like. The classic work of Engels, *The Origin of the Family, Private Property, and the State*, using evidence from primitive societies, proved that private property and similar phenomena all were the products of history, following the sequence of coming into being, developing, and passing away. It, thus, refuted the bourgeois theory which regarded their existence as eternal.

To this way of thinking, the highest goal of the study of archaeology should be "to prove that ancient Chinese history followed Marxist social developmental theory" and to prove the inevitability of the extinction of the private economic system. These, of course, are legitimate issues for academic study, but, taken as a foregone conclusion, they cannot be verified and lack substance. Xia Nai emphasized this point of view because of the demands of contemporary politics. The theoretical legitimacy of the Chinese Communist regime, just as in Communist regimes elsewhere in the world, was mainly derived from the "inexorable historical law," or, in other words, from the theory of unilineal evolutionism. According to "Marxist social developmental theory," human society evolved through the sequence of primitive band, matrilineal clan, patrilineal clan, slave society, feudal society, capitalist society, and, finally, socialist society. The succession of these stages is similar to a natural phenomenon. It is "objective law" and thus cannot be changed by human intervention. If "socialism" is the final end-result of human society, naturally people have no choice but to tolerate the control of the Communist Party and all its policies, carried out, as they are, under the banner of "socialism." Recognizing this background, we can understand why the diverse archaeological discoveries from these thirty years were all explained by this one model. This academic paradigm is directly connected with maintaining the extant political system.

In terms of the archaeological theory of the historical period, Mao's idea to "take class struggle as the key link" was actualized in archaeological practice. Xia Nai (1972:41) explained this principle as follows:

The Great Leader Chairman Mao teaches us, "people, and the people alone, are the motive power for the creation of world history." Laboring people are the masters of history. They invented social wealth and culture. But in slave societies and feudal societies their accomplishments were seized by exploiting classes and they, themselves, were subjected to cruel exploitation. We archaeologists must follow the guide of Marxism, Leninism, and the thought of Mao Zedong, conscientiously fulfilling the great guiding principle of Chairman Mao, to "make the past serve the present." We must adopt the viewpoint of class and class struggle to investigate social phenomena reflected in archaeological data, to wipe out all the abominable influences of the distortion of history by the bourgeois and other exploiting classes, to reverse "the reversed history," and to resume "the reality of history." Let archaeology better serve the politics of the proletariat.

This passage was written during the Cultural Revolution, and, as such, should perhaps be regarded as a temporary expedient of this radical time. But neither Xia Nai himself nor the scholars who expounded his thoughts after his death ever question this opinion. It still influences Chinese archaeology today. Surely now we have the right to analyze it as a part of the theory of Marxist/Maoist archaeology.

In class society, the laboring people truly were exploited and persecuted by the dominant ruling classes, and their inventions usually were ignored by historians. Hence, in archaeology it is necessary to pay special attention to the social, economic, and cultural situations of the laboring people who constituted the majority of the population. Under the actual conditions of ancient society, however, the main achievements of politics, literature, art, religion, and science were initiated, designed, and accomplished by professional politicians, writers, artists, religious figures, and scientists. Over-emphasizing the direct contribution of the laborers in order to "reverse history" everywhere inevitably diminishes the accomplishments of these higher social strata, ignoring them as the products of the exploiting class. This deficiency exactly characterizes Chinese archaeology. At its extreme, this prejudice developed into the frenzied "Movement of Eradicating the 'Four Olds'" (consisting of: old ideology, old customs, old traditions, and old habits) during the Cultural Revolution. At that time, the Red Guards, incited by Mao Zedong, destroyed numerous valuable cultural relics and antiquities and created an unprecedented disaster for Chinese history.

In another sense, the antagonistic relationship among different classes was not the only connection between individuals during early historic times. Other social, political, and economic interactions also took place, and, under certain conditions, these relations also influenced the process of history. Even among the different classes, the interaction was not always opposed, but also interdependent and perhaps symbiotic. It is inappropriate to apply the contemporary "class struggle theory" of Mao Zedong to ancient society; to set laboring people against other social classes, especially against intellectuals; and to regard this perspective as the one correct guiding theory of Chinese archaeology.

According to Xia Nai, Chinese archaeology must sever connections with earlier historical studies, as well as with all relevant contemporary foreign studies. Only by so doing can Chinese archaeology "wipe out all the abominable influences of the distortion of history by bourgeois and other exploiting classes." This view, that Chinese archaeology should abrogate all historical traditions and world archaeological theory, was the basis for the "closed-door policy" carried out during this thirty-year period. Unfortunately, the implementation of this guiding principle created inestimable losses in Chinese archaeology.

Xia Nai's expressed goal for archaeology was "to serve the politics of the proletariat," or, in other words, to serve the policy of the Communist Party. In practice, this vulgarized archaeology, eradicating its objectivity and scientific character. Carried to its extreme, the absurdity of such goals was demonstrated by numerous events during the Cultural Revolution. These included: "Meeting for Recalling Past Suffering and Thinking over the Source of Present Happiness" as conducted at the excavation sites of ancient elite tombs;[5] "Using the Antiquities Stored in the Temple of Confucius in Qufu County to 'criticize Lin Biao[6] and Confucius'" (Pu Ren 1974); and "To Criticize the So-Called 'Theory of Innate Genius of Lin Biao' as Illustrated by the History of the Making of Stone Tools" (Du and Dong 1974). Such examples illustrate the disastrous effects of Xia Nai's directive.

II Nationalist issues in Chinese archaeology: external and internal debates

Archaeology is probably the science most associated in the minds of the Chinese people with cultural patriotism owing to its social and historical background. China is a country which values history and tradition and in which ancestor worship prevailed for an extended period. Antiquities inherited from former generations not only meant wealth, but also embodied political and ritual significance. For example, bronze *zhong* (bells) or *ding* (tripods) were regarded as "State Ritual Treasures" in ancient China, denoting the legitimacy of political authority and rule. According to Chinese ethics, if the descendants could not preserve the remains of their ancestors, their shame expanded to become the great misfortune of the state. In China, the collection of antiquities, practiced since the earliest dynastic periods by both the government and elite families, was probably associated with this tradition.

Beginning in the mid-nineteenth century, the escalating encroachment on Chinese territory by western imperialist countries created resentment among the Chinese toward certain foreign polities. As a result, a vast number of antiquities were stolen and smuggled out of the country and became the means of profit for unscrupulous dealers, and this looting damaged the self-respect of the Chinese people. Archaeology appeared as a new science in China shortly after the May Fourth Movement. This anti-imperialist, anti-feudal Movement broke out in 1919, while the first scientific archaeological excavations – at the Neolithic site at Yangshao village in Henan province – were undertaken in 1921. Consequently, the anti-imperialist sentiments of the May Fourth Movement strongly influenced Chinese archaeology from its very beginning (Xia Nai 1979b:193–6). Against this background, the sensitivity of Chinese archaeologists to issues of national identity and self-respect can be understood as both natural and correct.

Owing to certain objective and subjective causes, Mao Zedong implemented a comprehensive anti-Western policy after 1949. Hence, the already extant anti-imperialism of the Chinese was intentionally expanded and exaggerated, ultimately becoming total anti-foreignism. Unavoidably, Chinese archaeology was affected by this campaign. To some degree, it became colored by nationalism, and normal international academic exchange was seriously impeded.

To satisfy the needs of nationalism, certain Chinese archaeologists adopted a pragmatic attitude in their study. Although they never overtly discussed any western theory, in reality they usually adopted different approaches and viewpoints, according to particular problems. These included, for example, the two main theories of Western archaeology: indigenous evolutionism and cultural diffusionism. These theories were applied, along with the related concepts of monism and pluralism for the origin of culture and civilization, to two distinct topics: the interaction of Chinese cultures with non-Chinese societies (those exterior to China); and the relationships of cultures within China (interior). It must be understood that these two categories are delineated by China's modern political borders.

The external problem concerns all the ancient cultures within present-day Chinese territory and their relations with cultures beyond China's borders. In this respect, certain Chinese scholars emphasized the indigenous origin and the complete independent sequence of the development of Chinese culture. In a paper on the origin of civilization, An Zhimin (1987:455) said:

> Formerly some scholars had an opinion that the origin of world civilization was monistical. For example, the main advocator of diffusionism, Elliot Smith, took

Egypt as the single origin of world civilization. He held that all the accomplishments of human beings diffused from Egypt.

But, An continued:

along with the development of archaeology, pluralism prevailed . . . Although the standards for classifying centers of civilization vary according to different schools of thought, they all agree that human civilization arose in several loci. The cultures in these centers originated independently but, at the same time, influenced each other and thus gradually expanded the sphere of civilization.

China was one of these original centers. "At present, the fact that Chinese civilization developed independently is accepted by all academics." I quite agree with such an argument and wish to observe that this perspective is an example of multilinear evolutionism.

When we emphasize the independent origin and development of Chinese civilization, we should, however, consider another fact. Chinese civilization originated and developed within a larger world. External influences, especially from western and southern Asia, should be considered in the study of Chinese archaeology as well. During the thirty years reviewed here, however, the attitude of some Chinese archaeologists toward this interaction was not very objective. There was no serious discussion in China concerning the possibility of a foreign origin of some technologies, such as bronze casting and iron casting. If an opinion was expressed by foreign scholars regarding the possibility of external influence with respect to other cultural elements, some Chinese scholars reacted with indignation. They inevitably connected this kind of discussion with politics and made normal academic debate, which might have proven fruitful, impossible.

The most salient example of this aborted dialogue is the discussion of the origin of painted Neolithic pottery. Owing to the lack of comparative materials, the Swedish archaeologist J.G. Andersson in the 1920s suggested that the painted pottery of the Yangshao culture had diffused from the Anau culture of western Asia (Andersson 1923). In 1943, when more data had become available, Andersson corrected his error, and sincerely criticized his earlier interpretation:

It is not unfounded but rather disgraceful when we Europeans, working under a superiority bias that lacks proportion and perspective speak of "Herrenvölker" who brought a superior culture to China. Who are the Chinese? In four parts of the Old World, in Egypt, in Irak–Iran, in NW India and in China there arose at the dawn of the metal ages high cultures, the remains of which seem to us grand and marvelous. What has become of these ancient civilizations? In Egypt, in Mesopotamia, on the plateaus of Iran, in Punjab and Sind: desert, dust and oblivion. Only in China is there an unbroken succession of the same race, of the same culture starting with Yang Shao via Anyang up through the dynasties to the present day, the same race, virile, industrious and peace-loving. Several times the Chinese were subjugated by warrior-barbarians. But they always emerged again, through armed defense or peaceful penetration, in freedom and strength. Should we not approach their initial sites with caution and reverence? (1943:291)

This modest attitude with its high praise of ancient Chinese civilization clearly shows that Andersson's initial error stemmed from making a premature inference from insufficient data. This is a common phenomenon in scientific research and is pardonable, as long as the writer is willing to revise his theories when contradictory evidence comes to light. This Andersson did.

The criticism of Andersson by Chinese scholars began in 1937. In "The Analysis of the Longsham Culture and the Yangshao Culture," Yin Da (1955:118) wrote:

The emergence of new data can supplement or correct the existing cognition. This is a universal role of scientific development and archaeology is not an exception. Ten years ago Andersson first studied Chinese Neolithic culture and collected some materials. But due to the limitation of contemporary data, his inferences about the Yangshao and Qijia cultural sites were not exactly true.

This opinion constitutes normal scholarly criticism.

After 1949 Andersson still was regarded as an advocate of the "Western origin of Chinese culture," even though he had already altered his initial conclusion. The sharp criticism continued for decades. For example, in 1972, An Zhimin (p. 36) asserted:

The discovery of the Yangshao culture declared the bankruptcy of the fallacious theory that "China has no Stone Age." Some reactionary bourgeois scholars shifted the chronology of the Yangshao culture, vainly attempting to find new grounds for the reactionary theory of the "Western origin of Chinese culture." . . . In 1925, Andersson published his "six stage theory," placing the Yangshao culture in the late Neolithic or Chalcolithic age, and estimating its date as 3200–2900 BC. Later, he catalogued the Yangshao culture as late Neolithic, but still dated it as late as 2200–1700 BC.

It is difficult to justify this criticism on any grounds. Having checked many materials, I cannot find evidence showing that any serious Western archaeologist still proposes that "China has no Stone Age" in the twentieth century. The appellation of "reactionary bourgeois scholar" to Andersson represents entirely an example of political vitriol and should not be included in any academic discussion.[7]

In addition, some Chinese academic authorities reacted from political motives concerning the foreign scholars who believed that certain Chinese cultural elements may have originated elsewhere; consequently, their attitude was quite hostile. For example, there is an opinion that Chinese copper and bronze casting technology may have originated in western Asia. Considering that the earliest known copper and bronze metallurgy did emerge there (Xia Nai and Wang Zhongshu 1986:16), this argument must be considered, although it is not yet proven. Instead of serious discussion, Xia Nai (1979c:9–10), however, denounced it as the "clamor" of "the imperialists and the so-called archaeologists of the revisionist Soviet Union." L.S. Vasil'ev, an historian of the former Soviet Union, proposed that the conception of the zodiac was transmitted into China from the West in the Shang dynasty (Vasil'ev 1976). Xia Nai refuted this opinion. He concluded (1979c:50):

> we do not deny that influences existed between the cultures of different nations in ancient times. But the historian of the Soviet Union talks nonsense that the conception of the twenty-eight *su* [lunar lodges] in ancient China was borrowed from the Western zodiac. This is a vain attempt to renew the long-discredited theory of the alleged Western origin of Chinese civilization, to create anti-China public opinion by distorting the truth. Faced with the objective facts, this intention, fraught with ulterior motives, must meet disgraceful failure.

This kind of threat, which associated any concrete academic problem with the aggression of imperialism, was not intended to intimidate foreign scholars, since western academics were unlikely to yield to Chinese political coercion. For Chinese scholars, however, the inherent meaning of these sentences was powerful enough to make them treat these topics as taboo. I do not deny that in the foreign imperialistic abuse of China some foreign scholars played the role of accomplice. I also agree that some parts of certain foreign academic works denigrate Chinese culture or misrepresent Chinese history. In such cases, it is necessary for Chinese scholars to refute these distortions. But the refutations should be practical, realistic, and reasonable, not impetuous and invective, and this is exactly the distinction between real national self-respect and narrow nationalism.

Concerning the development of cultures "interior" to China, some Chinese scholars no longer adhere to the Marxist/Maoist dictated sequence of cultural development in different ecological regions within present-day Chinese territory; rather, they inordinately emphasize the importance of the cultures of the middle and lower Yellow River valley, the so-called "Central Plain Region" of Chinese history (for later trends, see Falkenhausen this volume). The developmental impetus for the cultures in other regions came from the Yellow River valley. An Zhimin (1984:936) argued: "As early as the prehistoric period, human activities, centering in the Yellow River valley, developed continuously. Especially the cultures flourishing in the Neolithic Age established the foundation of Chinese civilization." As for the relationships between Chinese cultures in other regions and the cultures in the Yellow River valley, An Zhimin (1979:403) asserted:

> Taking the Yellow River valley as the center of ancient Chinese culture, neither denies that there were ancient remains and long cultural traditions in other areas, nor does it contradict that they made positive contributions in the formation of the Chinese cultural assemblage. But in their developmental process they were influenced and propelled by the advanced cultures in the Yellow River valley. Thus the Yellow River valley always was the center of Chinese culture. After the emergence of the classes and the state, this was more prominent.

I concur that during the earliest three dynasties in China – the Xia, Shang, and Zhou dynasties – the center of Chinese civilization was the Yellow River valley. But in the prehistoric period, the situation may have been different. During the Palaeolithic period, for example, the earliest known fossils of *Homo erectus*, namely *Homo erectus yuanmouensis*, dated to 1.7 million years ago, were found in Yunnan province. At that early time, it is difficult to maintain that this local culture was influenced by the cultures in the Yellow River valley. During the Neolithic period, the regional cultures of the Yangtze River valley, such as the Hemudu culture (*c.* 5000 BC), the Majiabang culture (*c.* 4325–3230 BC), and the Liangzhu culture (*c.* 2800–1900 BC), in terms of their productive technologies, artistic inventions, and social institutions, were all comparable with that in the Yellow River valley. From these data we can see that two interacting yet distinguishable traditions developed simultaneously in the Yellow River and Yangtze River valleys. Each of these had its advantages and characteristics. We are unable to say which is the more advanced and which is the more backward, or which is central and which is peripheral. In the fourth edition of his *Archaeology of Ancient China*, K.C. Chang borrowed the term "interaction sphere" from North American archaeology to describe the relationships between all the late Neolithic regional cultures of China. He explained the reason for the adoption of this term (1986:242): "because this prehistoric sphere formed the spatial core of the historical China and because all the regional cultures must have played a part in forming the historical Chinese civilization that was unified under the Qin and Han dynasties." This objective analysis undoubtedly is correct.

The territory of modern China occupies almost the entire eastern part of the Asian continent. The area is vast and the geography is complex. From the sub-Arctic climate of the utmost north to the tropical climate of the south, the different ecological zones reflect great diversity. In ancient times, cultures developed in response to the ecological environment of their particular regions. According to the theory of evolutionism, these local cultures could have independently developed their own individual sequences. An Zhimin declared that only "the cultures flourishing in the Neolithic Age" in the Yellow River valley "established the foundation of Chinese civilization." The development of other regional cultures "was influenced and propelled by the advanced cultures in the Yellow River valley." In fact this assertion violates the principle of evolutionism, and reflects diffusionism and the belief in single cultural origins. Similar to evolutionism, diffusionism has many different schools, but, in general, this theory asserts that human culture only emerged from several distinct centers. Cultures in other regions were the products of diffusion from the main centers (Harris 1968:373–92). Why is it that in the prehistoric period the cultures in the Yangtze River valley paralleled those in the Yellow River valley, yet in the historic period the center of Chinese civilization was limited to the latter? This is a problem requiring further research and will not be addressed here, owing to limitations of space (see Tong 1994).

During the thirty years from 1949 to 1979, the political situation in China demanded the obedience of local, especially peripheral, regions to the political center Beijing, which is located on the Yellow River plain; emphasized the centralization of power; and stressed the cultural superiority of the Han people, the inhabitants of the Yellow River valley in ancient times. Considering that the goal of Chinese archaeology at this time was "to serve the politics of the proletariat," the opinions of An Zhimin should not be regarded as accidental.

The nationalism of some Chinese academic authorities is reflected not only in the underlying philosophy that guides their work, but in their refusal to cooperate with any Western scholar, including technological collaboration. During these thirty years, Western scholars could not obtain any supplementary data beyond the material published in the three national journals (namely *Kaogu*, *Wenwu*, and *Kaogu xuebao*); local journals were not available to foreigners. In addition, Western students who majored in Chinese archaeology and studied in Chinese universities could not participate in field work. This is common knowledge.

A typical case occurred in 1981 when Sichuan University contracted an agreement for a joint project with K.C. Chang of Harvard University, a project which was supported by the National Science Foundation of the United States. The aim of the project was to launch a long-term interdisciplinary research program focussing on a single geographic region or several regions in China and to study the beginnings and development of early agricultural communities. In the process of this cooperation, the Americans were to have established laboratories in China to carry out analytical work that could not be performed in existing laboratories in China. Chinese students and technicians would have been invited to the

United States for training in specific tasks. Because of a Chinese legal regulation at that time banning foreign nationals from archaeological field work, the Americans agreed not to participate physically in the excavations, and all recovered data would be Chinese property and remain in China. This was a project which would have opened a totally new field of archaeological research at that time and would have promoted the technology of Chinese archaeology. No matter what results were produced, it would, at least, not have harmed Chinese archaeology in any respect. Nevertheless, Xia Nai bitterly opposed this plan, and the project came to a premature end. In the process of his rejection, Xia Nai did not even read the proposal. His rejection was not based on the project itself, but on a dogmatic opposition to any cooperation with westerners in archaeology. He did not evaluate the project from a scientific aspect, but rather used his administrative power to prohibit it directly. This course of events typically demonstrates the paternalism of certain administrators of archaeology, and their exclusionary objectives.[8]

III The "Golden Age" of Chinese archaeology

In his papers, Xia Nai mentioned several times that the thirty years reviewed here could be considered "the Golden Age of Chinese archaeology." In 1984, under his direction, the Institute of Archaeology of the Academy of Social Science of China published an article entitled "The Golden Age of Chinese Archaeology" (Zhongguo Shehui Kexueyuan Kaogu Yanjiusuo 1984). As a Chinese archaeologist, I am elated and honored at every achievement of Chinese archaeology, and I also agree with the facts cited in this article. Even so, I have reservations regarding the designation of that period as a "Golden Age." From 1949 to 1979, the discoveries of Chinese archaeology are quite unprecedented, because large-scale industrial and agricultural construction projects provided the opportunities for the discoveries, and Chinese archaeologists diligently completed the work. Both in quality and in quantity, the archaeological finds in China attracted the attention of the world. For these reasons, it is accurate to characterize this period as the "Golden Age" of archaeological *discovery*.

Although discovery is an important component of archaeology, archaeological practice does not end there. In order to evaluate the total archaeological achievement of a certain country during a certain period, the following three fields should be considered in addition to noting new finds: the scientific nature of the guiding theory; the creativity of the study; and the advancement of research facilities and methodology. I maintain that during this thirty-year period deficiencies in these three areas undermined some of the acclaim attached to the material discoveries. Problems plagued development in all these areas.

Mention already has been made of the profound negative influence of the unilineal evolutionary theory and the class struggle concept of Mao Zedong on Chinese archaeology. Until now, many Chinese archaeologists still avoid discussing theoretical problems, let alone developing new theories. And yet the guiding theory of Chinese archaeology, as described by Xia Nai, was not as scientific as he suggested. This rigid and sterile theory inevitably hindered research. During these thirty years, the work of most Chinese archaeologists was confined to the materials themselves and concerned with such goals as dating, definition, and the determination of function. Of course, all of these aspects are important and are the basis for further archaeological study. As Xia Nai (1979b:196) correctly suggested, "we should not study only artefacts, but also the natural environment. We must study ancient social, economic, and cultural institutions through archaeological data in order to discover the laws of the development of human society." It can be seen from the archaeological practice at that time, however, that some Chinese research was merely formulaic and dealt in generalities.

In fact, in a country such as China, with its vast land, various ethnic groups, and diversity of social types, researchers, if they managed to liberate their thinking and free themselves from Morgan's models, could use the abundant new unearthed materials to obtain more reliable and colorful conclusions about the ancient societies of the different peoples inhabiting the disparate ecological regions.

Regarding field work, the lack of a concrete guiding theory and valid, testable scientific hypotheses meant that the excavation schedules, the selection of materials, and the types of record keeping all followed a fixed pattern. Many valuable phenomena were ignored. Some research data were totally discarded, especially materials concerning the natural environment, such as floral and faunal remains, as well as other materials not considered to be cultural relics. It is helpful to review a passage written by Yin Da (1963:580–1) in the 1960s:

> Recently I participated in the work of editing a Chinese history. The first issue is the primitive society. Among many problems, the most embarrassing and most difficult one is the tribal system. We have checked all the available archaeological reports and papers, trying to reconstruct the framework of Chinese tribal society, but we met with great difficulty even at the beginning. A great deal of information was stereotyped, limited to a few simple, fragmentary artefacts, or obscure remains, which provided no scientific evidence. I hope that in the future field archaeologists will consider this problem seriously: how can we gather archaeological materials which might reflect the society of a certain culture more completely and systematically?

The problem Yin Da raised here is not technological, but theoretical. No serviceable guiding theory existed then to direct archaeological work. Has the situation since improved? This is a question we Chinese archaeologists must honestly consider.

In general, there was little improvement during this thirty-year period in terms of research facilities, tools, and methodology. Techniques and implements used in field work virtually stagnated at the level of the early 1950s, as taught by Xia Nai and others in the various Archaeological Study Courses conducted at that time. These reflected the field methods of Western archaeology in the 1930s. Xia Nai mentioned many new technologies in his paper "Thirty Years of Chinese Archaeology," but the majority of them were not popularized. Except for a few institutions in Beijing, all the local archaeological teams remained very backward in terms of their excavation techniques, digging tools, laboratory equipment, and restoration and storage methods. Even relatively low-cost procedures, such as flotation or computer data processing and analysis could not be popularized, owing to the ignorance of the administrators. The need for technological improvements in Chinese archaeology is nearly critical for a great country with so many antiquities from her glorious past civilizations.

A necessary role of research should be to report newly unearthed archaeological materials completely and expeditiously. But for several objective reasons, Chinese archaeologists frequently cannot do that. Each Chinese province is approximately equal to a large European country either in area or in population. Yet, during this thirty-year period, only a few archaeologists – ranging from two or three to no more than a dozen – in each provincial museum were qualified to conduct excavations and write reports. In 1957, Guo Moruo (1957:2) pointed out: "Archaeological materials were unearthed so rapidly and in such quantity that the work of processing and analysis could not keep pace. This is a serious problem." In addition, during these thirty years, successive political campaigns occupied most of the working time of archaeologists, who were already seriously short-handed. This circumstance too produced grave consequences: the vast amount of data was not quickly processed; or only a brief description was provided, lacking precise details. Unearthed materials were packed away in store rooms year after year. As time passed, labels became mixed, and original records were lost. From the scientific perspective, much important data was eventually reduced to indecipherable rubbish. As far as I am aware, this phenomenon was common in almost every Chinese museum.

During these thirty years, the archaeological finds in China were really quite amazing. But even dealing just with these discoveries, it is necessary to adopt a more modest attitude. As Xia Nai (1979a:392) correctly noted:

if the unearthed artefacts are national treasures, they are an inheritance from our ancestors. That was the contribution of the ancient Chinese. But in the process of excavation, if we do not work meticulously, observe carefully, and record scientifically, then excavation can become a destructive activity.

In fact, many important archaeological discoveries in China, including the Han tomb number 1 of Mawangdui and the terracotta warriors of the First Emperor, which astounded the whole world, were not carried out by professionals, but by the common people. They were not the result of scholarly scientific projects. Hence, when we evaluate the accomplishments of Chinese archaeology, we should distinguish the materials themselves from the quality of the excavations and research. The former was the invention of our ancestors, and the latter is the true reflection of our current level of scholarship. Thanks to the ancestors of the Chinese, China enjoys exceptional advantages, possessing exquisite and abundant underground treasures. If the minds of Chinese archaeologists were not shackled, if they could get equipment at least commensurate with the level of China's scientific position as a whole, and if they could be permitted to cooperate with foreign academics, in order to exploit technological opportunities not currently available in China – then it is possible to imagine that Chinese archaeology could advance rapidly to a higher level.

To use the words of the Chinese, the "Great Cultural Revolution" was "a great revolt against culture." During these tumultuous ten years, the destruction of the "Four Olds" was carefully planned and organized. The thoroughness of this campaign is revealed by the fact that almost every concerned household was searched. Thus, not only the monuments and relics on the ground were seriously damaged, but private antiquarian collections were almost entirely destroyed. Our national cultural treasures never sustained such heavy losses during the five-thousand-year history of Chinese civilization, including periods of foreign invasion or civil strife. This unspeakable waste cannot be expressed by such empty statements as "the development of archaeology [in this period] inevitably met great obstruction" (Institute of Archaeology 1984:866). Conscientious Chinese archaeologists should seriously review this historical period, collect detailed statistics, and publish the consequences of that "revolution." Only by so doing can we account for this to our ancestors and descendants.

In fact, the destruction of cultural relics and antiquities and the persecution of archaeologists has not been limited merely to the "Cultural Revolution." In former campaigns, such as "Land Reform" and "Anti-Corruption," Chinese private antiquarian collections suffered many losses. This is even acknowledged by Guo Moruo (1957:2) who admitted that "In the process of a great revolutionary campaign like Land Reform, how could antiquities and ancient books not be damaged!" Although some misfortunes are inevitable during periods of great social turbulence, the records of the events themselves should not be erased. In the 1950s, there were only a few formally trained and accomplished archaeologists in China. But in the "Anti-Rightists Campaign," some of them were incriminated as "Rightists" and suffered cruel persecution. Internationally famous scholars, such as Chen Mengjia and Zeng Zhaoyu, committed suicide. That such tragedies happened in this "Golden Age" should not be forgotten by later generations.

IV Conclusion

Since the Third Plenary Session of the Eleventh Central Committee of the Chinese Communist Party, the sensible leaders of China raised the slogans of "Bring Order out of Chaos" and "Reform and Opening," and declared the principle that "practice is the one single standard for the examination of truth." The late general secretary Hu Yaobang (1982:38) incisively observed:

> The Cultural Revolution and the "leftist" errors committed prior to it exerted profound influence and caused serious harm. In the process of denouncing and criticizing two of the counterrevolutionary groups – those respectively headed by Jiang Qin and Ling Biao – we must eradicate all the errors of the Cultural Revolution and the errors of the "leftist" trend prior to it.

Responding to his call, Chinese academia, including the branches of history, philosophy, economics, law, literature, and religion, reviewed the damage caused by the "leftist" trend and dogmatism of the past thirty years. Many honest scholars repeatedly appealed for the elimination of "leftist" interference and fought for academic freedom. While this course is long and indirect, the struggle for the freedom and purity of science is just unfolding. Strangely enough, in this national renaissance, some academic authorities of Chinese archaeology consistently remain aloof from this movement. For example, in many of his papers and articles that summarized Chinese archaeology during this period, Xia Nai always emphasized the achievements of Chinese archaeology, stressing the so-called "Golden Age," while exempting the Cultural Revolution.[9] He neither mentioned the detrimental policies of the Communist Party, even those recognized by current Party leaders, nor admitted that some shortcomings and problems still plagued Chinese archaeology. This approach, which isolated archaeology from the social and political milieu and used some facts while concealing others, clearly is neither practical nor realistic.

Although I have suggested some shortcomings and problems of Chinese archaeology during this thirty-year period, I do not intend to deny the great achievements cited at the beginning of this paper. If some events and persons are criticized, the one censured first is the author himself. As a practicing Chinese archaeologist, I admit that the work I conducted and the papers I wrote then were inevitably colored by the political climate of the time. While mentioning some deficiencies, I must emphasize my great respect for the many archaeologists who choose to devote their lives to field work. Their pay is low and the working conditions bad. Their arduous, never-ending labor is the true basis from which the achievements of Chinese archaeology derive. Hu Yaobang (1982:38) said:

> Due to the influence of the "leftists" and the thoughts of small-scale producers, for a long period of time there has been a pervasive, erroneous view held by many members of our Party, despising education, science, and culture and discriminating against intellectuals. It seriously obstructs the construction of the spiritual and material civilization in our country.

Had the Chinese Communist Party valued and protected archaeologists during the past years – even if not providing them with better working conditions, at least subjecting them to fewer political campaigns and allowing them more time for productive work – then their achievements would have far surpassed their current level. In the process of summarizing the history of Chinese archaeology of this period, Xia Nai did not demand any changes in policy by the ruling party towards his science. He did not ask that existing conditions be improved, that archaeologists be better rewarded, or that a more tolerant academic atmosphere be created, but rather required that Chinese archaeologists "must have the spirit of devotion" (1985:481–4). This biased exhortation is both unfair and unjustified.

This paper cites many opinions of Xia Nai and expresses several viewpoints different from his. The reason for these repeated references to Xia Nai is that, during the time period under discussion, he was the highest administrator of Chinese archaeology. The influence of his words and actions was profound and pervasive on Chinese archaeologists. As the most famous archaeologist in China, his academic achievements are known by everyone. But no man in this world is perfect. As a Chinese intellectual who held such a high post in a political sphere that sought to control absolutely the thoughts not only of the common people, but also of government officials themselves, he had to adapt himself to the specific political climate, perhaps, at some times, even going so far as to cater expediently to these circumstances. While Xia Nai was an outstanding scholar, he was at the same time an activist in the Anti-Rightist Campaign in 1957 and "joined the Communist Party at the battlefront" in 1959 at "the high tide of class struggle." His authority derived mainly from the authority of the Party; his leadership in archaeology was the concretized leadership of the Party. As such, it is inconceivable that he was never affected by "leftist" trends, never enacted "leftist" policies, or never catered to "leftist" intentions. It should be recognized that his actions were not always correct and free from political intent. In recording history, we must attempt to be objective. It is not necessary to conceal the truth in order to save the dignity of the respected elders.

NOTES

1 The author wishes to thank Penny Rode for her assistance in the composition of the English version of this paper.
2 These slogans occur in a number of articles written by Xia Nai during the 1950s (Xia Nai 1955, 1957a, 1957b, 1957c, 1958). Significantly, these articles are omitted from Xia Nai's official bibliography, which is attached to Wang Zhongshu's biography of Xia Nai (Wang Zhongshu 1986:13–24).
3 Jiang Qing was the wife of Mao Zedong. Kang Sheng and Chen Boda were Mao's assistants for ideological control.
4 Guo Moruo was the late President of the Chinese Academy of Sciences.
5 See Zhongguo Renmin Jiefangjun Moubu 1972.
6 In the late 1960s Lin Biao was the legal successor of Mao Zedong. In 1971 he fell out of favor and mysteriously died in Mongolia.
7 As a matter of fact, until the 1980s, some academic administrators in China still manufactured certain imaginary enemies, then seriously denounced them. For instance, at a meeting held in 1982 for the discussion of the proposed programs of Chinese social science, Ma Hong, the former president of the Academy of Social Science of China, gave a lecture. He said (Ma 1984:15):

> compared with the other social sciences, archaeology does not seem closely connected with current practices. But in reality this is not true. For example, regarding the origin of Chinese culture and civilization, some foreign scholars are still talking endlessly. They chatter that Chinese culture and civilization perhaps came from the west, the north, or the south. Their "western origin theory," "northern origin theory," or "southern origin theory" are all nonsense with ulterior motives.

As far as I know, in the past half-century some foreign scholars do advocate that one or several cultural elements diffused to ancient China from the outside, but no scholar holds that all Chinese culture or civilization came from another place. Using an "imaginary enemy" to spur the political militancy of Chinese archaeology, in fact, deceives Chinese archaeologists.
8 Details regarding this event will be forthcoming in a future publication.
9 Even during the Cultural Revolution, Xia Nai himself was not much affected by this evil storm. Beginning with 1970, when universities and scientific institutions were still closed, and the majority of intellectuals were imprisoned in "cowsheds" or sent to the countryside for re-education, he was personally appointed by Prime Minister Zhou Enlai to receive foreign guests and to visit Albania, Mexico, and Peru, carrying out "Chairman Mao's revolutionary line in foreign affairs" (see

Xia Nai 1977). Consequently, Xia Nai did not endure the personal suffering of so many intellectuals of the period, nor did he share their hatred and resentment of the Leftist regime that persecuted them.

12 The regionalist paradigm in Chinese archaeology

Lothar von Falkenhausen

A nationalist interpretive framework, emphasizing the antiquity, uniqueness, purity, and importance of Chinese civilization, is so basic to the pursuit of history and archaeology in China that it would seem a moot exercise to expound on it.[1] If our objective is to lie in sounding out the intellectual atmosphere of present-day Chinese archaeological practice, it may be more relevant, as well as more interesting, to explore how subtle inter-regional tensions within the country have lately been symbolically played out through the public presentation of archaeological data. This is the main task of this chapter.[2] We shall, however, never veer far from the topic of nationalism in archaeology; understanding the new regionalist paradigm in Chinese archaeology may indeed help us to perceive in more general terms how nationalism has come to be culturally reconfigured in China during the eighties and early nineties.

I New frameworks of interpretation

During the last decade, the study of prehistoric and early historical archaeology in China has undergone a change of paradigm. Until the late seventies, all of Chinese civilization had been perceived as originating from a narrowly circumscribed area along the middle reaches of the Yellow River, from where it gradually spread outward. This mononuclear model has now given way to a geographically much more broadly based interpretation of Chinese cultural origins, in which early developments in virtually all of China proper (excluding border areas still inhabited by minority populations) are seen as interlinked and are collectively taken as ancestral to the dynastic civilization of China.

The Western public has been able to follow the emergence of this new interpretative scheme through the four editions of K.C. Chang's *Archaeology of Ancient China*, which has been, over three decades, the best synthesis of Chinese archaeology available in any language. The first edition (Chang 1963) held that agriculture in China started in a "Nuclear Area" at the confluence of the Wei, Fen, and Yellow Rivers, and drew a straight line from there to the rise of complex society and dynastic civilization. This centralistic evolutionary model persists, albeit in ever-attenuated form, in the second and third editions (Chang 1968 and 1977). It was abandoned in the most recent, fourth, edition (Chang 1986). Here the author gives equal treatment to early agricultural remains in a number of different regions throughout northern and southern China. To explain the rise of complex society, Chang introduces the concept of a "Chinese Interaction Sphere." He describes how "in both north and south China . . . beginning around 4000 BC the several regional cultures, which had indigenous origins and distinctive styles, became interlinked in a larger sphere of interaction" (Chang 1986:241). "By this time we see why these cultures are described together: not just because they are located within the borders of the present-day China, but because they were the initial China" (p. 234). Though primarily devised to account for developments in late prehistoric China, such a view of the cultural historical process as emanating from an intercommunicative network of coevolving regional traditions can also be fruitfully applied to the subsequent "Three Dynasties" of the Chinese Bronze Age.

In China, even as recently as the beginning of the 1980s, such a view of the past still had an aura of heterodoxy. At the time it was associated mostly with Su Bingqi and his students (e.g. Su Bingqi 1983:225–34 *et passim*; Yu Weichao 1985). In recent years, however, the new model of interpretation has found wide acceptance in the archaeological community, even though there are still some conservative holdouts. Its adoption was triggered, first and foremost, by important discoveries in various provinces which, as they multiplied over the last two decades, became more and more difficult to accommodate into the earlier mononuclear framework. Yet one may doubt that the mere realization that a regional-developmental model fits the evidence better than a centralistic one would have sufficed to bring about the fundamental reorientation of scholarship that has been underway. It is my contention, instead, that this development may have been decisively conditioned by changes in the ideological and administrative structures in which archaeologists have been doing their work. Just as the earlier mononuclear model of cultural development, derived from a millennia-long tradition of dynastic historiography stressing the unity of the realm (Pulleyblank 1964), was in many essential respects the necessary outgrowth of the exaggerated bureaucratic centralism of the Maoist era, the idea of an "interaction sphere" symbolically embodies the decreased degree of political control by the center in the wake of Deng Xiaoping's economic reforms.

Rather than enforcing a cultural hierarchy in which the "cradle" of dynastic civilization in parts of Henan and Shaanxi took precedence over all other areas, the new model empowers the outlying provinces.[3] It has the distinct political advantage of acknowledging that various parts of China all played a role in laying what Chang calls the "foundation of civilization" in this part of the world. In this way, a much larger part of the country than before is legitimized as ancestral to the cultural mainstream and to the textbook accounts of Chinese history. Instead of coercing unity from the center, regionalism encourages voluntary integration. In the political culture of China; where over many centuries the past has been used to provide a normative projection of the present, this is neither accidental nor unimportant. With due caution, the new view of the past may be viewed as a more "pluralistic," even a more "democratic" one – two adjectives liberally used by foreign journalists with reference to China during the time preceding the events of June 1989.

II Recent administrative reorganization

If we are to understand the implications of the new regionalism in Chinese archaeology, we must take cognizance, first of all, of recent infrastructural changes in the organization of archaeological work in China. From the early fifties through the late seventies, almost all important field research in the country was undertaken under the auspices of Beijing-based institutions, among which the Institute of Archaeology (Kaogu Yanjiusuo) of the Chinese Academy of Social Sciences (Zhongguo Shehuikexueyuan)[4] has traditionally occupied the paramount position. The provincial museums, which had their own archaeological teams, would participate in such ventures, but were rarely capable of mounting major excavation projects on their own. These provincial institutions, placed under the central administration of the State Bureau of Cultural Relics (Guojia Wenwuju) in the Ministry of Culture (Wenhuabu), were mainly charged with the local storage of archaeological relics and the preservation of ancient monuments and sites.

This has changed. Gradually, since *c.* 1979, the provincial archaeological teams have been separated from their respective museums, becoming fully fledged provincial archaeological institutes.[5] As of 1990, this had been accomplished in every province except for Tibet. The new provincial institutes, most of which are named "Institutes of Cultural Relics and Archaeology" (Wenwu Kaogu Yanjiusuo),[6] have, in principle, become the only work units (*danwei*) in their respective provinces authorized to undertake archaeological excavations;[7] national-level units now have to obtain excavation permits through them. While the activities of both the provincial museums and the provincial archaeological institutes continue to be coordinated and, in part, funded by the State Bureau of Cultural

Relics in Beijing, most crucial decisions bearing on the work of these institutions are being made at the provincial level.

Within their respective provinces, the newly founded Institutes are in charge of the salvage excavation projects mandated by law in conjunction with public works, which provide a lucrative source of revenue. As money centrally administered through the Bureau of Cultural Relics has recently become extremely scarce, salvage excavations have become the major opportunity for field work in China. Universities and Beijing-based research institutions, if they are to partake of these resources, have to go through the provincial institutes, which, as a result, have lately become the major players in Chinese field archaeology.

As a consequence of the new regionalized administration, field archaeologists employed in the provinces have risen in status. Their newly gained independence from the museums has heightened their institutional prestige, giving them more direct access to the authorities, the ability to dispose of their own funds, and the opportunity to concentrate on field work without the need to consider museum priorities. All this has certainly had a positive influence on the quality of archaeological work at the provincial level. Professionalism and solidarity among provincial field workers have additionally been fostered by the establishment of new regional networks of formal and informal intellectual exchange. New professional associations of archaeologists have been sponsored by some provincial institutes, imitating, on a regional level, the nationwide Association for Chinese Archaeology (Zhongguo Kaoguxuehui). There are also semi-official organizations for the study of local cultures (e.g., the Society for Chu Studies), which operate under local auspices without an explicit mandate from Beijing – a development that would have been unthinkable only a few years ago. These societies have held many conferences, to which, in contrast with the exclusive attitude of the Association for Chinese Archaeology, they are often keen on inviting foreign participants, both as a means of boosting their prestige and as sources of financial support (*via* special foreigners' registration fees, to be paid in foreign currency). Undoubtedly, such activities are enriching and enlivening the study of ancient China, as well as attracting international interest to regionalist modes of interpretation.

Perhaps the most important new vehicle of communication at the local level are new specialized periodicals. Until the late seventies, archaeological publication had been virtually monopolized by the "three great journals" published in Beijing: *Wenwu* ("Cultural Relics"), *Kaogu* ("Archaeology"), and *Kaogu Xuebao* (*Acta Archaeologica Sinica*). Recently, however, provincial museums and the newly independent provincial archaeological institutes have taken to publishing their own journals, and there now exists at least one for every province, except for Gansu and Tibet;[8] a number of similar publications have started to appear even at a sub-provincial level. These journals are an important source for probing the intellectual dimensions of the regionalist paradigm.

I will, hereafter, define and contextualize some tendencies in recent Chinese archaeological thought that stem from the new regionalist modes of interpretation. My remarks are informed by extensive readings in the regional archaeological journals (many of which are unavailable in the West) during my 1990–1 sojourn at the Institute of Archaeology in Beijing.[9] It is hard to generalize about these publications as they greatly differ from one another in their standards of editing; but they often tend to mix archaeological reports and research articles of genuine scholarly interest with quirky, idiosyncratic, and sometimes far-out pieces of work that would have no chance of being published elsewhere. Items of the latter sort can often highlight some inherent dangers and absurdities of regionalist interpretations, as well as the political uses to which they may be put. They remind us that products of modern-day scholarship – even in archaeology, a discipline regarded by many outsiders as one of the driest fields of academe – must be taken as historical documents conditioned by contemporary ideological and socio-economic pressures.[10]

III Official provincial sequences and cultures

Many articles recently published in the regional journals concentrate on cultural phenomena within their provinces, stressing those features that distinguish them from neighboring provinces. Much energy is being expended, for instance, on establishing which archaeologically recognizable cultural traits in a given locality are homegrown, as opposed to those that may have been diffused from elsewhere; here, local scholars predictably tend to emphasize the autochthonous element. Specialized studies on such topics, as well as a flurry of new regional syntheses (such as Zheng Shaozong 1989 on Hebei; An Jinhuai 1990, Cai Jinfa 1990, Hu and Song 1990, and Yang Chaoqing 1990 on Henan; Peng Shifan 1987 on Jiangxi; Zhang Xuehai 1989 on Shandong; Wang Kelin 1986 on Shanxi; and those assembled by the State Bureau of Cultural Relics in Beijing 1991a), have opened up valuable new perspectives on Chinese archaeology.

Ironically, however, these new studies often perpetrate a tendency toward a new regionalist form of centralism: for one of the priorities of provincial archaeologists appears to lie in constructing cultural master sequences specific for each province. Imposed on finds from the entire province, these provincial-level schemes are just as unilinear as the former nationwide mononuclear model; finds from areas outside the jurisdiction of that province's archaeological authorities are, if at all possible, excluded from their definition.

Since the areas occupied by ancient cultures and ethnic groups cannot necessarily be expected to have coincided with the political subdivisions of post-1949 China, such province-based master sequences create confusing distortions. It is even more unrealistic to suppose that, within a geographically unified area such as China proper, separate provincial cultures could have arisen and flourished in isolation from one another. The provincial sequences, furthermore, tend to suggest a false sense of continuity when there may well have been shifts in the location of centers, which in turn would have been reflected in the geographical alignment of cultures. Further complications are created by the pervasive and indiscriminate superimposition of ancient ethnonyms onto archaeological remains. Let me illustrate this state of affairs by some examples.

In prehistoric archaeology, for instance, one often has the impression that twentieth-century political geography plays an important role in determining the nomenclature of Neolithic cultures. One well-known instance is the use of the terms Dawenkou and Qinglian'gang for the same middle Neolithic culture, which occupied most of Shandong and northern Jiangsu provinces. Field workers in Jiangsu, where the culture was first identified in the fifties, have always referred to it by the site of Qinglian'gang in their province, but archaeologists in Shandong (as well as their colleagues from Beijing institutions) consider the Shandong site of Dawenkou as the type-site. To those who have to rely on published reports, this is highly confusing.[11] Neither side claims a difference in substance between the two cultures, but settling on a unified nomenclature continues to be impossible for reasons of regional prestige.

Similar, but somewhat more complex problems have beset the study of regional cultures of the Bronze Age, a field in which the recent break with earlier scholarly habits has been especially marked. For prehistoric archaeology, even the old, centralist model had allowed for a certain amount of heterogeneity, while the early historical periods had to be accommodated in the standard, unilinear historical sequence. Now, by contrast, archaeologists no longer hesitate to dwell on archaeological remains that have no parallel with the centers of Shang and Zhou civilization. While the old shibboleth of the local cultures' "close relationship" with the dynastic courts in the Yellow River basin is still being invoked at times, this is sometimes done for regionalist motives (see below).

On the northern edge of the geographical extent of the Chinese Bronze Age, for instance, new materials permit us to point out, at Shang sites of Hebei province, connections to cultures in the Chinese northeast and beyond – features that distinguish the Hebei remains from the contemporary Shang capitals in central Henan; this has been shown in a series of thoroughly researched articles by Tang Yunming (1987, 1988a, 1988b). Bronze Age phenomena in south China that had not previously received their fair share of attention include, in the time contemporary with the Shang, the Sanxingdui culture of Sichuan (Chengdu 1989; for an introduction in English, see Bagley 1988) and the Wucheng culture of Jiangxi (see Beijing 1975 and 1991b; Bagley 1992); and, in a somewhat later period, the mounded tombs (*tudunmu*) and the patterned hard-fired pottery of the lower Yangtze River system (Song Yongxiang 1986; Yang Debiao 1988; Xuanzhou 1988; Chen Yuanfu 1991), and the Wuyishan boat burials in northern Fujian (Fuzhou 1980, 1991). How to conceptualize these local cultures, however, as well as the differences between them, continues to create difficulties.

Archaeologists working on the Bronze Age in South China, for instance, while not denying the significant cultural impact on the region of the dynastic civilization in the Yellow River basin, have recently shifted their assessment of the incoming northern traits; the latter are no longer regarded *a priori* as evidence of northern conquest or immigration, but as acting upon preexisting local populations in a variety of ways. In this connection, the stylistic differences, previously often disregarded, between regionally produced ritual bronzes and those imported from the dynastic centers have come into focus.[12] For instance, in an article on bronzes from southeast China, Peng Shifan (1988) points out that a great deal of northern influence is visible at an early stage, contrasting with ever-decreasing similarity later on; he deftly proceeds to argue, citing Marx, that this development toward stylistic independence testifies to an awakening revolutionary spirit of the oppressed masses in the south, who rose up at some point against cultural domination by alien ethnic groups in the north. Despite the strident formulation (and the obvious contemporary subtext), such a view of cultural dynamics in terms of inter-ethnic conflict and cultural assertion is not without interest (for more cautious formulations, see Bagley 1992).

In itself, the shift in emphasis to the local populations constitutes a promising new departure; but, owing not least to the agenda of the regionalist centralism mentioned above, the quest to identify – and identify with – these ancient local populations has led to considerable fantasizing. Ancient states and ethnic groups that are documented in early texts have come to be used as convenient tags for symbolic reference, with the result that, in a number of provinces, archaeologists have virtually equated the ancient history of the region with the name of one such nationality. A non-exhaustive list of such officially privileged ancient populations includes the Eastern Yi in Shandong, Jin in Shanxi, Chu in Hubei, Wu in

Jiangsu, Yue in Zhejiang, Min (or Min Yue) in Fujian, Luo Yue in Guangxi, Ba and Shu in Sichuan (often fused into a single "Ba-Shu" nation, perhaps so as to do justice to the present-day unification of the territory), and Dian in Yunnan (Map 3). Bronze Age archaeological cultures, initially defined on the basis of their material characteristics, have, in the process, been associated with ancient ethnonyms; e.g., the above-mentioned Sanxingdui culture with Shu and the Wucheng culture and the later cultures of southeastern China with Yue.

The identification of ethnic groups on the basis of their material remains is a legitimate archaeological concern, though it is not an easy matter because of complexities inherent in the very concept of ethnic identity. This issue and its theoretical ramifications have been well presented with respect to the Yue in south China by Heather Peters (1990 and forthcoming). However reasonable it may sometimes appear it simply cannot be assumed *sans phrase* that an archaeological culture defined on the basis of its material remains reflects a distinct ethnic unit. In any case, such identifications must be clearly lodged in time and space, and, to be fully convincing, they should be linked to specific evidence from inscriptions and/or the classical texts (see Tong 1982). Identifications of this sort have proved possible in some restricted areas for limited time periods, for the most part toward the end of the Bronze Age.

Recent writers promoting a regionalist agenda, on the other hand, appear to have engaged in a quite different process of reasoning. On the basis of a superficial interpretation of textual sources, they begin by assuming that archaeological remains in a particular province are identical to a certain ancient state or ethnic group; from here they proceed to a mechanical definition of all finds in the province as the archaeological "culture" of that group. Little concern is typically given to whether the finds thus jumbled together actually constitute a coherent complex of material traits co-occurring regularly over a certain area, or whether they differ systematically from phenomena in areas outside the administrative boundaries of the province. Some articles published in the provincial journals go to absurd lengths in their quest to substantiate the homology of one nationality with a certain province and to deny other provinces a claim to that nationality. Ji Zhongqing (1982), for instance, exclusively lodges the state of Wu in Jiangsu, explaining that Wu only later and temporarily occupied adjoining areas now belonging to other provinces.

This is problematic for a variety of reasons. The identification of everything in a province as connected with one particular pet nationality often results in the quite unwarranted marginalization of other cultural, ethnic, or political entities located in that province that do not have the good fortune of being situated in the vicinity of the present-day political

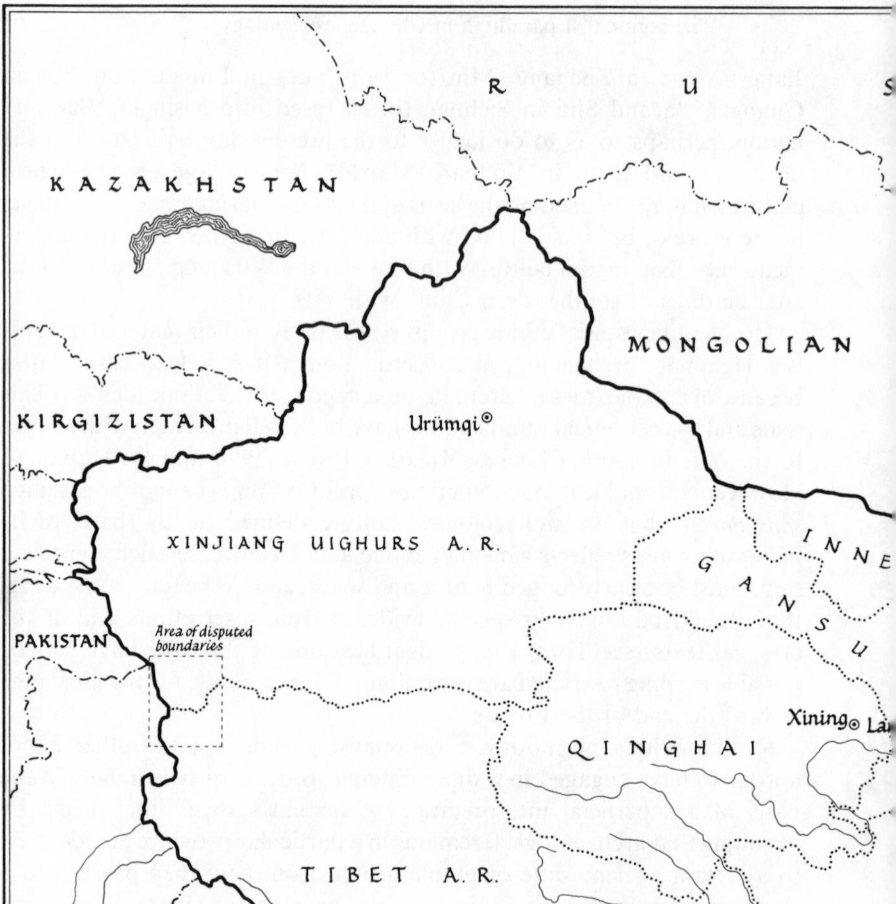

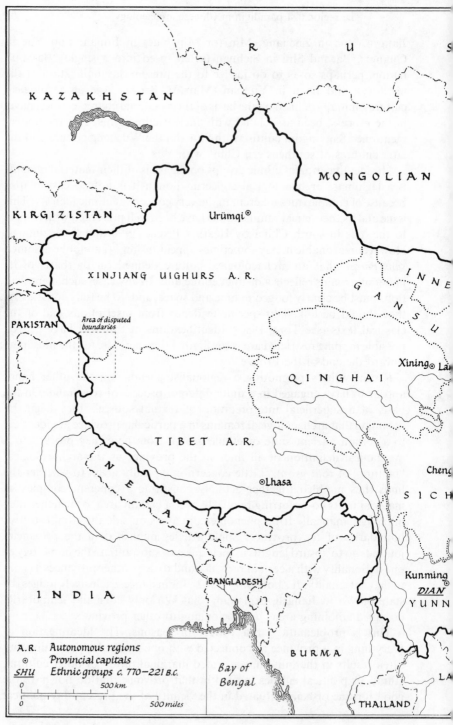

3 China's administrative divisions, showing major states and ethnic groups of the Eastern Zhou period (*c.* 770–221 BC)

S I A
PUBLIC
HEILONGJIANG
Harbin
JILIN
Changchun
Shenyang
LIAONING
NORTH KOREA
Sea of Japan
ONGOLIA A.R.
Hohhot
BEIJING
TIANJIN
Bo Hai
HEBEI
Shijiazhuang
Yinchuan
Taiyuan
SHANXI
Huang-he
Jinan
EASTERN YI
SHANDONG
SOUTH KOREA
JAPAN
Huang Hai
JIN
QIN
Xi'an
ZHOU
SHAANXI
Zhengzhou
HENAN
JIANGSU
WU
ANHUI
Nanjing
SHANGHAI
Hefei
East China Sea
CHU
HUBEI
Wuhan
YUE
Hangzhou
Chang Jiang
BA
ZHEJIANG
Nanchang
Changsha
HUNAN
JIANGXI
MIN
YUE
Fuzhou
UIZHOU
Guiyang
FUJIAN
Taibei
TAIWAN
GUANGXI-ZHUANG A.R.
GUANGDONG
Guangzhou
Xi Jiang
LUO
YUE
Nanning
HONG KONG (Br. occ.)
Macao (Port. occ.)
TNAM
South China Sea
HAINAN
CHINA
Guangzhou
South China Sea
The South China Sea Islands

centers. Particularly objectionable, moreover, is the tendency, in many articles, to go beyond the time frame of available textual documentation and to equate prehistoric remains with the historical ancient nationalities. The above-mentioned identification of the mid- to late second-millennium BC Sanxingdui culture in Sichuan with the Shu nationality is a typical example. Even though the Shu kingdom did flourish in the same geographical area, it did not arise until sometime after 700 BC; and the archaeological record for the half-millennium separating Shu from the much earlier Sanxingdui Bronze Age is still unclear. In a fascinating article, Sun Hua (1990) attempts to establish the cultural continuity between the two, based on hypothetical reconstructions of ancient clans, totemistic interpretations of art motifs, and highly speculative extrapolations from much later texts. Ultimately, this sort of reasoning remains unsatisfactory, as well as suspicious. The fact remains that the archaeological record shows few if any significant similarities between the Sanxingdui culture and the remains of the Shu kingdom. The use of the label "Shu" (or even "proto-Shu") in connection with the latter seems to stem primarily from the will to create a coherent and unilinear master-sequence. In some provinces, even Neolithic materials are similarly identified with ethnic groups from the classical texts.

IV An example: the "Jin culture" of Shanxi

Let us briefly examine one prominent instance of how an ancient ethnonym has been turned into a catch-all category of identification for all archaeological finds from one province: the case of Jin in Shanxi province. The concept of a "Jin culture," which has come to permeate the regional journal of Shanxi province, *Wenwu Jikan* (formerly *Shanxi Wenwu*), was launched in a major way in 1985 at a conference held at Houma, introducing archaeologists from all over the country, including leading figures from institutions in Beijing (no foreigners), to the results of excavation and surveys that had been undertaken near the historical centers of the Jin state since the late fifties. The volume of proceedings from this conference (Taiyuan 1986) is an interesting document. In his concluding address, Wang Kelin, then the director of the Shanxi Provincial Institute for Cultural Relics and Archaeology, traced the history of the ancient nation of Jin over almost ten thousand years through a continuous Shanxi-based archaeological sequence from late Palaeolithic through early imperial times (see Wang Kelin 1986; 1989). In a nutshell, Wang described how the best in cultural trends from surrounding areas converged upon "Jin" during the prehistoric period; how "Jin culture" found its first historical expression in China's earliest dynasty, the Xia (traditional dates 2205–1767

BC); and how, later on, the state of Jin served as the main pillar of the Zhou royal house – finally to become, with the foundation of the Chinese Empire, a central constituent of the Han nation.

As contrasted with this sweeping archaeological definition of Jin, historians have traditionally used that term in a much more restricted sense. Centered along the lower reaches of the Fen River, the historical state of Jin was an important polity founded at the beginning of the Zhou dynasty (*c.* 1050 BC) and ruled by a branch of the Zhou royal house. Having occupied center stage during the political struggles of the Springs and Autumns period (770–450 BC), Jin broke up into three separate kingdoms during the fifth century BC. The history of the state thus spans approximately six centuries.

The former territory of Jin is almost entirely contained within present-day Shanxi province; excavations since the fifties have recovered a number of settlements, cemeteries, and workshop sites that can be identified with Jin on the basis of reliable historical-geographical or epigraphic evidence.[13] But while Jin was unquestionably of major importance in the cultural history of the area during the first half of the first millennium BC, it should be noted that other ancient polities coexisted with Jin in present-day Shanxi during that time (some of them conquered by Jin in the course of the centuries). There were also unassimilated non-Zhou groups such as the Di in the Taihang mountains, as well as nomadic or semi-nomadic populations in the area now constituting the northernmost part of the province. In regarding all of these as manifestations of an ancient "Jin culture," archaeologists in Shanxi simplify an historically complex situation, unduly exaggerating the importance of Jin at the expense of the other ancient polities and ethnic groups in the province.

The extension of Jin into much earlier protohistoric and prehistoric periods is likewise historically extremely doubtful. To lend support to this line of argument, Wang goes to considerable lengths trying to prove that the place-name Jin was used with reference to Shanxi even in pre-Zhou times; this he does through dubious etymological speculations combined with facetious interpretations of Late Shang oracle bone graphs. The effort to link the semi-legendary Xia dynasty as an important element to "Jin culture" lends an extra twist to the matter, coopting central features of mainstream textbook historical accounts for Shanxi and enhancing the national prominence of the area. To buffer up the primacy of Shanxi to Xia civilization, another local scholar, in an article on the historical geography of the Xia, has taken great pains to locate the origins of the Xia and its earliest capitals in the province, dismissing the proposed locations of alleged Xia capitals in Henan as either mistaken or late and of secondary importance (Qu Yingjie 1989).

This is not the place for a full-scale investigation into the ancient cultural history of Shanxi; let it simply be stated that, although attractive for political reasons, the officially propounded regionalist vision of ancient cultural developments in Shanxi is entirely fictitious. Both the geographical and the temporal definitions of "Jin culture" pose unsurmountable historical problems. There is, moreover, no intrinsic reason to assume either ethnic homogeneity or continuity of domination within all of present-day Shanxi over the long timespan claimed for "Jin culture." The imposition of such a standard interpretive framework on the archaeological evidence is motivated by extraneous concerns. When Shanxi archaeologists assert that the Jin state was the most loyal supporter of the Zhou kings, a bastion of ritual orthodoxy against encroaching barbarism (e.g., from the southern state of Chu), and the wellspring of classic Chinese philosophy, such statements call for a rereading in contemporary terms such as the Beijing government, Hong Kong capitalism, and Communism.

V Regional supremacism and the place of archaeologists

Justified though its adoption may have been by the archaeological evidence, the recent regionalist focus in Chinese archaeology has, thus, not entailed a mere cold-blooded reevaluation of archaeological data. An attitude that we may call regional supremacism, stemming from a politically motivated exaggeration of regionalist interpretations, influences the way in which many provincial archaeologists now present and explain their data, both in scholarly and in non-scholarly contexts. Their wars of proxy involving ancient nationalities and states are a very serious matter in terms of present-day discourse – both in the context of the provinces' quest for greater autonomy and in defining the place of archaeology and its practitioners in the life of the Chinese nation.

I should emphasize here that the identification of different ancient nationalities in each province does not (for the time being, at least) translate into a present-day ethnic separatism. In this respect, China may differ somewhat from other areas covered in the present volume. Within the ongoing scholarly and political discourse, the unity and homogeneity of the Chinese nation is axiomatic, and formulations that might conjure up questions of ethnic identity in the present era are strictly taboo. Historians and archaeologists concur that all the nationalities mentioned in the ancient texts were long ago fused into the Han nationality.[14] When concentrating their efforts on enhancing an ancient nationality such as Jin, then archaeologists are not claiming that present-day inhabitants of Shanxi are in any way ethnically distinct from other Chinese. Neither should, for example, one scholar's attempt to derive the origins of the Shang dynasty from the far-away northeastern provinces of China (Zhang Boquan 1987) be misread as questioning the "Chinese" ethnicity of the Shang royal house.[15] At issue is, instead, the historical importance of a particular region in the formation of Chinese civilization, which, symbolically reified in archaeological cultures, is conceived as a metonym of the present-day power and prestige of the political unit that happens to contain that region, and of its ruling authorities.

To understand the archaeological reasoning under the regionalist paradigm, we must briefly explore how Chinese archaeologists, as members of a specific professional group, present their tradition and heritage, and how they configure their own position in contemporary society. With regard to social position and educational background, Chinese archaeologists appear to be a fairly homogenous group. Even though archaeological training is currently available at twelve universities in China, the curricula differ little from institution to institution, with Beijing University's Archaeology Department being the trendsetter. Linked horizontally, like all Chinese intellectuals, by ties of solidarity among fellow-students, and vertically by bonds of loyalty to their teachers, Chinese archaeologists operate within a rather uniform scholarly discourse, characterized, above all, by a deeply ingrained adherence to a Morgan/Engels type of social evolutionism.

The inter-regional competitive posturing under the regionalist paradigm, then, does not reflect the existence of contending local schools of archaeologists. Instead, I would suggest that the present situation should be seen principally in terms of the archaeologists' economic situation in the eighties and early nineties. The subtext of the debate is one of lobbying for scarce resources (see Olsen 1992). Like other members of the Chinese intelligentsia, archaeologists are at present confronting formidable problems: their living standards have steadily eroded during the past decade as government salaries have been allowed to slip way out of pace with steadily rising prices (Link 1992). At work, archaeologists are facing an ever more serious shortage of funds in the face of sky-rocketing field work costs. To secure support, they have to convince the archaeological authorities in Beijing that their respective regional tradition is more worthy of attention than others because of its uniquely important contributions to national culture; and the regional non-archaeological authorities must be convinced that archaeology in the area under their supervision should be generously supported because it reveals a glory outshining those of other areas in China – a glory that might be put to use, e.g., in attracting foreign investment.

To see how archaeologists approach the powers that be, we may take a look at a 1986 special issue of *Jianghan Kaogu*, the regional archaeological journal of Hubei province, entitled with the slogan "Strengthen the legal system, protect cultural relics." This special issue, which was not distributed to regular subscribers, was published on the occasion of a provincial-level meeting of Communist cadres constituting the "leadership" (*lingdao*) in cultural affairs. As the overwhelming majority of these party functionaries lack any interest whatsoever in culture, the contributors to the issue make every attempt to touch on the one point on which they may be expected to be sensitive: power. Besides flattering photos of the participants and the texts of their official speeches, the issue contains short articles on archaeology in the province, phrased at an intellectual level markedly below that normally maintained by this journal. Among them, an article entitled "National-level superlatives and world-level superlatives among the archaeological discoveries in Hubei" (Guo Dewei 1986) is of interest as a particularly flagrant example of regional supremacism: a *Guinness Book of Records*-style enumeration of "firsts." Some examples: the Neolithic site of Qujialing yielded the earliest "eggshell-thin pottery" in China; the site of Panlongcheng (near Wuhan) is the best-preserved Shang city in China; the largest bronze *yue* axe, the largest jade *ge* weapon, and the earliest piece of carved lacquer in the world have been found in tombs near there; Chongyang county sports the earliest known bronze drum; the former Chu capital of Jiangling is the first such site in China where an ancient city gate was excavated, and the only one where a wooden watergate has been unearthed; it features the greatest concentrations of wells, of Chu tombs, and, within the tombs, of ancient bamboo objects, bronze swords, inscribed bamboo slips, and ancient silk textiles anywhere . . . For a scholar, dwelling on such matters – which frequently strike one as contrived in any case – would not constitute a priority; but this is the only sort of information that will be sure to impress politicians eager to brag about "results." The pressure to outdo their colleagues in other areas and to identify as many such superlatives as possible must weigh heavily on many archaeologists, especially those charged with administrative tasks.

The lobbying for official support by archaeologists in Hubei has met with gratifying success. Archaeological activity in the province has been focussed on Chu, a state that flourished in the Middle Yangtze region during much of the first millennium BC, and which (in spite of the existence of many other important early states in the province) has been turned into the official cultural mascot of the Hubei archaeological authorities. The provincial government has recently sponsored much scholarly activity in Chu studies, including an international conference held in Wuhan in 1988. A veritable flood of publications on all imaginable aspects of Chu has appeared in the province (e.g. Fang Yousheng 1988; He Hao 1989; Hou Dejun 1990; Huang Dexin 1983; Peng De 1991; Shi Quan 1988; Wang

Guanghao 1988; Wei Chang 1989; Wuhan 1987 and n.d. a and b; Zhang Zhengming 1988; Zhang Zhengming 1984 – to list merely some recent book-length items).

In the process, Chu and the antecedent "proto-Chu" have been styled into a "superculture" supposedly encompassing the regional Bronze Age cultures throughout southern China, including phenomena that other archaeologists have associated with various other ancient nationalities, such as Yue, Ba, and Xu; some Hubei archaeologists would like to see all these as regional manifestations of "Chu civilization" (for a critique, see Li Ling 1993). This archaeologically encoded claim to a Hubei hegemony over neighboring provinces has not gone unchallenged, however. One strategy has been to argue for the importance of areas outside of Hubei to Chu history; archaeologists in Henan, for example, have pointed out that the earliest political centers of Chu, according to historical accounts, may have been located in the southern part of their province (Pei Mingxiang 1983; Zhao Shigang 1983; and other contributions to Zhengzhou 1983; see also Cao Guicen 1990) – a suggestion that seems to find some support in recent archaeological finds. Somewhat more surprisingly, a similar claim to being the original seat of the Chu polity, based on much less solid evidence, has also been put forward on behalf of Anhui province, which hosted the Chu capitals during the final half-century or so of its history. Local Anhui scholars have found reasons to argue that, in moving to their province, the Chu royal house actually returned to its ancestral seats (Ding Bangjun 1986; Zhang Jingguo 1988). Given the priorities of the ongoing discourse, it seems likely that their argument is mainly motivated by regional supremacism, aiming to boost Anhui's standing with respect to Hubei.

VI The peripheries usurping the mainstream

Besides bringing out – and sometimes exaggerating – the intrinsic importance of provincial evidence at the expense of the traditional "mainstream," another means to direct the spotlight of attention to the provinces is to relocate events central to the textbook accounts of orthodox historiography into areas heretofore deemed peripheral. Though potentially in contradiction with one another, both approaches are equally acceptable to an audience that is interested, above all, in matters of prestige; proclaiming both at the same time enables the regionalist scholars and their official sponsors to have their cake, and eat it too.

Examples of articles purporting to turn certain regions into the center stage of Chinese national history abound in the provincial periodicals; their reasoning is mainly based sometimes on reinterpretations of traditional historical geography, at other times on archaeological evidence. Let us briefly consider here some examples from Liaoning province. Zhang Boquan's (1987) attempt to derive the Shang royal house from that far northeastern region has already been mentioned. Zhang voices the opinion that the middle Neolithic Hongshan culture in western Liaoning and southeastern Inner Mongolia corresponds to Di Ku, one of the mythical sage rulers of high antiquity, who was the First Ancestor of the Shang. This sort of attempt to buffer up ancient legends by associating them with specific geographical sites has a long history in China; in the twentieth century, Chinese as well as foreign scholars have proceeded to rationalize the mythical figures by historicizing them as various predynastic "clans."

Going a step beyond Zhang Boquan, Jin Yue (1986/7 and 1989) has located the whole lot of the mythical Five Emperors in the northeast. The author's rationale for this highly unorthodox theory is an archaeological one: in his opinion, the sophisticated ritual structures and the splendid jades found at sites of the Hongshan culture prove that the northeast must have played the paramount role at the earliest stage of Chinese history; only this area was therefore fit to be the residence of the sage rulers. The limitations of his regionalist perspective allow Jin conveniently to ignore the existence of other splendid Neolithic remains in different parts of China, and his commitment to considering everything within the present-day geographical boundaries of China as pertinent to traditional textbook accounts of Chinese history would probably prevent him from even considering the possibility of doubting that Hongshan was directly ancestral to later Chinese civilization (cf. Akiyama 1988). Like Zhang, Jin, in a different article (1990), proceeds to link Liaoning province intimately with the Shang dynasty, locating in the province various principalities known from the Shang oracular records and emphasizing their close relationship with the Shang dynastic court.

Correlating archaeological finds from the provinces with the data of orthodox historiography was the principal interpretive strategy under the earlier mononuclear, centralist approach. With the rise of the regionalist paradigm, the same sort of reasoning continues to be employed, but the goal of the method has been turned on its head: instead of drawing the peripheries into a narrowly conceived center, the centers of national history are now moved into a variety of different areas. Whereas, in earlier decades, finds from all over China were pooled to extol the unified national tradition, the national tradition now explains and enhances piecemeal regional schemes of cultural development. Such a situation is bound to create numerous different readings of historical and mythical events for which only one sort of interpretation had previously been allowed.

Such provincial reinterpretations of the textbook accounts of history would be unthinkable if the central government were still inclined to enforce its former monopoly over the manipulation of the historical orthodoxy. This, however, is no longer the case. In the decades after 1949, archaeology has been used by the Communist regime as a means of "proving" the universal correctness of the Engelsian blueprint of social development for Chinese history. Recently, by contrast, as the government has ever more single-mindedly defined its self-image in terms of the success of its economic reforms, there has been a marked decline of interest in ideology in general, and in its symbolic legitimation through archaeology in particular. The provinces have picked up the shreds.

The preceding survey suggests that the new interpretive strategies in Chinese archaeology that I have called the regionalist paradigm have arisen chiefly in response to current political realities and needs. Regionalist argumentation in archaeology, for all its apparent separatism, neither overtly nor covertly challenges Chinese nationalism; rather, it is a manifestation thereof. Regionalist supremacism is nothing but a new expression of the same fervently loyal stance that archaeologists have had to adopt in order to gain official support and legitimation ever since the inception of modern archaeology in China some seven decades ago. The current imbalances in the perception of the archaeological record are perhaps a necessary dialectic element that one may expect in any paradigm change.

NOTES

1 For an assessment of the impact of traditional historiography on Chinese archaeology, which has strong connections with nationalism, see Falkenhausen 1993a.
2 This article was first presented at the annual meeting of the American Anthropological Association in Chicago on November 23, 1991. For helpful comments I am grateful to Bettina Arnold, Philip J. Ivanhoe, and David N. Keightley.
3 In this paper, I use the word "province" as encompassing all provincial-level political units, including, besides the provinces properly speaking, the "Autonomous Regions" (Xinjiang, Ningxia, Inner Mongolia, Guangxi, and Tibet) and the "Special Municipalities" (Beijing, Tianjin, and Shanghai).
4 Until 1977, the present Academy of Social Sciences formed part of the Academy of Sciences (Zhongguo Kexueyuan).
5 In theory, the provincial archaeological institutes are now charged with the recovery, and the provincial museums with the storage and conservation, of archaeological finds. However, owing to systemically inbuilt inter-institutional frictions (*maodun*), archaeological institutes everywhere in China are refusing to turn over "their" materials, keeping them instead in their own storage facilities. While the museums are holding on to their archaeological collections accumu-

lated earlier, they now have few avenues left to expand, except by acquisition of "scattered antiques" (*liusan wenwu*) from private owners. Control and ownership of archaeological finds has become a matter of explosive potential recently as their material value has become an issue; for the idea of allowing Chinese institutions to sell off "less important" holdings on the international market is being discussed more and more seriously.

6 The only two differently named institutions that I am aware of are the Provincial Institutes of Archaeology of Shaanxi and Shanxi provinces (Shaanxi/Shanxi Sheng Kaogu Yanjiusuo) and the Henan Provincial Institute of Cultural Relics (Henan Sheng Wenwu Yanjiusuo; the so-called Henan Provincial Institute of Archaeology [Henan Sheng Kaogu Yanjiusuo], a branch of the provincial Academy of Social Sciences, has no connection with the State Bureau of Cultural Relics and is not entitled to engage in field work).

7 In some areas there exist sub-provincial units authorized to undertake minor field work on their own initiative, e.g. the Municipal Archaeological Team of the city of Luoyang.

8 First attempts at publishing regional archaeological journals may be traced to the fifties, but such activity did not start in earnest until after the Cultural Revolution. Since *c.* 1980, some of the regional journals have become available for subscription abroad; others are only circulated internally (*neibu*). Most do not appear on a regular schedule. For a bibliographic overview, see Falkenhausen 1993b.

9 This research was funded by a post-doctoral fellowship from the J. Paul Getty Foundation. I should like here to express my gratitude to the Foundation for its generous support.

10 This is, of course, nothing new. In the early seventies, for instance, scholars were compelled to criticize Confucius and to sprinkle their articles with boldface quotations from the writings of Mao and the Marxist-Leninist classics, often in such a clumsy fashion that outside readers would find themselves wondering whether the authors could have possibly believed what they wrote. The regionalist slant of some recent articles warrants a similar skepticism; Western scholars might overlook this fact if they are duped by the superficial affinity of the new Chinese regionalist interpretive models to those advocated in post-diffusionist Western archaeology.

11 K.C. Chang, having referred to Qinglian'gang only in the first edition of *The Archaeology of Ancient China* (1963:107), introduced both Qinglian'gang and Dawenkou as geographically distinct cultures in the second edition (1968:135–9) and as chronologically separate stages in the third (1977:158–60), finally settling on Dawenkou as the exclusive name in the fourth edition (1986:196).

12 So far, comparatively little notice has been taken of the pioneering studies by non-Chinese specialists on this subject, such as Kane 1974/5, Hayashi 1980, Bagley 1980 and 1987, and Rawson 1990.

13 Deplorably, none of this evidence has yet been properly reported upon (for a convenient summary, see Beijing 1984:273, 278–81, 291–2), the only exception being a cache of inscribed treaty slips from Houma. All too rarely do provincial archaeologists bother to buffer up their regionalist viewpoints with full archaeological reports. Notable exceptions are two archaeological reports

recently published in Shandong (Jinan 1982 and 1987).

14 Chinese archaeologists generally refrain from identifying materials bearing on the really existing present-day frictions between the Han and their neighbor nationalities. In view of the currently unstable minorities situation, it is perhaps no accident that the regionalist paradigm does not so far seem to have much affected the archaeology of the minority areas of China (especially Xinjiang and Inner Mongolia). Another reason may be the nature of the evidence available and the relatively recent formation of the ethnic groups now dominant in those areas; for the Uighurs and Mongols are not directly descended from the preceding populations of those regions, which are reflected through the majority of archaeological finds.

15 There is a great difference between such a stance and the theories of the Korean historian Yun Nae-hyŏn (1982), who claims that the Shang were Tungus (and hence, in terms of Yun's own nationalist agenda, "Korean"). Even if there were scholarly merit to such an idea, it would be sure to be condemned by Chinese scholars.

13 The politics of ethnicity in prehistoric Korea

Sarah M. Nelson

Archaeology in Korea is viewed, as it is elsewhere in east Asia, as a branch of history rather than anthropology. One consequence of this position is that attention to the remote past has been focussed largely on Korean ancestors: who they were in reference to Chinese historic documents; and how and when they came to the Korean peninsula. By the time of the formation of states in the southern Korean peninsula and the Japanese islands, a fully Korean presence in the peninsula is assumed, and the identity of Koreans within the peninsula is complete.

Questions of ethnic origins have thus been paramount in terms of approaches to prehistory in Korea, and in the past answers have been found with reference to mythology and by appeal to ancient texts. More recently, archaeology has been asked to supply some answers to ethnic questions, or in some cases archaeology has been used to validate the established mythological or legendary constructs regarding the original ancestors. At this intersection of mythology, history, and archaeology lie many problems for the interpretation of the past. Political and nationalistic motivations for preferring one interpretation over another, although more covert than overt, are at the heart of these problems.

Although ethnicity is called upon to validate political claims in many places, Korea's particular variation on the theme helps to illuminate the way ethnicity in the past is and has been approached. Generally, Koreans look for a single ancestral antecedent, and implicitly assume that a Korean ethnic group existed outside the Korean peninsula before its migration to the peninsula.

Almost any archaeology or ancient history text makes clear that the purpose of archaeology in Korea is the search for Korean ethnicity, expressed as the history of the Korean people. An extended example of this approach to archaeology can be found in *Recent Archaeological Discoveries in the Republic of Korea*. Kim Won-yong, the doyen of Korean archaeology, devotes more than half of the introductory chapter to a summary of the Korean "race" and its derivation. The reader learns that the people are Tungusic Mongoloids, and the language belongs to the

4 Northeast Asia and the Korean peninsula

Altaic family, which also includes Mongolian, Turkic, and Tungusic. These statements are followed by a description of the Neolithic inhabitants of the Korean peninsula, who are said to be not Koreans but Palaeo-Siberians. The identity of the Palaeolithic people is left unspecified, but presumably they were also not Koreans. Next we learn about the real Koreans, who were called Yemaek (the Korean pronunciation of the Chinese characters Wei-Mo, or Kuai-Mo according to Kim). According to this scenario, the Yemaek entered Korea from Manchuria in about 1000 BC, bringing with them distinctive bronze swords, dolmens, stone cists, and new pottery types. Kim stresses the bear cult, and makes some linguistic comparisons to emphasize his point.

Kim also asserts that "the Yemaeks in northern Korea maintained their traditional nomadic pattern of life, but those who settled in southern Korea had become sedentary farmers by 300 BC." The nomadic notion is another theme which is emphasized in the formation of Korean ethnicity. This theme will be touched upon later.

The Three Kingdoms, traditionally dated from 57 BC to AD 668, are then all ascribed, despite their differences, to Yemaek descendants. Kim ends this section by summarizing: "Korean culture, however, retained its northern traits throughout her history largely due to a *remarkable ethnic homogeneity*" (Kim 1983:2–3, emphasis mine).

This citation of Kim's work is not intended to call into question his enormous and important pioneering contributions to Korean archaeology, nor the right of Koreans to define their own archaeology in accordance with their own national goals. I also do not wish to leave the impression that every archaeologist in Korea subscribes equally to the ethnic theory I have outlined here, although it is very widespread, and examples could be multiplied. My point is, however, that an approach which begins with ethnic homogeneity and reads it into the past is incompatible with Western standards of archaeological interpretation, and makes discussion of archaeological evidence less than fruitful.

My own interpretations of Korean archaeology, which differ substantially from those described above (e.g. Nelson 1982, 1993), are not the point I wish to emphasize here. Rather, I wish to examine the concept of ethnicity as it is used as an interpretive device in Korea. I will explore the roots of this concept in the recent past, and consider the consequences of this approach for Korean archaeology.

There is no doubt that Korea is unusual in having a homogeneous population, with no national minorities or lingering aboriginals speaking different and unrelated languages, as is the case in both China and Japan. The Korean language has regional dialects, but they are mutually understandable throughout the peninsula and into the Korean Autonomous Region of Yanji, in Jilin Province, China. The Korean language is entirely congruent with people who consider themselves Koreans. Furthermore, although Korean is classified as a Tungusic language, among whose relatives is Manchu, it is distinct from the other languages, and clearly has had a long separate history (Miller 1980). Therefore, it is not the insistence upon Korean ethnicity in the present with which I wish to take issue, but rather I wish to consider the effect on interpretations of the past of reifying Koreanness.

The concept of a nation having a mixed background, with various ethnicities contributing to a new blend (for example the waves of immigration into the British Isles), is considered to be unlikely in the Korean case because of this apparent homogeneity of the present population. Generally, Korean archaeologists and historians, in seeking a single ancestral group which migrated into the peninsula, assume that something like Koreanness existed in the previous homeland. Although I have never seen this view explicitly stated, these ancestral Koreans are implicit in the model of the nomadic Yemaek people, who brought the Korean language and culture into the Korean peninsula. This emphasis on ethnic purity causes the interpretation of archaeological evidence to be a history of population movements, only one of which (the last) is important because it is relevant to understanding the formation of the Korean people. However, a people can become homogeneous. The Korean homogeneity of the present could have been forged from diverse elements, as indeed the archaeology seems to indicate when viewed apart from this dominant ethnicity paradigm.

The causes of this emphasis on Korean ethnicity extending back into the mists of time are complex and historic. The most important of these reasons is probably the most recent: the present division of Korea into approximately equal halves – the south influenced by capitalism and the north by communism. While many deep differences divide the two Koreas, they are equally intent on reunification, and equally insistent that Koreans are the same wherever they may live. Divided Korea is uniquely a result of global Cold War politics – perhaps the last remaining vestige – and is unrelated to its prior history. A country which had done its best to avoid involvement in international affairs (once known as "The Hermit Nation" [Bishop 1905]) was caught up in a division, and later a war, for which there was no local agenda. The present condition of a divided Korea is thus an affront to the sensibilities of Koreans. Families affected by the division are a continuous theme of films, fiction, magazines, and newspapers.

The common wish for reunification, however, does not produce identical archaeological interpretations in North and South Korea. For example, the emphasis in the North on *juche*, self-reliance, spawns a rejection of any Chinese presence in the peninsula, while the South has few scholars who would dispute the Han dynasty Chinese commanderies (108 BC to 330 AD) as historical fact. Furthermore, while interpretations of Korean archaeology are somewhat influenced by evolutionism in the South and Marxism in the North, the underlying emphasis on eternal Koreanness makes the two archaeologies more alike than different.

A second root of the insistence on Korean ethnicity is the Japanese colonization of Korea from 1910 to 1945, which intensified a fierce national pride, especially in reaction to the sometimes derogatory Japanese accounts of ancient Korea. The first deliberate archaeology in Korea was done early in this century by Japanese scholars, who had their own agenda for the interpretations of the Korean past. Part of this involved justification of the colonization of Korea, which was understood as having "belonged" to Japan in the very ancient past. Among the many Japanese interpretations of Korean–Japanese relationships in the past, the worst affront to Korean sensibilities is the Japanese insistence that the Yamato state in

Japan held part of southern Korea under the name of Mimana (Grayson 1977). The Koreans call this region Kaya (or Karak), and according to Korean histories it was a loose confederation of six small kingdoms, Korean to the core, which the Silla kingdom conquered one by one, completing the last conquest in 562.

The Kwanggaeto stele, a monument inscribed with Chinese characters extolling the exploits of a king of Koguryo (one of the Three Kingdoms) in AD 414, is widely believed in Korea to have been defaced by the Japanese who discovered and reerected it, so that the "mythical" (according to Koreans) invasions from Wa (the name for southern Japan in the Chinese chronicles) would be given historical validity (Hong 1988:231–6). The fact that no such polities as Korea or Japan existed at this time is irrelevant to the dispute, which is based on present national boundaries.

Other interpretations of Korean archaeology were based on Japanese perceptions as well. Because Japanese scholars were loath to recognize any debt to Korea in their own cultural past, they created an extremely short time depth for Korean state formation and denied a Korean Bronze Age. Furthermore, since bronze and iron appear to have been exported from Korea simultaneously into Kyushu, the southernmost island of Japan, in the Yayoi period, it was deemed necessary to declare that Korea likewise had no Bronze Age, but went directly from the Neolithic stage to the Iron Age. Japan and Korea were seen as simultaneously receiving an advanced culture from China, rather than that culture being seen as having been successively passed from China first to Korea and then to Japan. Western interpretations have more often followed Japanese than Korean models, perhaps because Western scholars tend to be more familiar with the Japanese view (Nelson 1989).

The third, most muted but still effective strand in the emphasis on Korean ethnicity is a Sinocentric view of history. Korea has stood in a dependent relationship to China at least since the Han dynasty commandaries on the Korean peninsula, 108 BC to AD 313. By the time Silla took control of the entire peninsula in 668 with the help of the Tang dynasty, China was seen as elder brother to the younger brother Korea, not interfering in internal affairs, but nevertheless validating the king's right to rule. Korea had looked to China originally for the civilizing influences of writing and religion. China's writing system long antedated Korea's alphabetic *han'gul*, and many facets of the governing system, the educational system, and even religion (Buddhism) and philosophy (Confucianism) came to Korea from China. Consequently, there is a strong dependence on China when it comes to historical interpretation. Furthermore, the earliest written references pertaining to Korea are found in Chinese sources, while the earliest Korean histories relate to the Three Kingdoms period, and are described in Confucian or Buddhist-influenced writings.

Thus, Korea has looked to Chinese documents more than to archaeology as the key to the ancient past. This led to a privileging of Chinese historical writings about archaeological discoveries. Myths, legends, and history are interwoven in these documents, as they are in Korea's own histories, the *Samguk Sagi* (History of the Three Kingdoms) and the *Samguk Yusa* (Memorabilia of the Three Kingdoms). Although these documents were written in the twelfth and thirteenth centuries, they were probably based on earlier documents now lost. One strand of archaeological interpretation, therefore, attempts to match archaeological discoveries with the written record.

Koreans have not been interested in world prehistory, nor in the comparative history of humankind, but in unearthing and validating their own past. The ethnogenesis of Koreans, however, is not the point, for Korean ethnicity is seen as eternal, not as an emergent process. Few archaeologists consider the *formation* of Koreanness within the Korean peninsula, for it is not possible to contemplate a time when Koreanness did not exist. Rather, Korean ethnicity is sought outside the peninsula, and the ethnic group which entered the peninsula is usually seen as a single people, entering relatively suddenly and spreading out quickly. Deriving from the "nomadic" fringes of China, the mythology demands that ethnic Koreans arrived with rice agriculture and bronze.

This insistence upon eternal Korean ethnicity might seem trivial, but there are consequences for archaeological method and theory, as well as for interpretations of the past. Furthermore, although there is no current bloodshed over the nationalism inherent in these ideas, implicit territorial claims are nevertheless staked (Sohn *et al.* 1987), ready to be acted upon under different circumstances. The interpretive implications will be considered first, in order to illuminate the consequences for method and theory.

In general, stages in Korean prehistory are perceived as covering long stretches of time, and as being relatively static. Each stage is seen as a great event, superseded by the next event. The great stair steps of history occur in orderly progression. There is a tendency to emphasize similarities within a stage, masking both temporal and spatial variation, and to emphasize differences between adjacent stages. However, the search for the original homeland of Korean ethnicity plays out differently in different time periods.

I The Siberian connection

Since Palaeolithic and Neolithic sites are declared to represent Palaeo-Asiatics – that is, non-Koreans – until recently they have been less investigated than later sites and their study poorly financed. However, status accrued to Palaeolithic archaeology with the discovery of the site of Chon'gongni, where a few classic handaxes challenged the previous dogma that northeast Asia was backward in the production of patterned stone tools (Movius 1948). Thereby the study of the Palaeolithic was legitimized, and the presence of stone tools "more developed" than those of China became a source of national pride, as well as the reported antiquity of the site. (The original age estimate was half a million years.)

The only scrap of legendary prehistory which might be said to apply to Korea in the Neolithic is the story of Tangun, preserved in the *Samguk Yusa* (Ilyon 1972). The Tangun legend is a creation story, involving a tiger and a bear – both female, and both wanting to become the mother of humanity (or perhaps just the mother of Koreans, this distinction not being made). The bear wins by perseverance and adherence to ritually imposed sanctions, and becomes the mother of Tangun with the aid of the God of Heaven. Tangun teaches all good things, especially agriculture and sericulture; lives for one thousand years; and becomes a spirit presiding over Chonji, Heavenly Lake, a high crater lake which is found approximately in the middle of the current border between Korea and China. This is thin material for Neolithic reconstructions.

In contrast, the archaeological scenario for the Neolithic is based almost entirely on pottery. Both the pottery and the potters were traditionally assumed to have entered Korea from Siberia. Comb-marked pots made in simple conical shapes have been found in the vicinity of Lake Baikal in Siberia as well as in Korea, and the connection between the two was made without regard to what had been or might be found in the intervening territory. No concern was shown for establishing reasons for the migration, or for considering ecological similarities or differences between the reputed homeland and the ultimate destination. No interest in temporal differences is evident, either.

When this theory was established, it was believed that Palaeolithic evidence did not exist in Korea, making it imperative to derive Neolithic inhabitants from outside the peninsula. Even after a Palaeolithic presence in Korea had become well established, the Neolithic intrusion model has been sustained by the Palaeolithic Gap – a period of time in the early Holocene when Korea has had no archaeological evidence of human inhabitants. However the Palaeolithic Gap is rapidly closing. A surprising number of Mesolithic sites have recently been found in several different environmental settings, and sites with pottery are producing ever earlier dates, so that the gap is diminishing, and perhaps will turn out to have been only an artefact of the paucity of archaeological research in Korea. But the most telling point is that several of the pre-pottery sites are stratigraphically beneath pottery-bearing layers, with the continuity of stone tool types and food refuse strongly suggesting a continuity of culture. However, so far the discoveries of Mesolithic sites have had little effect on the Siberian hypothesis, which continues to be the official version of Korean prehistory.

Korean Neolithic pottery, although often called Chulmun, meaning "comb-marked," actually has a striking amount of variation in the beginning stages as judged by radiocarbon dates (Nelson 1992). This variation should serve as a caution to any interpretation of a single migration of a single pottery-using people into the peninsula. The earliest dated pottery is on the east coast. It has flat bases and is decorated on the shoulders with stamped or impressed motifs. In the southeast there is a large percentage of plain pottery, and in the northeast incised designs occur but they are not usually made with a toothed implement. None of these east coast ceramics bear much relationship to Siberian pottery, but more closely resemble widespread early coastal ceramics found in Japan and China. It is evident that boats were in use at the beginning of the Holocene in Japan (Ikawa-Smith 1986), so the mechanism for transmission is not mysterious. The coastal location of the earliest Korean sites is another reason to link these regions together.

Only the west coast pottery is properly designated Chulmun. It was made on conical, open-mouthed shapes with pointed or rounded bases. The west coast pottery resembles some Siberian pottery in its overall shape, but the inspiration for it can probably be found much closer at hand, across the Yellow Sea and in the Liaodong peninsula of China (Nelson 1990). Some of these sites have not only comb-incised and impressed pottery, but also square hearths bordered with cobbles, a characteristic found in most Korean sites. Recent discoveries in northeastern China produce ever earlier possible prototypes for Chulmun pottery.

II The Chinese connection

Chinese writings include the names of four individuals or groups which are frequently claimed for Korean ancestors. The first of these is Kija (Jizi in Chinese), a member of the royal Shang clan who appears in the Zhou chronicles (Wu 1982:311). Owing to his meritorious behavior the Zhou conqueror granted Kija – despite his relation to the defeated Shang king – permission to take a retinue of followers to the northeast and found a new state called Choson. Kija has been claimed for Korea on these documentary grounds alone. If Choson was in the Korean peninsula, there is not a shred of archaeological evidence discovered so far. In particular, one would expect this prince of Shang to have brought with him bronze vessels and writing, both of which are noticeable by their total absence in Korea for several hundred years after the fall of the Shang dynasty. Possible evidence of Kija has been found in the Yan state, however, near modern Beijing, and it is sometimes argued that the territorial extent of Choson included the Liaodong peninsula and the region around Beijing (e.g. Yoon 1986).

The second group believed to be Korean ancestors by some scholars is the Dong-I, or Eastern Barbarians, who are most often located in Shandong (Hsu and Linduff 1988:14), on the basis of ancient Chinese writings. Some Koreans not only have claimed that the Dong-I were Koreans, but also have gone so far as to assert that the Shang dynasty was Dong-I and that, therefore, the Koreans invented the first Chinese writing (e.g., An 1974). Although oracle bones (without writing) have been found in Korea, a linguistic difficulty with this interpretation immediately springs to mind, for the oracle bone language is clearly Chinese, not merely in the ideograms but also in the grammatical structure. Pictograms and ideograms would be an unlikely vehicle for an agglutinative language like Korean.

Even leaving extravagant claims aside, there are few useful hypotheses regarding the Dong-I as Korean ancestors which could be tested archaeologically. However, if the Dawenkou culture in Shandong represents the Dong-I, as is the scholarly consensus, the Korean hypothesis becomes even less tenable, for tripod vessels, an important element in the Dawenkou complex, are not found in Korea until a millennium later.

The Dong-hu are yet another group named in Chinese documents and frequently claimed for Korean ancestors. Located in eastern Liaoning during the Zhou period, they were well placed for a Bronze Age sweep into Korea. Frequently they are equated with the Yemaek, listed at least once as a branch of the Dong-hu. Most often advanced as specifically Korean ancestors are the Yemaek themselves (as noted above), who are seen as a Tungusic tribal group. The Yemaek also appear once in Chinese documents as one of the nine tribes of the Dong-I, muddying the water a bit.

The *Wei Ji* (compiled 233–97) places the Yemaek in the Korean peninsula at the time of the Han commanderies in the first century BC (Parker 1890), giving them a specifically Korean identity at least by that time. These Yemaek are said to have had seven cities and forts. Obviously it is not easy to apply names from textual materials to archaeological sites. However, at least it seems likely that a group by this name occupied a part of northwestern Korea by Han dynasty times. The problem comes in the use of the name Yemaek to apply to Bronze Age peoples throughout the Korean peninsula as much as 1500 years earlier (Kim Won-yong 1986:19; Choi Mong-lyong 1984). For example, Kim writes: "The Koreans of the Late Bronze Age were all the same Yemaek people, but historical records almost give us the impression that the southern Yemaek, called Han . . .

were ethnically different from the northern nomadic Yemaek." A different interpretation sees the Yemaek as Koguryo ancestors, arising in southern Manchuria (which was the Koguryo homeland archaeologically as well as historically) by the ninth century BC (Rhee 1992).

Archaeological finds on the Korean peninsula suggest more complex origins for this time period just as they do for the Chulmun period. The Megalithic Age, sometimes problematically called the Bronze Age, begins with Mumun pottery accompanied or shortly followed by stone cist graves and dolmens. Rice agriculture and bronze may have entered the peninsula later, not necessarily together or even from the same direction (Kim Won-yong 1982). It is useful to examine each of these archaeological manifestations to see whether the Yemaek, or any single ethnic group, can reasonably be invoked as responsible for all of them.

Mumun or Plain Coarse pottery first appears in the southern coastal area of Korea at about 2000 BC in recalibrated radiocarbon dates (Nelson 1992). In this region Mumun has simple shapes with a round base and a wide mouth with a double rim. Necked jars and flowerpot-shaped plain pottery vessels appear in the northwest and center of the peninsula by 1500 BC, while jars with very small flat bases are found further to the northwest. There is clearly *not* a single diffusion of Mumun from the north. Regional styles are simply regional, and do not exhibit progressive changes or sequential time periods.

The change in Korean pottery styles from decorated to undecorated begins around 2000 BC in the south, and perhaps 1500 BC on the west coast. The pottery is thicker than Chulmun and appears to have different cultural roots, although some linear incising is found on Mumun vessels, a fact which has been argued to represent a vestige of Chulmun and therefore cultural continuity (Choe 1982). The stone tool inventory now includes polished forms almost exclusively. Well-made projectile points, semi-lunar knives, daggers, awls, chisels, axes, and adzes dominate the assemblages. Houses are larger than previous ones, and in a few places in west-central Korea longhouses have been excavated, with multiple hearths down the long axis. Villages are located on the sides of hills, as they are today, leaving the flatter land near rivers for growing crops.

Megalithic monuments are an important feature of the Mumun period. They consist mostly of dolmens, constructed like a rectangular house in the north, but consisting of only a large boulder above the ground in the southern form. The earliest C14 date from a dolmen is 2400 BC, but this date stands alone and is likely to be an error. From the bulk of C14 dates it would seem that the heyday of dolmen building was about 1500 to 500 BC. Most of the dolmens are burial markers. The ones shaped like stone houses (called *shipeng*, literally stone houses, in Liaoning) probably contained an above-ground burial. Southern dolmens were usually erected above a stone cist grave.

The Yemaek, as newcomers to the peninsula, must be found elsewhere. Manchuria (the Dongbei to Chinese) provides the putative homeland. Archaeological sites with broad similarities to Korean sites of the Megalithic period can be found in both Liaoning and Jilin provinces of China. The most obvious of these are the stone cist burial sites, which are widespread in both places. Contents of the cists are standardized in Korea, including one or two burnished red jars, polished stone daggers, and a necklace of tubular jades with a single *gokok*, or curved bead. Probably these burials represent an elite segment of the population, since there are not enough of them to account for burial of the entire population (Nelson 1993).

Dolmens are also found in Manchuria, as well as throughout Korea, but the Manchurian dolmens are fewer and tend to be more carefully constructed. There is no obvious reason to suppose that dolmens went from northeastern China to Korea instead of the other way around. In fact, if we assume that there is an evolution from crude to polished, then the Manchuria dolmens should be later than those in Korea. The complex of burial goods found in dolmens is distinctly Korean, yet there is a whole book dedicated to deriving the dolmens from outside Korea (Kim Byong-mo 1981). Again, the culture is seen as intrusive *in toto* rather than looking for a partially or totally indigenous base with multiple migrations from various places. The documented Yemaek area on the east coast is, in fact, the region with the *fewest* dolmens.

Rice is found in Korean sites definitely by 1000 BC and quite possibly a thousand years earlier (Choe 1991). Its movement into Korea is traced either by means of the distribution of semi-lunar reaping knives through northern China and Manchuria (Choe 1982), or according to finds of grooved adzes from southern China to Korea (Kim Won-yong 1982). The Yemaek along the east coastal strip of Korea are said to have raised the five cereals, including rice (Parker 1890), but of course this is much later than the identified archaeological rice.

Bronze is another element which is associated with Mumun pottery and dolmen burials. A particular style of bronze dagger, called Yoyong (Liaoning) style, has been found in southern Korea as well as in Liaoning. This is adduced as evidence that the Yemaek "tribe" formed in Manchuria and later moved into the Korean peninsula. Few Korean bronzes have been found in datable contexts, so typological analysis has substituted uneasily for firm dates, but recent dated excavations place the daggers in Korea about the same time as Liaoning – in the Spring and Autumn period of the Zhou dynasty (Rhee 1984).

Fixing on the Yemaek as the only tribal group that entered Korea in the Megalithic/Bronze Age surely oversimplifies the case. The marked regional variation in both pottery and burial types suggests different ethnicities, although these differences are obscured by Korean terminology.

By the Warring States period (403–221 BC), the presence of Yen "knife money," which is found in far northwestern Korea, suggests the possibility of commerce, trade, or even Chinese settlers. Han dynasty writings indicate some northern Chinese settlement in the Korean peninsula, and even provide a motive – the Han monopoly on iron may have motivated traders to explore and locate sources of ore outside the Han jurisdiction. Wiman, a historical figure who founded a state referred to as "Wiman Choson" (to distinguish it from the earlier, more shadowy Ancient Choson), does not appear to have been a pedigreed Korean himself (Gardiner 1969). Some North Korean archaeologists, however, prefer to consider Wiman to have been a "pure" Korean. They even deny that the Han Chinese ever conquered any part of the Korean peninsula, instead seeing the rich graves of Lelang in Chinese style as those of noble Koreans with Chinese trade goods, copying upper-class Chinese (Pearson 1978).

After the Han dynasty established the Lelang Commandery on the Korean peninsula in 108 BC, Chinese chroniclers were able to have a closer view of southern Korea. Both the *Wei Ji* and the *Hou Han Shu* record ethnographic partial descriptions of the inhabitants of the south. These histories mention some similarities among various Korean groups, as well as a fair amount of diversity. As they formed, the Korean Three Kingdoms, which probably all spoke some form of proto-Korean, were separated by cultural differences and did not let their commonalities prevent them from waging wars of conquest among themselves. These differences, as we have seen above, have been explicitly denied.

III The Japanese connection

The migration of peoples continues to be an important theme in relation to Japan as well. From the Korean perspective, movement is seen only from north to south: Manchuria to Korea; and Korea to Japan. The emigrants from the peninsula established agriculture on Kyushu in early Yayoi times, exported a stratified society and warfare in later Yayoi, and brought enlightenment to the Kofun period. Thus the formation of early states in the Japanese islands is attributed in Korea to migratory Koreans. However, the Japanese presence on the peninsula in the Three Kingdoms period is hotly denied, especially in the form of the Mimana outpost (according to Japanese sources), as well as in the form of invading armies. The controversy over the Kwanggaeto stele, noted above, is part of this contention.

IV Conclusion

The insistence on migration as an explanation of the peopling of Korea to the virtual exclusion of other mechanisms for culture change has an important political dimension. Desire for reunification of the two Koreas probably underlies the emphasis on the exclusivity of the Korean culture in the past as well as in the present. Proposing the migration of the whole Korean people into the peninsula at one time from some other previously established homeland is an assertion that allows a kind of Koreanness to have been established from time immemorial. Perceiving the development of Korean culture from a number of diverse sources is not at all congenial to this perspective. Even if it had occurred a very long time ago, the formation of Korea from any amalgamation of peoples cannot be acknowledged. The Korean people simply are, and always have been.

The rejection of a theory that the Neolithic inhabitants might have practiced horticulture is related to the notion of real Korean ethnicity as well. Neolithic discoveries tend to be slighted, and their interpretation as anything other than a poor beginning is unwelcome. Why attribute any form of inventiveness to these non-ancestors?

Internal inconsistencies in the interpretation of the evidence is the result of these several strands of interpretation. For example, there is a certain shiftiness in the presentation of Tangun. As the progenitor of the Korean people, he needs to be assigned to the beginning period in the Korean peninsula, and so he is mythically described. This equates Tangun with the Chulmun or Neolithic period in Korea.

But as soon as a shift is made from myth to archaeology, inconsistencies appear. For example, since Neolithic inhabitants of the peninsula are not seen as Korean ancestors, but as a thin population that was soon overrun or possibly exterminated by the Yemaek invaders (Kim Won-yong 1982), Tangun cannot be one of those Palaeo-Asiatics. What happens to Tangun? He becomes one of the Yemaek. However, the association of Tangun with bear worship creates an awkwardness which is most often ignored, for the circumpolar bear cult is ascribed to Palaeo-Asiatics.

The asserted nomadism of the first Koreans is also part of the need to find Korean ethnicity outside the peninsula. It seems to be easier to conceive of a group moving in its entirety if it is nomadic to begin with, than to imagine people with land and crops making such a move. The reputed nomadism in Manchuria, however, is not substantiated with archaeological finds. In fact, permanent settlements are the norm in Manchuria for some seven thousand years (Nelson, in preparation).

I would like to conclude by suggesting that the political need to find distinctiveness and wholeness in Korean culture in the past, as well as in the present, has been detrimental to archaeological interpretation. In this climate it has been difficult, if not impossible, for Korean archaeologists to develop theory with regard to the formation of ethnicity, even though this is a major focus of interpretation in Korean archaeology.

This outcome is particularly disappointing, since theories of ethnicity in the prehistoric past are not well developed anywhere. Ethnicity is problematic even in ethnography, and it is even more difficult to understand using archaeological data. The origins of specific ethnicities, however, should be reachable with archaeological data (Auger *et al.* 1987).

Some suggestions have been made with regard to entry into this problem. For example, ritual and culinary practices may be reflected in archaeological finds (Santley *et al.* 1987), and continuity of house style (provided there is no environmental reason for the change) and clothing may also reflect ethnic dimensions. Another promising line of inquiry would deal with stylistic boundaries between non-functional artefacts or decorative patterns on functional artefacts. Korean archaeology is in a position to make an important contribution to the development of theory regarding ethnicity in the past, if it can shed its insistence on ethnic Koreanness from time immemorial.

14 Nationalism and postwar Japanese archaeology

Clare Fawcett

In August 1945 the Japanese people, crushed by years of war and numbed by the final horrors of Hiroshima and Nagasaki, awaited the arrival of the Allied Forces. Within a few months the work of rebuilding postwar Japan would begin. Part of this process involved the creation of a new vision of the Japanese people's national identity, a new image of what it meant to be Japanese.

In this paper I will trace the relationship between postwar Japanese archaeology and this new sense of Japanese national identity. I will argue that in the aftermath of World War II, Japanese archaeologists believed that their discipline could prevent a revival of emperor worship and extreme nationalism by using material remains to rewrite ancient Japanese history. This approach, which focussed on the retrieval and description of primary data, was highly empirical. In the 1950s and 1960s, a goal of archaeological work was to collect and organize materials excavated through academic research projects. Later, during the 1970s and 1980s, information began to come mainly from administrative rescue excavations. Archaeologists found themselves unable to keep up with the constant need both to excavate sites threatened with destruction and to publish the results in a form accessible to the general public. Consequently, archaeological information has gradually been incorporated into a broader discourse, one which revolves around the definition of a new Japanese national identity.

The aims of this paper are: first, to draw a picture of the changing socio-political context of Japanese archaeology in the postwar period; secondly, to describe how the empiricism of post-war research – a reaction to prewar nationalism – has resulted in contemporary archaeological work being extremely descriptive; and thirdly, to show how this trend has led to archaeological results being incorporated into a discourse which molds a new national identity (and some would say a new nationalism) for Japan.

I Nationalist ideology and archaeology before 1945

To understand postwar Japanese archaeology one must know something of prewar ultra-nationalist ideology and how it affected the study of history and prehistory in Japan prior to 1945. Prewar Japanese nationalist ideology was founded on the premise that the Japanese emperor was a sacred being descended from the gods. Individual Japanese were thought to owe complete allegiance to the emperor, an embodied god and the symbolic father for all Japanese subjects.

The strength of prewar nationalist ideology was such that official explanations of the origins of the imperial line, the Japanese state, and the Japanese people could not be questioned. These explanations were based on two texts, the *Kojiki* and the *Nihon shoki*, both of which had been compiled during the seventh and eighth centuries and were based on ancient myths and legends.

Archaeology did exist in prewar Japan. From the late 1860s through the 1880s, archaeologists tried to tie artefacts to peoples by attempting to identify which prehistoric groups could have made the early Jomon pottery (*c.* 10,000–300 BC) found throughout the archipelago (Ikawa-Smith 1982). As imperial ideology became more entrenched during the 1890s, however, these research questions faded away until archaeologists were limiting their investigations to the detailed description and typological classification of artefacts with no mention of the people who might have made them.

II Japanese archaeology during the Occupation period

The first few years of the Allied Occupation of Japan (1945–52) were a time of limited activity for archaeologists. By 1948, however, just three years after the end of the Pacific War, there were 109 archaeological excavations reported in Volume 1 of *Archaeologia Japonica: The Annual Report of the Japanese Archaeologists Association.* Most of these excavations were small scale. They were either directed by professional university archaeologists assisted by students, college or public school archaeology clubs and other interested amateurs or they were conducted by amateur archaeologists, many of whom were school history teachers or local civil servants (Nihon Kokogaku Kyokai 1951:35–119). Despite limited time and funding – most of the funding for these projects came out of the pockets of the archaeologists themselves – these men (and they were all men) were generally careful researchers who provided invaluable information about Japanese prehistory. These early archaeologists were ardent students of the Japanese past who went about their work with profound dedication. They had a mission – to rewrite the history of Japan unsullied by the myths of prewar nationalist ideology.

The best-known excavation to be carried out during the Occupation period was that of the Yayoi period (300 BC–AD 300) Toro site in Shizuoka Prefecture. Some of the funding for the excavation of Toro came from the municipal and prefectural governments, but most was provided by the national government which, in 1948, recognized the importance of the site for Japan by presenting the excavators with a substantial grant of 700,000 yen (Fujita 1951:4).

The Toro site excavation was carried out between 1947 and 1950. It was important for a number of reasons. First, the excavation was reported in newspapers throughout Japan, giving the Japanese people an awareness of archaeology, buried cultural properties, and the scientific study of the ancient past (Niiro 1986:216). This public interest and awareness encouraged the Japanese government seriously to consider funding archaeological work. Secondly, the Toro excavation was a multi-disciplinary, cooperative project which involved scholars from a variety of universities and disciplines throughout Japan (Fujita 1951:4; Tsuboi 1986:485). Finally, the project set a precedent in theoretical orientation since the archaeologists who excavated Toro were determined to show that, in the postwar period, the study of Japanese ancient history would be based on the systematic excavation and analysis of material remains (Fujita 1951:3; Takahashi 1980:192). At Toro, archaeologists established one of the important premises of postwar archaeology: that the writing of Japanese ancient history should be based on the excavation and analysis of empirical evidence using scientific methods rather than on the study of ideological documentary evidence as had been the case prior to 1945.

In 1950, the Law for the Protection of Cultural Properties was passed by the Japanese Diet (Bunkacho Bunkazai Hogo Bu 1989:224). After this only those individuals whose work was judged, by their peers, to be of professional quality were granted permission to direct archaeological excavations. Since there were few full-time jobs for professional archaeologists in universities or in government offices dealing with cultural properties, many of the individuals directing excavations in the late 1940s and into the 1950s continued to make a living working not at archaeology but at other jobs. For these "amateurs," archaeology was an important aspect of their personal identity. Often, they accorded as much or more importance to their role as "archaeologist" as to their job as teacher or government employee. This was reflected in the fierce dedication they had to the discipline. Ultimately, the work of these amateurs laid the foundation for understanding the culture history of the Japanese islands and contributed to a tradition of public interest and involvement in archaeology.

In the early postwar period, particularly during the late 1940s and the first half of the 1950s, historical materialist analyses of history, based on the work of Japanese Marxist historians, became popular among Japanese archaeologists. One of the reasons for this was the general acceptance of Marxist political philosophy among Japanese intellectuals, of whom archaeologists and historians formed a subgroup (Nishi 1982:94). Many historians and archaeologists accepted Marxist theory after 1945 because Marxism was one of the only intellectual traditions whose advocates had continued to criticize imperial ideology through the prewar and war years. Consequently, in the immediate postwar period, Marxists and Marxist philosophy were seen as untainted by prewar ideology and were therefore considered acceptable. Marxist interpretations of ancient history provided a change from the ultra-nationalist history written prior to and during the war.

Marxism also became an important part of the landscape in electoral politics after 1945. Support for the Japan Communist Party grew rapidly, and the socialists, some of whom were philosophically Marxist, participated in a coalition government for fifteen months during 1947–8 (Totten 1983). However, with the advent of purges of Marxists in academia and elsewhere during the late 1940s and early 1950s, electoral support for the Japan Communist Party and the socialists decreased (Nishi 1982:251; Totten 1983:11).

Marxist interpretations were of special interest to archaeologists working in western Japan, where the nature of the archaeological material encouraged discussions of the origins of the Japanese state. The academic implications of a turn toward historical materialism are not important for my discussion here. More important is that archaeology, a discipline whose data base is composed of excavated remains rather than documents, was seen as crucial for the creation of a new version of Japanese history, which would put to rest the prewar versions of history based on notions of sacred imperial descent.

Another important aspect of postwar Marxist archaeology was the linking of theory to practice through the "people's history movement." The "people's history movement" was an effort by Marxist historians and archaeologists to confront increased repression of socialist thought from 1948 to 1952 by the Supreme Commander of the Allied Powers (SCAP, the Occupation government) and, after 1952, by conservative Japanese politicians (Yoshida 1984:50). The purposes of the movement were to involve historians in both educational and scientific research by developing a form of historical research which would bring together scholars, students, and local people to write historical studies of the Japanese common people in their local regions and workplaces. The "people's history movement" was supported mainly by young scholars and students rather than by established historians and archaeologists. It lasted only four years. Nevertheless, the movement implanted in the consciousness of the Japanese public and historians the idea that public involvement in the creation of history is important (Yoshida 1984).

The Tsukinowa Kofun (Burial Mound) site, which dates to the Kofun period (*c.* AD 300–600) is the best example of the "people's history movement" in archaeology (Kondo 1960; 1983a; 1983b). The project was directed by archaeologists from Okayama University. The goal of the Tsukinowa excavation was to involve people of different ages, social classes, and backgrounds in the excavation of a site and, in doing so, to promote the democratic study of history and social studies (Yoshida 1984:45). In 1953 10,000 people from the towns and villages near the site participated in the excavation (Kondo 1960:418). Unlike Toro, Tsukinowa was not financed by the Japanese government but by the local people through their village council and other associations (Kondo 1983a:22).

Thus, at Tsukinowa, the empiricist tradition of Japanese archaeology was tied to the idea of archaeological remains as a reservoir of information about the Japanese people's history. Historical knowledge, furthermore, was to be created by and for the Japanese people; it was not to be controlled by Japan's ruling political and business elites. The widespread acceptance of this paradigm is what leads many archaeologists to say that postwar Japanese archaeology has Marxist foundations. It has also resulted in a realization by postwar archaeologists that archaeological data are closely linked to social and political issues.

Yet, not all early postwar archaeologists were Marxist in orientation, although all were quick to deny the validity of imperial worship ideology for the interpretation of ancient Japanese history. For the first few years after the war, many of the professional archaeologists teaching in the universities were relatively conservative individuals who had done research and taught in prewar Japan. Many of these people had steered clear of the political implications of their work by stressing the formal study of the archaeological record. For a large number of archaeologists, both professional and amateur, the scientific interpretation of archaeological remains continued to involve inductive and descriptive methods of analysis. The goal of most postwar researchers was to sort artefacts into types and then describe their spatial and chronological variation. Many amateurs made crucial contributions to the development of this Japanese prehistoric culture history at a local level. Archaeologists believed that this kind of empirical work was a first step toward understanding Japanese history. When excavations, such as that at the Toro site, began to produce data on prehistoric diet, archaeological goals were expanded to include the reconstruction of prehistoric lifestyles. Thus, early postwar Japanese archaeology focussed on the excavation, description, and analysis of material remains as a way of creating Japanese history, free from imperial nationalist ideology.

III The beginnings of rescue archaeology

With the withdrawal of the Allied Forces in 1952, Japan's conservative political and business elites once again took firm control of the country. Throughout the 1950s they retained power with promises to develop the nation and raise the standard of living for all Japanese citizens. For many Japanese, development held hope for a better life and an escape from the poverty of the postwar period. After its formation in 1955, the Liberal Democratic Party (LDP) remained in power, despite vocal opposition from the socialists and communists over the 1960 renewal of the United States–Japan Mutual Security Treaty. Early enthusiasm for the LDP's policy of industrial development at all costs began to wane in the 1970s, when Japanese citizens realized that rapid economic and industrial growth in the 1950s and 1960s had resulted in pollution, the destruction of natural and historical environments, and severe hazards to public health. At this point, the government began to reduce pollution levels through strict controls to which businesses, in general, adhered and by moving polluting heavy industries to other parts of Japan or abroad.

Land development began to change the face of Japan in the late 1950s. With increasing economic prosperity, public and private construction projects destroyed more and more archaeological sites (Inada 1986; Kihara 1974:13). They did this despite the 1950 Law for the Protection of Cultural Properties. Site destruction worried archaeologists and historians, who argued that developers were destroying evidence needed to create and support a scientific version of the Japanese people's early history. In general, archaeologists, many of whom clung to the paradigm outlined by Marxist historians after the war, opposed the LDP government's philosophy of capitalist development at all costs. They pointed out that cultural properties which could provide scholars with information needed to create a history of Japan that was untainted by emperor-worship ideology were essential elements of Japanese culture and should be protected.

Although all archaeologists criticized site destruction resulting from development rather than research on principle, there were, in practice, two responses to this new situation. A small number of vocal archaeologists rejected the government's push for development and the destruction of archaeological sites through excavations. They argued that, by encouraging rescue excavations, the Japanese government was destroying evidence that could potentially be used to undermine any return of emperor-worship nationalism. Consequently, they retained a radical position and lobbied for site preservation at all costs. In the eyes of this first group of archaeologists, most of whom adhered to the historical materialist tradition, archaeological excavation, unless absolutely necessary, should be conducted only in the context of research aimed at providing the Japanese people with an understanding of their own history.

The majority of archaeologists took another approach to the large-scale site destruction resulting from economic growth and the accompanying development projects. They agreed to excavate some threatened sites, vocally demanded protection for select ones, and, with the help of the media, publicized cases where developers destroyed sites without excavation. Thus, they pushed the Committee for the Protection of Cultural Properties (CPCP), the national government agency administrating the Law for the Protection of Cultural Properties, to offer protection for more sites of national importance, while they accepted contracts to dig less important sites on land which was irreversibly slated for development.

These archaeologists were the mainstream, who formed the core of the Japanese Archaeological Association and staffed national and private university archaeology departments. Although they continued to adhere to the postwar notion of archaeology as a means of rewriting the Japanese people's history and archaeology as an empirical science – a paradigm that had originally been defined within the context of the postwar Marxist tradition – they transformed this message by blending it with a liberal-democratic philosophy that accepted the necessity of economic growth and development despite the destruction of cultural properties. To understand this transformation, it is essential to remember that many archaeologists in this group, as part of the growing Japanese urban middle-class, were members – albeit lowly members – of the new Japanese ruling elite. Although their positions as intellectuals (and later as low-level bureaucrats) gave them less power than those in key business or bureaucratic positions, as professors in national and highly acclaimed private universities, they certainly were, and continue to be, active in defining national identity in postwar Japan.

Consequently, in the late 1950s and throughout the 1960s, many university-based archaeologists were willing to excavate sites when development projects threatened their destruction. These archaeologists justified excavation by pointing out that it was their duty, as archaeologists, to salvage as much as possible from such sites. Many archaeologists accepted that not all sites could be preserved and felt that, as long as they had enough time and money to do adequate excavation, they should participate in this kind of work. Of course, archaeologists also realized that the large-scale excavation of sites made possible by development funding would provide information about Japanese prehistory which would otherwise be unavailable. Some stated openly that this information would help advance the discipline of archaeology. What archaeologists did not often mention when discussing the necessity of excavating threatened sites was that, in many cases, receiving a contract for a large salvage project could provide the individual archaeologist with information that would eventually further his career in academia or later, in the growing administrative archaeology system. Furthermore, these contracts were financially lucrative.

In summary, in the 1960s, we see the development of a group of archaeologists, who, in the late 1960s and 1970s, will go on to build the contemporary administrative system and then become leaders in the fields of academic and administrative archaeology. While there is considerable variation within this group, in general they retain the ideals of the earlier Marxist-based paradigm of archaeology as a way of rewriting the Japanese people's history and a belief in archaeology as an empirical discipline. On the other hand, they accept and work within the liberal-democratic tradition of postwar Japan and certainly do not consider themselves "Marxist archaeologists."

IV The creation of an administrative archaeology system and the control of archaeological knowledge within Japan

The late 1960s was a time of change in the structure of Japanese archaeology and in the position of archaeology within Japanese society. Protests by radical students, who accused their professors of compromising professional standards by agreeing to do salvage excavations, and frustration among mainstream archaeologists, who realized that they could not do adequate rescue excavations with limited funds and staff, encouraged mainstream archaeologists to push the government to reform archaeological administration. Archaeological administrators working within government agencies, such as the Committee for the Protection of Cultural Properties until 1968 and the Agency for Cultural Affairs after that, were already aware of these problems and were also searching for ways to improve the system of administrative rescue archaeology. Thus, in the late 1960s, when the government began to provide more money to build a structure for administrative archaeology, administrators and archaeologists from the newly created Agency for Cultural Affairs worked to build an effective administrative system.

The administrative system they designed was structured so that the prefectural boards of education were given the main responsibility for deciding which sites should be preserved and which should be excavated. Officials of the national-level Agency for Cultural Affairs were asked to work with prefectural officials to find money to preserve sites judged to be important cultural remains of the Japanese people. National and prefectural-level officials were given the task of negotiating between developers and archaeologists to ensure that enough time and money were allocated to carry out adequate excavations on sites destined for destruction. Excavation was carried out by a variety of groups and foundations associated with the prefectural and local levels of government.

As the new structure for the administration of buried cultural properties became a reality, universities throughout Japan expanded their programs to train the hundreds of archaeologists who were to carry out the vast number of rescue excavations anticipated in the future. The professors who taught in these programs were predominantly mainstream archaeologists, who emphasized the ideal of research into Japanese history as a moral imperative for archaeologists. Consequently, students were sent into the archaeological administrative workforce knowing that they were supposed to be concerned with research.

By the mid-1970s, the composition of the archaeological community had changed dramatically. With the expansion of the administrative system, there were jobs available for the many individuals who, in earlier years, would probably have become amateur archaeologists. In consequence, the importance of amateur archaeology decreased. Academic archaeologists remained influential because of their role as teachers and their acknowledged research expertise, although, since the mid-1970s, they have been outnumbered by administrative archaeologists.

It was in the late 1960s and early 1970s that archaeologists saw a substantial and rapid increase in government support for excavation. Unfortunately, as in the late 1950s and 1960s, this offer of money to create an extensive infrastructure for rescue work, a system which would be funded largely by developers, placed archaeologists in a contradictory position. The new administrative system assured archaeologists of adequate funding for excavation, analysis, and site reporting. In this way, it seemed to provide archaeologists with expanded opportunities to conduct research into the Japanese past.

On the other hand, because administrative rescue archaeology was closely regulated and institutionalized, decisions about which sites should be preserved, which should be excavated and how these excavations should be done came to be even more tightly controlled by administrators working through the prefectural boards of education and the national Agency for Cultural Affairs. Since, by the mid-1970s, a large proportion of Japan's archaeologists were working within the administrative system, individual archaeologists had much less control over their own research goals than did earlier amateur or university-based archaeologists.

In addition, once the administration system was in place, many archaeologists became reluctant to protest about site destruction. This was because they recognized that the administrative rescue system was providing money to do excavation work that often yielded results which, when analyzed within the context of broader research goals, could provide a better understanding of Japanese history. Furthermore, because archaeologists had helped to create the administrative system and were integral parts and beneficiaries of it, they were reluctant to complain. But, while archaeologists working in the administrative system appreciated the funding that allowed them to do more excavation than they had ever thought possible, they soon became aware that technical excavation work left little time for analysis and synthetic research. They also realized that, as they did more excavation, an increasingly large number of sites were being irrevocably destroyed. Thus, they were left in a situation where the ideal of site preservation or, at least, adequate research excavation, continued to be at the root of the archaeological paradigm, but the reality of archaeological work was rescue excavation.

V The development of Nihonbunkaron

In the early 1970s, there was a Japan-wide florescence in the study of things Japanese. This interest, which is expressed in all forms of popular culture as well as in some academic works, has been called alternatively Nihonron, Bunkaron and Nihonbunkaron, a term which has been aptly translated by Moeran (1989:183) as "discussions of the Japanese." Nihonbunkaron purports to define the uniqueness of Japanese culture, society, and national character (Befu 1984:66). It also stresses the stereotyped notion that Japanese society is structured around a consensus or group model (Mouer and Sugimoto 1986). Anthropologists writing about Nihonbunkaron have pointed out that the number of writings of this type has greatly increased since the early 1970s (Befu 1984; Mouer and Sugimoto 1986). One explanation for this is that these ideas are a response to Japan's increased interaction with Western nations, an interaction that creates a need within Japan for national self-determination (Befu 1983). The definition of Japanese culture as unique and homogeneous provides a way of distancing the country from Western nations and denying any possibility of comparison between Japan and the West. In addition, the view of Japan as a homogeneous society which works through consensus serves the needs of elites within Japan since it upholds the idea that Japanese people should cooperate with authorities for their own good and that of Japan (Mouer and Sugimoto 1986).

There are many contradictions in Nihonbunkaron. Japanese society is obviously not homogeneous – ethnic minorities such as the Ainu and Koreans exist. Nor are all Japanese middle-class as some would like to believe. When studying Japanese prehistory and history, it soon becomes obvious that many aspects of Japanese culture were introduced to the archipelago from outside and that a model of cultural, racial, and linguistic uniqueness and homogeneity can easily be challenged. Nevertheless, the premise upon which many discussions of the Japanese rest is that of discovering the true origins of the essence of the Japanese people and culture; that is, the origins of Japanese ethnicity and nationality.

VI Asuka Mura and the Japanese national identity

One of the best examples of the use of archaeological materials to create a sense of Japanese national identity was the creation of the historical area of Asuka Mura by Japanese political and business elites. The Asuka area is located in the central part of Nara Prefecture on the main island of Honshu. This small region, which today encompasses four semi-rural villages, is filled with archaeological sites and historic monuments dating from the sixth and seventh centuries (Asuka Historical Museum 1978; Kidder 1972; 1973). The only written records which describe the history of this period – a time of crucial importance since it was during these years that the Japanese state was probably originally formed – are semi-mythological accounts from the *Kojiki* and *Nihon shoki*.

In the late 1960s and early 1970s, at about the same time that the administrative rescue archaeology system was created, two government ministries, the Prime Minister's Office and the Ministry of Construction, began to show interest in developing Asuka Mura into a national historical park area. They were supported and joined in their attempt by members of the Japanese business elite, including executives of companies such as Matsushita Electric and the private Kintetsu train line. The theme for this park was to be Asuka as the "hometown of the Japanese people."

Despite opposition from many of the Asuka area's residents who worried about how residing in a national park site would affect their lives, the Asuka area was developed as a major historic park. The extent to which Asuka has become a symbol designed to create a new Japanese national identity is shown by the following passage from a pamphlet published by the Asuka Preservation Foundation:

> In various nations there are various histories and traditions rooted in the nation's heart, the people's spirit and the people's character. Asuka is a land which must be called the home of the Japanese heart (*Nihon kokumin no kokoro no furusato*). It was here, in the area often housing the capital city during the century between the reigns of Emperor Suiko and Emperor Temmu, that a great reformation took place. It was here that the foundation of the ancient nation of Japan was gradually solidified. And it was here that, with the introduction of Buddhism and other aspects of culture from the Asian continent, the ancient culture of Japan blossomed. In Asuka, where one can touch the ancient palaces and burial mounds, we can truly

feel ancient Japanese history. And here, the contemporary environment evokes the historical environment described by the songs of the Man'yoshu. In Asuka we can recall ancient Japan. (Asuka Hozon Zaidan 1981:1)

The development of a historic park in the Asuka area was significant because it was a clear example of the use of archaeological and ancient historical sites to define a postwar Japanese national identity. After the discovery, in Asuka, during the early 1970s, of the Takamatsuzuka tomb – an eighth-century monumental burial site that demonstrated clear links between political elites in Japan, the states of the Korean peninsula and mainland China – archaeological news began to appear regularly on the front pages of Japanese national newspapers. Television news programs began to cover local excavations, and archaeological themes became more common in all forms of popular culture.

Although archaeologists appreciated the publicity they and their discipline were receiving, they were somewhat ambivalent about the presentation of archaeological and ancient historical news by newspaper and television reporters. Their professional explanations of new discoveries and excavation projects were filtered through the mass media in such a way that the reports were more interesting to the public, but less historically accurate.

Some archaeologists saw the media's "archaeology boom" of the early 1970s as an attempt by Japanese elites to turn the Japanese people's attention away from domestic political problems and toward a new pride in past and present accomplishments of the Japanese nation and people. Others believed that the sudden interest of the media and the public in archaeology reflected the closer contact people throughout Japan had with archaeological sites as a result of the rapid increase in the number of sites being excavated by archaeologists working in the new administrative archaeology system. Another explanation for this sudden interest in archaeology could be that, with Japan's growing economic prosperity and integration into world political, economic, and cultural systems, the Japanese people were becoming more interested in defining who they were as Japanese within their local neighborhoods, as Japanese within the nation of Japan, and as Japanese within the international sphere. These questions can be partially answered through archaeology.

In summary, by the early 1970s, archaeologists had compromised their early postwar attempt to preserve Japanese sites from destruction by accepting money to excavate from public and private developers. Furthermore, they had lost some, although certainly not all, control of the way in which crucial aspects of Japanese history were presented and explained to the public. By accepting controlled rescue excavation as a viable option in a national program of buried cultural property management, archaeologists sacrificed much of the critical edge of their discipline. Archaeological knowledge was accepted by the liberal-democratic establishment of Japan as a useful and non-threatening means of defining Japanese national identity, as seen at Asuka Mura.

This trend continues today. By the mid-1980s, a large number of archaeologists, some based in prefectural and local boards of education excavation units, others in non-profit, public foundations (Bunkazai Senta, that is, Cultural Property Centers), and a small minority at universities, museums and research institutes, found themselves working hard to dig and analyze the thousands of sites being threatened annually by destruction throughout Japan. In 1987, for example, archaeologists excavated 21,755 sites throughout Japan. Of these, only 409 were academic excavations while 21,346 were administrative rescue projects (Nara Kokuritsu Bunkazai Kenkyujo Maizo Bunkazai Senta 1989:1). Interviews I conducted in 1986 with archaeologists working in the administrative rescue system, in academic posts, and at national research institutes and museums show that archaeologists still cling to the postwar ideal of archaeology as the empirical study of the Japanese people's history. This theme underlies all of their work. Yet, the changing social, political, and economic contexts of archaeology and the nation of Japan have resulted in archaeologists, particularly those who work in the administrative rescue system, losing control over the presentation of archaeological information to the public. In this way, archaeological knowledge is being transformed into another means of creating Japanese national identity.

Japanese political and business elites exercise tremendous power over archaeology through the auspices of the Japanese state, though I do not believe that this socio-political context of archaeology completely controls the organization of the discipline or the research of archaeologists. Nevertheless, in the case of Japan, the state and business elites have shaped the kinds of research archaeologists do, the way they structure and organize their work, and the use of archaeological results in the public realm – particularly the use of archaeology to define Japanese national identity.

In the prewar era, this control was obvious. It was manifested through the dismissal or even arrest of archaeologists who questioned official versions of history based on the myth of imperial sanctity. Although archaeologists themselves did not necessarily believe this myth, they turned away from archaeological research related to the imperial line and focussed instead on detailed classificatory studies of archaeological materials, studies which were less threatening to the state ideology. In the prewar period, the control the Japanese state had over archaeological research and interpretation was overt.

In the postwar period, particularly since the late 1960s and early 1970s, archaeology has once again come under the control of the Japanese state. This control, however, is quite subtle. Early postwar archaeology was characterized by its sense of mission to create a history for the Japanese people and a radical stand *vis-à-vis* the development plans of the conservative Japanese political and business elites. Through the 1950s and early 1960s, these elites reacted to archaeologists' and the public's calls for site preservation by saving a few key sites and providing limited time and funds to excavate others. By the late 1960s, however, a number of influential LDP politicians and business leaders had become interested in the origins of the Japanese nation and Japanese people. Archaeology, which was able to produce information on precisely these topics, became a field worthy of notice and funding. Funding was provided through the prefectural and national administrative archaeology systems, which pleased most archaeologists. They were less happy about the funding provided to preserve Asuka Mura, which came directly from the national government by way of the Ministry of Construction or from the Asuka Zaidan (Asuka Foundation), a foundation created by the business community.

From the late 1960s, therefore, archaeology began to feed into a new form of Japanese nationalism, a nationalism that is not focussed on the emperor (although the imperial family does remain of interest), but which has as its central theme the notion of the Japanese people as a cohesive and homogeneous "ethnic" group. We see in the postwar period a reformatting of the ideological system used to create a sense of cohesion and homogeneity among the Japanese people and to deny internal social conflict. Nationalist ideology has been transformed from a system of belief based on the notion of *kokutai* (the national body), in which the Japanese people were seen as a "family" linked to the emperor in a paternalistic bond, to a vision of the Japanese people as descended from the "original Japanese," who created the "roots" of the Japanese nation. Paralleling this general ideological transformation, we see a transformation within the field of archaeology, from neutral work that did not threaten the imperial myth to work that feeds into the myth of homogeneity.

The question that arises is how consciously elites have used and controlled archaeology. In my opinion, control manifests itself on two levels. On the first level, we can say that the themes archaeologists explore and the way archaeology is used in the broader public realm of the mass media and the tourist industry have been consciously and actively controlled by elites. This control is manifested through the funding for research focussing on Japanese origins and the preservation of specific sites linked to this theme. Asuka Mura is only the most obvious example of this form of control. Of course, for the individuals and organizations who provide the funding and for those doing the research, this work appears to be objective. Archaeologists and historians are simply answering questions about the origins of the Japanese people, which, in the eyes of researchers and in the eyes of the Japanese people as a whole, is a valid research goal. Nevertheless, to understand how archaeology is being shaped by the need of the Japanese elites to neutralize conflict and opposition throughout Japanese society, one has to look at the overall effect of the ideology of Japanese homogeneity in contemporary Japan.

The second and more subtle level at which Japanese government and business controls archaeology is through its policy of funding empirical research. This is seen in the structure of the administrative rescue system, which favors total site excavation and detailed description over synthetic problem-oriented research. It is also demonstrated by the recent increase in funding aimed at the development of scientific techniques of data collection and data organization. The overall effect of this emphasis on detail over theory is that, over successive intellectual generations, Japanese archaeology is losing its critical edge. Archaeologists, particularly those working in the administrative system, are becoming technicians, unable, or not interested, to look at their data with a synthetic or critical eye. This kind of control is not overt; Japanese elites did not consciously set out to neutralize archaeologists. Nevertheless, this has been the result of this focus on data.

Many questions remain unanswered. What, for instance, is the relationship between archaeologists and the mass media? Many professional archaeologists write popular books or magazine articles on archaeological themes, organize museum displays, and appear on television talking about their work. How does the work of these professionals feed into this new image of Japanese national identity? How is archaeology incorporated into the teaching of Japanese history in schools? Does archaeology define only national identity or are archaeological data incorporated into discussions of local or regional identity? Finally, how does the Japanese public interpret and understand the work of archaeologists and the popular presentation of archaeological research? These are questions for future research.

Part V

Commentary

15 Promised lands and chosen peoples: the politics and poetics of archaeological narrative[1]

Neil Asher Silberman

As the essays in this volume demonstrate so clearly, images and symbols from the past play conspicuous and powerful roles in the present. In the many twentieth-century examples cited here by the authors, we can see how archaeological finds become battle-banners of modern ethnic groups and nations; how the dubious evidence of ancient ethnic migrations and diffusions can be used to legitimize modern territorial expansion and ethnic cleansing; how patterns of archaeological funding and scholarly interest can place interest on certain politically useful sites and certain classes of evidence; and how archaeological interpretation can often both reflect and reinforce the centralizing policies of emerging nation-states. Yet this chapter will attempt to show that such nationalist bias in archaeological research and interpretation is neither a regional aberration nor merely a curable symptom of an identifiable scholarly disease. It will argue that archaeology has by its nature an unavoidable political dimension – and that nationalism is simply one of many possible manifestations of its character as *both* a scientific and a political enterprise.

Although most of the chapters in this volume deal with regions with long historiographical traditions, where images of ancient enmity have fueled modern ethnic or political conflict, archaeology can also be seen to manifest its political character in superficially peaceful surroundings and "shallow" historical contexts. G.W. Bowersock's patronizingly ethnocentric observation (1988:190; also cited in Kohl 1993:181) that "America is most unusual in its lack of feeling for the contemporaneity of ancient history," and is thus inherently different from those Middle Eastern nations that still shed blood over ancient grudges, misses an important point. Archaeological finds from Mount Vernon or Monticello may – for the elite represented by the Society of Mayflower Descendants or the Daughters of the American Revolution – have no less emotional impact or political utility (Marling 1988) than the Tomb of Philip for a modern Greek Macedonian politician (Silberman 1989) or a neo-Babylonian palace for a modern Middle Eastern chief of state (Lewis 1989). The artefacts and human remains recently excavated at the Little Bighorn National Battlefield in Montana are no less evocative for the Lakota Sioux or the Northern Cheyenne because they date only from AD 1876 (Silberman in press; Linenthal 1983). When it comes to modern beliefs and behavior, "ancientness" may lie in the eye of the beholder. How ancient, after all, is the historical mythmaker's "once upon a time?"

The main focus of interest of the contributors to this volume is on the influence that nationalism has exerted (and still exerts) on professional standards of behavior and research traditions *within* the discipline. This chapter will, in contrast, attempt to view the phenomenon from an outside perspective – that of society at large. Its primary interest will be on forms of archaeological interpretation that gain currency among the general public, conveyed in such media as schoolbook texts, guided tours through national parks, museum displays, and popular literature (for some general studies of this subject, see, for example, Friedman 1992, Lowenthal 1985, Leone 1981, and Lewis 1975). Whether spoken, written, or visually depicted, these interpretations usually take the form of narratives: sequences of archetypal story elements, didactically arranged with clear beginnings, middles, and ends. And whether describing the archaeology of Jerusalem, Croatia, or Colonial Williamsburg, these archaeologically based stories often address politically evocative themes.

Bruce Trigger's classic article, "Alternative Archaeologies: Nationalist, Colonialist, Imperialist" (1984) was among the first to highlight some common archaeological story patterns that are linked to specific political contexts. "Nationalist" archaeology, in Trigger's view, is the most common of the traditions and tends to emphasize the decisive historical role of the presumed ancestors of modern ethnic groups or nations. This is obviously a pattern that most of the chapters in this volume describe. "Colonialist" archaeology is characteristic of areas settled by Europeans since the sixteenth century and tends to denigrate the historical role of displaced aboriginal peoples. "Imperialist" archaeology is usually an expansionist national tradition that spreads under the aegis of a military or economic superpower that presumes it possesses an understanding of the mechanics of global historical change. To construct a typology of stories, however, is certainly not to suggest that standards of scientific observation are irrelevant or that the purveyors of archaeological interpretation bear no moral or social responsibility for the practical application of their ideas. If archaeological interpretation is indeed a form of political discourse (Shanks and Tilley 1987b; Patterson 1995), it should be subject to the same standards of public accountability as other forms of public expression – in addition to its obligation to adhere to scholarly standards of logic and evidence.

In most cases, egregious political bias in archaeological interpretation –

usually linked to far more significant human rights abuses – is fairly easy to identify. The evil and murderous implications of Nazi archaeology and anthropology (documented by Arnold and Hassmann and by Anthony in this volume and by Proctor 1988), the tight ideological control exercised by the Soviet state over theoretical discussion (Shnirelman, this volume), and the pervasive racism of many European scholars who laid the foundations for the archaeology of southern Africa (Hall 1984), to enumerate just a few examples, are symptoms of far more pervasive political crimes. In the area of the archaeological and political world with which I am most familiar, the Near East, it is possible to trace a long history of politically inspired archaeology that has been harmful to both archaeological resources and ethnic minorities (Silberman 1990, 1991). But what of the cases in which reasonably well-grounded archaeological interpretation can be shown to foster legitimate national pride, ethnic awareness, or communal solidarity? At what point does the interplay of scientific research and modern political contexts become undesirable or even dangerous? This article will suggest that a scholar's responsibility to speak out on these questions lies in his or her willingness to criticize archaeological narratives as *both* scientific hypotheses and literary texts.

I The archaeologist with a thousand faces

In all of the discussions of politically inspired and ideologically potent archaeological stories contained in this volume, one tale remains omnipresent, but is never explicitly discussed. It is the fable of the Archaeologist as Hero – one of the basic narrative forms through which archaeological finds are brought to the public, in varying degrees of elaboration and detail. As an adventure story with a moral, it legitimizes the exploration of hidden places and sanctions the removal of long-hidden antiquities. As a genre of travel writing, it often emphasizes the local population's ignorance or hostility to the archaeologist's endeavor and places the scholar's persistence in a heroic light (on a parallel colonial genre, see Smith 1983). From often humble beginnings, and often with a childhood fascination for antiquity, the archaeologist leaves familiar surroundings to undergo exacting professional training under a series of mentors and when armed, at last, with the intellectual weapons of the profession, sets off for unfamiliar or exotic realms, braving opposition and danger to solve an ancient mystery. The lives of such real-life archaeologists as Austen Henry Layard, Heinrich Schliemann, Arthur Evans, and Howard Carter have lent themselves to this style of retelling (the classic being, of course, Ceram 1951), as have such fictional heroes as John Cullinane (Michener 1965) and Indiana Jones.

This narrative pattern should be familiar from works on ancient mythology and folklore by James Frazer (1922), Vladimir Propp (1968), and Robert Graves (1948), among others. The most recent and by far most widely disseminated variation is Joseph Campbell's "monomyth" (1949, 1988). In this distillation of a story form known from many eras and many cultures, Campbell writes (1949:245–6):

> The mythological hero, setting forth from his commonday hut or castle, is lured, carried away, or else voluntarily proceeds to the threshold of adventure. There he encounters a shadow presence that guards the passage. The hero may defeat or conciliate this power and go alive into the kingdom of the dark . . . Beyond the threshold, then, the hero journeys through a world of unfamiliar yet strangely intimate forces, some of which severely threaten him (tests), some of which give magical aid (helpers). When he arrives at the nadir of the mythological round, he undergoes a supreme ordeal and gains his reward . . . or again – if the powers have remained unfriendly to him – his theft of the boon he came to gain . . . The final work is that of return. If the powers have blessed the hero, he now sets out under their protection (emissary); if not, he flees and is pursued (transformation flight, obstacle flight). At the return threshold, the transcendental powers must remain behind; the hero re-emerges from the kingdom of dread. The boon he brings restores the world . . .

Although Campbell's sweeping claims for the universality of this mythic pattern have been subject to criticism for modern ethnocentrism and sexism (Gill 1989), such criticisms should not impede its utility for understanding the frequently ethnocentric and sexist archaeological narratives of the nineteenth and twentieth centuries. The same basic pattern of adventure is endlessly repeated; whether it is Heinrich Schliemann singlemindedly digging at Hissarlik assisted faithfully by his wife Sophia; Frederick Catherwood and John Lloyd Stephens hacking their way through a Guatemalan jungle; Henry Layard outwitting a one-eyed pasha; Yigael Yadin mobilizing a massive expedition to uncover the ancient fortress of Masada; or Ivor Noel Hume following clues to come upon the grisly secret of Martin's Hundred – the repetitive narrative pattern of archaeologist as hero suggests that our culture has developed an effective literary form to legitimize sudden changes or revelations in our understanding of the past. And despite its occasional inversion in popular films and novels that see the archaeologist as a reckless intruder into realms that should not be violated (after the pattern established in the 1932 film *The Mummy*; see Solomon 1978:160–3), I would argue that the heroic narrative pattern deeply colors the general public's understanding of all archaeological work.

Likewise, as palaeoanthropologist Misia Landau has shown in her examination of early theories of human evolution, the folktale can serve as a model not only for stories of scholarly discovery, but in many cases for the scholarly interpretations themselves (1991). In her analysis of the competing evolutionary theories of Darwin, Huxley, Haeckel, Keith, and Elliott Smith, she shows that all these scholars' explanations take the form of narratives in which the primate ancestor of mankind is always the hero; the sequence of evolutionary stages is the adventure; and the transformation of the primate ancestor into a fully modern human is always the end. Yet as she compares these narrative theories, it is the differences in details, characters, and emphasis – rather than the shared literary form – that Landau finds significant. She suggests that narrative analysis may provide an effective way of revealing important differences between rival scientific hypotheses by clarifying their inner logic, choice of causation, and final outcome (1991:177).

Landau's insight on the importance of narrative as the carrier of basic meaning has obvious significance for archaeology. For just as *Homo habilis*, the Neanderthals, or the Cro-Magnons can be seen as "heroes" of scholarly folktales, so can the Minoans, the Incas, or the ancient Israelites. Indeed, it would perhaps not be too great a leap to see some of the most familiar regional archaeological syntheses as the adventures of a "chosen people" in the search for their promised land. Descriptions of competing narratives fill this volume: the diffusion of the Indo-Europeans (Anthony); the origins of the Koreans (Nelson); the cultural achievements of Copper Age society in Portugal (Lillios); and ethnic relations and predominance in the Caucasus (Kohl and Tsetskhladze). In fact, examples can be found in every chapter, since both "nationalist" and non-nationalist interpretations can be seen as rival narratives. Certainly all of these theories must be judged on how they are constrained by the evidence, but there is another level of interpretation in which stories can at least be compared. Most stories focus on the historical development of a specific ethnic group, society, or regional culture, yet what makes some "nationalist" and others more objective? I would suggest that the connected story of archaeologist-as-hero is the crucial factor; when the discoverer proclaims his or her connection to a modern population that claims descent from the group under study, the archaeological narrative is transformed from mere historical description into something of a political essay. The evocative juxtaposition of ancient glory and modern resurrection by a modern descendant (usually across a long period of desolation or political subjugation) creates a compound fable of national resurrection in which the historical existence of neither ancient society nor its putative modern successor possesses full meaning by itself (Silberman 1991).

II Epics of inevitability

Although all of the chapters in this volume deal with the archaeology of the present century, the potent narrative messages conveyed by archaeologists can be traced to the very beginnings of the discipline. Most historians of science place those beginnings in the Renaissance, and a number have highlighted its political context (Trigger 1989a; Rouse 1965). Since at the end of the Middle Ages, in the thirteenth and fourteenth centuries, the High Gothic movement, particularly in France, based its spiritual and temporal power on a *rejection* of the classical past, the growth of interest among southern European – particularly Italian – scholars in precisely the historical period that had been rejected can be seen as a conscious movement of protest. Ciriaco de' Pizzacoli of Ancona, the scholar most often credited with the "invention" of archaeology, traveled through Italy, Greece, Asia Minor, and Egypt during the later fifteenth century collecting ancient inscriptions and carefully sketching archaeological remains. A possibly apocryphal story about him is nevertheless revealing. When a priest asked him what he thought he was doing, Ciriaco told him, "I go to awake the past" (MacKendrick 1952:134). And it was precisely the past that the powers-that-be had neglected that he chose to resurrect. Thus the emergence of an interest in the relics of Greek and Roman antiquity in concert with a new political interest in classical ideals and social norms set early archaeology apart from the haphazard collecting expeditions of curious noblemen, pilgrims, and kings (see also Sklenar 1983).

The implicit political message eventually became more focussed throughout the seventeenth and eighteenth centuries. With the spread of methodical archaeological exploration across Europe, antiquarian enthusiasm often reflected and reinforced emerging feelings of local patriotism. The search for ancient artefacts and monuments was now closely linked to efforts at their identification as the handiwork of historically documented peoples – to whom the searcher felt akin (Trigger 1989a:48–52; Michell 1982). Needless to say, this was the first great age of archaeological nationalism, since it was the first great age of nationalism itself (Smith 1986). Antiquarians pored over medieval records, collected folk traditions, and mapped and measured ancient barrows, hillforts, and stone circles. The scientific value of this work varied greatly (Lynch and Lynch 1968). But all the work, good or bad, fostered a public awareness (naturally quite limited at first) of the archaeologists' dramatic "resurrection" of the material culture of certain ancient groups, whether they be regional, ethnic, or political (Díaz-Andreu, this volume; Anderson 1983; Smith 1986:191–208).

Naturally, older traditions of antiquarianism continued to exist alongside the nationalist: classical connoisseurship continued (Vickers 1987; Stoneman 1987) and classical ideals were still cherished, but by the late eighteenth and early nineteenth centuries, these practices were increasingly linked to a broader imperial enterprise (Bernal 1987). Greek and Roman literature (and of course the Bible) had long been seen as the spiritual inheritance of Western Christendom, and a physical bond between Europe and the lands of the eastern Mediterranean had been forged since the end of Antiquity by stolen or "translated" relics (Geary 1990) and standardized pilgrimage routes (Sumption 1975). With the spread of the modern European empires, however, pilgrimage began to be replaced by a new kind of exploration in which the object was to construct alternative landscapes by empirical observation and historical research, rather than faith (Silberman 1982). At least superficially, classical and biblical archaeology seemed quite distinct from the archaeology of Europe. Indeed, early proponents of biblical archaeology self-consciously attempted to counter the historical doubts cast on the veracity of the Scriptures by Darwin's theories and by evolutionary European archaeology (Moorey 1991:18; Silberman 1982). Yet the same juxtaposition of past and present that gave power to the nationalistic narratives can be distinguished in biblical and classical archaeology as well. The modern discovery of the ancient splendors of the Near East by trained European and American scholars seemed to put Europe and America – rather than modern Egyptians, Palestinians, Turks, or Iraqis – in the position of legitimate heirs (Larsen 1987). And the birthright was seen not only as spiritual or historical but imperial as well (Said 1978).

As Trigger and other historians of science have repeatedly stressed, archaeology and anthropology have long been fundamentally divided between the romantics – looking backward fondly to their favorite chosen peoples and golden ages – and the evolutionists – often looking ahead (Trigger 1981, 1989a, 1989b; Stocking 1987; Carpenter 1950). In certain respects, this divide was geographical as well as philosophical, with classical and biblical archaeology tending toward the romantic and an increasing proportion of prehistoric European archaeology, evolutionary. The personal dimension of the controversy, especially in England, is well illustrated by the fact that the Duke of Argyll, a champion of the theory of cultural degeneration in European prehistory, was also one of the founding members of the Palestine Exploration Fund (Gillespie 1977; Silberman 1982:86). There is, of course, a political and economic context for this philosophical conflict; the metaphor of progress supported the ambitions of a new entrepreneurial middle class that sought to challenge the dominance of a landed elite (Trigger 1989a:84–6; Gordon 1968).

From a strictly narrative standpoint, however, the contrast between the two schools of thought may be somewhat overdrawn. The evolutionist, in seeing all of humanity as a chosen people, writes no less of a patriotic narrative. The barely disguised political subtexts of the various late nineteenth-century theories about the place of the Neanderthals in human evolution, for example, was hardly less powerful or polemical because of their apparent universality (Hammond 1980). Thus whether dealing with the ancient cultures of a single country, nation, region, or all of humanity, the standard archaeological narrative requires that a certain ancient trait be identified, celebrated as noble and timeless, and linked to the present across a long period of ignorance or neglect. The "new" archaeology of evolution showed that the dramatic technological changes then transforming the world through steam and steel, through railroads, suspension bridges, and factories, were a natural and even inevitable part of history. While nationalism is an important and venerable use of this form of archaeological narrative, it is not the only one. Indeed, it might be said that all archaeological stories – be they classical, biblical, nationalist, or evolutionary – can be read as narratives of the inevitability of certain lands to be conquered and the right of certain people to rule.

III Rebuilding the past

We have heard many times in this volume about traditional folktales being supplemented or supplanted by archaeological explanation (for example, Nelson, Kaiser, Kohl and Tsetskhladze, Díaz-Andreu), in the interests of modern ruling elites. It is interesting to note a similar sequence of abandonment of literal belief in traditional myths – and their gradual replacement by positivistic history and archaeology – occurring in locales as diverse as post-medieval Europe, nineteenth-century Japan and China, and, newly emergent, late twentieth-century Asian and African nation-states. In most cases, the reason for this transformation is ascribed to the self-evident superiority of empirically gathered data (as in Posnansky 1982), in other cases to the search for self-justifying political metaphors. Yet it may be argued that the choice of archaeology as a medium for historical self-identification is culturally conditioned and bears a significance that transcends its scientific achievements or specific national context. With the advance of industrialization based on European models and with the construction of modern roads, factories, schools, and water systems, every would-be modern nation naturally seeks to build a "modern" past for itself.

In many cases, the new rulers are members of the indigenous population that has long been dispossessed of a meaningful role in local archaeology (for the case of Egypt, see Reid 1985). Archaeology had traditionally been used by colonial or metropolitan institutions as an instrument of power, to make the rule of a certain chosen people seem timeless and therefore inevitable. In the Near East, Africa, and North America, archaeological narratives often depicted the modern populations as fairly recent usurpers who occupied and in many cases desolated and put an end to the country's golden age (for the Near East, Silberman 1991; for Africa, Hall 1984; for North America, Trigger 1980). In the post-colonial age all this had to be changed. And thus began a process of redressing the perceived historical powerlessness – not by returning to the old epics or inventing a new story, but by following the familiar and venerable archaeological precedent of devoting time, funds, and official sanction to the celebration and presentation of a new chosen people and celebrating a new golden age (Silberman 1990).

For every new nation-state ready to construct for itself a modern saga, both scientific and literary conventions must be observed. All over the world, archaeology students are trained in broadly similar systems of excavation and analysis of data (broadly similar at least in comparison to non-archaeological forms of historical reflection), similarly structured national departments of antiquities are established, and national park services set up to preserve, present, and interpret selected archaeological remains to the general public (for examples and discussion of this process, see Miller 1980). The irony is that, even if regional historical traditions were initially different or modern national identities are in conflict, they are nonetheless made vivid and politically potent by structurally similar narratives. The emotional power of archaeology in Israel, Saudi Arabia, Syria, Cyprus, Turkey, Greece, and the regions of the former Yugoslavia, for example, is that they all implicitly link the present to a particular golden age. And it is important not to overlook a subtle internationalist dimension that exists side-by-side with the nationalist particularism in the new nations of the post-colonial world. The uniqueness and self-contained character of the older folk traditions, with their often surrealistic creatures and miraculous causation, made it difficult to compare and synchronize various national histories. But now, since the archaeology of every new nation addresses *both* a domestic and an international audience, the comparative antiquity of certain peoples or the speed with which they climbed the evolutionary ladder are as important as the celebration of specific events from their history. Thus each new nation must now construct its past with the C14 dates, regional typologies, and anthropological generalization that attempt to make its historical achievements instantly and universally comprehensible.

As contributors to this volume have suggested, the transformation of the past from "traditional" to "modern" is seldom achieved without considerable internal opposition. In most cases, certain power groups within the society in its pre-state form zealously guard their exclusive right to interpret the past. These are often figures of religious authority, whose prestige is derived from familiarity with sacred oral or written texts. Archaeology, with its potential independence from written texts and its wondrously tangible relics, threatens the bases of such specialized, sacred learning. As a result, religious authorities will in some cases attempt to restrict or suppress archaeological activities; in other cases, the religious authorities and their political allies will attempt to utilize archaeological excavations or archaeological monuments to reinforce their own preeminence (as in the case cited by Aronoff 1986). But in either case, the battle over archaeological public interpretation must be seen for what it is: a struggle for power between rival groups in the fluid conditions of an emerging nation-state. Archaeological remains, when preserved and presented to the public, are almost always monuments either to generalized notions of progress or of *someone's* inalienable historical and political rights.

IV From patriotic shrines to theme parks

While the struggle of modern peoples to gain or maintain statehood continues to provoke inter-ethnic bloodshed in the Balkans, the Middle East, and Central Asia, new archaeological challenges confront nation-states whose existence is no longer in doubt. It is striking how many cherished and potent national myths have been recently challenged on archaeological grounds. Masada and Custer's Last Stand (Cohen 1982; Scott *et al.* 1989) are two famous cases in which both factual and metaphorical aspects of the traditional interpretation have come under attack. Likewise, in recent reappraisals of the character of the ancient Israelite conquest of Canaan (Finkelstein 1988), the initial interaction of Dutch colonists and Khoikhoi people of South Africa (Schrire 1988), the supposed economic emancipation of African-Americans in the post-Civil War period (Orser 1988), or the many other examples of overturned nationalist mythmaking cited in this volume, criticism of traditional archaeological interpretation can easily become a barely masked metaphor for criticism of the state.

There are naturally far more serious threats to state power, and they too can have their impact on the pursuit of archaeology. Early hopes that statehood will provide a ready pathway to industrialization, modernization, and prosperity can lead to disillusionment and economic crisis when the impact of reckless development, environmental degradation, and the social dislocation of rapid urbanization begin to be felt (Harvey 1989). For many semi-industrialized nations, particularly those with abundant beaches, wildlife, or archaeological remains, the advantages of encouraging tourism from Japan, Western Europe, and North America seem almost irresistible (for a wide selection of case studies, see Hachlili and Killebrew 1993). At first glimpse, tourism seems a relatively harmless enterprise that can attract welcome foreign currency without the mobilization of a large industrial workforce or the depletion of precious natural resources (Lowenthal 1985). Yet what modern mass tourism often does do – and this is its significance to the historical development of archaeological narrative – is to force the nation to become a parody of itself.

In his instructive and enlightening book, *Reshaping America: Public Memory, Commemoration, and Patriotism in the Twentieth Century* (1992), the social historian John Bodnar traces the rise of the National Park Service in its continual attempts to expand its role in the interpretation of American history. Like other agencies of the federal government, the Park Service has only been able to justify this enlargement of its staff and budget by expanding its bureaucratic responsibilities. And since the performance of the National Park Service – like national parks authorities in most countries – is judged at least partly by attendance figures at its major attractions, the desires and expectations of its potential clients must be taken into account in every major development plan (Foresta 1984). This is particularly problematic in the selection and subsequent presentation of archaeological and historical sites. Needless to say, when market share and market orientation influence government decisions to "create" archaeological attractions, a nation's archaeological narratives are deeply affected. Since the object in selecting sites is to encourage high attendance and tourist revenue, fiercely nationalist archaeology may be counterproductive to attracting outsiders. Interpretations or symbols that have unpleasant or controversial implications may be avoided. In addition, ephemeral prehistoric sites and mudbrick constructions that are difficult to preserve for public viewing will often be excluded, leaving the emphasis on large-scale, impressive, masonry constructions. In the Mediterranean, to take one region as an example, that means sprawling marble-column-filled classical sites.

For a nation like the Republic of Cyprus, with its obvious political attachment to images of Greek antiquity, the extensive excavation and presentation of classical cities like Paphos, Kition, and Ammathus are clearly linked to a modern national self-consciousness (Silberman 1989). In the case of Ephesus and the other Hellenistic-Roman cities of modern Turkey, of Baalbek in Lebanon, or Jerash and Petra in Jordan, the associations to the modern population are more ideologically ambiguous, yet their lucrative drawing power for tourists has a long history. Far more complex and in some ways troubling is the case of a major excavation project now underway in Israel, which, if successful, may herald an era of strictly utilitarian archaeology – directed neither by nationalist ideology nor by the scholarly agenda, but by domestic politics and the hope for economic benefit (Shanks 1990). At the modern development town of Beth Shean (the site of the ancient biblical city of Beth Shean and the Hellenistic and Roman city of Nysa-Scythopolis), the lure of tourism and the problem of high unemployment have been the primary motivations for a massive archaeological dig. Supervised jointly by the Israel Antiquities Authority and the Hebrew University of Jerusalem, and using untrained labor from the local labor exchange, these excavations have uncovered virtually the entire civic center of the ancient city during the past eight years. Whether this site will succeed as a major tourist attraction will depend not only on the finds and presentation, but also on the vagaries of tourist flow, airline fares, and Western fears of international terrorism. What is certain, however, is that economic considerations can open the way to an era in which archaeological resources are selectively exploited, not for scientific or ideological reasons but according to someone's idea of what sells.

The technological and fiscal achievements of public presentation at such sites as the Jorvik Viking Centre in York, England, or Colonial Williamsburg in Virginia, USA, are impressive, and it may be assumed that, as in an earlier age of archaeological exploration, when European and American archaeologists were called upon to train new generations of local scholars to excavate and update the nation's history, so museum planners and exhibit designers will be regularly called in to help merchandize a nation's past. And, consciously or unconsciously, they will shape the historical interpretation of every site. In a bitter international competition for tourist dollars, unpleasantness, inequality, brutality, and evil are no selling cards. For understandable commercial reasons much of what is negative in the historical record will, on occasion, have to be eliminated. The historical fantasies of potential customers will have to be fed.

Yet the late twentieth-century government antiquities departments, tourist ministries, and private foundations that attempt to market their archaeological sites as products are, it might be argued, unable by their bureaucratic natures to forge a coherent narrative message about their sites. Recent studies of the processes of historical interpretation and presentation in America demonstrate that although the historians, architects, designers, and Park Service officials all have genuine concern for effectively presenting their sites to the public, power is shared, responsibility is fragmented, and the scholars and government planners are forced to reconcile their divergent priorities (see the essays in Blatti 1987). The result is that restored historic and archaeological sites – even such evocative locales as Ellis Island in New York Harbor – often express in their signage and exhibits not a single narrative vision but the babel of modern corporate compromise (Bodnar 1986). In the best tradition of electronic age expression, the presentations at interactive archaeological sites and museums do not present a logical line of causation, but rely on the non-narrative association of emotions with things. The future of archaeological interpretation – and perhaps even of historical interpretation, as illustrated by the ambitious plans for Disney's "American" theme park in northern Virginia – may thus no longer lie in the competing narratives of nation-states and would-be peoples, but between archaeological sites that bear ideological messages and those that are designed for profit alone.

V The future of archaeological narratives

From trends emerging in the last decade of the twentieth century, at least two more types can be added to Trigger's typology of alternative archaeologies. The first is the kind of "touristic archaeology" just described – in which attendance figures and revenue expectations are no less significant than scholarly insights. The second type might be an "archaeology of protest," that springs from forces that *oppose* the nation-state. In addition to the examples of counter-narratives cited above, one might mention, among many examples, how recent studies of the material culture of American slavery and plantation life in the seventeenth and eighteenth centuries (and its links to the cultures of Africa) have helped foster historical awareness in many African-American communities (Horton and Crew 1989); how the archaeological investigation of the post-medieval Palestinian village has laid the foundation for a new national scholarly tradition (Ziadeh 1987); and how the right to preserve and interpret traditional Hawaiian archaeological sites has become a focal point of the activism of local groups (Friedman 1992).

In a sense, Trigger's typology can also be seen as a potential sequence, composed of narrative building blocks. Nationalist, Colonialist, Imperialist are descriptions of major transformations that a nation state may undergo. The end and even order of the sequence is uncertain, as are the roles that post-statehood tourism and internal protest may play. Archaeological narratives cannot help but be constructed in contemporary idiom, with emphasis on each society's specific hopes and fears. As the essays in this volume have shown, archaeologists sometimes wear the uniforms of patriots and crusaders. They may also, in different circumstances, become imperial agents, revolutionaries, or tourist shills. Archaeology, the most visual of the historical disciplines, is inescapably didactic. And unless scholars come to appreciate the full complexity of its political and ideological associations, their well-intentioned calls for the eradication of nationalist bias in archaeological interpretation may merely pave the way for the discipline's exploitation by other, even more transcendent ideologies.

NOTE

1 This essay is dedicated, in gratitude, to the memory of Professor Aharon Kempinski of Tel Aviv University, an innovative archaeologist and a tireless crusader for human rights. Over the years, I benefited greatly from Professor Kempinski's friendship, his erudition, and his healthy skepticism of conventional wisdom. Many of the political and ideological themes explored in this essay were first formulated in my conversations with him. Aharon Kempinski died on July 3, 1994, at the start of an era of profound political challenge for both Israelis and Palestinians. His intellectual energy and moral courage will surely be missed.

16 Romanticism, nationalism, and archaeology

Bruce G. Trigger

European thought has been dominated for over 200 years by a pervasive dichotomy between rationalism, universalism, and positivism on the one hand and romanticism, particularism (or "alterity"), and idealism on the other. The first of these philosophical packages was initially associated with French liberalism, the second with German reaction (Dumont 1991). Both ethnic nationalism and post-modernism (which in archaeology is the essence of post-processualism) are products of the romantic side of this polarity.

I Archaeology, idealism, and relativism

Post-processualism remains a minority position in archaeology, but derives considerable prestige from the preeminence of post-modernism in comparative literature and its dissemination throughout the humanities and social sciences (Hunt 1989; Laudan 1990; Rose 1991). Post-processualism propagates the idea that, because every decoding of a message is another encoding, all truth is subjective (Tilley 1990:338). It thereby transforms relativism into an absolute principle. Because of this, many post-processualists conclude that there is no difference between knowledge and faith and further deny the validity of distinguishing science from magic and religion (Barnes 1974, 1977). Archaeologists such as Shanks and Tilley have concluded that the only goal of their research can be a political one (Shanks and Tilley 1987a:195). In their view, the aim of archaeological discourse should be to disempower political and intellectual elites by affirming the relativism, and hence the equal validity, of all explanations of the past (Bapty and Yates 1990; Shanks 1992; Shanks and Tilley 1987a, 1987b, 1989; Tilley 1990, 1991; Ucko 1990). These archaeologists view themselves as being politically progressive and struggling against the reactionary tendencies of powerful, establishment colleagues. Yet, as the papers in this volume clearly illustrate, the history of archaeology reveals that the political uses that have been made of that discipline's "findings" have promoted bigotry, violence, and destruction at least as often as they have promoted social justice. In the context of extreme relativism, it becomes very difficult, if not impossible, to justify political programs in a reasoned fashion.

That archaeologists should find themselves in such an impasse is at least as much the fault of processual archaeologists allowing their commitment to extreme positivism and ecological determinism to epiphenomenalize human cognition, as it is the result of excessive romanticism and idealism. By dismissing perceptions, beliefs, and cultural traditions as significant factors shaping human behavior, processual archaeologists left a void in the study of prehistory that encouraged the development of radical, alternative forms of explanation. Only recently has it become evident that these two forms of explanation complement one another (Preucel 1991; Renfrew and Bahn 1991; Trigger 1989a; Willey and Sabloff 1993). Both extremes might have been avoided had archaeologists paid more attention to the history of their discipline.

Long ago, the archaeologist Gordon Childe, who was strongly committed to a materialist view of human behavior, argued that the world human beings adapt to is not the real world but the world as they imagine it to be. Childe accepted the idealist claim that human perception is organized and rendered meaningful in terms of categories that for the most part are learned within the context of cultural traditions that are specific to particular societies and to various social groups (Childe 1949:5–19). He argued, for example, that the British system of government in the nineteenth century, with its bicameral parliament and constitutional monarch, could not be explained entirely in terms of nineteenth-century British capitalism. Instead, it had to be accounted for as a system that had evolved over many centuries and been modified in the course of the nineteenth century only sufficiently to adapt it to the novel social and economic realities of that era (Childe 1936:98).

At the same time, Childe argued that no cultural system will survive for long if there is not a reasonable congruence between the imaginary and the real worlds. Ideas are tested by their observed utility and their ability to serve human needs and desires (Childe 1956:106–18). Individuals about to bump into a stone wall will stop not simply because they know from experience, or being told, that they may seriously injure themselves but also because they can see an actual wall ahead of them. Childe's position annihilated the opposition between positivism and idealism. He did not provide a detailed account of how ideas and observed reality relate to one another, but avoided the twin dangers of ecological and cultural determinism by viewing cultural traditions as simultaneously being: 1. the means by which individuals cope with their environment; 2. an inertia that opposes change; and 3. intellectual formulations that are transformed as individuals and groups seek to cope with environmental challenges and achieve new goals. Determining more precisely the nature of the relations between cultural traditions and social action remains a major problem for the social sciences and is a subject of much heated debate. Yet it remains clear that ideas, many of them derived from specific cultural traditions, are a source of knowledge and attitudes that play a major role in guiding human behavior.

Childe also acknowledged that circumstances arise in which traditional knowledge is inadequate to guide or reshape human behavior. He believed that such knowledge could be adaptively functional or dysfunctional. In extreme situations, what people believe may limit their responses to novel challenges to the extent that it severely inhibits their ability to compete with groups who hold alternative beliefs (Childe 1947:65–76, 81). Childe's views apply equally to particular nationalisms, to specific forms of archaeological interpretation, and to entire cultural systems.

In terms of archaeological practice, Childe's epistemology suggests that there can be a productive dialogue between the conscious or unconscious beliefs of the archaeologist and what Alison Wylie (1982) and others (Watson 1990:683) describe as the resistance of the archaeological record. Even though the preoccupations of archaeologists play a major role in determining such basic matters as what they do or do not perceive as evidence and the ways that they classify such evidence, the very fact that archaeologists must take account of material that they did not create themselves imposes significant limitations on their imaginations. It is absurd to maintain that there are no empirical limits to the manner in which archaeologists can responsibly interpret their data.

Another dichotomy that has perhaps outlived its usefulness is that drawn between the internal and external factors that shape archaeological thought (Welter 1965). Archaeologists have to adapt to a work environment that is composed of political and economic, as well as intellectual, factors. Political conditions may formally or informally constrain what archaeologists say about their data. Some interpretations of archaeological data may result in greater economic or social rewards than do others. The art historian Barry Lord (1974) has demonstrated the important role that patronage has played in encouraging the development of some artistic styles and the disappearance of others. Yet the interpretation of the past is also powerfully shaped by internal factors, such as what archaeologists individually and collectively believe they know about the past and what techniques they have at their disposal for recovering, analyzing, and interpreting archaeological evidence. There is also the physical evidence of the past, which instead of merely changing, increases incrementally over time.

The archaeological understanding of the past is clearly influenced by all these factors, although it is uncertain how they relate to each other in specific situations. What is clear, however, is that what archaeologists say about the past is not simply a reflection of their ethnic or class prejudices or what a patron or authority figure wishes, even if the latter is in a position to be politically or economically coercive. It is also a product of the state of the discipline in specific places and at particular times. Furthermore, all of these factors are channeled through the idiosyncratic understanding and personalities of individual archaeologists. Nicholai Marr's ideas about linguistics and prehistory may have been punitively supported by the Soviet government because these ideas were perceived to accord with that government's internationalist policies in the 1920s and 1930s. Yet, as Shnirelman points out in this volume, Marr's ideas were not originally formulated with that goal in mind. It is quite possible that, had a number of theories that were reasonably congenial to state policy been available, the Soviet government might have selected another of them. What is favored at any given time is a product not only of specific economic and social conditions but also of ongoing, and sometimes competing, traditions of archaeological research. The complex ways in which internal patterns of research and external conditions intersect ensure that the development of archaeology does not occur in a unilinear fashion and that the paths it follows can never be predicted easily or with any assurance.

II Archaeology and nationalism in historical perspective

Nationalism is only one of many political forces that have impacted on archaeology, and a relatively recent one. Its seeming antiquity results from its having incorporated ethnic stereotypes that in some cases are thousands of years old (Wailes and Zoll, this volume). Throughout much of recorded human history royal families and ethnic groups have sought to bolster their prestige by invoking mythical links to the gods or to some glorious human past. In the medieval period, these claims took the form of claiming descent from individuals named in the Bible or in Greek and Roman mythology. After Renaissance scholarship had discredited this approach and drawn attention to ancient buildings and works of art as sources of historical information, Kings Christian IV of Denmark (reigned 1588–1648) and Gustavus II Adolphus of Sweden (reigned 1611–32) promoted antiquarian research as part of the political and military rivalry that followed the separation of their kingdoms in 1523. Still earlier, the Tudor monarchs of England had sought prestige by favoring the critical Renaissance scholarship of the itinerant Italian historian Polydore Vergil, even though his research undermined the historicity of medieval claims that were highly flattering to the British people and more particularly to the Tudor dynasty (Ferguson 1993).

In general, Renaissance scholarship used antiquarian studies less for nationalistic purposes than to legitimize political changes by providing them with classical precedents. For example, the development of democratic and princely governments in opposition to feudalism in northern Italy was justified as conforming to forms of political organization that could be shown to have existed prior to the decline of the Roman empire (Slotkin 1965:x). Likewise, in Japan, the Kokugaku (or National Learning) movement, which began in the late seventeenth century and emphasized the study of Japanese history and antiquities, played a major role in subverting Tokugawa feudalism and bringing about the restoration of Imperial rule in the late nineteenth century (Hoffman 1974). On the other hand, scholars in India manifested little interest in either history or antiquarian studies in pre-colonial times. While Arab culture strongly promoted the study of history, its stigmatizing of the pre-monotheistic period as a *jahiliya*, or Age of Darkness, effectively discouraged the development of a scholarly interest in antiquarianism.

As Díaz-Andreu points out in this volume, western European nationalism was the product of a process of economic and social change that gradually came to invest *de facto* sovereignty in the entire population of states rather than in their rulers and their families. In France, this view developed within the context of Enlightenment philosophy, which played a major role in precipitating the French Revolution. Enlightenment philosophy originally envisaged all human beings as potential beneficiaries of progress (Slotkin 1965:423). The French republic sought to export its new and "better" way of life to neighboring peoples. Edward Said (1978) to the contrary, many of the French revolutionary leaders who supported Napoleon's invasion of Egypt in 1798 had long regarded Egypt as a source of ancient wisdom, a view that was prevalent in the masonic lodges to which many of them belonged (Curl 1982:83–8). They also believed that social and legal reforms, especially with respect to property, would allow modern Egyptians to enjoy the same benefits that these reforms were assumed to be bringing to the peoples of western Europe (Herold 1962:15–16). The French revolutionaries may have been totally ethnocentric in their admiration for their own cultural and political achievements, but they also believed in the ability of all human beings to share in the progress of the Enlightenment.

The scientific archaeology that replaced an object-oriented antiquarianism in western Europe, beginning in the early nineteenth century, reflected the universalism of the Enlightenment. While the archaeology that initially developed in Scandinavia, Scotland, and Switzerland was not devoid of patriotic embellishments, its main theme was cultural evolution rather than ethnic history. This was even more true of the Palaeolithic archaeology that developed in England and France from the 1850s. The main aim of evolutionary archaeology was to document the archaeological record of human achievements back to their oldest and simplest beginnings and hence to demonstrate the historicity of the conjectural developmental schemes of Enlightenment philosophers. As Darwinian evolution opened up new theoretical perspectives concerning human biological origins, this task acquired greater urgency and social importance (Trigger 1989a:73–102). The findings of evolutionary archaeology helped to alter irreversibly a scientific understanding not only of human biological and cultural origins but of human nature as well.

An evolutionary perspective, albeit a much modified one, survived the undermining of a faith in the capacity of all peoples to share in human progress which resulted from the growing racism that accompanied the expansion of colonialism in the course of the nineteenth century. As Europeans came to exploit much of the rest of the world, the western European middle class began to doubt that all peoples could benefit from technological progress. Darwinian evolutionism was utilized to denigrate the capacity for development of aboriginal peoples by comparison with Europeans and to provide a new, scientific respectability to the racial prejudices that colonists had long directed against the American Indians. Under the leadership of John Lubbock, a little understood archaeological record was construed to support the view that Europeans were, as a result of thousands of years of biological evolution, capable of promoting and benefiting from cultural progress, while the aboriginal peoples they were supplanting in the Americas, Africa, Australia, and the Pacific were incapable of doing so. Hence the exploitation and replacement of these peoples by European settlers was viewed as facilitating the biological as well as the cultural development of the entire human species. Lubbock's scheme was a universal one, built upon a racist view of human capabilities (Trigger 1989a:110–47).

As nationalism became politically more important from the late 1860s, it began to play a more prominent role in shaping archaeological research. In western Europe industrialization was producing increasing class conflict, giving rise to trade unionism, demands for political reform, broader suffrage, and educational opportunities, and spawning international socialist and communist movements that proclaimed the solidarity of the working classes. To counteract these trends, conservative elements sought to emphasize ideas that stressed the historical and biological unity of nations and to direct blame for economic and social problems against other national groups. Romantically inclined western European intellectuals called on all to take pride in their nation state and regard the historical, cultural, and biological heritage that its citizens shared as being more important than the class antagonisms that were threatening the social order. At the same time, ethnic nationalism grew stronger in eastern Europe, as local elites sought freedom from the dynastic regimes that still controlled that region (Trigger 1989a:148–74). In each of these countries, social theorists sought to celebrate the authenticity of their ethnic cultures, which they associated with their origins as a people (Mudimbe 1988:115). Being far more influenced by the conservative values of romanticism than by the liberal ones of the Enlightenment, the nationalist movements in eastern Europe stressed ethnicity more than they did the ideas of universal human rights, which continued to temper nationalism in western Europe and North America (Gellner 1983; Taylor 1992). At the same time, nationalism began to develop in various colonial settings, as well as in countries, such as Japan and China, that were resisting European domination.

Under the impetus of nationalism, archaeology abandoned a primary focus on evolution and concentrated on interpreting the archaeological record as the history of specific peoples. This resulted in the development of culture-historical archaeology. Archaeological cultures were defined and many were identified as prehistoric manifestations of historically known peoples, whose development and movements could be traced in the archaeological record. European archaeologists sought to lengthen the pedigrees of their own national or ethnic groups and to glorify these groups by comparison with neighboring peoples. Usually this took the form of identifying a particular people with a succession of specific archaeological cultures leading into the remote past and drawing attention to the special achievements of these cultures. Some German archaeologists emphasized the apparent lack of non-German peoples in their homeland during the historical period and projected this situation back into prehistory as evidence of their racial and ethnic purity. They argued that this purity made them superior to other Indo-European peoples, who had migrated elsewhere and mingled to varying degrees with allegedly inferior non-Indo-Europeans. British archaeologists and historians, on the other hand, maintained that repeated invasions had provided the material which allowed selective processes to create a people and culture superior to any other (Rouse 1972:71–2). Nationalism had a positive effect on archaeology inasmuch as it encouraged archaeologists to trace spatial variations in the archaeological record more systematically than they had done previously. Such variations had generally been ignored by unilinear evolutionists.

Yet the culture-historical approach was also adopted in countries, such as the United States, where archaeologists had no ethnic or emotional bonds to the peoples whose remains they were studying. In such places, the main attraction of the culture-historical approach was its capacity to account for geographical variation in the archaeological record and growing evidence of change that could not be explained in terms of unilinear evolution. Slowly but surely, the culture-historical approach resulted in a greater appreciation of the flexibility and adaptability of aboriginal American cultures in prehistoric times (Trigger 1989a:186–95). Hence, while the origins of cultural-historical archaeology were rooted in nationalism, not all culture-historical archaeology was nationalistic. It was in connection with these less nationalistic approaches that archaeologists most quickly concluded that it was difficult, if not impossible, to trace ethnic identity in the archaeological record without the aid of written records.

The heterogeneous nature and origins of nationalism suggest that archaeology influenced by it is not likely to be a unitary phenomenon and that the relations between this type of archaeology and political movements are extremely complex. Around the world, nationalistic archaeology has varied in content, importance, and its relations to the political process. The production of archaeological knowledge has only been regulated in detail for nationalistic purposes by a relatively small number of regimes. The most flagrant example is the Soviet Union between the 1930s and the 1950s, where, as Shnirelman has chronicled, Slavic archaeology received extensive state patronage as a basis for counteracting German claims of prehistoric superiority and for promoting a new image of the Soviet Union as a Russian-centered, rather than a multi-ethnic, federation. Yet the detailed ideological control of archaeology by the Soviet Communist Party both preceded and outlived this phase. Nazi Germany provides a second example, although the surveillance of the work of individual archaeologists seems to have been less intensive there than it was in the Soviet Union. Likewise, the ultra-nationalist regime that controlled Japan in the 1930s and early 1940s did not dictate precisely how archaeological data were to be interpreted, although it dismissed and even imprisoned archaeologists whose work cast doubt on the divine origin of the imperial family. The main result of this policy was to encourage archaeologists to describe, rather than to interpret, prehistoric finds, an attitude which Fawcett (this volume) suggests has persisted to the present. She also argues that since World War II the Japanese government has encouraged the use of archaeological findings to support the concept of the unity of the nation, as expressed in the common origins and history of the Japanese people rather than the emperor. This resembles the role played by archaeology in late nineteenth- and early twentieth-century Europe. In the early decades of the Communist regime in China, the state used archaeology to reinforce a centrist and extremely chauvinist view of Chinese history that was conducive to national unity, although this traditional view was disguised by an overlay of Marxist evolutionism (Tong, this volume).

In other states, the freedom of archaeologists has been curtailed less by state control than by popular expectations. This is particularly true of nation states that are seeking to establish themselves or experiencing a severe crisis. Archaeology, focussed on the period of the Old Testament, has encouraged the founding and development of the state of Israel. In addition to enjoying widespread popular support among Israelis, it has supplied symbols, such as the Herodian fortress at Masada, that have come to play major roles in the rituals of the Israeli state. The goals of Israeli archaeology have meant that very little state support is accorded to the study of the archaeology of the Christian and particularly the Islamic periods, since this would be counterproductive from a nationalistic point of view (Silberman 1989). In other countries, such as Korea, nationalism has provided a lasting framework for archaeological research (Nelson, this volume). Yet this is mainly in the sense that archaeologists have assumed that the goal of their discipline is to study the history of a specific people. Apart from this general focus, they have not been under intensive pressure from either the state or public opinion to produce specific results. While archaeological discoveries, initiated by Europeans, have long encouraged a pride in India's past among its educated elite, there is even less evidence of nationalism influencing the practice of Indian archaeology, which still seems to be regarded as an exotic discipline (Chakrabarti 1988).

In most European countries, nationalist archaeology was developed by a small number of archaeologists, who were often amateurs (Díaz-Andreu, Lillios, this volume). Their work frequently attracted the approval and support of political movements and of governments, most of which were politically right-wing. While this support was important, it often did not last long, because either the regimes did not survive or their leaders soon lost interest in archaeology. Despite some interest in German prehistory by politicians such as Field Marshal Paul von Hindenburg (Sklenar 1983:152), Gustaf Kossinna fought an uphill battle against the prestige that German universities traditionally had accorded to the study of classical and Near Eastern archaeology. It was only after the Nazis came to power in 1933 that his brand of archaeology received substantial patronage from the German government (Anthony, Arnold and Hassmann, this volume). Even then, if Albert Speer (1971:41) is to be believed, Hitler, whose architectural tastes were decidedly neoclassical, privately expressed contempt for the study of German prehistory.

There is also disagreement about the focus of nationalistic investigations. As the Soviet Union has weakened, growing ethnic conflicts, especially in the Caucasus region, have encouraged the manipulation of archaeological data by various ethnic groups, often in a highly irresponsible manner (Kohl and Tsetskhladze, this volume). In China the focus of archaeology has shifted from a centrist to a provincially based view as political conditions have changed and sources of patronage have become more decentralized (Falkenhausen, this volume). In Spain the impact of nationalist archaeology has been blunted by disagreement among archaeologists as to whether it should relate to the nation-state or to smaller ethnic groups (Díaz-Andreu, this volume). In former Yugoslavia political developments have focussed archaeology on various ethnic groups, whereas in Romania and Bulgaria it has been concentrated on the dominant ethnic groups at the expense of minorities (Kaiser, this volume). While some archaeologists have noted the development of a multi-national perspective in western European archaeology (which may constitute a new focus for "nationalism") (Kristiansen 1990), Lillios (this volume) suggests that European economic and political union may intensify rather than diminish the archaeological expression of traditional nationalisms.

In Africa we also encounter nationalist archaeology that, as a result of being formulated in the context of decolonization, is transnational in its expression. The emphasis of Chaikh Anta Diop and his followers on deriving African civilization as a whole from a Black Egyptian prototype has diverted attention from growing archaeological evidence of the important indigenous cultural achievements of the various peoples of West Africa and the continent as a whole (Diop 1974; Holl 1990:301–4). Ironically, in the Republic of South Africa the white minority government's desire to court international prestige by sponsoring high-quality archaeological research has resulted in finds that contradicted the Afrikaner myth of having arrived in that country prior to the Bantus (Hall 1990).

The main impact of nationalism has been to influence the questions about the past that archaeologists are prepared to ask or not ask and the amount of evidence that is required to sustain a particular position. On the positive side, nationalistic archaeology has stimulated asking questions about local cultural configurations and ethnicity that evolutionary and colonially oriented archaeologists did not consider worthwhile. On the negative side, it has encouraged the misinterpretation of archaeological data for political purposes and ignoring equally important aspects of human history. While it is possible to identify some of the conditions that are favorable to the development of nationalistic archaeology, the relations between archaeology and nationalism are complex and largely unpredictable.

III Nationalism and archaeological objectivity

Many of the papers in this volume are highly critical of nationalistic approaches in archaeology. They see a commitment to nationalism as consciously or unconsciously distorting the past, limiting the questions that are asked, and artificially determining the units to be studied. Von Falkenhausen (this volume) documents how in China identical archaeological assemblages are being identified with different ethnic groups in different provinces, while very different assemblages are being identified with a single ethnic group within a single province. In southeastern Europe ethnic rivalries have led to the same cultures being given different names in neighboring countries (Kaiser, this volume). Weigand (n.d.) has argued that the modern national border between the United States and Mexico has distorted the interpretation of the prehistory of that region. Differing national perspectives have likewise distorted the interpretation of prehistoric and protohistoric aboriginal relations along what is now the frontier between Canada and the United States.

It is argued more fundamentally that nationalistic archaeology rests on false assumptions about the nature of the archaeological record. We must assume that in the past, as at present, ethnicity was a complex, subjective phenomenon. It consists of a self-assigned group identity, which may change relatively quickly and may or may not correspond with attributes that are observable in the archaeological record. In the past, archaeologists frequently were tempted to trace ethnicity in the archaeological record by assuming congruency between race, language, and culture. This often involved believing that the differentiation of all three resulted from the break-up of single ethnic groups. Anthropologists have long known that these are independent variables, which may follow similar or very different trajectories of change (Boas 1940; Sapir 1921:221–5; Trigger 1968:7–13). They have also observed that neighboring peoples who share nearly identical material cultures may assert a number of different ethnic or tribal identities, as was the case among the Pueblo Indians of the southwestern United States or the Plains Indians in the nineteenth century. Less frequently, peoples with different economies and material cultures may claim the same ethnic identity (Murdock 1959:415–16). Because of the subjective nature of ethnic identity, it is difficult to trace in the archaeological record in the absence of supplementary historical evidence. It is equally difficult to ascertain what language was associated with most prehistoric archaeological cultures. These are problems that are limited not only to nationalistic archaeology but to any culture-historical archaeology that addresses problems of prehistoric linguistic or ethnic identity.

This calls into question what Kohl and Tsetskhladze (this volume) have labelled the "essentialist" bias of nationalist archaeology: the belief that peoples and cultures continue to exist "forever" in recognizable forms. Sarah Nelson (this volume) has examined the problems posed for Korean archaeology by what she regards as the unrealistic assumption of a Korean ethnic identity extending far back into prehistoric times. Japanese archaeologists similarly tend to believe in the unbroken continuity and homogeneity of their national history. Timothy Kaiser (this volume) has shown how an essentialist approach to archaeology in many parts of southeastern Europe was reinforced after World War II by Soviet archaeology's insistence on viewing human history as a series of local parallel developments.

While Childe's *Dawn of European Civilization* (1925) established an internationally recognized standard for the study of culture history, Childe quickly concluded that his goal of using archaeological data to determine the place of origin of the Indo-European-speaking peoples was probably unattainable. He also decided that the culture-historical approach, which sought to trace the history of ethnic groups in the archaeological record, precluded addressing many more interesting questions relating to sociocultural development in prehistoric times. Childe described culture history as the archaeological equivalent of political history but, like some of the more innovative historians of the 1920s, he believed it necessary to transcend political issues and study social and economic history (Childe 1930:240–7; 1958). Doubtless he would have welcomed the still later popularity of intellectual history.

Since the 1920s, archaeologists have devoted much attention to studying subsistence patterns, technology, trade, and social and political organization in prehistoric times. They have also addressed general questions concerning cross-cultural uniformity in human behavior and cultural change, to what extent cultures can be studied as adaptive systems, the status of population increase as a factor bringing about cultural change, and the impacts that adjacent cultures have upon one another. More recently, archaeologists have investigated still more erudite issues, such as the relations of material culture to social behavior, the role played by subjective factors such as religious beliefs in channelling human behavior, and the relative value of positivist and idealist epistemologies for explaining human behavior (Binford 1989; Hodder 1991b; Renfrew and Bahn 1991). These developments, which have drawn archaeology into the mainstream of theoretical debates in the social sciences, are far removed from the particularizing concerns of the culture-historical approach associated with nationalistic archaeology. In the course of doing these things, archaeologists have also developed important new techniques for eliciting behavioral information from archaeological data, as well as benefiting from advances in the physical and biological sciences.

Childe specifically valued studying the development of new technologies and social organization and how neighboring cultures had influenced each other as ways to overcome the chauvinism and intellectual limitations of a culture-historical approach. Following the coming to power in Germany of the National Socialist regime, he became increasingly concerned with the dangers that the culture-historical approach posed for the collective welfare of all human beings, especially when it was combined with racism and aggressive nationalism (Childe 1933a, b).

Extreme relativists maintain that all archaeological interpretations are subjective creations, which are scarcely constrained, if at all, by archaeological evidence. They assume that egregious errors of archaeology's past, such as the Moundbuilder myths of North America or attributing the prehistoric stone ruins of Zimbabwe to Semitic colonists, have become evident to us mainly because they are remote in time and we no longer accept the premises on which they were based (Hall 1990:59–63; Kuklick 1991; Silverberg 1968). It may be, however, that many of the excesses associated with nationalistic approaches to archaeology have occurred not simply because of the socially determined beliefs of archaeologists but in situations where the knowledge of the archaeological record was extremely limited or where archaeological data were intentionally ignored and distorted for propagandistic reasons. Kohl and Tsetskhladze (this volume) suggest that both processes are currently in play in the Caucasus. Long ago I argued that negative stereotypes of the American Indians hindered the development of American archaeology and biased efforts to interpret the archaeological record. Yet, over time, accumulating archaeological evidence revealed the untenable nature of a static view of American prehistory and began to call into question the assumptions and stereotypes on which that view was based (Trigger 1980).

I do not suggest that interpretations of archaeological data can ever be free from social and political presuppositions, which influence the questions that archaeologists ask, what evidence they note, how they treat such evidence, and what answers they are predisposed to find congenial. But I do suggest that, as archaeology develops, it acquires a larger data base and new methodologies that in turn act as constraints upon the imagination of the archaeologist. These developments permit archaeologists to challenge former interpretations, on the grounds either that they were based on inadequate information and have failed to stand the test of new finds or that the data were wrongly interpreted. For most scientists the ability to be challenged in this manner is a crucial test of the scientific status of an explanation (Popper 1959). Moreover, as Anthony points out in this volume, most interpretations of past human behavior can be approached from a number of different directions, employing different data bases and different analytical techniques. The convergence of the findings of several different and independent approaches provides a further, though not necessarily an infallible, warrant for the objectivity of the results (Murdock 1959:1–47).

The claim by archaeologists to be able to falsify interpretations on the basis of new evidence or by means of new techniques of analysis is dismissed by extreme relativists as an untenable manifestation of elitism and intellectual hegemony, which must be resisted with counterclaims that all interpretations of the past are subjective and hence there is no way to demonstrate that the insights of a professional archaeologist are necessarily superior to those of anyone else (Ucko 1990:xix–xx). In reality, the much decried intellectual hegemony of professional social scientists is largely precluded by their inability to agree among themselves about the nature of high-level theory. Yet the history of archaeology reveals, in addition to follies and reflections of the biases of different periods, an irreversibly changing understanding of the past that has been shaped by the constraining influence of a growing body of archaeological data. Far from being a collective delusion, this growing understanding is a sign that archaeology has something positive and worthwhile to contribute to an understanding of human development in the past and hence of the conditions in which human beings now find themselves (Trigger 1989a:396–407). In this way, archaeology can assist the development of the societies that sustain it and hopefully of all humanity.

Relativism, subjectivism, and idealism have important roles to play in the study of human behavior. Our relationship to the natural world is symbolically mediated and the cognitive maps that facilitate our behavior are a subtle product of culturally conditioned learning which can to some degree be reformulated as a result of individual experience. Yet, if positivism and rationalism have in the past been guilty of trying to make human behavior appear unduly regular and treating it as nothing more than a series of responses to external, largely environmental, constraints, Lewis Pyenson (1993:107) rightly observes that "radical relativism . . . diminishes our common humanity." Neither romanticism nor rationalism has a monopoly when it comes to explaining the archaeological record, any more than does a positivist or an idealist epistemology.

Nationalism, despite its renewed importance as a source of group identity during the current period of dramatic economic, political, and ideological changes, is only one of many issues that are challenging human beings. It is also a phenomenon of recent origin. It is therefore a concept of importance to modern people, including archaeologists, rather than to the people who created the archaeological record and hence a factor influencing archaeological research rather than an object of archaeological investigation. While the related concept of ethnicity *was* of importance to prehistoric peoples, it was a subjective concept that archaeologists cannot hope to study to any significant degree in the absence of specifically relevant historical or ethnographic data. Fortunately, there are many more appropriate problems that archaeologists who lack access to other sorts of data are equipped to investigate.

Even when we include the archaeology that was practiced in Germany during the National Socialist period, nationalistic archaeology has been no more an accomplice in inflicting suffering on human beings than have other forms of archaeology. These include colonialist archaeology, which sought to lend credence to racism and the denial of human rights to peoples in many parts of the world, and the Marxist archaeology that was practiced in the former Soviet Union as part of what Leo Klejn (1991:70) has described as a politics of alienation, domination, exploitation, and repression. Wittingly or unwittingly, processual archaeology, by denying the significance of culturally specific experiences, has played a role in devaluing local cultures and promoting a universalistic outlook that has served the far from altruistic goals first of American and then of international capitalism. Because of their geographical and ideological parochialism, specific expressions of nationalistic archaeology tend to oppose and undermine one another, while many other ideological archaeologies claim universal significance. It is much harder for archaeologists to recognize and overcome such general biases.

IV Nationalism and archaeologists

Archaeologists are unable to divorce their view of the relationship between archaeology and nationalism from what nationalism means to them as individuals. As a result of the crimes currently being committed in the name of various ethnic loyalties in many parts of the world, it is scarcely surprising that nationalism is widely viewed as an atavistic force that threatens world peace. Yet it is the duty of all social scientists to try to understand, rather than simply to respond emotionally to such phenomena. Nationalism, by promoting a sense of group unity, has played many different roles during the last 250 years. When combined with an awareness of the dignity of all human beings, it has helped to provide the basis for resisting colonial and dynastic oppression and for creating a more broadly based popular sovereignty that promotes political freedom as well as social, economic, and intellectual development. Without these rationalistic constraints, however, it has often served to justify and promote intolerance, aggression, and theft.

Nationalism also has assumed historical importance as the most potent intellectual weapon for countering the Marxist program for world revolution. During World War I, European workers, who had been bombarded for two generations with nationalistic propaganda, generally supported their national governments rather than taking advantage of the situation to join together, as many Marxists had expected them to do, to overthrow the ruling classes. During World War II, Stalin acknowledged the ideological weakness of Marxism when he turned to nationalism to rally effective opposition to the Nazis. In recent years, nationalism has played a significant role in dismembering the Soviet Union and the collapse of Communist control.

Nationalism continues to promote group identity and provide meaning for individuals during a period of intense global change and uncertainty, but, like Islamic fundamentalism, it is a backward-looking philosophy. The most powerful force in the modern world is an international economy that increasingly is breaking free of control by national governments and attempting to dictate a self-interested social and political agenda to all nations (Marchak 1991). By diverting attention from the task of creating a new political order that is able to match the power of these multinational corporations, nationalism serves the interest of these economic forces. On the other hand, radical nationalism threatens to destroy the precarious world order on which multinational corporations rely to make profits.

Nationalism is not a unitary concept but one that affects individual human beings in different ways and to different degrees. How we perceive both our personal circumstances and nationalism affecting our lives determines our attitude toward this manifestation of group unity. Because of this, archaeologists must recognize that their personal attitudes toward archaeology's relations with nationalism are affected by what they understand to be in their self-interest.

Before archaeologists pass a final judgment on their discipline's role in specific nationalistic ventures, they must take account of their own biases. One thing, however, is certain. Whatever their personal views may be, either of particular ethnic conflicts or of the current world situation, nothing justifies the deliberate distortion of the archaeological record or its misinterpretation to serve political ends. Doing this diminishes not only the stature of the offending archaeologist but also that of the archaeological profession. The editors of this volume help to resolve the dilemma between professional and political responsibility when they argue that an archaeologist can accept a potentially damaging archaeological interpretation as the most plausible, while condemning a state policy that bends and distorts that interpretation for questionable political ends.

Archaeologists may not always be able to distinguish sensible interpretations of their data from erroneous or irrational ones. Yet they always have a moral duty to try to do so, especially in situations where biased or irrational interpretations can be used to justify one group of people inflicting pain or injustice on another. This is no less true of gender or racial issues than it is of ethnic ones. By unmasking erroneous interpretations of the past and avoiding the temptation to champion biases on the basis of too little evidence, archaeologists can enhance the status of their discipline and its ability to act as a positive force in human history. Archaeology in the service of nationalism has undoubtedly sometimes contributed to our understanding of the past and promoted worthy causes. Yet, as many of the chapters in this volume demonstrate, nationalist archaeology, both in the past and at present, has been an accomplice in inflicting a vast amount of suffering on human beings. We must seriously question the status of a relativism that refuses to take account of such behavior.

Bibliography

Åberg, Nils 1921 *La Civilisation énéolithique dans la péninsule ibérique*, vol. 25. Uppsala: Vilhelm Ekmans Universitetsfond.

Academia Portuguesa da História 1937–8 *Boletim*. Lisbon.

Academy of Sciences of Armenia SSR 1988 *Nagornii Karabakh: Istoricheskaya Spravka*. Erevan.

Agaev, E. 1987 *Baku: A Guide*. Moscow: Raduga.

Akhundov, D.A. 1985 Otlichitelnye cherty i simbolicheskie osobennosti stel kavkazskoi Albanii. In *Vsesoyuznaya Arkheologicheskaya Konferentsiya "Dostizheniya Sovetskoi Arkheologii v XI Pyatiletke,"* pp. 77–8, abstracts of papers, vol. 1, Baku.

Akiyama, Shingo 1988 Kôzan bunka-to Sen-Kôzan bunka: Sekihô Kôzan kôko, sono ichi. *Koshi Shunjû* 5:2–26.

Aksenova, E.P. 1990 Izgnannoe iz sten Akademii (N.S. Derzhavin i akademicheskoe slavyanovedenie v 30-e gody). *Sovetskoe Slavyanovedenie* 5:69–81.

Aksenova, E.P. and M.A. Vasilev, 1993 Problemy etnogonii slavyanstva i ego vetvei v akademicheskikh diskussiyakh rubezha 1930–1940-kh godov. *Slavyanovedenie* 2:86–104.

Alekperov, A.K. 1990 The Azerbaidzhanians. In *Soviet Anthropology and Archaeology*, edited by M.M. Balzer and H.B. Paksoy, pp. 19–26. Summer, 29(1).

Alexander, J.A. 1980 First-Millennium Europe Before the Romans. In *The Cambridge Encyclopedia of Archaeology*, edited by A. Sherratt, pp. 222–6. Cambridge: Cambridge University Press.

Alexander, J.J.G. 1978 *A Survey of Manuscripts Illuminated in the British Isles*, vol. 1, *Insular Manuscripts 6th to the 9th Century*. London: Harvey Miller.

Alijarov, S.S. 1990 On the Genesis of the Azerbaidzhanian People (Toward a Formulation of the Problem). In *Soviet Anthropology and Archaeology*, edited by M.M. Balzer and H.B. Paksoy, pp. 34–68. Summer, 29(1).

Alonso del Real, C. 1946 Función social del arqueólogo. *Il Congreso Arqueológico del Sureste Español*:33–43.

Alpatov, V.M. 1991 *Istoriya odnogo mifa. Marr i Marrism*. Moscow: Nauka.

Altstadt, A.L. 1992 *The Azerbaijani Turks: Power and Identity under Russian Rule*. Stanford, CA: Hoover Institution Press.

Alvarez Barrientos, J. and G. Mora Rodríguez 1985. El final de una tradición. Las falsificaciones granadinas del siglo XVIII. *Revista de Dialectología y Tradiciones Populares* 40:163–89.

An Ho-sang 1974 *The Ancient History of the Korea Dong-I Race*. Seoul: Institute of Baedal (Korean) Culture.

An Jinhuai 1990 Shinianlai Henan Xia-Shang kaogu de faxian yu yanjiu. *Hua Xia*

Kaogu 3:11–16.

An Zhimin 1972 Lüelun woguo xinshiqishidai wenhua de niandai wenti (On the Chronology of the Neolithic Cultures in China). *Kaogu* 6:35–44, 47.

1979 Lüelun sanshinianlai woguo de xinshiqishidai kaogu (Chinese Neolithic Archaeology in the Past Thirty Years). *Kaogu* 5:393–403.

1984 Lüelun Huabei de zaoqi xinshiqu wenhua (On the Early Neolithic Cultures in North China). *Kaogu* 10:936–44.

1987 Shilun weming de qiyuan (Discussion on the Origin of Civilization). *Kaogu* 5:453–7.

Anderson, B. 1983 *Imagined Communities: Reflections on the Origins and the Spread of Nationalism*. London: Verso.

Andersson, J.G. 1923 An Early Chinese Culture. *Bulletin of the Geological Survey of China* 5:1–68.

1943 Research into the Prehistory of the Chinese. *Bulletin of the Museum of Far Eastern Antiquities* 15:1–304.

Anonymous 1950 A estação pre-histórica de "Covo de Almeida." *Notícias de Portugal* 162:14.

Anthony, David W. 1986 The "Kurgan Culture," Indo-European Origins, and the Domestication of the Horse: A Reconsideration. *Current Anthropology* 27(4):291–313.

1990 Migration in Archaeology: The Baby and the Bathwater. *American Anthropologist* 92(4):895–914.

1991a The Archaeology of Indo-European Origins. *Journal of Indo-European Studies* 19 (3 & 4):193–222.

1991b Settlement Hierarchy and Power in the Cucuteni-Tripoly Culture, 4500–3500 B.C. Invited Paper, 56th Annual Society for American Archaeology Conference, New Orleans.

Aptekar', V.B. 1928 Na putyakh k marksistskoi lingvistike. *Vestnik Kommunisticheskoi Akademii* 28(4):254–78.

Aragão, Rui 1985 *Portugal: O Desafio Nacionalista. Psicologia e Identidade Nacionais*. Lisbon: Teorema.

Arce, J. and R. Olmos (eds.) 1991 *Historiografía de la Arqueología y de la Historia Antigua en España (siglos XVIII–XX)*. Madrid: Ministerio de Cultura.

Areshian, G.E. 1992 Armenian and Indo-European Cosmogonic Myths and Their Development. In *Proceedings of the Fourth International Conference on Armenian Linguistics*, edited by J.A.C. Greppin, pp. 1–36. Delmar, NY: Caravan Books.

Arnold, Bettina 1990 The Past as Propaganda: Totalitarian Archaeology in Nazi Germany. *Antiquity* 64(244):464–78.

1992 Germany's Nazi Past: How Hitler's Archaeologists Distorted European Prehistory to Justify Racist and Territorial Goals. *Archaeology* July/August:30–7.

Aronoff, M.J. 1986 Establishing Authority: The Memorialization of Jabotinsky and the Burial of the Bar-Kochba Bones in Israel under the Likud. In *The Frailty of Authority*, edited by M.J. Aronoff, pp. 105–13. New Brunswick, NJ: Transaction Books.

Artamonov, M.I. 1939 Dostizheniya Sovetskoi arkheologii. *Vestnik Drevnei Istorii*

2:122–9.

1940a Institut Istorii Materialnoi Kultury v 1939 godu. *Kratkie Soobshcheniya Instituta Istorii Materialnoi Kultury* 4:63–6.

1940b Spornye voprosy drevneishei istorii slavyan i Rusi. *Kratkie Soobshcheniya Instituta Istorii Materialnoi Kultury* 6:3–14.

1947 Arkheologicheskie teorii proiskhozhdeniya indoevropetisev v svete ucheniya N.Ya. Marra. *Vestnik Leningradskogo Universiteta* 2:79–106.

1948 K voprosu o proiskhozhdenii vostochnykh slavyan. *Voprosy Istorii* 9:97–108.

1949 K voprosu ob etnogeneze v sovetskoi arkheologii. *Kratkie Soobshcheniya Instituta Istorii Materialnoi Kultury* 29:3–16.

1950 *Proiskhozhdenie slavyan*. Leningrad: Vsesoyuznoe Obshchestvo po rasprostraneniyu politicheskikh i nauchnykh znanii.

Artizov, A.N. 1992 Nikolai Nikolaevich Vanag (1899–1937 gg.). *Otechestvennaya Istoriya* 6:95–109.

Asuka Historical Museum 1978 *Guide to the Asuka Historical Museum*. Nara National Cultural Properties Research Institute, Nara, Japan. (Translated by W. Carter.) Asuka Historical Museum, Nara Prefecture.

Asuka Hozon Zaidan 1981 Tobu tori no Asuka (Asuka of the Flying Bird). In *Asuka: Hozon 10 Nen no Ayumi*. Pamphlet of the Asuka Hozon Zaidan, pp. 1–2. Nara Prefecture. (In Japanese.)

Auger, Reginald, Margaret F. Glass, Scott MacEachern, and Peter H. McCartney (eds.) 1987 *Ethnicity and Culture*. Proceedings of the Eighteenth Annual Chacmool Conference. The University of Calgary Archaeological Association.

Avtorkhanov, A. 1964 Denationalization of the Soviet Ethnic Minorities. *Studies on the Soviet Union* 6(1):74–99.

1991 *Imperiya Kremlia*. Minsk-Moscow: Polifact-Druzhba narodov.

Ayvazian, A. 1990 *The Historical Monuments of Nakhichevan*, trans. by Maksoudian, K.H. Detroit: Wayne State University Press.

Bachof, Otto 1965 Die "Entnazifierung." In *Deutsches Geistesleben und Nationalsozialismus*, edited by Andreas Flittner, pp. 195–216. Tübingen: Rainer Wunderlich Verlag.

Backhouse, Janet 1981 *The Lindisfarne Gospels*. Ithaca, NY: Cornell University Press.

Bagley, Robert W. 1980 The Appearance and Growth of Regional Bronze-Using Cultures. In *The Great Bronze Age of China*, edited by Fong Wen, pp. 109–17. New York: Metropolitan Museum of Art.

1987 *Shang Ritual Bronzes in the Arthur M. Sackler Collections* (Vol. 1 of *Ancient Chinese Bronzes in the Arthur M. Sackler Collections*). Cambridge, Mass.: Harvard University Press.

1988 Sacrificial Pits of the Shang Period at Sanxingdui in Guanghan County, Sichuan Province. *Arts Asiatiques* 43:78–86.

1992 Changjiang Bronzes and Shang Archaeology. In *International Colloquium on Chinese Art History, 1991, Proceedings: Antiques, Part I*, pp. 209–54.

Balzer, M.M. 1992 Turmoil in the Northern Caucasus: The Maikop Archaeology Debate. *Soviet Anthropology and Archeology*. Winter, 30(3).

Balzer, M.M. and H.B. Paksoy 1990 A Region in Turmoil: Azerbaidzhanian Historical Ethnography. *Soviet Anthropology and Archaeology*. Summer, 29(1).

Bankoff, Arthur and H. Greenfield 1984 Decision-Making and Culture Change in the Yugoslav Bronze Age. *Balcanica* (Belgrade) 15:9–31.

Bapty, I. and T. Yates (eds.) 1990 *Archaeology after Structuralism: Post-Structuralism and the Practice of Archaeology*. London: Routledge.

Barandiarán, I. 1988 *Enciclopedia general ilustrada del País Vasco*, Vol. 1, *Prehistoria: paleolítico*. San Sebastián: Ed. Auñamendi.

Barandiarán, J.M. 1917 Investigaciones prehistóricas en la Diócesis de Vitoria. *Euskal Erria* 77:386–92, 431–42.

1932 Paralelo entre lo prehistórico y lo actual en el País Vasco. Investigaciones en Balzola y en Gibijo. *Anuario de Eusko-Folklore* 12.

1934 *Euskalerriko Lehen Gizona*. Colecc. Zabalkundea. Serie de Ciencias, Bellas Artes y Letras no. 3. Ed. Auñamendi.

Barnes, B. 1974 *Scientific Knowledge and Sociological Theory*. London: Routledge.

1977 *Interests and the Growth of Knowledge*. London: Routledge.

Barth, F. (ed.) 1969 *Ethnic Groups and Boundaries*. Boston: Little, Brown.

Bayard, D. 1978 15 Jahre "New Archaeology": Eine Kritische Bersicht. *Saeculum* 29:69–106.

Bede 731. *A History of the English Church and People*. 1955 translation by Leo Sherley-Price. Harmondsworth: Penguin Books.

Befu, H. 1983 Internationalization of Japan and Nihon Bunkaron. In *The Challenge of Japan's Internationalization: Organization and Culture*, edited by H. Mannari and H. Befu, pp. 232–66. Nishinomiya and Tokyo: Kwansei Gakuin University and Kodansha International Ltd.

1984 Civilization and Culture: Japan in Search of Identity. In *Japanese Civilization in the Modern World: Life and Society*, edited by T. Umesao, H. Befu, and J. Kreiner, pp. 59–75. Senri Ethnological Series 16. Osaka: National Museum of Ethnology.

Beijing 1975 Jiangxi Qingjiang Wucheng Shang-dai yizhi fajue jianbao. *Wenwu* 7:51–71.

1978 *Houme mengshu*. Beijing: Wenwu.

1984 *Xin Zhongguo de kaogu faxian he yanjiu*. Beijing: Wenwu.

1991a *Wenwu kaogu gongzuo shinian*. Beijing: Wenwu.

1991b Jiangxi Xin'gan Dayangzhou Shang-mu fajue jianbao. *Wenwu* 10:1–16.

Benac, A. 1972 Some Aspects of the Migrations of Cultures in Northwestern Balkan. *Balcanica* 3:1–10.

Beramendi, J.G. 1981a *Vicente Risco no nacionalismo galego*, vol. 1, *Das orixes a afirmación plena*. Santiago de Compostela: Edicions do Cerne.

1981b *Vicente Risco no nacionalismo galego. 2. Escisión-unidade-escisión*. Santiago de Compostela: Edicions do Cerne.

Bernal, M. 1987 *Black Athena*, vol. 1, *The Fabrication of Ancient Greece 1785–1985*. New Brunswick, NJ: Rutgers University Press.

Bernshtam, A.N. 1935 Proiskhozhdenie turok. *Problemy Istorii Dokapitalisticheskikh Obshchestv* 5–6:43–54.

Bernstein, S.B. 1989 Tragicheskaya stranitsa iz istorii slavyanskoi filologii (30-e gody). *Sovetskoe Slavyanovedenie* 1:77–82.

Binford, L.R. (ed.) 1972 *An Archaeological Perspective*. New York: Seminar Press.

1989 *Debating Archaeology*. San Diego: Academic.

Bishop, Isabella Bird 1905 *Korea and Her Neighbours*. London: John Murray.

Blakey, M.L. 1990 American Nationality and Ethnicity in the Depicted Past. In Gathercole and Lowenthal (1990), pp. 38–48.

Blatti, J. (ed.) 1987 *Past Meets Present: Essays About Historic Interpretation and Public Audiences*. Washington, DC: Smithsonian Institution Press.

Blindheim, Charlotte 1984 De fem lange ar pa Universitets Oldsaksamling. *Viking*, Tidsskrift for Norren Arkeologi, 48:27–43.

Boas, F. 1940 *Race, Language and Culture*. New York: Macmillan.

Bodnar, J. 1986 Symbols and Servants: Immigrant America and the Limits of Public History. *The Journal of American History* 73:137–51.

1992 *Remaking America: Public Memory, Commemoration, and Patriotism in the Twentieth Century*. Princeton: Princeton University Press.

Bogaevski, B.L. 1931 K voprosu o teorii migratsii. *Soobshcheniya Gosudarstvennoi Akademii Istorii Materialnoi Kultury* 8:35–8.

Bogoraz-Tan, V.G. 1928 *Rasprostranenie kultury na zemle*. Moscow-Leningrad: Gosizdat.

Bollmus, Reinhard 1970 *Das Amt Rosenberg und Seine Gegner: Zum Machtkampf im Nationalsozialistischen Herrschaftssystem*. Studien zur Zeitgeschichte. Stuttgart: Institut für Zeitgeschichte dva.

Boriskovski, P.I. 1934 Fashiziruyushchayasya nauka. *Problemy Istorii Dokapitalisticheskikh Obshchestv* 9–10:197–203.

Bosch Gimpera, P. 1915 *El problema de la cerámica ibérica*. Comisión de Investigaciones Paleontológicas y Prehistóricas 7. Madrid.

1932 *Etnologia de la Península Ibèrica*. Barcelona: Ed. Alpha.

1937 *"España." Conferencia dada por Pedro Bosch Gimpera, rector de la Universidad de Barcelona*. Valencia: Anales de la Universidad de Valencia.

Bournoutian, G.A. 1983 The Ethnic Composition and the Socio-Economic Condition of Eastern Armenia in the First Half of the Nineteenth Century. In *Transcaucasia: Nationalism and Social Change*, edited by R.G. Suny, pp. 69–86. Ann Arbor: University of Michigan Press.

1992 Review of A.L. Altstadt's *The Azerbaijani Turks: Power and Identity under Russian Rule*. *Armenian Review* 45(3):63–9.

Bouza Alvarez, J.L. 1981 *Introducción a la museología*. Madrid.

Bowersock, G.W. 1988 Palestine: Ancient History and Modern Politics. In *Blaming the Victims: Spurious Scholarship and the Palestinian Question*, edited by E.W. Said and C. Hitchens, pp. 181–92. New York: Verso.

Briusov, A. Ya. 1940 *Istoriya drevnei Karelii*. Moscow: Istoricheskii Muzei.

1952 *Ocherki po istorii plemen evropeiskoi chasti SSSR v neoliticheskuyu epokhu*. Moscow: AN SSSR.

Bromlei, Iu. V. 1990 Improving National Relations in the USSR. In *The Soviet Multinational State: Readings and Documents*, edited by M.B. Olcott, pp. 63–72. Armonk, NY: M.E. Sharpe. (Originally appeared in *Kommunist*, 1986, no. 8.)

Broxup, M.B. 1992 *The North Caucasus Barrier: The Russian Advance Towards the*

Muslim World. New York: St. Martin's Press.

Buda, A. (ed.) 1984 *Problems of the Formation of the Albanian People, Their Language and Culture*. Tirana: Academy of Sciences.

Bunkacho Bunkazai Hogo Bu 1989 *Maizo Bunkazai Hakkustu Chosa no Tebiki (Handbook of Buried Cultural Property Excavation)*, 16th edition. Tokyo: Kokudo Chiri Kyokai. (In Japanese.)

Burney, C. 1979 Meshkinshahr Survey. *Iran* 17:155–6.

Butts, D.J. 1990 Nga Tukemata: Nga Taonga o Ngati Lahungunu (The Awakening of the Treasures of Ngati Kahungunu). In Gathercole and Lowenthal (1990), pp. 107–17.

Bykovski, S.N. 1931a O classovykh kornyakh staroi arkheologii. *Soobshcheniya Gosudarstvennoi Akademii Istorii Materialnoi Kultury* 9–10:2–5.

1931b O roli izucheniya yazykovykh yavlenii v borbe za novuyu istoriyu materialnoi kultury. *Soobshcheniya Gosudarstvennoi Akademii Istorii Materialnoi Kultury* 11–12:4–7.

1931c Yafeticheskii predok vostochnykh slavyan – kimmeriitsy. *Izvestiya Gosudarstvennoi Akademii Istorii Materialnoi Kultury* 8(8–10):1–99.

1932 Plemya i natsiya v rabotakh burzhuaznykh arkheologov i istorikov i v osveshchenii Marksizma-Leninizma. *Soobshcheniya Gosudarstvennoi Akademii Istorii Materialnoi Kultury* 3–4:4–18.

1933 K peresmotru arkheologicheskoi terminologii. *Problemy Istorii Materialnoi Kultury* 5–6:10–12.

Bynon, T. 1977 *Historical Linguistics*. Cambridge: Cambridge University Press.

Cai Jinfa 1990 Shinianlai Henan Qin Han kaogu de faxian yu yanjiu. *Hua Xia Kaogu* 3:30–40, 92.

Campbell, J. 1949 *The Hero With a Thousand Faces*. Princeton: Princeton University Press.

Campbell, James, Eric John and Patrick Wormald (General Editor: James Campbell) 1982 *The Anglo-Saxons*. Ithaca, NY: Cornell University Press.

1967 Introduction. In *Myth, Religion, and Mother Right: Selected Writings of J.J. Bachofen*, trans. by Ralph Manheim, pp. xxv–lvii. Princeton: Princeton University Press, for the Bollingen Foundation.

1988 *The Power of Myth*. New York: Doubleday.

Cao Guicen 1990 Henan Chu wenhua de faxian yu yanjiu. *Hua Xia Kaogu* 3:63–7, 47.

Carneiro, R. 1978 Political Expansion as an Expression of the Principle of Competitive Exclusion. In *Origins of the State: The Anthropology of Political Evolution*, edited by R. Cohen and E. Service, pp. 205–23. Philadelphia: Institute for the Study of Human Issues.

Caro Baroja, J. 1957 Sobre ideas raciales en España. In *Razas, pueblos y linajes*, edited by J. Caro Baroja, pp. 141–54. Madrid: Ed. Revista de Occidente.

1992 *Las falsificaciones de la Historia (en relación con la de España)*. Biblioteca breve. Barcelona: Ed. Seix Barral.

Carpenter, E.S. 1950 The Role of Archaeology in the 19th-Century Controversy Between Developmentalism and Degeneration. *Pennsylvania Archaeologist* 20:5–18.

Carr, R. 1982 *Spain 1808–1975*, second edition. Oxford: Oxford University Press.

Carrière d'Encausse, H. 1978 Determinants and Parameters of Soviet Nationality Policy. In *Soviet Nationality Policies and Practices*, edited by J. Azrael, pp. 39–59. New York: Praeger.

Carvalho, Antonio 1989 Para a história da arqueologia em Portugal. *Arquivo de Cascais* 8:75–150.

1991 Arqueologos e investigação arqueológica em Cascais entre 1940 e 1960. In *Actas das IV Jornadas Arqueologicas (Lisboa 1990)*. Lisbon: Associação dos Arqueólogos Portugueses, pp. 267–75.

Castelos Paredes, J. 1990 A aparición do rexionalismo na Galicia de fin de seculo, a sua estructura mental e o acondicionamiento social. *Dársena* 2:41–9.

Ceram, C.W. 1951 *Gods, Graves, and Scholars*. New York: Knopf.

Cernyh, E.N., L.I. Avilova, T.B. Barceva, L.B. Orlovskaia and T.O. Tenejsvili 1991 The Circumpontic Metallurgical Province as a System. *East and West* 41(1–4):11–45.

Chakrabarti, D.K. 1988 *A History of Indian Archaeology from the Beginning to 1947*. New Delhi: Munshiram Manoharlal.

Champion, T., C. Gamble, S. Shennan and A. Whittle 1984 *Prehistoric Europe*. Orlando: Academic.

Chang Kwang-chih 1963 *The Archaeology of Ancient China*. New Haven: Yale University Press.

1968 *The Archaeology of Ancient China*, second edition. New Haven: Yale University Press.

1977 *The Archaeology of Ancient China*, third edition. New Haven: Yale University Press.

1986 *The Archaeology of Ancient China*, fourth edition. New Haven: Yale University Press.

Chapman, J. 1994 Destruction of a Common Heritage: The Archaeology of War in Croatia, Bosnia and Hercegovina. *Antiquity* 68(258):120–6.

Chatterjee, P. 1993 *The Nation and Its Fragments*. Princeton: Princeton University Press.

Cheboksarov, N.N. 1944 Etnicheskaya antropologiya Germanii. *Kratkie Soobshcheniya Instituta Etnografii* 1:55–62.

Chechenov, I.M. 1992 On the Study of the Ancient History and Archaeology of the Northern Caucasus. In Balzer (1992), pp. 67–8.

Chen Yuanfu 1991 Lianglei tudunmu guanxi zhi tantao – tudunmu ruogan wenti tantao zhi yi. *Hangzhou Kaogu* 2:13–19.

Chengdu 1989 *Sichuan Wenwu: Sanxingdui yizhi yanjiu zhuanji*. (Special issue on Sanxingdui).

Chernij, E.N., L.I. Avilova, T.B. Bartseva, L.B. Orlovskaia and T.O. Teneishvili 1990 El sistema de la Provincia Metalurgica Circumpontica. *Trabajos de Prehistoria* 47:63–101.

Chervonnaya, S.M. 1992 *Abkhaziya – 1992:* . . . Moscow: Mosgopechat' Press.

Childe, V.G. 1925 *The Dawn of European Civilization*. London: Kegan Paul.

1926 *The Aryans*. New York: Knopf.

1929 *The Danube in Prehistory*. Oxford: Clarendon.

1930 *The Bronze Age*. Cambridge: Cambridge University Press.

1933a Is Prehistory Practical? *Antiquity* 7:410–18.
1933b Races, Peoples and Cultures in Prehistoric Europe. *History* 18:193–203.
1936 *Man Makes Himself* (2nd edition 1941, 4th edition 1965.) London: Watts.
1947 *History*. London: Cobbett.
1949 *Social Worlds of Knowledge*. London: Oxford University Press.
1950 *Prehistoric Migrations in Europe*. Instituttet for Sammenlignende Kulturforskning. Serie A: Forelesninger XX. Oslo: H. Aschehoug and Co. (W. Nygaard).
1956 *Society and Knowledge*. New York: Harper.
1958 Retrospect. *Antiquity* 32:69–74.
Chivilikhin, V. 1982 *Pamyat'. Roman-Esse. Roman-gazeta*, no. 16 (950), no. 17 (951). Moscow: Goskomizdata SSSR.
Choe Chong-pil 1982 The Diffusion Route and Chronology of Korean Plant Domestication. *Journal of Asian Studies* 41(3):519–30.
1991 A Critical Review of Research on the Origin of Koreans and Their Culture. *Han'guk Sangkosa Hakbo* 8:7–43.
Choi Mong-lyong 1984 Bronze Age in Korea. *Korea Journal* 24:23–33.
Cirković, S. 1988 Albanci u ogledaju južnoslovenskih izvora. In *Iliri i Albanci*, edited by M. Garašanin, pp. 323–40. Beograd Srpska Akademija Nauka i Umetnosti.
Cirujano Marín, P., T. Elorriaga Planes, and J.S. Pérez Garzón 1985 *Historiografía y nacionalismo español 1834–1868* Madrid: Centro de Estudios Históricos. Consejo Superior de Investigaciones Científicas.
Clarke, D. 1968 *Analytical Archaeology*, second edition. London: Methuen.
Cohen, S.J.D. 1982 Masada: Literary Tradition, Archaeological Remains, and the Credibility of Josephus. *Journal of Jewish Studies* 33:385–405.
Cole, J. and E. Wolf, 1974 *The Hidden Frontier: Ecology and Ethnicity in an Alpine Valley*. New York: Academic.
Comissão Executiva dos Centenários 1940 *Congresso do Mundo Português*. Lisbon.
Comşa, E. 1960 Considérations sur le rite funéraire de la civilisation de Gumelnitsa. *Dacia* 4:5–30.
1975 Quelques problèmes concernant la période de transition vers l'âge du bronze dans l'est de la Roumanie et le sudouest de l'URSS. *Acta Archaeologica Carpathica* 15:133–44.
1976 *Bibliografia Neoliticului de pe Territoriul României*. Vol. 1. Bucharest: Biblioteca Muzeologica.
1977 *Bibliografia Neoliticului de pe Territoriul României*. Vol. 2. Bucharest: Biblioteca Muzeologica.
Condurachi, E. 1964 *Rumanian Archaeology in the 20th Century*. Bucharest: Bibliotheca Historica Romaniae.
Costa, J. 1917 *Ultimo día del paganismo y primero de . . . lo mismo*. Madrid: Biblioteca Costa.
Čović, B. 1959 Tragovi preistoriski migracija u sjeveroistočn o j Bosni. *Članci i Gradta* 3:5–22.
Creamer, H. 1990 Aboriginal Perceptions of the Past: The Implications for Cultural Resource Management in Australia. In Gathercole and Lowenthal (1990), pp.

130–40.

Crişan, I. 1969 *Ceramica daco-getică cu speciala privire la Transilvania*. Bucharest: Editiones Stiintifica.

Crumley, Carole L. 1974 *Celtic Social Structure: The Generation of Archaeologically Testable Hypotheses from Literary Evidence*. Anthropological Papers 54. Ann Arbor: Museum of Anthropology, University of Michigan.

Curl, J.S. 1982 *The Egyptian Revival: An Introductory Study of a Recurring Theme in the History of Taste*. London: Allen and Unwin.

Daicoviciu, H. 1979 L'Epoque classique de la civilisation des Daco-Gètes. In *La Civilisation classique des Daco-Gètes*, edited by V. Capitanu, H. Daicoviciu, E. Iaroslavschi, C. Pop, M. Turcu, and N. Vlassa, pp. xiii–xxxi. Brussels: Musées Royaux d'Art et d'Histoire.

d'Encarnação, José 1979 *The Prehistoric Caves of Alapraia*. Coimbra: Estoril Coast Tourist Board.

Denich, B. 1993 Unmaking Multi-ethnicity in Yugoslavia: Metamorphosis Observed. *Anthropology of East Europe Review* 11(1–2):43–53.

Dennell, R.W. and Webley, D. 1975 Prehistoric Settlement and Land Use in Southern Bulgaria. In *Palaeoeconomy*, edited by E.S. Higgs, pp. 97–109. Cambridge: Cambridge University Press.

Derzhavin, N.S. 1944 *Proiskhozhdenie Russkogo naroda*. Moscow: Sovetskaya Nauka.

1946 *Slavyane v drevnosti*. Moscow-Leningrad: AN SSSR.

Diakonoff, I.M. 1984 *The Pre-History of the Armenian People*. Delmar, NY: Caravan.

Diamond, Irene and Gloria Feman Orenstein (eds.) 1990 *Reweaving the World: The Emergence of Ecofeminism*. San Francisco: Sierra Club Books.

Díaz-Andreu, M. 1993 Theory and Ideology: Spanish Archaeology under the Franco Regime. *Antiquity* 67:74–82.

Diem, D. Hermann 1965 Nachwort. In *Deutsches Geistesleben und Nationalsozialismus*, edited by Andreas Flittner, pp. 237–40. Tübingen: Rainer Wunderlich Verlag.

Dietler, Michael 1994 "Our Ancestors the Gauls": Archaeology, Ethnic Nationalism, and the Manipulation of Celtic Identity in Modern Europe. *American Anthropologist* 96(3):584–605.

Ding Bangjun 1986 Jianghuai diqu Chu wenhua kaogu shulüe. *Wenwu Yanjiu* 2:62–6.

Diop, C.A. 1974 *The African Origin of Civilization: Myth or Reality*. Westport, Conn.: Lawrence Hill.

Dobrescu, M. 1979 Avant-propos. In *La Civilisation classique des Daco-Gètes*, edited by V. Capitanu, H. Daicoviciu, E. Iaroslavschi, C. Pop, M. Turcu and N. Vlassa, pp. x–xi. Brussels: Musées Royaux d'Art et d'Histoire.

Du Yubing and Dong Qi 1974 Shijian chu zhenzhi – shiqi fazhan de lishi shi dui "tiancailun" de chedi fouding (Genuine Knowledge Comes from Practice – the History of the Making of Stone Tools is the Thorough Negation for the "Theory of Innate Genius"). *Wenwu* 4:7–28.

Dumitrescu, H. 1958 Deux nouvelles tombes cucuténiennes à rite magique découvertes à Traian. *Dacia* 2:407–23.

Dumitrescu, V. 1970 A propos l'ancienne culture néolithique de Roumanie. *Studii şi Cercetari Istorie Veche* 21:187–99.

Dumont, L. 1991 *L'idéologie allemande: France-Allemagne et retour* (Homo Aequalis 2). Paris: Gallimard.

Dundua, G.F. 1987 *Numizmatika antichnoi Gruzii.* Tbilisi: Metsniereba.

Duplá, A. and Emborujo, A. 1991 El Vascocantabrismo: mito y realidad en la historiografía sobre el País Vasco en la antigüedad. In Arce and Olmos (1991), pp. 107–12.

Dzhaparidze, O. 1989 *Na zare etnokul'turnoi istorii Kavkaza.* Tbilisi: Tbilisi University Press.

Edelman, M. 1964 *The Symbolic Uses of Politics.* Urbana: University of Illinois Press.

Efimenko, P.P. 1923 Doistoricheskaya arkheologiya, ee zadachi i perspektivy v oblastnom izuchenii. *Kraevedenie* 2:93–8.

Efirov, S.A. 1989 Sotsialnyi nartsissizm. In *V chelovecheskom izmerenii*, edited by A.G. Vishnevskii, pp. 25–52. Moscow: Progress.

Eggert, Manfred K.H. 1978 Prähistorische Archäologie und Ethnologie: Studien zur amerikanischen New Archaeology. *Praehistorische Zeitschrift* 53:6–164.

Ehrich, R. 1965 *Chronologies in Old World Archaeology.* Chicago: Chicago University Press.

Eisler, Riane 1987 *The Chalice and the Blade.* San Francisco: Harper and Row.

1990 The Gaia Tradition and the Partnership Future: An Ecofeminist Manifesto. In Diamond and Orenstein (1990), pp. 23–34.

Elon, Amos 1994 Politics and Archaeology. *New York Review of Books*, September 22, 1994:14–18.

Enciclopédia Luso-Brasileira de Cultura 1973 Lisbon: Verbo.

Enciclopedia Universal Ilustrada Europeo-Americana 1924 Various volumes. Madrid, Barcelona: Ed. Espasa-Calpe.

Engels, F. 1884 *The Origin of the Family, Private Property and the State* (rev. 4th edn, 1894). Stuttgart: Dietz.

Evans, Christopher 1989 Bersu's Woodbury 1938 & 1939. *Antiquity* 63:436–50.

Falkenhausen, Lothar von 1993a On the Historiographical Orientation of Chinese Archaeology. *Antiquity* 67:839–49.

1993b Serials on Chinese Archaeology Published in the People's Republic of China: A Bibliographical Survey. *Early China* 17, forthcoming.

Fang Yousheng (ed.) 1988 *Chu Zhanghuatai xueshu taolunhui lunwenji*, Wuhan: Wuhan Daxue Chubanshe.

Fawcett, C. 1990 *A Study of the Socio-Political Context of Japanese Archaeology.* Ph.D. dissertation, McGill University, Montreal, Canada.

Fedorov, G.B. 1948 Obsuzhdenie knigi professora P.N. Tretyakova "Vostochnoslavyanskie plemena." *Vestnik Drevnei Istorii* 4:117–24.

Fedotov, G.P. 1992 Novyi idol. G.P. Fedotov. *Sudba i grekhi Rossii.* St. Petersburg: Sofiya, 2:50–62.

Ferguson, A.B. 1993 *Utter Antiquity: Perceptions of Prehistory in Renaissance England.* Durham: Duke University Press.

Finkelstein, I. 1988 *The Archaeology of the Israelite Settlement.* Jerusalem: Israel Exploration Society.

Florescu, A. 1966 Sistemul de Fortificare al Aşezarilor Cucuteniene din Moldova. *Archeologia Moldovei (Iaşi)* 4:23–37.

Foanaota, L. 1990 Archaeology and Museum Work in the Solomon Islands. In Gathercole and Lowenthal (1990), pp. 224–32.

Foresta, R.A. 1984 *America's National Parks and Their Keepers*. Washington, DC: Resources for the Future.

Formozov, A.A. 1993 Arkheologiya i ideologiya (20–30-e gg.). *Voprosy Filosofii* 2:70–82.

Foss, M.E. 1952 *Drevneishaya istoriya Severa evropeiskoi chasti SSSR*. Moscow: AN SSSR.

Fowler, D.D. 1987 The Uses of the Past: Archaeology in the Service of the State. *American Antiquity* 52:229–48.

Fox, R.G. 1985 *Lions of the Punjab: Culture in the Making*. Berkeley: University of California Press.

Frazer, J.G. 1922 *The Golden Bough*. New York: Macmillan.

Friedman, J. 1992 The Past in the Future: History and the Politics of Identity. *American Anthropologist* 94:837–59.

Fryer, Peter and Patricia McGowan Pinheiro 1961 *Oldest Ally: A Portrait of Salazar's Portugal*. London: Dennis Dobson.

Fuchs, S. 1937 *Die griechischen Fundgruppen der frühen Bronzezeit, und ihre ausvartigen Beziehungen*. Berlin.

Fujita, R. 1951 Kokogaku ippan (Archaeological Movements). In *Nihon Kokogaku Nempo*, edited by the Nihon Kokogaku Kyokai, pp. 3–17. Tokyo: Seibundo-Shinkosha. (In Japanese with English title.)

Fuzhou 1980 Fujian Chong'an Wuyishan Baiyan yadongmu qingli jianbao. *Fujian Wenbo* 3:3–8.

1991 *Fujian Wenbo zengkan*. (Special issue devoted to the study of ancient boat burials in Fujian.)

Gadamer, Hans-Georg 1978 The Historicity of Understanding as Hermeneutic Principle. In *Heidegger and Modern Philosophy*, edited by Michael Murray, pp. 161–258. New Haven: Yale University Press.

Gadlo, A.V. 1968 Problema Priazovskoi Rusi i sovremennye arkheologicheskie dannye o Yuzhnom Priazove 8–9kh vekov. *Vestnik Leningradskogo Universiteta*, seriya istorii, yazyka i literatury, 14(3):55–65.

Gadon, Elinor W. 1989 *The Once and Future Goddess: A Symbol For Our Time*. New York: Harper and Row.

Gamkrelidze, G. 1985 "Epokha Antichnosti (Graeco-Roman)" or "Iberian-Colchian epokha." In *Problems of Georgian Archaeology*, vol. 3, pp. 123–6. Tbilisi (in Georgian).

Gamkrelidze, T.V. and Vyach. Vs. Ivanov. 1984 *Indoevropeiskii yazyk i indoevropeitsy*, 2 vols. Tbilisi: Tbilisi State University Press.

Gamsakhurdia, Z. 1991 There Is No Ossetia in Georgia. In *The Georgian Messenger* 1(4):1.

Garašanin, D. 1972 *Bronzano Doba Srbije*. Belgrade: Narodni Muzej.

Garašanin, M. 1954 Iz istorije mladjeg neolita u Srbiji i Bosni. *Glasnik Zemaljskog Muzeja u Sarajevu* 9:5–39.

1974 *Praistorija na Tlu Srbije*. Belgrade: Nolit.

1988 Nastanak i poreklo Ilira. In *Iliri i Albanci*, edited by M. Garašanin, pp. 9–80. Belgrade: Srpska Akademija Nauka i Umetnosti.

Garašanin, M. (ed.) 1979 *Praistorija Jugoslavenskih Zemalja II: Neolit*. Sarajevo: Akademija Nauka i Umjetnosti Bosne i Hercegovine.

García Casado, S. 1987 Algunas reflexiones acerca del problemático nacionalismo español. *Cuadernos de Alzate* 5:37–44.

García de Cortázar, F. and Azcona, J.M. 1991 *El nacionalismo vasco*. Biblioteca Historia 16. Madrid: Ed. Historia.

Gardiner, Kenneth Herbert James 1969 *The Early History of Korea*. Honolulu: University of Hawaii Press.

Gasper, Philip 1990 Explanation and Scientific Realism. In *Explanation and Its Limits*, edited by Dudley Knowles, pp. 285–95. Cambridge: Cambridge University Press.

Gathercole, P. and D. Lowenthal (eds.) 1990 *The Politics of the Past*. London: Unwin Hyman.

Gaul, James Harvey 1948 *The Neolithic Period in Bulgaria*. American School of Prehistoric Research, Bulletin 16. Cambridge, Mass.: Peabody Museum of Harvard University.

Geary, P.J. 1990 *Furta Sacra: Thefts of Relics in the Central Middle Ages*. Princeton: Princeton University Press.

Geertz, Clifford 1973 *The Interpretation of Cultures*. New York: Basic Books.

Gellner, E. 1983 *Nations and Nationalism*. Oxford: Basil Blackwell.

1988 The Stakes in Anthropology. *American Scholar* [1]:17–30.

Gening, V.F. 1982 *Ocherki po istorii sovetskoi arkheologii*. Kiev: Naukova Dumka.

Georgiev, G. 1961 Kulturgruppen der Jungstein- und Kupferzeit in der Ebene von Thrazien (Südbulgarien). In *L'Europe à la fin de l'âge de pierre*, edited by J. Böhm and S. DeLaet, pp. 45–100. Prague: Czechoslovak Academy of Sciences.

1965 Die Entwicklung der älteren prähistorischen Kulturen Südbulgarien. In *Ethnogénèse des peuples balkaniques*, edited by G. Georgiev. *Studia Balcanica* 5:21–35. Sofia.

Gero, J. 1985 Socio-Politics and the Woman-at-Home Ideology. *American Antiquity* 50:342–50.

Geyushev, R.B. 1986 *Arkheologiya Azerbaidzhana* (in Azeri Turkish with Russian résumé). Baku: Ishi.

Gill, B. 1989 The Faces of Joseph Campbell. *New York Review of Books*, September 28.

Gillespie, N.C. 1977 The Duke of Argyll, Evolutionary Anthropology, and the Art of Scientific Controversy. *Isis* 68:40–54.

Gilman, Antonio 1981 The Development of Social Stratification in Bronze Age Europe. *Current Anthropology* 22(1):1–23.

(in press) Recent Trends in the Archaeology of Spain. In *The Origins of Complex Societies in Late Prehistoric Iberia*, edited by K. Lillios. Ann Arbor: International Monographs in Prehistory.

Gimbutas, Marija 1970 Proto-Indo-European Culture: The Kurgan Culture during the Fifth, Fourth, and Third Millennia B.C. In *Indo-European and the Indo-Europeans*, edited by G. Cardona, H.M. Hoenigswald and A. Senn, pp. 155–97. Philadelphia: University of Pennsylvania Press.

1973 Old Europe c. 7000–3500 B.C.: The Earliest European Civilization before the Infiltration of the Indo-European Peoples. *Journal of Indo-European Studies* 1:1–21.

1974 *The Gods and Goddesses of Old Europe*. Los Angeles: University of California Press.

1977 The First Wave of Eurasian Steppe Pastoralists into Copper Age Europe. *Journal of Indo-European Studies* 5:277–338.

1980 *The Early Civilization of Europe*. UCLA Monographs for Indo-European Studies 131. Private circulation.

1989a Women and Culture in Goddess-Oriented Old Europe. In Plaskow and Christ (1989), pp. 63–71.

1989b *The Language of the Goddess*. London: Thames and Hudson.

Gómez Santacruz, S. 1935 *Numancia. Sus guerras. Exploración de sus ruinas. El Museo Numantino*. Soria.

Gordon, M.A. 1968 The Social History of Evolution in Britain. *American Antiquity* 39:194–204.

Goryainov, A.N. 1990 Slavyanovedy – zhertvy repressii 1920–1940 godov: Nekotorye neizvestnye stranitsy iz istorii Sovetskoi nauki. *Sovetskoe Slavyanovedenie* 2:78–89.

Graham, L.R. 1967 *The Soviet Academy of Sciences and the Communist Party, 1927–1932*. Princeton: Princeton University Press.

1987 *Science, Philosophy, and Human Behavior in the Soviet Union*. New York: Columbia University Press.

Gran Enciclopedia Gallega 1984 Santiago de Compostela: Ed. Silveiro Cañada.

Grande Enciclopédia Portuguesa e Brasileira 1935 Lisbon: Editorial Enciclopedia, Ltda.

Grant, Madison 1916 *The Passing of the Great Race, or The Racial Basis of European History*. New York: Scribner's.

Graves, R. 1948 *The White Goddess*. New York: Farrar, Straus, Giroux.

Grayson, James H. 1977 Mimana: A Problem in Korean Historiography. *Korea Journal* 7(8):65–8.

Grekov, B.D. 1953 *Kievskaya Rus*. Leningrad: Gospolitizdat.

Grekov, B.D. and Y.V. Bromlej 1952 Izuchenie istorii Kryma. *Vestnik AN SSSR* 8:71–5.

Guliev, Dzh. B., G.A. Madatov and A.A. Nadirov 1984 *Sovetskaya Nakhichevan*. Baku: Azerbaidzhanskoe Gosudarstvennoe Izdatelstvo.

Gumilev, L.N. 1960 *Khunnu*. Moscow.

1967 *Drevnie tyurki*. Moscow: Nauk.

1992 *Drevnyaya Rus i Velikaya step*. Moscow: Mysl.

1993a *Etnosfera. Istoriya lyudei i istoriya prirody*. Moscow: Ekopros.

1993b *Ot Rusi k Rossii*. Moscow.

Guo Dewei 1986 Hubei kaogu faxian de quanguo zhi yu shijie zhi zui. *Jianghan Kaogu*. Special issue (zengkan):54–6.

Guo Moruo 1957 Women jianchi wenwu shiye de zhengque fangxiang (We Must Persist in the Correct Direction of Archaeology). *Wenwu Cankao Ziliao* 9:1–2.

Guseinov, M.M. 1985 *Drevnii Paleolit Azerbaidzhana*. Baku: Elm.

Habermas, J. 1973 *Legitimation Crisis*. Boston: Beacon.

Hachlili, R. and Killebrew, A. (eds.) 1993 *Interpreting the Past: Presenting Archaeological Sites to the Public*. Haifa, Israel: University of Haifa Press.

Hagen, Anders 1985/6 Arkeologi or politik. *Viking, Tidsskrift for Norren Arkeologi*, 49:269–78.

Hall, M. 1984 The Burden of Tribalism: The Social Context of Southern African Iron Age Studies. *American Antiquity* 49:455–67.

1990 "Hidden History": Iron Age Archaeology in Southern Africa. In *A History of African Archaeology*, edited by P. Robertshaw, pp. 59–77. London: Currey.

Halpern, J. 1993 Introduction. *Anthropology of East Europe Review* 11(1–2):5–13.

Halpern, J. and Hammel, E. 1969 Observations on the Intellectual History of Ethnology and Other Social Sciences in Yugoslavia. *Comparative Studies in Society and History* 11:17–26.

Hammel, E.A. 1992 The Yugoslav Labyrinth. *Center for Slavic and East European Studies Update* (May). Berkeley: Center for Slavic and East European Studies, University of California.

Hammond, M. 1980 Anthropology as a Weapon of Social Combat in Late-Nineteeenth-Century France. *Journal of the History of the Behavioral Sciences* 16:118–32.

Hardin, Clyde L. and Alexander Rosenberg 1982 In Defense of Convergent Realism. *Philosophy of Science* 49(4):604–15.

Harding, A.F. 1983 The Bronze Age in Central and Eastern Europe: Advances and Prospects. In *Advances in World Archaeology*, vol. 2, edited by F. Wendorf and A. Close, pp. 1–50. New York: Academic.

Härke, Heinrich 1989a The Unkel Symposia: The Beginnings of a Debate in West German Archaeology? *Current Archaeology* 30:406–10.

1989b Die anglo-amerikanische Diskussion zur Gräberanalyse. *Archäologisches Korrespondenzblatt* 19:185–94.

1990 Die deutsche Sitzung bei TAG 90: Eine Auseinandersetzung mit Vergangenheit, Gegenwart und Zukunft des Faches in Deutschland. *Archäologische Informationen* 13(2):224–9.

1991 All Quiet on the Western Front? Paradigms, Methods and Approaches in West German Archaeology. In *Archaeological Theory in Europe: The Last Three Decades*, edited by Ian Hodder, pp. 187–222. London: Routledge.

Harris, Marvin 1968 *The Rise of Anthropological Theory: A History of Theories of Culture*. New York: Thomas Y. Crowell.

Harvey, D. 1989 *The Condition of Postmodernity*. Oxford: Basil Blackwell.

Hassmann, Henning 1990. Bericht über die Tagung der Ur- und Frühgeschichtsstudentinnen und -studenten 29.6–1.7.1990 in Göttingen. *Archäologische Informationen* 13(2):221–3.

(n.d.) Archaeology in the Third Reich. In *Archaeology, Ideology and Society: The German Experience*, edited by H. Härke. New Directions in Archaeology. Cambridge: Cambridge University Press.

Hayashi Minao 1980 In-Seishû jidai-no chihôkei seidôki. *Kôkogaku Memoir*:17–58.

He Hao 1989 *Chu mieguo yanjiu*. Wuhan: Wuhan Chubanshe.

Heidegger, Martin 1959 *An Introduction to Metaphysics* (original 1935, revised 1953), trans. by Ralph Manheim. New Haven: Yale University Press.

Hencken, Hugh 1955 *Indo-European Languages and Archaeology*. American Anthropological Association Memoir 84.

Hernández-Gil, D. 1983 Datos históricos sobre la restauración de monumentos. In *50 años de protección del patrimonio histórico artístico 1933–1983*, Madrid: Ministerio de Cultura.

Herold, J.C. 1962 *Bonaparte in Egypt*. New York: Harper and Row.

Hill, Jonathon D. 1992 Contested Pasts and the Practise of Archaeology: Overview. *American Anthropologist* 94(4):809–15.

Hobsbawm, E.J. 1983a Introduction: Inventing Traditions. In Hobsbawm and Ranger (1983), pp. 1–14.

1983b Mass-Producing Traditions: Europe, 1870–1914. In Hobsbawm and Ranger (1983), pp. 263–308.

1992a *Nations and Nationalism since 1780*, second edition. Cambridge: Cambridge University Press.

1992b Ethnicity and Nationalism in Europe Today. *Anthropology Today* 8(1):3–13. (Text of an address given at a plenary session of the American Association Meetings, Chicago, Illinois, November 1991, with comments by K. Verdery and R. Fox.)

Hobsbawm, E. and T. Ranger (eds.) 1983 *The Invention of Tradition*. Cambridge: Cambridge University Press.

Hodder, I. 1982a Theoretical Archaeology: A Reactionary View. In Hodder (1982b), pp. 1–16.

1984 Archaeology in 1984. *Antiquity* 58:25–52.

1985 Postprocessual Archaeology. In *Advances in Archaeological Method and Theory*, vol. 8, edited by M.B. Schiffer, pp. 1–26. Orlando: Academic.

1986 *Reading the Past: Current Approaches to Interpretation in Archaeology*. Cambridge: Cambridge University Press.

1987 La arqueología en la era postmoderna. *Trabajos de Prehistoria* 44:11–26.

1990 *The Domestication of Europe: Structure and Contingency in Neolithic Societies*. Oxford: Basil Blackwell.

1991a Interpretive Archaeology and Its Role. *American Antiquity* 56(1):7–18.

1991b *Reading the Past: Current Approaches to Interpretation in Archaeology*, second edition. Cambridge: Cambridge University Press.

Hodder, I. (ed.) 1982b *Symbolic and Structural Archaeology*. Cambridge: Cambridge University Press.

Hodges, Richard 1982 *Dark Age Economics: The Origin of Towns and Trade A.D. 600–1000*. London: Duckworth.

Hoffman, M.A. 1974 The Rise of Antiquarianism in Japan and Western Europe. *Arctic Anthropology* 11 (supplement):182–8.

Holl, A. 1990 West African Archaeology: Colonialism and Nationalism. In *A History of African Archaeology*, edited by P. Robertshaw, pp. 296–308. London: Currey.

Hong Wontack 1988 *Relationship between Korea and Japan in Early Period: Packche and Yamato Wa*. Seoul: Ilsimsa Publisher.

Horton, J.O. and S.R. Crew 1989 Afro-Americans and Museums: Towards a Policy of Inclusion. In *History Museums in the United States*, edited by W. Leon and R. Rosenzweig, pp. 215–36. Urbana: University of Illinois Press.

Hou Dejun 1990. *Chu-guo kexuejishushi-gao*. Wuhan: Hubeisheng Wenwu Kaogu Yanjiusuo.

Hroch, M. 1985 *Social Preconditions of National Revival in Europe*. Cambridge: Cambridge University Press.

Hsu Cho-yun and Katheryn M. Linduff 1988 *Western Chou Civilization*. New Haven and London: Yale University Press.

Hu Yaobang 1982 Quanmian kaichuang shehuizhuyi xiandaihua jianshe de xin jumian (Open Up a New Prospect of Modern Socialist Construction). *Zhongguo Gongchandang di Sier Ci Quanguo Daibiao Dahui Wenjian Huibian* (Documents of the Twelfth National Congress of the Communist Party of China), p. 38. Beijing: Renmin Chubanshe.

Hu Yongqing and Song Guoding 1990 Jinshinianlai Henan Liang-Zhou kaogu suo xinfaxian. *Hua Xia Kaogu* 3:17–29.

Huang Dexin 1983 *Chu-guo shilüe*. Wuhan: Huazhong Gongxueyuan Chubanshe.

Hughes, Kathleen 1971 Evidence for Contacts between the Churches of the Irish and English from the Synod of Whitby to the Viking Age. In *England before the Conquest: Studies in Primary Sources Presented to Dorothy Whitelock*, edited by Peter Clemoes and Kathleen Hughes, pp. 49–67. Cambridge: Cambridge University Press.

Hunger, Ulrich 1984 *Die Runenkunde im Dritten Reich: Ein Beitrag zur Wissenschafts- und Ideologiegeschichte des Nationalsozialismus*. Europäische Hochschulschriften Reihe 111: Geschichte und Ihre Hilfswissenschaften. Frankfurt: Peter Lang.

Hunt, L. 1989 Introduction: History, Culture, and Text. In *The New Cultural History*, edited by L. Hunt, pp. 1–22. Berkeley: University of California Press.

Ikawa-Smith, Fumiko 1982 Co-traditions in Japanese Archaeology. *World Archaeology* 13(3):296–308.

1986 Late Pleistocene and Early Holocene Technologies. In *Windows on the Japanese Past: Studies in Archaeology and Prehistory*, edited by Richard J. Pearson, pp. 199–216. Ann Arbor: Center for Japanese Studies, University of Michigan.

Ilyon 1972 *Samguk Yusa: Legends and History of the Three Kingdoms of Ancient Korea*, trans by Tae-Hung Ha and Grafton K. Mintz. Seoul: Yonsei University Press.

Inada, T. 1986 Iseki no hogo (Site protection). In *Nihon Kokogaku 7: Gendai to Kokogaku*, edited by Y. Kondo *et al.*, pp. 71–132. Tokyo: Iwanami Shoten. (In Japanese.)

Institut . . . 1992 1937 god. Institut Krasnoi Professury. *Otechestvennaya Istoriya* 2:119–46.

Isaković, A. 1988 Uvodna reć. In *Iliri i Albanci*, edited by M. Garašanin, pp. 5–6. Belgrade: Srpska Akademija Nauka i Umetnosti.

Isklyuchitelno zamechatelnyi akt 1992. Isklyuchitelno zamechatelnyi akt bratskoi pomoshchi. Dokumenty i materialy o peredache Krymskoi oblasti iz sostava RSFSR v sostav SSSR (yanvar–fevral 1954). *Istoricheskii Arkhiv* 1:39–54.

Izvestiya, no. 12, January 21, 1994.

Jalhay, E. and A. do Paço 1945 El castro de Vilanova de San Pedro. *Actas y Memórias de la Sociedad Española de Antropologia, Etnográfia, y Préhistória,*

Madrid, 1945, vol. 20, pp. 5–91.
Jankowska, N.B. 1991 Asshur, Mitanni and Arrapkhe. In *Early Antiquity*, edited by I.M. Diakonoff, pp. 228–60. Chicago: University of Chicago Press.
Jelavich, B. 1982 *History of the Balkans*, vol. 1, *Eighteenth and Nineteenth Centuries*. Cambridge: Cambridge University Press.
Ji Zhongqing 1982 Qiantan Wu wenhua he xian-Wu wenhua. *Nanjing Bowuyuan Jikan* 4:1–7.
Jin Yue 1986/7 Yanshan fangguo kao (Parts I and II). *Liaohai Wenwu Xuekan* 1986 (2):66–76, 29 and 1987 (1):84–94.
1989 Beifang wudi wenhua kao. *Liaohai Wenwu Xuekan* 2:40–52.
1990 Lun Dongbei Shang-dai qingtongqi fenqi, xingzhi he tedian. *Liaohai Wenwu Xuekan* 2:55–66.
Jinan 1982 *Qufu Lu-guo Gucheng*. Jinan: Qilu Shushe.
1987 *Linyi Fenghuangling Dong-Zhou-mu*, Jinan: Qilu Shushe.
Johnsen, Harald and Olsen Bjørnar 1992. Hermeneutics and Archaeology: On the Philosophy of Contextual Archaeology. *American Antiquity* 57(3):416–36.
Jones, W.R. 1971 England Against the Celtic Fringe: A Study in Cultural Stereotypes. *Journal of World History* 13(1):155–71.
Jovanović, B. 1972 The Autochthonous and Migrational Components of the Early Neolithic in the Iron Gates. *Balcanica* 3:49–58.
1974a Mladje gvozdeno doba. In *Praistorija Vojvodine*, edited by B. Brukner, B. Jovanović and N. Tasić, pp. 277–316. Novi Sad: Institut za Izučavanje Istorije Vojvodine.
1974b Ekonomska i društvena organizacija praistoriskih zajedenica Vojvodine. In *Praistorija Vojvodine*, edited by B. Brukner, B. Jovanović and N. Tasić, pp. 317–36. Novi Sad: Institut za Izučavanje Istorije Vojvodine.
K predstoyashchemu sezdu 1931 K predstoyashchemu Vsesoyuznomu sezdu po arkheologii i etnografii. *Soobshcheniya Gosudarstvennoi Akademii Istorii Materialnoi Kultury* 8:2–3.
Kane, Virginia C. 1974/5 The Independent Bronze Industries in the South of China Contemporary with the Shang and Western Chou Dynasties. *Archives of Asian Art* 28:77–107.
Karimullin, A. 1988 *Tatary: etnos i etnonim*. Kazan: Tatar Book Publishing.
Kater, Michael 1974 *Das Ahnenerbe der SS: 1935–45 ein Beitrag zur Kulturpolitik des Dritten Reiches*. Studien zur Zeitgeschichte, Institut für Zeitgeschichte. Stuttgart: Deutsche Verlagsanstalt.
Kaukhchishvili, T.S. 1979 Written Sources on "Colonization" of the Eastern Black Sea Littoral. In *Problems of Greek Colonization of the Northern and Eastern Black Sea Littoral*, pp. 294–304. Tbilisi.
Kavoukjian, M. 1987 *Armenia, Subartu and Sumer: The Indo-European Homeland and Ancient Mesopotamia*. Published privately with the support of the Malkhassian Foundation, Montreal.
Kay, Hugh 1970 *Salazar and Modern Portugal*. New York: Hawthorn Books.
Kedourie, E. 1988 [1966] *Nacionalismo*. Colección Estudios Políticos. Centro de Estudios Constitucionales. Madrid. [1979 *Nationalism*. London: Hutchinson.]
Kendrick, T.D. 1938 *Anglo-Saxon Art to A.D. 900*. London: Methuen.
Khalikov, A. Kh. 1992 *Kto my – bulgary ili tatary?* Kazan: Kazan Press.

Khudyakov, M.G. 1931 Finnskaya expansiya v arkheologicheskoi nauke. *Soobshcheniya Gosudarstvennoi Akademii Materialnoi Kultury* 11–12:25–9.

Kidder, J.E. 1972 *Early Buddhist Japan*. London: Thames and Hudson.

1973. Asuka and the Takamatsuzuka Tomb. *Archaeology* 26(1):24–31.

Kihara, K. 1974 Doro kensetsu to bunkazai (Road Construction and Cultural Properties). *Kosokodoro to Jidosha* 17(2):12–16. (In Japanese.)

Kim Byong-mo 1981 A New Interpretation of Megalithic Monuments in Korea. In *Megalithic Cultures in Asia*, edited by B.M. Kim, pp. 164–89. Seoul: Hanyang University Press.

Kim Won-yong 1982 Discoveries of Rice in Prehistoric Sites in Korea. *Journal of Asian Studies* 41(3):513–18.

1983 *Recent Archaeological Discoveries in the Republic of Korea*. Tokyo: The Centre for East Asian Studies, UNESCO.

1986 *Art and Archaeology of Ancient Korea*. Seoul: The Taekwang Publishing Company.

Kirigin, B. 1992 Issa i JNA. *Obavijesti* 24(1):51–5.

Kleeman, G. 1986 Ist die Kunst auf der Alb entstanden? *Stuttgarter Zeitung*, no. 7, January 10, 1986.

Klejn, L.S. 1974 Kossinna im Abstand von vierzig Jahren. *Jahresschrift Mitteldeutscher Vorgeschichte* 58:7–55.

1991 A Russian Lesson for Theoretical Archaeology: A Reply. *Fennoscandia Archaeologica* 8:67–71.

Kohl, P.L. 1992 Ethnic Strife: A Necessary Amendment to a Consideration of Class Struggles in Antiquity. In *Civilization in Crisis: Anthropological Perspectives*, vol. 1, *Essays in Honor of Stanley Diamond*, edited by C.W. Gailey, pp. 167–80. Gainesville: University of Florida Press.

1993 Nationalism, Politics, and the Practice of Archaeology in Soviet Transcaucasia. *Journal of European Archaeology* 1(2):181–8.

Kondo, Y. 1983a Tsukinowa Kofun no hakkutau (1) (The Tsukinowa Kofun Burial Mound Excavation (1)). In *Minzoku to Mimikazari*, edited by Y. Kondo, pp. 20–3. Tokyo: Aoki Shoten. (In Japanese.)

1983b Tsukinowa Kofun no hakkutau (2) (The Tsukinowa Kofun Burial Mound Excavation (2)). In *Minzoku to Mimikazari*, edited by Y. Kondo, pp. 24–7. Tokyo: Aoki Shoten. (In Japanese.)

Kondo, Y. (ed.) 1960 *Tsukinowa Kofun (The Tsukinowa Kofun Burial Mound)*. Okayama: Tsukinowa Kanko Kai. (In Japanese with English summary.)

Kontselidze, O. 1991 Petra, or –. *Kobuleti* (district newspaper), p. 1. (In Georgian.)

Korell, Dieter 1989 Zum Wesen der Vor- und Frühgeschichte. *Mannus*, Deutsche Zeitschrift für Vor- und Frühgeschichte, 55(3):169–84.

Korošec, J. 1957 Kultura in kulturna skupina v predgovini. *Arheološki Vestnik* 8:95–8.

Kossack, Georg 1992 Prehistoric Archaeology in Germany: Its History and Current Situation. *Norwegian Archaeological Review* 25(2):73–109.

Kossinna, Gustaf 1911 *Der Herkunft der Germanen: Zur Methode der Siedlungsarchäologie*. Mannus-Bibliothek 6. Würzburg: Kabitzsch.

Kosso, Peter 1991 Method in Archaeology: Middle-Range Theory as Hermeneutics. *American Antiquity* 56(4):621–7.

Krichevski, E. Yu. 1931 Burzhuaznaya arkheologiya v sovetskom muzee. *Soobshcheniya Gosudarstvennoi Akademii Materialnoi Kultury* 9–10:62–71.

1933 Indogermanskii vopros arkheologicheski razrashonnyi. In *Iz istorii dokapitalisticheskikh formatsii*, edited by S.N. Bykovski *et al.*, pp. 158–202. Moscow and Leningrad: Gossotsecizdat.

Kristiansen, K. 1990 National Archaeology in the Age of European Integration. *Antiquity* 64:835–8.

von Krosigk, Hildegard Gräfin Schwerin 1982 *Gustav Kossinna*: Der Nachlass – Versuch einer Analyse. Offa – Ergänzungsreihe Bd. 6. Neumünster: Karl Wachholtz Verlag.

Krupnov, E.I. 1960 *Drevnyaya Istoriya Severnogo Kavkaza*. Moscow: Academy of Sciences.

KSIE 1950 Kratkie Soobshcheniya Instituta Etnografii, 12.

Kuklick, H. 1991 Contested Monuments: The Politics of Archaeology in Southern Africa. In *Colonial Situations: Essays on the Contextualization of Ethnographic Knowledge* (History of Archaeology 7), edited by G.W. Stocking, Jr, pp. 135–69. Madison: University of Wisconsin Press.

Kushner (Knushev), P. 1927 Nuzhno li izuchat obshchestvennye formy. *Istorikmarksist* 6:206–14.

Laing, Lloyd and Jennifer Laing 1979 *Anglo-Saxon England*. London: Routledge (pagination here from Granada 1982 paperback edition).

Landau, M. 1991 *Narratives of Human Evolution*. New Haven: Yale University Press.

Larsen, M.T. 1987 Orientalism and the Ancient Near East. *Culture and History* 2:96–115.

Laudan, L. 1990 *Science and Relativism: Some Key Controversies in the Philosophy of Science*. Chicago: University of Chicago Press.

Lawton, Thomas (ed.) 1991 *New Perspectives on Chu Culture during the Eastern Zhou Period*. Washington, DC: Arthur M. Sackler Gallery.

Leone, M.P. 1981 Archaeology's Relationship to the Present and the Past. In *Modern Material Culture: The Archaeology of Us*, edited by R.A. Gould and M.B. Schiffer, pp. 5–14. New York: Academic Press.

Leone, M.P., P.B. Potter and P.A. Shackel 1987 Toward a Critical Archaeology. *Current Anthropology* 28(3):283–302.

Levenok, V.P. 1941 Arkheologicheskie raboty Trubachevskogo muzeya. *Kratkie Soobshcheniya Instituta Istorii Materialnoi Kultury* 10:95–9.

Lewis, B. 1975 *History Remembered, Recovered, Invented*. Princeton: Princeton University Press.

Lewis, P. 1989 Ancient King's Instructions to Iraq: Fix My Palace. *New York Times*, April 19.

Li Ling 1993 On the Typology of Chu Bronzes. Translated and edited by Lothar von Falkenhausen. *Beiträge zur Allgemeinen und Vergleichenden Archäologie*, forthcoming.

Li Shu 1983 Makesizhuyi yu Zhongguo lishixue (Marxism and Chinese Historical Science). *Lishi yanjiu* 2:3–16.

1985 *Zaisiji* (A Collection of Reconsiderations). Beijing: Zhongguo Shehuikexue chubanshe.

Lichardus, J. 1988 Der Westpontische Raum und die Anfänge der Kupferzeitlichen Zivilisation. In *Macht, Herrschaft, und Gold: Das Gräberfeld von Varna und die Anfänge einer neuen Europäischen Zivilisation*, ed. by G.W. Költzsch and J. Lichardus, pp. 79–130. Saarbrücken: Moderne Galerie des Saarland-Museums.

Linenthal, E.T. 1983 Ritual Drama at the Little Bighorn: The Persistence and Transformation of a National Symbol. *Journal of the American Academy of Religion* 51:267–81.

Link, Perry 1992 *Evening Chats in Beijing*. New York: W.W. Norton.

Lomsadze, Sh. 1989 *Meskheti i Meskhi*. Tbilisi: Tbilisi University Press.

Lord, B. 1974 *The History of Painting in Canada: Toward a People's Art*. Toronto: NC Press.

Lordkipanidze, O. 1982 *Arkheologiya v Gruzinskoi SSR*. Tbilisi: Metsniereba.

1989 *Nasledie Drevnei Gruzii*. Tbilisi: Metsniereba.

1991 *Archäologie in Georgien: von der Altsteinzeit zum Mittelalter*. Weinheim: VCH, Acta Humaniora.

Loukatos, D. 1978 Tourist Archeofolklore in Greece. In *Folklore in the Modern World*, edited by R.M. Donson, pp. 175–82. The Hague: Mouton Publishers.

Lowenthal, D. 1985 *The Past is a Foreign Country*. Cambridge: Cambridge University Press.

Lynch, B.D. and T.F. Lynch 1968 The Beginnings of a Scientific Approach to Prehistoric Archaeology in 17th and 18th Century Britain. *Southwestern Journal of Anthropology* 24:33–65.

Ma Hong 1984 Zuohao guihua gongzuo, kaichuang zhexue shehui kexue yanjiu de xin jumian (Create a Good Programme, Open Up a New Prospect for the Study of Philosophy and Social Science), edited by the Chinese Academy of Social Science. *Kaichuang Shehui Kexue Yanjiu de Xin Jumian* (Open Up a New Prospect for the Study of Social Science), p. 15. Beijing: Zhongguo Shehuikexue Chubanshe.

McCann, William J. 1988 The National Socialist Perversion of Archaeology. *World Archaeology Bulletin* 2:51–4.

1990 "Volk und Germanentum": The Presentation of the Past in Nazi Germany. In Gathercole and Lowenthal (1990), pp. 74–88.

MacCannell, D. 1976 *The Tourist: A New Theory of the Leisure Class*. New York: Schocken Books.

McConnell, B.E. 1989 Mediterranean Archaeology and Modern Nationalism: A Preface. *Revue des Archéologues et Historiens d'Art de Louvain* 22:107–13.

McFarlane, Adrian A. and N. Samuel Murrell 1988 Influences of the 19th-Century Hermeneutics of Consciousness on Subsequent Modes of Understanding. *Correlatives* 2:4–17.

McGuire, Randall H. 1992 *A Marxist Archaeology*. San Diego: Academic.

MacKendrick, P. 1952 A Renaissance Odyssey: The Life of Cyriac of Ancona. *Classica et Medievalia* 13:131–45.

MacKenzie, R. 1990 The Development of Museums in Botswana: Dilemmas and Tensions in a Front-line State. In Gathercole and Lowenthal (1990), pp. 203–13.

McNairn, Barbara 1980 *The Theory and Method of V. Gordon Childe*. Edinburgh:

Edinburgh University Press.

Máiz, R. 1984 *Alfredo Brañas*. Vigo: Ed. Galaxia.

Mannheim, K. 1936 *Ideology and Utopia: An Introduction to the Sociology of Knowledge*. New York: Harcourt, Brace and World.

Maravall, J.A. 1981 *El concepto de España en la Edad Media*. Madrid: Centro de Estudios Constitucionales.

Marc-7 (Dupré, X., O. Granados, E. Junyent, X. Nieto, N. Rafel and F. Tarrats) 1986a L'arqueologia catalana – I. El procés de consolidació de l'arqueologia catalana. *L'Avenç* 90:139–45.

1986b L'arqueologia catalana – II. De la postguerra als anys setanta. *L'Avenç* 91:224–31.

1986c L'arqueologia catalana – i III. Reorganització i nous impulsos, 1975–1985. *L'Avenç* 92:291–7.

Marchak, M.P. 1991 *The Integrated Circus: The New Right and the Restructuring of Global Markets*. McGill-Queen's University Press, Montreal.

Marinescu-Bîlcu, S. 1982 Au sujet de quelques opinions d'auteurs étrangers sur le Néo-Énéolithique de Roumanie. *Dacia* 26:153–6.

Markovin, V.I. 1992a Disputed Points in the Ethnogenetic Study of Northern Caucasus Antiquities (The Maikop Culture). In Balzer (1992), pp. 7–28.

1992b A Reply to Articles Submitted in Connection with the Discussion of the Maikop Culture. In Balzer (1992), pp. 79–84.

Marling, K.A. 1988 *George Washington Slept Here: Colonial Revivals and American Culture*. Cambridge, Mass.: Harvard University Press.

Marr, N. Ya. 1915 Kavkazskii kulturnyj mir i Armeniya. *Zhurnal Ministerstva Narodnogo Prosveshcheniya* 62:280–330.

1927 Rasselenie yazykov i narodov i vopros o prarodine turetskikh yazykov. *Pod Znamenem Marksizma* 6:18–60.

1931 Chto daet yafeticheskaya teoriya istorii materialnoi kultury? *Soobshcheniya Gosudarstvennoi Akademii Istorii Materialnoi Kultury* 11–12:7–24.

1933 *N.Ya. Marr. Izbrannye raboty*. Moscow and Leningrad: AN SSSR, 1.

1934 O lingvisticheskoi poezdke v Vostochnoe Sredizemnomore. Moscow and Leningrad: OGIZ.

1935 *N.Ya. Marr. Izbrannye raboty*. Moscow and Leningrad: AN SSSR, 5.

Martínez Navarrete, M.I. 1993 *Teoría y Práctica de la Prehistoria: Perspectivas desde los Extremos de Europa (Theory and Practice of Prehistory: Views from Edges of Europe)*, edited by M. Isabel Martínez Navarrete. Universidad de Cantabria, CSIC: Santander.

Martirosian, A.A. and R.M. Munchaev 1968 Review of S.A. Sardarian's *Pervobytnoe obshchestvo v Armenii. Sovetskaya Arkheologiya* 3:255–62.

Marx, K. 1954 *Capital*, vol. 1. Moscow: Progress Publishers (original 1867).

Megaw, Ruth and Megaw, Vincent 1989 *Celtic Art from Its Beginnings to the Book of Kells*. London and New York: Thames and Hudson.

Mélida, J.R. 1908 Excavaciones de Numancia. *Revista de Archivos, Bibliotecas y Museos* 8.

Merpert, N. Ya. 1958 Gunny v Vostochnoi Evrope. Ocherki istorii SSSR. In *Krizis rabovladelcheskoi systemy i zarozhdenie feodalizma na territorii SSSR III–IX v*, edited by B.A. Rybakov, pp. 151–66. Moscow: AN SSSR.

MESA Newsletter 1993 Open letter to Slobodan Milosevic, Predsednik Republike Srbije, Yugoslavia, by The Committee on Academic Freedom of the Middle East Studies Association of North America. January. 15(1).
MESHAG n.d. *The Evolution of Armenian Alphabet*. (Poster). Fresno, CA: MESHAG Printing, Publishing and Bookstore.
Meshchaninov, I.I. 1928 O doistoricheskom pereselenii narodov. *Vestnik Kommunisticheskoi Akademii* 29(5):190–238.
1931a Teoriya migratsii i arkheologiya. *Soobshcheniya Gosudarstvennoi Akademii Istorii Materialnoi Kultury* 9–10:33–9.
1931b Kromlekhi u slavyan. *Soobshcheniya Gosudarstvennoi Akademii Istorii Materialnoi Kultury* 7:14–16.
1935 N.Ya. Marr kak lingvist. *Problemy Istorii Dokapitalisticheskikh Obshchestv* 3–4:20–8.
Michell, J. 1982 *Megalithomania*. Ithaca: Cornell University Press.
Michener, J. 1965 *The Source*. New York: Random House.
Miclea, I. and R. Florescu 1980 *Geto-Dacii: Strămosii Românilor, Vestigii milenare de cultură sşi arta*. Bucharest: Editura Meridiane.
Mikolajczyk, A. 1990 Didactic Presentations of the Past: Some Retrospective Considerations in Relation to the Archaeological and Ethnographical Museum, Lodz, Poland. In Gathercole and Lowenthal (1990), pp. 247–56.
Milisauskas, S. 1986 Selective Survey of Archaeological Research in Eastern Europe. *American Antiquity* 51(4):779–98.
Miller, D. 1980 Archaeology and Development. *Current Anthropology* 21:709–26.
Miller, Daniel and Christopher Tilley (eds.) 1984 *Ideology, Power and Prehistory*. Cambridge: Cambridge University Press.
Miller, Roy Andrew 1980 *Origins of the Japanese Language*. Seattle: University of Washington Press.
Miziev, I.M. 1986 *Shagi k istokam etnicheskoi istorii Tsentralnogo Kavkaza*. Nalchik: Elbrus Press.
1990 O sozdatelyakh maikopskoi kultury. *Sovetskaya Arkheologiya* 4:131–7.
Moeran, B. 1989 *Language and Popular Culture in Japan*. Manchester: Manchester University Press.
Mongait, A.L. 1948 Obsuzhdenie knigi P.N. Tretyakova "Vostochnoslavyanskie plemena." *Voprosy Istorii* 9:137–41.
1963 Vozniknovenie i pervye shagi sovetskoi arkheologii. *Istoriya SSSR* 4:75–94.
Moora, Kh. A. 1950 Voprosy etnogeneza narodov Sovetskoi Pribaltiki po dannym arkheologii. *Kratkie Soobshcheniya Instituta Etnografii* 12:29–37.
Moorey, P.R.S. 1991 *A Century of Biblical Archaeology*. Westminster/John Knox: Louisville, KY.
Morán, M. and F. Checa 1985 *El Coleccionismo en España*. Madrid: Ed. Cátedra.
Morgan, Lewis H. 1877 *Ancient Society*. New York: Holt.
Mouer, R. and Sugimoto, Y. 1986 *Images of Japanese Society: A Study in the Structure of Social Reality*. London: KPI Limited.
Movius, Hallam 1948 The Lower Palaeolithic Cultures of Southern and Eastern Asia. *Transactions of the American Philosophical Society* 38(4):329–420.
Mudimbe, V.Y. 1988 *The Invention of Africa: Gnosis, Philosophy, and the Order of Knowledge*. Bloomington: Indiana University Press.

Muradova, F.M. 1979 *Gobustan* (in Azeri Turkish with Russian résumé). Baku: Elm.

Murdock, G.P. 1959 *Africa: Its Peoples and Their Culture History*. New York: McGraw-Hill.

Murray, Michael 1978 *Heidegger and Modern Philosophy: Critical Essays*. New Haven: Yale University Press.

Museu Nacional de Arqueologia e Etnologia and Instituto Português do Património Cultural 1989 *Portugal das Origens à Epoca Romana*. Lisbon.

Nadinskij, P.N. 1951 *Ocherki po istorii Kryma*. Simferopol: Krymizdat, 1.

Nara Kokuritsu Bunkazai Kenkyujo Maizo Bunkazai Senta 1989. *Maizo Bunkazai Nyusu 66 (CAO News 66)*. Nara: Nara Kokuritsu Bunkazai Kenkyujo Maizo Bunkazai Senta. (In Japanese with English title.)

Nash, D. 1978 Territory and State Formation in Central Gaul. In *Social Organisation and Settlement*, edited by D. Green, C. Haselgrove, and M. Spriggs, pp. 455–75. Oxford: British Archaeological Reports, Int. Ser. 43.

Nelson, Sarah M. 1982 Recent Progress in Korean Archaeology. In *Advances in Old World Archaeology*, vol. 1, edited by Fred Wendorf and Angela Close, pp. 99–149.

1989 Review of *Relationship Between Korea and Japan in Early Period*, by Won-taek Hong. *Journal of Asian Studies* 3:636–7.

1990 Neolithic Sites in Northeastern China and Korea. *Antiquity* 64:234–48. (Also translated into Chinese.)

1992 Korean Archaeological Sequences from the First Ceramics to the Introduction of Iron. In *Chronologies in Old World Archaeology*, third edition, edited by R.W. Ehrich; vol. 1, pp. 430–8; vol. 2, pp. 417–24. Chicago: University of Chicago Press.

1993 *The Archaeology of Korea*. Cambridge: Cambridge University Press.

Nelson, Sarah M. (ed.) in preparation. *The Archaeology of Northeast China*.

Nenarokov, A.P. 1992 Krakh popytok prognosticheskogo analiza mezhnatsionalnykh otnoshenii. *Otechestvennaya Istoriya* 2:3–23.

Neretina, S.S. 1990 Smena istoricheskikh paradigm v SSSR (1920–1930 gg.). In *Nauka i Vlast*, edited by A.P. Ogurtsov and B.G. Yudin. Moscow: AN SSSR.

Nezhinskij, L.N. 1990 Byla li voennaya ugroza SSSR v kontse 20–kh – nachale 30-kh gg.? *Istoriya SSSR* 6:14–30.

Nihon Kokogaku Kyokai 1951 Hakkutsu oyabi chosa (Surveys and Excavations). *Nihon Kokogaku Nempo 1, Seibundo-Shinkosha*, Tokyo:35–119. (In Japanese.)

Niiro, T. 1986 Janarizumu to kokogaku (Journalism and Archaeology). In *Nihon Kokogaku 7: Gendai to Kokogaku*, edited by Y. Kondo *et al.*, pp. 169–208. Tokyo: Iwanami Shoten. (In Japanese.)

Nishi, T. 1982 *Unconditional Democracy: Education and Politics in Occupied Japan, 1945–1952*. Stanford: Hoover Institute Press, Stanford University.

Nordenfalk, Carl 1977 *Celtic and Anglo-Saxon Painting: Book Illumination in the British Isles 600–800*. London: Chatto and Windus.

1987 One Hundred and Fifty Years of Varying Views on the Early Insular Gospel Books. In *Ireland and Insular Art: A.D. 500–1200*, edited by Michael Ryan, pp. 1–5. Dublin: Royal Irish Academy.

Novak, G. (ed.) 1971 *Epoque préhistorique et protohistorique en Yougoslavie –*

Recherches et résultats. Belgrade: Arheološk o Društvo Jugoslavije.

O vreditelstve . . . 1937. O vreditelstve v oblasti arkheologii i o likvidatsii ego posledstvii. *Sovetskaya Arkheologiya* 3: v–x.

Oganesian, V.E. 1992 A Silver Goblet from Karashamb. In *Recent Discoveries in Transcaucasia*, edited by P.L. Kohl, pp. 84–102. *Soviet Anthropology and Archaeology*. Spring, vol. 30, no. 4.

Okakura, Kakuzo 1964 *The Book of Tea*. New York: Dover. (Original 1906.)

Olmos, R. 1992a La realidad soñada. La recuperación del pasado en la novela arqueológica española del siglo XIX. *Arqcrítica* 3:18–20.

1992b La arqueología soñada. Una mirada a la novela arqueológica de raíz decimonónica. *Revista de Arqueología* 140:52–7.

Olsen, B. 1986 Norwegian Archaeology and the People without (Pre-) History: Or How to Create a Myth of a Uniform Past. *Archaeological Review From Cambridge* 5(1):25–42.

Olsen, John W. 1992 Archaeology in China Today. *China Exchange News* 20(2):3–6.

O'Meara, J. Tim 1989 Anthropology As Empirical Science. *American Anthropologist* 91(2):354–69.

O'Regan, S. 1990 Maori Control of the Maori Heritage. In Gathercole and Lowenthal (1990), pp. 91–106.

Ormrod, J. 1993 North Caucasus: Fragmentation or Federation? In *Nations and Politics in the Soviet Successor States*, edited by I. Bremmer and R. Taras, pp. 448–76. Cambridge: Cambridge University Press.

d'Ors, E. 1911 Introducció al cicle de conferències d'Educació civil. *Revista Anyal* 7:7–12.

Orser, C. 1988 *The Material Basis of the Postbellum Tenant Plantation: Historical Archaeology in the South Carolina Piedmont*. Athens, Ga.: University of Georgia Press.

Ortiz de Urbina Montoya, C. and E. Pérez Olmedo 1991 La historiografía sobre Alvava romana en el siglo XIX. In Arce and Olmos (1991), pp. 113–16.

O'Shea, John 1992 Review of *The Domestication of Europe*, by Ian Hodder. *American Anthropologist* 94(3):752–3.

Paço, A. do 1941 As grutas do Poço Velho ou de Cascais. *Communicações dos Serviços Geológicos de Portugal* 22:45–84.

1942 [1970] A póvoa eneolítica de Vila Nova de S. Pedro. *Trabalhos de Arqueologia de Afonso do Paço*, vol. 1, pp. 275–330. Lisbon: Associaçao dos Arquéologos Portuguesos.

1947 Castro de Vila Nova de São Pedro. *Arqueologia e Historia* 3:31–80.

1954 Necrópole de Alapraia. *Anais* 6:28–140.

1957 Castro de Vila Nova de São Pedro. *Revista de Guimarães* 67:83–94.

1964 *O Povoado Préhistórico de Parede (Cascais)*. Cascais: Câmara Municipal de Cascais.

1966 O castro de Pedra do Ouro. *Anais* 16:117–52.

Paço, A. do and Maria L. Bártholo Arthur 1952 O castro de Vila Nova de São Pedro. *Broteria* 54:289–309.

Paço, A. do, Maria L. Bártholo Arthur and A. Brandão, 1959 Novos achados arqueológicos das grutas de Cascais. *Actas e Memórias do Congresso Nacional*

de Arqueologia 1º, Lisboa, 1958, pp. 147–59.
Paço, A. do and E. Jalhay 1935 [1970]. As grutas de Alapraia. *Broteria* 21:108–29.
Paço, A. do and E. Sangmeister 1956 Castro de Vila Nova de S. Pedro: VIII-campanha de escavações de 1955 (19a). *Arqueologia e Historia* 7:95–114.
Paço, A. do, E. da Cunha Serrão and E.P. Vicente 1957 Estação eneolítica de Parede (Cascais). *Congresso Luso-Espanhol para o Progresso das Ciencias*. Coimbra.
Paço, A. do and Maxime Vaultier 1943 Estação eneolítica do Estoril. *Congresso Luso-Espanhol, Porto, 1943*, pp. 118–29.
Palmer, Richard E. 1969 *Hermeneutics*. Evanston: Northwestern University Press.
Palvadre, M. Yu. 1933 Novoe uchenie o yazyke i finnougrovendenie. In *Iz istorii dokapitalisticheskikh formatsii*, edited by S.N. Bykovski *et al.*, pp. 45–55. Moscow and Leningrad: Gossotsecizdat.
Parker, E.H. 1890 On Race Struggles in Korea. *Transactions of the Asiatic Society of Japan* 23:137–228.
Pasamar Alzuría, G. and I. Peiró Martín 1991 Los orígenes de la profesionalización historiográfica española sobre la Prehistoria y la Antigüedad (tradiciones decimonónicas y tradiciones europeas). In Arce and Olmos (1991), pp. 73–8.
Passek, T.S. 1945 Drevnie pamyatniki v Pridneprove. *Vechernyaya Moskva*:229.
Patrushev, V. 1992 *Finno-ugry Rossii (II tys. do n.e. – nachalo II tys. n.e.)*. Ioshkar-ola: Mariiskoe Book Publishers.
Patterson, T.C. 1995 *Toward a Social History of Archaeology in the United States*. Harcourt Brace: Fort Worth, TX.
Pearson, Richard 1978 Lolang and the Rise of Korean States and Chiefdoms. *Journal of the Hong Kong Archaeological Society* 7 (1976–1978):77–90.
Pei Mingxiang 1983 Chu wenhua zai Henan fazhan de licheng. In Zhengzhou (1983), pp. 23–48.
Peikov, A. 1973 Za osnovite problemi na neolitnata revoluticija. *Arheologija* 2:1–6.
Peng De (ed.) 1991 *Chu yishu yanjiu*. Wuhan: Hubei Meishu.
Peng Shifan 1987 Jiangxi gudai wenmingshi gaishu. *Jiangxi Wenwu* 2:12–24.
1988 Lüelun Woguo nanfang Shang Zhou qingtongqi ji qi tese. *Wenwu Yanjiu* 3:35–41.
Pericot, L. 1934 *Historia de España: Geografía histórica general de los pueblos hispanos*, vol. 1, *Epocas primitiva y romana*. Barcelona: Instituto Gallach.
Peters, Heather 1990 Tattooed Faces and Stilt Houses: Who Were the Ancient Yeu? *Sino-Platonic Papers* 17.
(forthcoming) Ethnicity along China's Southwestern Borders. In manuscript.
Phillips, Patricia 1980 *The Prehistory of Europe*. Bloomington: Indiana University Press.
Piggott, Stuart 1965 *Ancient Europe: From the Beginnings of Agriculture to Classical Antiquity*. Chicago: Aldine.
del Pino, F. 1978 Antropólogos en el exilio. In *El exilio español de 1939. 6. Cataluña, Euzkadi, Galicia*, edited by F. del Pino, V. Riera Llorca, A. Manent, M. de Ugalde, R. Martínez López, J. Campos, and J.L. Abellán. Biblioteca Política Taurus 41. Madrid: Ed. Taurus.
Plaskow, Judith and Carol P. Christ (eds.) 1989 *Weaving the Visions: New Patterns in Feminist Spirituality*. San Francisco: Harper.

Pogozheva, A.P. 1983 *Antropomorfnaya Plastika Tripol'ya*. Novosibirsk: Akademiia Nauk, Sibirskoe Otdelenie.

Poliakov, Leon 1974 *The Aryan Myth: A History of Racist and Nationalist Ideas in Europe*. New York: Basic Books.

Popović, V. 1988 Albanija u kasnoj antici. In *Iliri i Albanci*, edited by M. Garašanin, pp. 201–50. Belgrade: Srpska Akademija Nauka i Umetnosti.

Popper, K.R. 1959 *The Logic of Scientific Discovery*. London: Hutchinson.

Posnansky, M. 1982 African Archaeology Comes of Age. *World Archaeology* 13:345–58.

Postman, N. 1985 *Amusing Ourselves to Death: Public Discourse in the Age of Show Business*. New York: Viking Penguin.

Potter, Parker 1992 Review of *Reading Material Culture: Structuralism, Hermeneutics and Post-Structuralism*, by Christopher Tilley. *American Antiquity* 57(3):556–7.

Prat de la Riba, E. 1978 [1906]. *La nacionalitat catalana*. Barcelona: Edicions 62 i Caixa de Pensions.

Prendi, F. 1966 La civilisation préhistorique de Maliq. *Studia Albaniae* 3:255–80.

Preucel, R.W. (ed.) 1991 *Processual and Postprocessual Archaeologies: Multiple Ways of Knowing the Past*. Occasional Paper 10. Carbondale: Center for Archaeological Investigations, Southern Illinois University at Carbondale.

Price, N.P.S. 1990 Conservation and Information in the Display of Prehistoric Sites. In Gathercole and Lowenthal (1990), pp. 284–90.

Proctor, R. 1988 From *Anthropologie* to *Rassenkunde* in the German Anthropological Tradition. In *Bones, Bodies, Behavior: Essays on Biological Anthropology. History of Anthropology*, vol. 5, edited by G.W. Stocking, pp. 138–79. Madison: University of Wisconsin Press.

Propp, V. 1968 *Morphology of the Folktale*. Austin: University of Texas Press.

Protiv . . . 1939 Protiv istoricheskoi kontseptsii Pokrovskogo, edited by B.D. Grekov. Moscow: AN SSSR, 1.

Pryakhin, A.D. 1986 Istoriya sovetskoi arkheologii:1917–seredina 1930 gg. Voronezh: Voronezhskii Universitet.

Pu Ren 1974 Xiri zunkong chongru de "shengdi," jinri Pilin Pikong de zhanchang (Formerly a Sacred Place for the Worship of Confucius and Confucianism – Currently a Battlefield for the Criticism of Lin Biao and Confucius). *Kaogu* 3:143–52.

Pulleyblank, Edwin G. 1964 The historiographical tradition. In *The Legacy of China*, edited by R. Dawson, pp. 143–64. Oxford: Oxford University Press.

Pyenson, L. 1993 Cultural Imperialism and Exact Sciences Revisited. *Isis* 84:103–8.

Qu Yingjie 1989 Xia-du kaoshu. *Wenwu Jikan* 2:37–42, 47.

Randsborg, Klavs 1980. *The Viking Age in Denmark: The Formation of a State*. New York: St Martin's.

Rappaport, Roy A. 1986 Desecrating the Holy Woman: Derek Freeman's Attack on Margaret Mead. *American Scholar* (3):313–47.

Rauschning, Hermann 1973 *Gespräche mit Hitler*, second edition. Vienna: Europa Verlag.

Ravdonikas, V.I. 1930 Za marksistskuyu istoriyu materialnoi kultury. *Izvestiya Gosudarstvennoi Akademii Istorii Materialnoi Kultury* 7 (3–4).

1932a Peshchernye goroda Kryma i gotskaya problema v svyazi so stadialnym razvitiem Severnogo Prichernomorya. *Izvestiya Gosudarstvennoi Akademii Istorii Materialnoi Kultury* 12 (1–8):5–106.

1932b Arkheologiya na sluzhbe u imperializma. *Soobshcheniya Gosudarstvennoi Akademii Istorii Materialnoi Kultury* 3–4:18–35.

1932c Arkheologiya na zapade i v SSSR v nashi dni. *Soobshcheniya Gosudarstvennoi Akademii Istorii Materialnoi Kultury* 9–10:12–23.

1935 Arkheologiya v Germanii posle fashistskogo perevorota. *Sovetskaya Etnografiya* 1:140–5.

Rawson, Jessica 1990 *Western Zhou Ritual Bronzes in the Arthur M. Sackler Collections*, vol. 2 of *Ancient Chinese Bronzes in the Arthur M. Sackler Collections* (2 vols.), Cambridge, Mass.: Harvard University Press.

Ray, K. 1986 Archaeological Praxis in West African Preservation: Senegambia 1981 *Archaeological Review From Cambridge* 5(1):58–76.

Reid, D.M. 1985 Indigenous Egyptology: The Decolonization of a Profession? *Journal of the American Oriental Society* 105:233–46.

Reinerth, Hans 1936a Unser Weg. *Germanen-Erbe* (Monatsschrift für deutsche Vorgeschichte).

1936b Das politische Bild Alteuropas: Aus der Arbeit der Nationalsozialistischen Vorgeschichtsforschung. *Germanenerbe*:66–75.

Renfrew, Colin 1972 *The Emergence of Civilization: The Cyclades and the Aegean in the Third Millennium B.C.* London: Methuen.

1986 Varna and the Emergence of Wealth in Prehistoric Europe. In *The Social Life of Things: Commodities in Cultural Perspective*, edited by Arjun Appadurai, pp. 141–68. Cambridge: Cambridge University Press.

Renfrew, A.C. and P. Bahn 1991 *Archaeology: Theories, Methods, and Practice*. London: Thames and Hudson.

Reshenije 1952 *Reshenije obedinennoi nauchnoi sessii Otdeleniya istorii i filosofii i Krymskogo filiala Akademii Nauk SSSR po voprosam istorii Kryma*. Simferopol: Krymizdat.

Reyero, C. 1989 *La pintura de historia en España*. Cuadernos Arte Cátedra 26. Madrid: Ed. Cátedra.

Rezepkin, A.D. 1992 Paintings from a Tomb of the Majkop Culture. *The Journal of Indo-European Studies* 20(1 and 2):59–70.

Rhee Song Nai 1984 Emerging Complex Society in Prehistoric Southwest Korea. Ph.D. Dissertation, University of Oregon.

1992 Secondary State Formation: The Case of Early Korea. In *Pacific Northeast Asia in Prehistory: Hunter-Fisher-Gatherers, Farmers, and Sociopolitical Elites*, edited by C.M. Aikens and S.N. Rhee. Seattle: Washington State University Press.

Riché, P. 1972 *Education and Culture in the Barbarian West, Sixth through Eighth Centuries*. Columbia, SC: University of South Carolina Press (1976 trans. by J.J. Contreni of third French edition).

Rodríguez Hidalgo, J.M. 1991 Sinopsis historiográfica del anfiteatro de Itálica. In Arce and Olmos (1991), pp. 91–4.

Rodríguez Morales, A., B. Escobar Pérez and E. García Vargas 1991 Historiografía de la estatuaria de Itálica. In Arce and Olmos (1991), pp. 95–8.

Rose, M.A. 1991 *The Post-Modern and the Post-Industrial: A Critical Analysis.* Cambridge: Cambridge University Press.

Rosener, Judy B. 1990 Ways Women Lead. *Harvard Business Review* November–December:119–25.

Roth, Uta 1987 Early Insular Manuscripts: Ornament and Archaeology, with Special Reference to the Dating of the Book of Durrow. In *Ireland and Insular Art: A.D. 500–1200*, edited by Michael Ryan, pp. 23–9. Dublin: Royal Irish Academy.

Rothfels, Hans 1965 Die Geschichtswissenschaft in den Dreissger Jahren. In *Deutsches Geistesleben und Nationalsozialismus*, edited by Andreas Flitner, pp. 90–107. Tübingen: Rainer Wunderlich Verlag.

Rouse, I.B. 1972 *Introduction to Prehistory: A Systematic Approach.* New York: McGraw–Hill.

Rouse, J.H. 1965 The Renaissance Foundations of Anthropology. *American Anthropologist* 67:1–20.

Rubinstein, N.L. 1939 Borba s antimarksistskimi izvrashcheniyami i vulgarizatorstvom v istoricheskoi nauke. *Pod Znamenem Marksizma* 5:165–80.

Rueda Muñoz de San Pedro, G. 1991 Francisco María Tubino (1833–1888) y la Revista de Bellas Artes. In Arce and Olmos (1991), pp. 59–63.

Ruiz Rodriguez, A. 1993 Present Panorama of Spanish Archaeology. In Martínez Navarrete (1993), pp. 307–26.

Ryan, Kathleen 1987 Parchment as Faunal Record. *M.A.S.C.A. Journal* 4(3):124–38.

Ryan, Michael 1991 The Early Medieval Celts. In *The Celts*, edited by Mario Andreose, pp. 621–37. Milan: Bompiani.

Rybakov, B.A. 1943 Rannyaya kultura vostochnykh slavyan. *Istoricheskii Zhurnal* 11–12:73–80.

1952 Problema obrazovaniya drevnerusskoi narodnosti v svete trudov I.V. Stalina. *Voprosy Istorii* 9:40–62.

1954 *Drevnyaya Tmutarakan i problema slavyanskoi kolonizatsii Priazovya. Tezisy dokladov na sessii Otdeleniya istoricheskikh nauk i Plenume Instituta istorii materialnoi kultury, posvyashchennykh itogam arkheologicheskikh i etnograficheskikh issledovanii 1953 g.* Moscow: AN SSR, 17–19.

Said, E. 1978 *Orientalism.* New York: Pantheon.

Salazar, Antonio de Oliveira 1946. *Discursos e Notas Politicas*, second edition. Coimbra: Coimbra Editora.

1963 *The Road for the Future.* Lisbon: SNI.

Sampaio, Albino Forjaz de 1926. *Porque me Orgulho de Ser Português.* Lisbon: Emprêsa Literária Fluminense.

Sánchez Ron, J.M. 1988 La Junta para Ampliación de Estudios e Investigaciones Científicas. Ochenta años después. In *La Junta para Ampliación de Estudios e Investigaciones Científicas. Ochenta años después* vol. 1, edited by J.M. Sánchez Ron, pp. 1–62. Madrid: CSIC.

Sanderson, Stephen K. 1990 *Social Evolutionism.* Cambridge, Mass.: Basil Blackwell.

Sangmeister, E. and Schubart, H. 1981 *Zambujal: Die Grabungen 1964 bis 1973.* Mainz am Rhein: Phillip von Zabern.

Santley, Robert S., Clare Yarborough and Barbara A. Hall 1987 Enclaves, Ethnicity, and the Archaeological Record at Matacapan. In *Ethnicity and Culture*, edited by R. Auger, M.F. Glass, S. MacEachern, and P.H. McCartney, pp. 85–100. Calgary: The University of Calgary Archaeological Association.

Sapir, E. 1921 *Language: An Introduction to the Study of Speech*. New York: Harcourt, Brace.

Sardarian, S.A. 1967 *Pervobytnoe obshchestvo v Armenii*. Yerevan.

Schnädelbach, Herbert 1984 *Philosophy in Germany, 1831–1933*, trans. by Eric Matthews. Cambridge: Cambridge University Press.

Schnapp, Alain 1977 Archäologie et nazisme. *Quaderni di Storia* 3(5):1–26.

1984 Gustaf Kossinna nach 50 Jahren: Kein Nachruf. *Acta Praehistorica et Archaeologica 1984/85*, 16/17:9–14.

Schrire, C. 1988 The Historical Archaeology of the Impact of Colonialism in 17th Century South Africa. *Antiquity* 62:214–25.

Scott, D.D., Fox, R.A., Connor, M.A. and Harmon, D. 1989 *Archaeological Perspectives on the Battle of the Little Bighorn*. Norman: University of Oklahoma Press.

Serrão, Eduardo da Cunha 1983 A estação pré-histórica de Parede: documentos inéditos sobre estratigrafia e estruturas (campanha de 1956). *O Arqueólogo Português* 4(1):119–48.

Serrão, Joaquim Veríssimo 1985 *Marcello Caetano: Confidências no Exílio*. Lisbon: Verbo.

Shafarevich, I. 1989 Dve dorogi k odnomu obryvu. *Novyi Mir* 7:147–65.

Shafer, B.C. 1955 *Nationalism: Myth and Reality*. New York: Harcourt Brace and World.

Shanks, H. 1990 Glorious Beth-Shean. *Biblical Archaeology Review* 16:17–31.

Shanks, M. 1992 *Experiencing the Past: On the Character of Archaeology*. London: Routledge.

Shanks, M. and C. Tilley 1982 Ideology, Symbolic Power, and Ritual Communication: A Reinterpretation of Neolithic Mortuary Practices. In *Symbolic and Structural Archaeology*, edited by Ian Hodder, pp. 129–54. Cambridge: Cambridge University Press.

1987a *Social Theory and Archaeology*. Cambridge: Polity Press.

1987b *Re-Constructing Archaeology*. Cambridge: Cambridge University Press.

1988 *Social Theory and Archaeology*. Albuquerque: University of New Mexico Press.

1989 Archaeology into the 1990s. *Norwegian Archaeological Review* 22:1–54.

Sharon, M. 1988 The Birth of Islam in the Holy Land. In *The Holy Land in History and Thought*, edited by Moshe Sharon, pp. 225–35. Leiden: E.J. Brill.

Shennan, Stephen 1982 Ideology, Change, and the European Early Bronze Age. In *Symbolic and Structural Archaeology*, edited by Ian Hodder, pp. 155–61. Cambridge: Cambridge University Press.

1989 Tendències en l'estudi de la Prehistòria Europea Recent. *Cota Zero* 5:91–101.

Sherratt, Andrew 1981 Plough and Pastoralism: Aspects of the Secondary Products Revolution. In *Pattern of the Past*, edited by Ian Hodder, G. Isaac, and N.

Hammond, pp. 261–305. Cambridge: Cambridge University Press.
1989 Review of *The Language of the Goddess*, by M. Gimbutas. *Antiquaries Journal* 69(2):345–6.
1991 Review of *The Domestication of Europe*, by Ian Hodder. *Antiquity* 65(248):742–3.

Shi Quan 1988 *Gudai Jing-Chu dili xintan*, Wuhan: Wuhan Daxue Chubanshe.

Shmagli, N.M. and M.Y. Videiko 1987 Piznotripil's'ke Poselennya Poblizu s. Maidanets'kogo Na Cherkashchini. *Arkheologiia* (Kiev) 60:58–71.

Shnirelman, V.A. 1992 Nauka ob etnogeneze kak mifotvorchestvo. A paper given for the conference "Myth and the Contemporary World" at the Institute of High Humanitarian Researches, Russian National Humanitarian University, Moscow, December 8–10.
1993a Archaeology and Ethnopolitics: Why Soviet Archaeologists Were So Involved in Ethnogenetic Studies. In *Interpreting the Past: Presenting Archaeological Sites to the Public*, edited by Ann Killebrew, p. 57. Haifa: University of Haifa Publications.
1993b Struggle for the Past: Ethnogenetic Studies and Politics in the USSR. 13th International Congress of Anthropological and Ethnological Sciences. Abstracts. Mexico City, July 29–August 4, p. 420.

Shul'ts, P.N. 1950. Istoriko-arkheologicheskie issledovaniya v Krymu. *Krym* 6:145–57.

Silberman, N.A. 1982 *Digging for God and Country*. New York: Knopf.
1989 *Between Past and Present: Archaeology, Ideology and Nationalism in the Modern Middle East*. New York: Henry Holt.
1990 The Politics of the Past: Archaeology and Nationalism in the Eastern Mediterranean. *Mediterranean Quarterly* 1:99–110.
1991 Desolation and Restoration: The Impact of a Biblical Concept on Near Eastern Archaeology. *Biblical Archaeologist* 54:76–87.
1993 From Masada to the Little Bighorn: The Role of Archaeological Site Interpretation in the Shaping of National Myths. In *Interpreting the Past*, edited by Ann Killebrew and Rachel Hachlili. Haifa: Haifa University Press.

Silva, Armando Coelho Ferreira da 1983 A idade dos metais em Portugal. *História de Portugal* 82:101–10.

Silverberg, R. 1968 *Mound Builders of Ancient America: The Archaeology of a Myth*. Greenwich, Conn.: New York Graphic Society.

Sinclair, P. 1986 Archaeology, Ideology and Development: Mozambican Perspectives. *Archaeological Review From Cambridge* 5(1):77–87.

Siret, Louis 1913 *Questions de chronologie et d'ethnographie ibériques*. Paris: Paul Geuthner.

Sklenar, K. 1983 *Archaeology in Central Europe: The First 500 Years*. New York: St. Martin's.

Slotkin, J.S. (ed.) 1965 *Readings in Early Anthropology*. New York: Viking Fund Publications in Anthropology 40.

Smirnov, A.P. 1953 K voprosu o Slavyanakh v Krymu. *Vestnik Drevnei Istorii* 3:32–45.

Smith, A.D. 1971 *Theories of Nationalism*. New York: Harper and Row.
1986 *The Ethnic Origins of Nations*. Oxford: Basil Blackwell.

Smith, W.D. 1983 The Colonial Novel as Political Propaganda: Hans Grimm's *Volk Ohne Raum. German Studies Review* 6:215–35.

Smolla, Günter 1980 Das Kossinna-Syndrome. *Fundberichte aus Hessen, 1979/80* 19/20:1–9.

Snodgrass, A. 1980 *Archaic Greece: The Age of Experiment*. London: Dent.

Soffer, O. 1985 *The Upper Paleolithic of the Central Russian Plain*. New York: Academic.

Sohn Pow-key, Pyon T'ae-sop, Han Yong-u, Yi Ki-dong, Im Hyo-jai 1987 Reflections on Studies in Ancient Korean History: Colloquium of Five Historians. *Korea Journal* 27(12):4–22.

Solomon, J. 1978 *The Ancient World in the Cinema*. New York: A.S. Barnes.

Song Yongxiang 1986 Jixi tudunmu chutan. *Wenwu Yanjiu* 2:45–50.

Speer, A. 1971 *Inside the Third Reich: Memoirs by Albert Speer*. New York: Avon Books.

Spretnak, Charlene 1990 Ecofeminism: Our Roots and Flowering. In Diamond and Orenstein (1990), pp. 3–14.

Srejović, D. 1972 *Europe's First Monumental Sculpture: New Discoveries at Lepsenski Vir*. London: Thames and Hudson.

1974 Mezolitske osnove neolitskih kultura u južn o m Podunavlu. *Materijali* 10:21–30.

Srejović, D. (ed.) 1988 *The Neolithic of Serbia: Archaeological Research 1948–1988*. Belgrade: Center for Archaeological Research, University of Belgrade.

Stalin, J.V. 1936 Politicheskii otchet Tsentralnogo Komiteta 16 Sezdu VKP(b). J.V. Stalin. *Voprosy Leninizma*, pp. 345–438. Moscow: Partizdat TsK VKP(b).

Sterud, E. and Ivey, M. 1973 The Development of Prehistoric Archaeological Research in the Balkan Peninsula. Paper presented at the 71st Annual Meeting of the American Anthropological Association.

Stipčević, A. 1986 Tout récit sur les Balkans commence par les Illyriens. *Iliria* 16(1):337–43.

1991 *Iliri: Povijest, Zivot, Kultura*, third edition. Zagreb: Školska Knjiga.

Stocking, G.W. 1987 *Victorian Anthropology*. New York: Free Press.

Stone, Merlin 1976 *When God Was A Woman*. San Diego: Harvest Books.

Stoneman, R. 1987 *Land of Lost Gods: The Search for Classical Greece*. Norman, OK: University of Oklahoma Press.

Stronach, D. 1981 Standing Stones in the Atrek Region: The Halat Nabi Cemetery. *Iran* 29:147–50 (with an appendix by W.R. Royce).

Su Bingqi 1983 *Su Bingqi kaoguxue lunshu xuanji*. Beijing: Wenwu.

Suleimenov, O. 1975 *Az i Ya*. Alma-Ata.

Sumption, J. 1975 *Pilgrimage: An Image of Medieval Religion*. Totowa, NJ: Rowman and Littlefield.

Sun Hua 1990 Shu-ren yuanliu-kao. *Sichuan Wenwu* 4:6–11 and 5:15–20.

Sun Shoudao 1983 Lun Zhongguo shishang "yuqishidai" de tichu – Hongshan wenhua yuqi yanjiu zhaji. *Liaoning Wenwu* 5:1–5.

1986 Liaoning dangqian kaogu yanjiushang de ba da keti (Part I). *Liaohai Wenwu Xuekan* 1:6–15.

Suny, R.G. 1988 *The Making of the Georgian Nation*. Bloomington and Stanford: Indiana University Press and the Hoover Institution Press.

1993a *Looking Toward Ararat: Armenia in Modern History*. Bloomington: Indiana University Press.

1993b *The Revenge of the Past: Nationalism, Revolution, and the Collapse of the Soviet Union*. Palo Alto: Stanford University Press.

Swietochowski, T. 1983 National Consciousness and Political Orientations in Azerbaijan, 1905–1920. In *Transcaucasia: Nationalism and Social Change*, edited by R.G. Suny, pp. 209–32. Ann Arbor: University of Michigan Press.

Taiyuan 1986 *Jin wenhua yanjiu zuotanhui jiyao*. Taiyuan: Shanxi-sheng Kaogu Yanjiusuo.

Takahashi, K. 1980 Hozon no rinen to hensen (2) Sengo (1945 nen iko) (Transitions in Postwar Preservation Policy (2) (after 1945)). In *Dai 2 Ji Maizo Bunkazai Hakusho*, edited by Nihon Kokogaku Kyokai, pp. 192–7. Tokyo: Gakugeisha. (In Japanese.)

Tang Yunming 1987 Lüelun Gaocheng Taixi Shang wenhua yicun. *Hua Xia Kaogu* 1:172–6.

1988a Taixi yizhi qiqi e yuanyuan ji yizhi wenhua xingzhi de tantao. *Hua Xia Kaogu* 2:62–7.

1988b Hebei Shang wenhua zongshu. *Hua Xia Kaogu* 3:61–70.

Taracena Aguirre, B. and A. Fernández de Avilés 1945. *Memorias sobre las excavaciones enel Castro de Navárniz (Vizcaya)*. Vizcaya: Junta de Cultura de la Exma Diputación de Vizcaya.

Tasić, N. 1974 Starije gvozdeno doba. In *Praistorija Vojvodine*, edited by B. Brukner, B. Jovanović, and N. Tasić, pp. 257–76. Novi Sad: Institut za Izučavanje Istorije Vojvodine.

Taylor, C. 1992 *Multiculturalism and the Politics of Recognition: An Essay*. Princeton: Princeton University Press.

Tekhov, B.V. 1980 *Tliiskii mogilnik*, vol. 1. Tbilisi: Metsniereba.

1981 *Tliiskii mogilnik*, vol. 2. Tbilisi: Metsniereba.

1985 *Tliiskii mogilnik*, vol. 3. Tbilisi: Metsniereba.

1988 *Bronzovye topory tliiskogo mogilnika*. Tbilisi: Metsniereba.

Thackeray, William M. 1854 *The Rose and the Ring; or The History of Prince Giglio and Prince Bulbo: a Fireside Pantomime for Great and Small Children*. New York: Platt and Peck.

Thieme, Paul 1958 The Indo-European Language. *Scientific American* (Oct.):63–74.

Thomas, Charles 1981 *A Provisional List of Imported Pottery in Post-Roman Western Britain and Ireland*. Special Report 7. Redruth, Cornwall: Institute of Cornish Studies.

Thomas, J. and A.W.R. Whittle 1986 Anatomy of A Tomb: West Kennett Revisited. *Oxford Journal of Archaeology* 5:129–56.

Thompson, E.P. 1966 *The Making of the English Working Class*. New York: Random House, Vintage.

Tikhanova, M.A. 1958 Goty v Prichernomorskikh stepyakh. Ocherki istorii SSSR. In *Krizis rabovladelcheskoi systemy i zarozhdenie feodalizma na territorii SSSR III–IX vv*, edited by B.A. Rybakov, pp. 130–7. Moscow: AN SSSR.

Tilley, C. (ed.) 1990 *Reading Material Culture: Structuralism, Hermeneutics and Post-Structuralism*. Oxford: Blackwell.

1991 *Material Culture and Text: The Art of Ambiguity*. London: Routledge.

Tishkov, V.A. 1992 The Crisis in Soviet Ethnography. *Current Anthropology* 33(4):371–94.

Todorova, Henrieta 1978 *The Eneolithic Period in Bulgaria*. Oxford: British Archaeological Reports, International Series 49.

1980 Klassifikatsiia i Chislovoi Kod Plastiki Neolita, Eneolita, I Rannei Bronzovoi Epokhi Bolgarii. *Studia Praehistorica* 3:43–64.

Todorova, H. and Nacheva, V. 1971 Psevdofirnisova keramika ot eneolitnoto nakolno selishte krai Ezerovo, Varnensko. *Arheologija* 2:66–75.

Todorova, H., Rindina, N.V. and Chernykh, E.N. 1977 Eneoliticheskii metall iz Golyamo Delchevo. *Soviet Archaeology* 1:15–27.

Tolstov, S.P. 1946 Drevneishaya istoriya SSSR v osveshchenii G. Vernadskogo. *Voprosy Istorii* 4:113–24.

1947a Sovetskaya shkola v etnografii. *Sovetskaya Etnografiya* 4:8–28.

1947b Iz predystorii Rusi. *Sovetskaya Etnografiya* 6–7:39–59.

1950 Osnovnye zadachi i puti razvitiya sovetskoi etnografii. *Kratkie Soobshcheniya Instituta Etnografii* 12:5–14.

Tong, Enzheng 1982 Slate Cist Graves and Megalithic Chamber Tombs in Southwest China: Archaeological, Historical, and Ethnographical Approaches to the Identification of Early Ethnic Groups. *Journal of Anthropological Archaeology* 1:266–74.

1989 Morgan's Model and the Study of Ancient Chinese Society. *Social Sciences in China* 2:182–205.

1994 Lun Zhongguo beifang yu nanfang wenming fazhan guiji zhi yitong (Northern China and Southern China: Two Trajectories of Social Development Toward Civilization). Paper presented at the International Conference on the Integration of Chinese Archaeology and History. Taiwan, January 1994.

Torres, S. 1992 Nacionalismo e historia. Emilio Castelar. In J. Varela (organizator). Course on "Nación y nacionalismo en España y en Europa". UNED Avila. Unpublished paper.

Totten, G. III 1983 Japan Communist Party. *Kodansha Encyclopedia of Japan 4*, pp. 11–12. Tokyo: Kodansha.

Tret'jakov, P.N. 1939 Arkheologicheskie pamyatniki vostochnoslavyanskikh plemen v svyazi s problemoi etnogeneza. *Kratkie Soobshcheniya Instituta Istorii Materialnoi Kultury* 2:3–5.

1940 Nekotorye voprosy etnogonii vostochnogo slavyanstva. *Kratke Soobshcheniya Instituta Istorii Materialnoi Kultury* 5:10–16.

1941a Slavyanskaya (dneprovskaya) expeditsiya 1940 g. *Kratkie Soobshcheniya Instituta Istorii Materialnoi Kultury* 10:120–4.

1941b Severnye vostochnoslavyanskie plemena. In *Etnogenez vostochnykh slavyan*, pp. 9–55. Moscow and Leningrad: AN SSSR.

Trigger, B.G. 1968 *Beyond History: The Methods of Prehistory*. New York: Holt, Rinehart and Winston.

1980 Archaeology and the Image of the American Indian. *American Antiquity* 45:662–76.

1981 Anglo-American Archaeology. *World Archaeology* 13:138–55.

1984 Alternative Archaeologies: Nationalist, Colonialist, Imperialist. *Man* 19:355–70.

1985 The Past as Power: Anthropology and the North American Indian. In *Who Owns the Past?*, edited by I. McBryde, pp. 11–40. Oxford: Oxford University Press.

1989a *A History of Archaeological Thought*. Cambridge: Cambridge University Press.

1989b Hyperrelativism, Responsibility, and the Social Sciences. *Canadian Review of Sociology and Anthropology* 26:776–97.

Trigger, B.G. and Glover, I. (eds.) 1981 *World Archaeology* 13(2):133–7.

Tringham, Ruth 1971. *Hunters, Fishers, and Farmers of Eastern Europe 6000–3000 BC*. London: Hutchinson University Library.

1974 The Concept of "Civilization" in European Archaeology. In *The Rise and Fall of Civilization*, edited by J. Sabloff and C.C. Lamberg-Karlovsky, pp. 470–85. Menlo Park: Cummings.

1991 Households With Faces: The Challenge of Gender in Prehistoric Architectural Remains. In *Engendering Archaeology: Women and Prehistory*, edited by Joan M. Gero and Margaret W. Conkey, pp. 93–131. Oxford: Basil Blackwell.

Tringham, Ruth, and Dusan Krstic (eds.) 1990 *Selevac: A Neolithic Village in Yugoslavia*. Monumenta Archaeologica 15. Los Angeles: UCLA Institute of Archaeology.

Tsetskhladze, G.R. 1992 Colchis and the Persian Empire: The Problems of Their Relationship. *Silk Road Art and Archaeology* 2.

1994 *Die Griechen in Colchis: historisch-archaeologische Abhandlung*. Berlin: Akademie Verlag.

Tsuboi, K. 1986 Problems Concerning the Preservation of Archaeological Sites in Japan. In *Windows on the Japanese Past: Studies in Archaeology and Prehistory*, edited by R.J. Pearson, G.L. Barnes, and K.L. Hutterer, pp. 481–90. Ann Arbor: Centre for Japanese Studies, University of Michigan.

Tsude, H. 1986 Nihon kokogaku to shakai (Japanese Archaeology and Society). In *Nihon Kokogaku 7: Gendai to Kokogaku*, edited by Y. Kondo *et al.*, pp. 31–70. Tokyo: Iwanami Shoten.

Turchaninov, G.F. 1971 *Pamyatniki pisma i yazyka narodov Kavkaza i Vostochnoi Evropy*. Leningrad: Nauka.

Ucko, P.J. 1990 Foreword. In Gathercole and Lowenthal (1990), pp. ix–xxi.

Udaltsov, A.D. 1943 Nachalnyi period vostochnoslavyanskogo etnogeneza. *Istoricheskii Zhurnal* 11–12:67–72.

1944 Teoreticheskie osnovy etnogeneticheskikh issledovanii. *Izvestiya AN SSSR*, ser. istorii i filosofii, 6:252–65.

1947a Proiskhozhdenie slavyan. *Voprosy Istorii* 7:95–100.

1947b Osnovnye voprosy etnogeneza slavyan. *Sovetskaya Etnografiya* 6–7:3–13.

1953 Rol arkheologicheskogo materiala v izuchenii voprosov etnogeneza v svete rabot J.V. Stalina o yazyke. In *Protiv vulgarizatsii marksizma v arkheologii*, edited by A.D. Udaltsov, pp. 9–18. Moscow: Akademii Nauk.

Uvarova, P.S. 1900 *Mogilniki Severnogo Kavkaza, Materialy po arkheologii Kavkaza*, vol. 8. Moscow.

van der Waals, J.D. 1969 *Praehistorie en Mythevormig*. Groningen: Wolters-

Noordhoff.
van Fraassen, B.C. 1980 *The Scientific Image*. Oxford: Clarendon.
Vasil'jev, L.S. 1976 *Problemy genesisa Kitajskoj civilizacii* (Problems Regarding the Genesis of Chinese Civilization). Moscow: Nauka.
Veit, Ulrich 1984 Gustaf Kossinna und V.G. Childe. Ansätze zu einer theoretischen Grundlegung der Vorgeschichte. *Saeculum* 35(3–4):326–64.
1989 Ethnic Concepts in German Prehistory: A Case Study on the Relationship between Cultural Identity and Archaeological Objectivity. In *Archaeological Approaches to Cultural Identity*, edited by S. Shennan. London: Unwin Hyman. *One World Archaeology* 10:35–56.
Vejmarn, E.V. and Strzheletskii, S.F. 1952 K voprosu o Slavyanakh v Krymu. *Voprosy Istorii* 4:94–9.
Verdery, K. 1983 *Transylvanian Villagers: Three Centuries of Political, Economic, and Ethnic Change*. Berkeley: University of California Press.
Vicent, J. 1982 Las tendencias metodológicas en Prehistoria. *Trabajos de Prehistoria* 39:9–53.
1990 El debat postprocessual: algunes observacions "radicals" sobre una arqueologia "conservadora." *Cota Zero* 6:102–7.
Vickers, M. 1987 Value and Simplicity: Eighteenth-Century Taste and the Study of Greek Vases. *Past and Present* 116:98–137.
Virchow, R. 1883 *Das Gräberfeld von Koban im Lande der Osseten, Kaukasus*. Berlin.
Wailes, Bernard 1989 Irish "Royal Sites" in Historical and Popular Tradition. Paper presented at the symposium The Meaning of Monuments (Peter S. Wells, Chair), 18 November. 88th annual meeting of the American Anthropological Association, Washington, DC.
Wallace, Anthony F.C. 1972 Paradigmatic Process in Culture Change. *American Anthropologist* 74(3):467–78.
Wang Guanghao 1988 *Chu wenhua yuanliu xinzheng*. Wuhan: Wuhan Daxue Chubanshe.
Wang Kelin 1986 Shanxi kaogu gongzuo de huigu yu zhanwang, Parts I and II. *Shanxi Wenwu* 1:4–14 and 2:1–14.
1989 Jin wenhua yanjiu. *Wenwu Jikan* 1:1–8.
Wang Zhongshu 1986 Xia Nai xiansheng zhuanlüe (Abbreviated Biography of Professor Xia Nai). In *Zhongguo kaoguxue yanjiu* bianweihui (Editorial Committee of *Archaeological Researches in China*), ed., *Zhongguo kaoguxue yanjiu – Xia Nai Xiansheng kaogu wushinian jinian lunwenji* (Archaeological Researches in China – A Collection of Papers in Commemoration of the Fifty Years of Prof. Xia Nai's Work in Archaeology), pp. 3–24. Beijing: Wenwu Chubanshe.
Watson, Burton 1961 *Records of the Grand Historian of China*, vol. 2. New York: Columbia University Press.
Watson, Patty Jo and Michael Fotiadis 1990 The Razor's Edge: Symbolic-Structuralist Archaeology and the Expansion of Archaeological Inference. *American Anthropologist* 92(3):629.
Watson, P., LeBlanc, S. and Redman, C. 1971 *Explanation in Archaeology: An Explicitly Scientific Approach*. New York: Columbia University Press.

Watson, R.A. 1990 Ozymandias, King of Kings: Postprocessual Radical Archaeology as Critique. *American Antiquity* 55:673–89.

Wei Chang (ed.) 1989 *Chu-guo jianshi.* n.p.: Zhongguo Dizhi Daxue Chubanshe.

Weigand, P. (n.d.) Idées Fixes: Attitudes about Disengagement, Ownership, and the 1848 Treaty of Guadalupe. Comments delivered at the symposium Nationalism, Politics, and the Practice of Archaeology. November. American Anthropological Association meetings, Chicago.

Welter, R. 1965 The History of Ideas in America: An Essay in Redefinition. *The Journal of American History* 51:599–614.

Werner, J. 1946 Las excavaciones del Seminario de Historia Primitiva del Hombre en 1941, en el cementerio visigodo de Castiltierra (Segovia). *Cuadernos de Historia Primitiva* 1(1):46–50.

Wilkes, J. 1992 *The Illyrians.* Oxford: Basil Blackwell.

Willett, F. 1990 Museums: Two Case Studies of Reactions to Colonialism. In Gathercole and Lowenthal (1990), pp. 172–86.

Willey, G.R. and J.A. Sabloff 1993 *A History of American Archaeology*, third edition. New York: Freeman.

Without author 1982 *Ciento cincuenta mil años de Prehistoria vasca. Gure herriaren lehen urratsak.* Alava: Diputación Foral de Alava.

Wixman, R. 1980 *Language Aspects of Ethnic Patterns and Processes in the North Caucasus.* Research Paper 191. Chicago: University of Chicago Press.

Wolf, E.R. 1982 *Europe and the People Without History.* Berkeley: University of California Press.

1984 Culture: Panacea or Problem? *American Antiquity* 49(2):393–400.

Wolfram, S. 1986 *Zur Theoriediskussion in der prähistorischen Archäologie Grossbritanniens.* Oxford: British Archaeological Reports 306.

Wormald, Patrick 1982 The Age of Bede and Aethelbald. In *The Anglo-Saxons*, edited by James Campbell, pp. 70–100. Ithaca, NY: Cornell University Press.

Wu, K.C. 1982 *The Chinese Heritage.* New York: Crown.

Wuhan 1987 *Chu wenhua yanjiulunji.* Wuhan: Jingchu Shushe.

n.d. a (*c.* 1984). *Chu-shi yanjiu zhuanji*, Wuhan: Hubei-sheng Chu-shi janjiuhui and Wuhan Shifanxueyuan Xuebao.

n.d. b (*c.* 1984). *Chu-guo biannianziliao.* Wuhan: Hubei-sheng Shehuikexueyuan Lishi Yanjiusuo.

Wylie, Alison 1989 Matters of Fact and Matters of Interest. In *Archaeological Approaches to Ethnic Identity*, edited by S.J. Shennan, pp. 94–109. London: Unwin Hyman.

1992 The Interplay of Evidential Constraints and Political Interests: Recent Archaeological Research on Gender. *American Antiquity* 57(1):15–35.

Wylie, M.A. 1982 Epistemological Issues Raised by a Structuralist Archaeology. In Hodder (1982b), pp. 39–46.

Xia Nai 1955 Pipan kaoguxuezhong de Hushipai zichanjieji sixiang (Criticize the Bourgeois Ideology of Hu Shi in Archaeology). *Kaogu Tongxun* 3:1–7.

1957a Yong kaogu gongzuo fangmian shishi jiechuang youpai huangyan (Expose the Lies of Bourgeois Rightists by Archaeological Facts). *Kaogu Tongxun* 5:1–4.

1957b Yong shishi jiechuan youpai huangyan (Expose the Lies of Bourgeois

Rightists by Facts). *Wenwu Cankao Ziliao* 7:7.

1957c Kaogu gongzuo de jinxi (The Present and the Past of Archaeology). *Wenwu Cankao Ziliao* 9:10–12.

1958 Kaogu gongzuo ye yao houjin baogu (Archaeology Also Needs to Stress the Present, Not the Past). *Kaogu Tongxun* 6:1–4.

1962 Xin Zhongguo de kaoguxue (Archaeology in New China). *Kaogu* 9:453–8.

1972 Wuchanjieji wenhuadagemingzhong de kaogu xinfaxian (The New Archaeological Finds during the Proletarian Cultural Revolution Period). *Kaogu* 1:29–42.

1977 Jin'ai de Zhou Enlai zongli dui kaogu wenwu gongzuo de guanhuai – Jinian Zhou zongli shishi yinzhounian (Our Esteemed and Beloved Premier Chou En-lai's Deep Concern for Archaeological Work – In Commemoration of the First Anniversary of Premier Zhou's Passing). *Kaogu* 1:5–8.

1979a Sanshinianlai de Zhongguo kaoguxue (Thirty Years of Chinese Archaeology). *Kaogu* 5:385–92.

1979b Wusi yundong he Zhongguo jindai kaoguxue de xingqi (The May 4th Movement and the Rise of Modern Archaeology in China). *Kaogu* 3:193–6.

1979c *Kaoguxue he kejishi* (Essays on Archaeology of Science and Technology in China). Beijing: Kexue.

1984 Shenme shi kaoguxue (What is Archaeology). *Kaogu* 10:931–5, 948. (English translation in *Chinese Sociology and Anthropology* 20(4):58–67.)

1985 Kaogu gongzuozhe xuyao you xianshen jingshen – Zai yijiubawunian sanyue yiri Zhongguo Kaoguxuehui diwuci nianhuishang de jianghua (Archaeologists Must Have the Spirit of Devotion – Address at the Fifth Conference of the Chinese Archaeological Association on March 1, 1985). *Kaogu* 6:481–4.

Xia Nai and Wang Zhongshu 1986 Kaoguxue (Archaeology). In *Zhongguo Da Baikequanshu, Kaoguxue* (Chinese Encyclopedia, Archaeology Volume), edited by Xia Nai *et al.*, pp. 1–21. Beijing: Zhongguo Dabaike Quanshu chubanshe.

Xuanzhou 1988 Nanling Qianfengshan tudunmu fajue jianbao. *Xuanzhou Wenwu* 6:9–13.

Yakobson, A.L. 1968 Review of G.N. Chubinashvili's *Razyskaniya po armyanskoi arkhitekture*. *Sovetskaya Arkheologiya* 3:262–70.

Yang Chaoqing 1990 Jinshinianlai Henan yuanshishehui kaogu de zhongyao faxian yu yanjiu. *Hua Xia Kaogu* 3:1–10.

Yang Debiao 1988 Shilun Wannan tudunmu. *Wenwu Yanjiu* 4:81–8.

Yin Da 1955 (original 1937) *Xinshiqishidai* (The Neolithic Age of China). Beijing: San Lian Publishing House.

1963 Xinshiqishidai kaogu gongzuo de huigu yu zhanwang (Review and Forecast of Chinese Neolithic Archaeology). *Kaogu* 11:577–89.

Yoon Nae-hyun 1986 *Ancient Korean History: A Reinterpretation*. Seoul: Ilchisa. (In Korean.)

Yoshida, A. 1984 Tsukinowa Kofun to gendai rekishigaku (The Tsukinowa Kofun and Historical Studies Today). *Kokogaku Kenkyu* 30(4):38–56. (In Japanese.)

Yu Weichao 1985 *Xian-Qin Liang-Han kaoguxue lunji*. Beijing: Wenwu.

Yun Nae-hyŏn 1982 *Chungguk'ui wonsisidae: sahoe songkyok'ui pyonch'on'ul*

chungsim'uro. Seoul (Tandae Ch'ulp'anbu).
Zadachi . . . 1953 Zadachi sovetskikh arkheologov v svete trudov J.V. Stalina po voprosam yasykoznaniya i ekonomicheskim problemam. *Sovetskaya Arkheologiya* 17:9–22.
Zekan, M. 1992 Muzej hrvatskih arheoloških spomenika – vojno-strateški cilj neprijatelja. *Obavijesti* 24(2):27–8.
Zhang Boquan 1987 Dui Liaoxi faxian wuqiannianqian de wenming shuguang de lishi lice. *Liaohai Wenwu Xuekan* 2:96–102.
Zhang Jingguo 1988 Lüelun Jianghuai diqu Xia Shang Zhou wenhua fenqi ji zushu. *Wenwu Yanjiu* 3:15–20, 46.
Zhang Xuehai 1989 Lun sishinianlai Shandong xian-Qin kaogu de jiben shouhuo. *Hai Dai Kaogu* 1:325–43.
Zhang Zhengming 1988 *Chu wenhua-zhi*. Wuhan: Hubei Renmin.
Zhang Zhengming (ed.) 1984 *Chu-shi luncong*. Wuhan: Hubei Renmin.
Zhao Shigang 1983 Chu-ren zai Henan de huodong yizhi. In Zhengzhou (1983), pp. 49–72.
Zheng Shaozong 1989 Hebei-sheng wenwu kaogu gonzuo shinian de zhuyao shouhuo. *Wenwu Chunqiu* 1/2:38–51, 37, and 3:41–5.
Zhengzhou 1983 *Chu wenhua yanjiu lunwenji*. Zhengzhou: Zhongzhou Shuhuashe.
Zhongguo Renmin Jiefangjun Moubu (A Certain Unit of the People's Liberation Army) 1972 Tantan canjia Qufu Hanmu he Zou Xian Mingmu fajue gongzuo de tihui (The Experience of Participation in the Excavations of the Han Tomb in Qufu County and the Ming Tomb in Zou County). *Wenwu* 5:37–8, 24.
Zhongguo Shehui Kexueyuan Kaogu Yanjiusuo (Institute of Archaeology, Chinese Academy of Social Sciences) 1984 Zhongguo kaoguxue de huangjin shidai (The Golden Age of Chinese Archaeology). *Kaogu* 10:865–71.
Zhukov, B.S. 1929a Voprosy metodologii vydeleniya kulturnykh elementov i grupp. In *Kultura i byt naseleniya Tsentralno-Promyshlennoi oblasti*, edited by V.V. Bogdanov and S.P. Tolstov, pp. 31–5. Moscow: Muzei Tsentralno-Promyshlennoi oblasti.
1929b Teoriya khronologicheskikh territorialnykh modifikatsii nekotorykh neoliticheskikh kultur Vostochnoi Evropy po dannym izucheniya keramiki. *Etnografiya* 1:54–77.
Ziadeh, G. 1987 The Present is Our Key to the Past. *Bir Zeit Research Review* 4:40–65.
Žile, I. 1992 Ratna razarnja spomeničke baštine u Dubrovniku i okolici. *Obavijesti* 24(1):30–7.
Znachenie . . . 1950 Znachenie trudov tovarishcha Stalina dlya izucheniya rannikh periodov istorii. *Kratkie Soobshcheniya Instituta Istorii Materialnoi Kultury* 32:3–6.
Zotz, L. 1933 Die Deutsche Vorgeschichte im Film. *Nachrichtenblatt für Deutsche Vorgeschichte* 9(4):50–2.
Zotz, T. 1986 Filmdokumente zur Zeitgeschichte: Wir Wandern mit den Ostgermanen. *Publikationen zu Wissenschaftlichen Filmen*. Sektion Geschichte – Publizistik. Series 6, Number 2, Göttingen: Institut für den Wissenschaftlichen Film.

Index